URBAN DESIGN FUTURES

EDITED BY MALCOLM MOOR AND JON ROWLAND

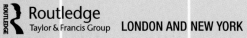

Routledge
Taylor & Francis Group
LONDON AND NEW YORK

URBAN
DESIGN
FUTURES

First published 2006
by Routledge
2 Park Square, Milton Park, Abingdon, Oxon, OX14 4RN

Simultaneously published in the USA and Canada
by Routledge
270 Madison Avenue, New York, NY10016

Routledge is an imprint of the Taylor & Francis Group, an informa business

Typeset in Info Text and Helvetica Neue Condensed
Designed by Crown Quarto
Printed and bound in China by Everbest Printing Co Ltd

British Library Cataloguing in Publication Data
A catalogue record for this book is available from the British Library.

Library of Congress Cataloging in Publication Data
A catalog record for this book has been applied for.

ISBN10 0-415-31877-7 (hbk)
ISBN10 0-415-31878-5 (pbk)
ISBN10 0-203-60172-6 (ebk)

ISBN13 978-0-415-31877-8 (hbk)
ISBN13 978-0-415-31878-5 (pbk)
ISBN13 978-0-203-60172-3 (ebk)

CITY PLANNING

BERNARD O'DONOGHUE

Carthago est delenda

Looked down on from the tower-top, it's fields
by other means: the street's the headland
where the mown hay has to be pulled back
making room for the tractor's clumsy, ribbed
back wheel. The Cathedrals, both persuasions,
face each other out across the skyline,
two swollen ricks, one of wheat, one barley.

So we, God's caretakers, are at liberty,
to reshape it or knock it all back down
and start again: to cut corners; leave fallow
the ground which only last year was (say)
the fruitful Eden where the Euphrates meets
the Tigris: to rub out the olive-drills
and rows of lights, the wide wrinkles of night-life.

And we're entitled too to smooth away
rough features, to erase them from the air
just as we'd brush the hair out of someone's eyes.
We make straight lines, arcing out from the centre,
just as in the old days we'd knock down
a fence between two fields and bulldoze it
into the quarry, covering the standing stone forever.

But you must have seen those light-maps, photographed
from space how the city's light shows up
by infra-red, and how the dark stays dark,
asleep at the edges. And those aerial pictures
of ringforts, how their subcutaneous
veins show through the earth's light covering
which has been hurriedly thrown over them.

CONTENTS

Prologue: City Planning Bernard O'Donoghue

Foreword Terry Farrell

List of illustrations viii
Contributors xi
Preface xiv
Acknowledgements xvii

Introduction Malcolm Moor 1

PART 1
Urban Design Comes of Age: The Bigger Picture 17

1 **Territories of Urban Design** 18
Alex Krieger
2 **Globalising Urban Design** 29
Tony Lloyd-Jones
3 **It's Sprawl, But It's MY Sprawl** 38
Harriet Tregoning
4 **Civitas: Traditional Urbanism in Contemporary Practice** 46
Paul Murrain
5 **The Planning System and the Delivery of Design Quality** 50
John Punter
6 **The ART of City Building** 57
David Rudlin

PART 2
Connecting Social Spaces: Creating the Public Realm 69

7 **Life, Spaces, Buildings – And in Said Order, Please** 70
Jan Gehl
8 **The Insecurity of Urbanism** 76
Tim Stonor
9 **The Street** 83
Adriaan Geuze
10 **Asian Commercialism and the Discovery of Place: The Lan Kwai Fong Story** 88
Alex Lui
11 **The Social Dimension of Urban Design** 94
Ken Worpole
12 **Men Shouldn't Decide Everything: Women and the Public Realm** 100
Mardie Townsend
13 **Post Modern Movement: The 'Inscribed' City** 106
Alain Cousseran
14 **Animal Urbanism and Homeopathic Architecture** 114
Lucien Kroll

PART 3
Sustainability Through Technology: Creating New Typologies 121

15 **What is the 'New Ordinary'?** 122
Bill Dunster
16 **A Vertical Theory of Urban Design** 135
Ken Yeang

PART 4
Networks Expand Choice: New Frameworks for Urbanism 141

17 **The Brand New Authentic Retail Experience: The Commercialization of Urban Design** 142
Richard Rees
18 **Place, Experience, Movement** 149
Andrew Cross
19 **Lower Lea Valley Olympic and Legacy Masterplans** 154
Jason Prior
20 **Giving Meaning to the Experience Economy** 159
John Worthington
21 **Ground Zero** 170
Thom Mayne

Conclusion: Urban Design Futures Jon Rowland 173

Index 190

FOREWORD

Speculating about the future of cities is an important critical endeavour for our times.

Our urban places, villages, towns, cities and metropolises are built slowly and by many hands. Planning them is an inexact art and the results range from effective to ineffective to the all too obviously downright damaging mistakes. But the importance of man's primary habitations and the future of the environment for all creatures on this globe necessitates that those who make urbanity their interest take stock, anticipate inevitable changes, speculate and then wherever possible plan in order to improve the eventual outcomes for us all. The evidence of successful speculation and planning is all around us, from the New Town in Edinburgh to Philadelphia's geometric grids, right up to the regeneration of the post-industrial landscapes of the world's urban docklands today.

This is an important book. It is unusual in that it is a book of beliefs and observations by some of the best practitioners and thinkers on urban design in the world. Its remit is global, the views of the authors reflect the social concerns of 'place' and the more dynamic ideas on form that are emerging from Europe, the Far-East and the US.

I cannot claim any credit for the excellent contributions to this book other than that it began as a result of a conversation at a happy gathering in my house where we were entertained by a jazz chanteuse and champagne. Of course, underlying this is my long association with Jon Rowland through the Urban Design Group. This important organisation brought many like minds together between the late 1980s and early 1990s at a time when the conjoined words of 'urban' and 'design' had to be expressed slowly with clear diction as the concept seemed to be new to most people – particularly political leaders and even, surprisingly, to many practitioners in the related fields, including architects, planners, engineers and landscape architects. Today of course it is another story, as many Prime Ministers and Presidents and their various ministers and departments declare their support for new initiatives in a worldwide urban renaissance.

With over half of the world's population now living in urban settlements and with our increasing acceptance that it is these settlements that are rapidly changing our climate and environment, the need for conjecture, imagination and debate on urban design futures is absolutely pressing and necessary. What's more the tools now at hand, particularly the electronic ones, make it much more possible to study the complexities, options and future projections of change that modern city planning involves. By simulating change and by engaging with a wide spectrum of those involved, choice and fairness in decision-making are made possible on scales that have not been achievable before. Urban design has come of age and the future is without doubt full of creative potential and discussion. This book is a catalyst for that debate.

TERRY FARRELL

April 2006

LIST OF ILLUSTRATIONS

0.1 Davygate, York
0.2 Vandalised garage court, Marsh Farm Estate, Luton
0.3 Residential towers in park, Rochdale Road, Manchester
0.4 Ring road severance, Bury
0.5 Retail boxes along inner ring road, Telford
0.6 Deck access housing, Gospel Oak, North London
0.7 Hammersmith flyover, West London
0.8 Field analysis of Central London's Georgian estates
0.9 Waterside development proposals, Buffalo, NY
0.10 Town square, Poundbury
0.11 Covent Garden fruit and vegetable market, London
0.12 Proposed development of Covent Garden Market, London
0.13 BedZED frontage to public realm, Sutton
0.14 New Bank Headquarters, Central, Hong Kong
0.15 Transport Development Zone Concept sketch
0.16 Place de l'Homme de Fer, Strasbourg
0.17 Renovation of Place de l'Homme de Fer
0.18 Circular tram station roof, Place de l'Homme de Fer
0.19 Guggenheim Museum, Bilbao, Spain
0.20 Icknield Loop Masterplan, Birmingham
0.21 Paris Plage, right bank of the Seine
0.22 Paris Plage, Hôtel de Ville to Pont Neuf
0.23 Shopping street, Brisbane
0.24 Student demo, Oxford Street, London
0.25 Pompidou Centre, Paris

1.1 The axis of the Champs Elysées seen from the Louvre
1.2 Grahame Park masterplan, Barnet, North London
1.3 Grahame Park, North London, Southern Square
1.4 Gloucester Docks masterplan
1.5 Gloucester Docks
1.6 Gloucester Docks
1.7 New traditionalism, Poundbury Estate, Dorchester
1.8 Public realm, Buchanan Street, Glasgow
1.9 Exchange Square, Millennium Quarter, Manchester
1.10 Gare du Nord Metro Interchange, Paris
1.11 Stratford City, London
1.12 Landscape urbanism, Der Strype, The Hague
1.13 *Woonerf* (home zone), Der Strype, The Hague
1.14 Visionary urbanism, Colindale, North London
1.15 Community participation, Cirencester, Gloucestershire

2.1 Unconscious urban design
2.2 Jakarta: commercial towers and informal squatter settlements
2.3 Shedland?, Washington, DC
2.4 Edge City? Dulles Airport, Washington, DC
2.5 Back-office-land, Washington, DC
2.6 Perilous shacks in Tucunduba, Belem, Brazil
2.7 Megacity downtown, Avenida Paulista, São Paulo, Brazil
2.8 Illegal land divisions in São Paulo, Brazil
2.9 Tucunduba, Belem, Brazil

5.1 Java Island, Amsterdam
5.2 Ira Keller Foundation Park, Portland, USA
5.3 False Creek North, Vancouver, Canada
5.4 Chillingworth Road, Islington, North London
5.5 The City of Sydney model, Australia

6.1 Temple Quay 2, Bristol, historic view of site
6.2 Temple Quay 2, Bristol, aerial view
6.3 Temple Quay 2, Bristol, masterplan
6.4 Bristol context figure-ground plan
6.5 New England Quarter, Brighton, aerial view
6.6 New England Quarter, Brighton, housing above Sainsbury's store
6.7 New England Quarter, Brighton, masterplan
6.8 Brighton context figure-ground plan
6.9 Southall Gasworks, Ealing, London, aerial view of proposals
6.10 Southall Gasworks, Ealing, London, masterplan
6.11 Aerial view, Southall Gasworks, Ealing, London
6.12 Marshall Mills, Leeds, masterplan
6.13 Marshall Mills, Leeds, new square
6.14 Marshall Mills, Leeds, aerial view
6.15 Oldham Beyond, Oldham, UK masterplan
6.18 Proposed Oldham theatre
6.19 Proposed new business quarter

7.1 Public bench, Copenhagen
7.2 Private moments, Copenhagen
7.3 Outdoor café in Strøget, Copenhagen
7.4 Bollards in Piazza del Campo, Sienna, Italy
7.5 Kalvebod Brygge waterfront, Copenhagen
7.6 Kalvebod Brygge, Copenhagen
7.7 The Deserted Street
7.8 Spokane, WA, USA
7.9 Clarksdale, MS, USA
7.10 A sunlit street, Copenhagen
7.11 Karl Johann Gaten, Stockholm
7.12 Aerial view of Aker Brygge, Oslo
7.13 Aker Brygge, Oslo
7.14 Aker Brygge, Oslo

7.15 Aker Brygge, Oslo
7.16 Strædet, pedestrian street in Copenhagen

8.1 Spatial integration map of central London
8.2 New central staircase for Trafalgar Square, London
8.3 Strategic design proposal for the historic core of Margate, UK
8.4 Margate, UK
8.5 Margate, UK
8.6 Strategic design proposal for the Brixton Town Centre Interchange, London
8.7 Masterplan for historic St Botolph's Quarter, Colchester, UK
8.8 Sketch of proposal for a new public space at Princes Circus, London
8.9 Princes Circus, London, sketch

9.1 Les Halles present entrances
9.2 Les Halles roof-lights
9.3 Les Halles landscape proposals
9.4 Les Halles, Paris, cross-section of proposals
9.5 Exciting night view of Les Halles proposals

10.1 Hong Kong aerial view showing Lan Kwai Fong
10.2 Lan Kwai Fong location plan
10.3 Elevation of D'Aguilar Street
10.4 Daytime scene enables street refurbishment to be visible
10.5 Night scene shows people, not buildings, are the centre of attention
10.6 Neon signs are Hong Kong's aesthetic

11.1 Waterloo Station, London
11.2 The Promenade Planté, Paris
11.3 Norr Mälarstrand, Stockholm
11.4 The northern section of Museum Park, Rotterdam
11.5 The same park in 2001, just after the bulldozers had finished their work
11.6 Victoria Square, Birmingham, UK
11.7 The Peace Gardens, Sheffield, UK
11.8 The closing of the main freeway along the Seine

12.1 Putting women's views on the design and planning agenda
12.2 Presentation on 'parental perceptions of the neighbourhood'
12.3 Focus group discussion
12.4 Low and high-rise housing, Raleigh Park, USA
12.5 Community tree planting

13.1 Orchestration of changes in scale in the 'inscribed' space of the street
13.2 'Inscribed' space restructured by the 'service' space
13.3 Giving meaning to an open space through treatment as an avenue
13.4 'Public' space can make up for the absence of a discernible streetscape
13.5 Landscaping as a means of restructuring open space
13.6 The 'service' space
13.7 The garden is, today, considered a major constituent of urbanism
13.8 The garden creates an image of the city
13.9 The garden structures the streetscape

14.1 Vauix-en-Velin, Lyons, France
14.2 Ecolonia, Alpha-aan-den Rijn, Netherlands
14.3 Ecolonia, Netherlands, public space
14.4 Ecolonia, Netherlands, private space
14.5 Ecolonia, Netherlands, built form
14.6 Ecolonia, Netherlands, context and ecology
14.7 Ecolonia, Netherlands, urban components
14.8 Bethoncourt-Montbeliard, France
14.9 Bethoncourt-Montbeliard, France, blocks remodelled
14.10 Bethoncourt-Montbeliard, France, casualness replaces banality
14.11 Bethoncourt-Montbeliard, France, elevation of block
14.12 Bethoncourt-Montbeliard, France, sketch of tower
14.13 ALEA Alençon, France
14.14 ALEA Alençon, France
14.15 ALEA, informal pathways
14.16 ALEA, social spaces
14.17 ALEA, the transformation

15.1 Volume house builders' output
15.2 Volume house builders' factory
15.3 UK urban sprawl
15.4 Internal view of BedZED living room
15.5 Computer section through BedZED
15.6 Cost-effectiveness plotted against thermal performance
15.7 Cross-section of BedZED building physics strategy
15.8 Site plan of BedZED
15.9 BedZED floor plan
15.10 Helios Road balconies
15.11 SkyZED, Wandsworth, aerial view
15.12 SkyZED, Wandsworth, aerial view
15.13 SkyZED, Wandsworth, cut-away perspective
15.14 ZEDquarter, King's Cross, aerial view of low-rise option from north
15.15 ZEDquarter, King's Cross, cross section
15.16 Broughton, coloured site plan
15.17 Perspective view from south
15.17 Street view showing ZED homes juxtaposed with traditional

16.1 A vertical theory of urban design, Georgian London
16.2 Sketches of Eco Tower, Elephant and Castle, London
16.3 Masterplan
16.4 Parks in the sky
16.5 High rise should have a multiplicity of uses
16.6 The application of urban design techniques

17.1 Niketown, Oxford Street, London
17.2 Selfridges, Birmingham's revitalised Bull Ring
17.3 Selfridges seen across Birmingham
17.4 Tesco and Tesco Express
17.5 Bournemouth Library
17.6 Cribbs Causeway, Bristol
17.7 Smaralind shopping centre, Reykjavik
17.8 Paradise Street, Liverpool
17.9 Waterfront City, Melbourne
17.10 Sheffield, new retail

18.1 Renault Parts Distribution Centre, Swindon, UK
18.2 Ontario Mills shopping centre, San Bernardino, California
18.3 Watling Street, Middle England, but could be anywhere
18.4 Droxford Business Park, Sunderland, UK

19.1 Olympic Park, aerial perspective
19.2 Olympic Park, aerial view
19.3 Legacy Masterplan
19.4 Olympic Masterplan
19.5 Village Plaza view
19.6 Stadium external view
19.7 The built environment legacy
19.8 Village water view
19.9 Sketch, Olympic Park
19.10 Sketch, legacy

20.1 Oresund Region
20.2 Twenty-first-century city
20.3 Retail park
20.4 SANE, study of distributed workspace
20.5 On-demand flexibility of pay-as-you-go
20.6 Aesthetic of mobility
20.7 Gateway to the city core
20.8 Ajax Stadium, Amsterdam
20.9 Papendorp, a greenfield site

21.1 West perspective
22.2 Cross-section
21.3 North perspective
21.4 Dynamic spaces
21.5 Canyon perspective

22.1 Kentlands,UK
22.2 BedZED
22.3 Ecolonia, Netherlands
22.4 Ecolonia, Netherlands
22.5 Telford Millennium Community masterplan, UK
22.6 Lewisham Gateway, UK, urban design framework
22.7 Lewisham Gateway, UK
22.8 Lewisham Gateway, UK
22.9 Bull Ring, Birmingham, UK
22.10 Bicester shopping village, Oxfordshire, UK
22.11 Paddington Basin development, London
22.12 Masterplan, Paddington Basin development
22.13 Paddington Basin development, London
22.14 Fairford Leys new community, Aylesbury, UK
22.15 Borneo, Sporenburg, Amsterdam
22.16 Morphosis competition entry for rebuilding of the Twin Towers, NYC
22.17 Olympic Park masterplan, East London
22.18 Las Vegas
22.19 Las Vegas

CONTRIBUTORS

Alain Cousseran is Director of Signes Paysage, which was established in 1990 in response to a growing demand for large-scale development: masterplans, town planning and studies for the integration of infrastructure and community amenities. He has taught at the Ecole Nationale Supérieure du Paysage and the Ecole Nationale des Ingénieurs des Techniques Horticoles et du Paysage, as well as receiving numerous awards including the Silver Medal of the City of Paris and the RIBA Award for the Thames Barrier Park in London.

Andrew Cross has an established reputation as a curator of contemporary art and has gained increasing acclaim as a photographer. He is interested in the less-observed landscapes, often at the urban periphery, that are at the heart of the country's economy. In 2000 he received two Arts Council of England Year of the Artist projects in Swindon and Enfield. He is currently completing a residency at the University of Sutherland and will be undertaking a residency at the Atlantic Center for the Arts in Florida. His photography has been featured in a number of magazines including *Themepark*, *Blueprint*, *FT Magazine* and *Sunday Telegraph Magazine*. His curatorial projects include Asia City, The Ladies Field Club, School Reunion and Real Places?

Bill Dunster is the creator of 'ZEDfactory', synthesising low environmental impact product development, architecture, masterplanning and financial appraisals. Following years of research and development into high-density zero fossil fuel urban regeneration, working with a local environmental business charity, the BioRegional Development Group, the BedZED scheme was presented to the Peabody Trust. In early 1999 a disused water treatment site was purchased from the local authority and both the BedZED project and Bill Dunster architects (BDa) began. Prior to forming BDa, Bill worked for Michael Hopkins and Partners for over fourteen years specialising in low energy and sustainable development. Bill spends much of his time trying to launch the concept of ZEDquarters – an urban regeneration concept for both new and existing communities interested in leading a one-planet lifestyle and workstyle.

Jan Gehl is Professor of Urban Design, and Director of the Centre for Public Space Research, the School of Architecture, the Royal Danish Academy of Fine Arts in Copenhagen, and President/Partner of GEHL Architects in Copenhagen. He has taught at universities in Edinburgh, Vilnius, Oslo, Toronto, Calgary, Melbourne, Perth, Berkeley, San Jose and Guadalajara and has acted as consultant in cities world-wide. He was awarded the Sir Patrick Abercrombie Prize for exemplary contributions to town planning and territorial development by the International Union of Architects as well as an honorary doctorate from Heriot-Watt University in Edinburgh.

Adriaan Geuze is a Professor in Architecture and Urban Design. He founded West 8 urban design and landscape architecture BV in 1987. After winning the prestigious Prix de Rome award in 1990, Adriaan, with his office West 8, established an excellent reputation at the international level with his unique approach to planning and design of the public environment. By founding the S.L.A. Foundation in 1992, Adriaan increased public awareness of the profession. He is regularly invited to lecture internationally. In 2002 the Veronica Rudge Green Prize for Urban Design was awarded to Adriaan.

Alex Krieger is a Professor in practice of Urban Design and the Chairman of the Department of Urban Planning and Design at the Graduate School of Design at Harvard University. He is a founding principal of Chan Krieger & Associates in Cambridge, Massachusetts, offering a full range of architectural, urban design, masterplanning and landscape architectural services. He has an extensive publications record, writing and commenting on issues from waterfront development to new urbanism to smart growth to civic and monumental space.

Lucien Kroll has worked in Brussels since 1952 with his Atelier d'Urbanisme d'Architecture et d'Informatique. He is best known for 'Meme', a building for students at the Medical Faculty in Brussels. He has been invited to work in Rwanda, France, Netherlands, Germany and in Italy on houses, schools, churches, monasteries, housing projects etc. He has published extensively and lectures around the world.

Tony Lloyd-Jones has more than thirty years experience of teaching and research in architecture and urban planning practice in the UK and internationally, with a focus on urban design and development planning. He is consulting Urban and Physical Planning Adviser to the Department for International Development and has advised the UK Government on human settlements matters at the United Nations since 1997. He is currently the international consultant to the Working Group on Urban Design for Sustainability, reporting to the EU Expert Group on the Urban Environment. He is a part-time senior lecturer in Urban Design and Development at the School of the Built Environment, University of Westminster, and research manager at the Max Lock Centre. He has conducted a number of urban development-related research projects and published papers and articles in journals and books world-wide.

Alex Lui is a Senior Adviser at Hysan Development Co. Ltd. a prime property investment and development company in Hong Kong. Prior to joining Hysan in 2002 he taught at the Chinese University of Hong Kong for a number of years on architecture, planning and urban design. He has also practised in Singapore and the United States. Some of his award-winning projects include the Hong Kong Industrial Technology Centre and the Jockey Club Environmental Technology Centre. He is involved in several large-scale commercial projects which form the core of a future pedestrian district in Causeway Bay, a major retail and commercial centre in Hong Kong.

Thom Mayne is founder and principal of Morphosis, based in Los Angeles. The practice came to prominence in the 1980s with the design of high-profile restaurants in the Los Angeles area. Thom has received twenty Progressive Architecture awards, and thirty-nine American Institute of Architects Awards, along with many other design honours including the Pritzker Prize in 2005. He has taught at Columbia, Harvard and Yale Universities, the Berlage Institute in Holland, and the Bartlett School of Architecture in London.

Malcolm Moor has qualifications in architecture from Nottingham University and urban design from Cornell University, New York, and is a member of the RIBA and RTPI. Malcolm has more than twenty-five years experience in the fields of urban design, architecture and town planning with expertise in masterplanning complex city centre sites. He has been a consultant to Jon Rowland Urban Design for the past six years, is a CABE Enabler, and a visiting urban design lecturer at Westminster University and was a contributor to the Compact City (2000).

Paul Murrain is currently Senior Design Director for The Prince's Foundation. Paul has carried out many consultancy commissions in complex inner-city sites and has collaborated with New Urbanist founders Andres Duany and Elizabeth Plater-Zyberk (DPZ) in the USA, Europe and Malaysia. He has also worked with Project for Public Spaces (PPS) in New York and was Urban Design Director at David Lock Associates from 1989 to 1993, and at Urban Initiatives from 1999 to 2002. He was Course Chairman at the Joint Centre for Urban Design, Oxford and joint author of *Responsive Environments: A Manual for Designers* (1985). He is a member of the Congress for New Urbanism in the USA.

Bernard O'Donoghue was born in Cullen, Co. Cork, in the depths of rural Ireland in 1945. He lived in the cities of Cork and Manchester briefly before settling in Oxford in 1965 where he teaches medieval English at Wadham College. He has published five volumes of poetry.

Jason Prior is the Regional Vice President of EDAW Europe. He is an urban designer, landscape architect and environmental planner, specialising in leading multi-disciplinary teams and providing integrated, broad-based solutions to a variety of complex design and planning projects. His experience includes design and implementation of major landscape, urban design and regeneration projects. Jason is leading the consultant team for the Lower Lea Valley Regeneration and Olympic Games Masterplan for the London Development Agency and was one of the key consultants responsible for the development framework, detailed masterplan and public realm strategy for Manchester City Centre following the 1996 bombing. He is an external examiner for the University of Greenwich and also a Commissioner for CABE Space.

John Punter is Professor of Urban Design at Cardiff University. He is the author of several books on urban design and planning, including *Planning Control in Western Europe* (1989), *Design Control in Bristol* (1990), *The Design Dimension of Planning* (1997), *Design Guidelines in American Cities* (1999) and *The Vancouver Achievement* (2003). His journal articles include detailed studies of the history and practice of aesthetic control in the UK, design control in Europe and current urban design initiatives in Australia. He is a Director of the Design Commission for Wales and Chair of their Design Review Panel.

Richard Rees is an architect/urban design director of Building Design Partnership (BDP) in London. He is a Fellow of the Society of Architectural Illustrators and has exhibited his masterplan drawings at the Royal Academy. His first major urban projects were undertaken in Hong Kong and included the Wanchai and Central Reclamation project on Hong Kong Island and Fanling New Town Centre, both now constructed. He is still working abroad and won a competition in 2002 for the redevelopment of a major dockland site in Melbourne, called Waterfront City. Richard was a major contributor to the BCSC Urban Task Force book, *Urban Design for Retail Environments* (2002) and he also lectures occasionally.

Jon Rowland has qualifications from the Architectural Association and Sussex University. He is an architect and Principal of the urban design practice JRUD. He has worked on major urban design projects including plans for the South Bank of London, masterplanning Telford

Millennium Community and the regeneration of Lewisham. He is co-author of *Designing Our Environment* and the author of *Community Decay*. He was Chairman of the Urban Design Group and is now a Regional Representative for CABE. He has advised the Crown Estate and English Partnerships on urban design and was a visiting lecturer at Oxford Brookes University.

David Rudlin is a planner and urban designer. He joined URBED in 1990 to head up the BURA best practice award-winning Little Germany Action project in Bradford. Since joining URBED, he has worked on numerous projects including masterplans in Brighton and Bristol, among others, and regeneration studies in places such as Swansea, Barnsley, Moss Side and Liverpool. He has written widely, including research projects for the Joseph Rowntree Foundation, the DETR, the Urban Task Force, the Housing Corporation and Friends of the Earth. David was a co-author of the groundbreaking *Hulme Guide to Development* and was also a founder member of the Homes for Change Housing Co-operative in Hulme. He is a founder member of CUBE (the Centre for Understanding of the Built Environment) in Manchester and a policy council member of the Town and Country Planning Association.

Tim Stonor is an architect and managing director of strategic design company Space Syntax, which he joined in 1995 after practising in London, Toronto, Paris and Newcastle. His work focuses on the analysis, design and evaluation of spatial masterplans, pedestrian movement systems and strategies for urban regeneration. He speaks regularly at international conferences and is an active director of Space Syntax Australia and Space Syntax Brussels.

Mardie Townsend is a Senior Lecturer in the School of Health Sciences at Deakin University, Melbourne, where she teaches in 'Public Health' and 'Family and Society'. Her research interests include: housing and homelessness; sustainability and health; human health benefits of interaction with nature; social and health impact assessment; and corporate social responsibility. Her current research into the human health benefits of interaction with nature includes exploring the effects of inequity in access to nature for the health and well-being of individuals, groups and communities. She has recently been involved in overseeing the development of a new community centre within an aged care facility designed to bring the outside world into the aged care facility and thus to break down the barriers between residents and the outside community.

Harriet Tregoning was appointed Special Secretary of the Maryland Governor's Office of Smart Growth in July 2001. As Special Secretary for Smart Growth, she acts as an advocate for Smart Growth and co-ordinates the State's comprehensive Smart Growth Initiative. Previously, Harriet was Secretary of the Maryland Department of Planning, where she emphasised strengthening links between transportation, land use and housing policies and contributed to Maryland's Smart Growth initiative, winning the prestigious 'Innovations in Government Award' from the Ford Foundation and Harvard's Kennedy School of Government. Harriet also served as the Director of the Urban and Economic Development Division of the US Environmental Protection Agency, where she founded the national Smart Growth Network.

Ken Worpole is one of Britain's most influential writers on urban social policy, and the author of many seminal reports and books. He has lectured and worked extensively in Europe, Australia and North America. His principal interests concern the quality of contemporary urban life, new forms of civil society, the planning and design of urban landscapes, the development of new kinds of institutions which support more convivial forms of democracy – and the pleasures of life in the open air. In 2001 he was appointed a member of the UK government's Urban Green Spaces Task Force. The same year he took on the role of English Editor to the UNCHS report *The State of the World's Cities*, published in New York in June 2001. In 2002 he was appointed as an expert adviser to the Historic Buildings and Land Panel of the Heritage Lottery Fund, and in 2003 to the Commission for Architecture and the Built Environment (CABE), notably on issues concerning the contemporary public domain.

John Worthington is a founder of DEGW, an international strategic design consultancy focused on enabling the process of change from the scale of the workplace to the city. He is currently chair of Building Futures, a joint CABE RIBA initiative, and Visiting Professor at the University of Sheffield and Chalmers University of Technology, Gothenburg. He is past President and current Patron of the Urban Design Group.

Ken Yeang is an architect specialising in the design and planning of signature buildings and masterplans that are green or ecologically-responsive. He has pioneered a new genre of tall buildings, referred to as the 'bioclimatic skyscraper'. Ken studied at the AA (the Architectural Association) School in London and completed his doctorate at Cambridge University. His doctoral work on ecological design was published by McGraw-Hill USA (in 1995) as a book, *Designing with Nature*. He is the author of several key books and articles on skyscraper and ecological design, including *The Green Skyscraper: The Basis for Designing Sustainable Intensive Buildings* (1999).

URBAN DESIGN FUTURES is a book about ideas. It is about the exciting ideas in urban design at the moment and it puts forward a series of provocative scenarios for directions in which urban design could evolve. These scenarios take the form of a series of 'think-pieces' on different aspects of urban design by leading practitioners and theorists. This book celebrates the plurality of thinking and approaches in urban design and recognises the emerging ideas on how to arrive at what we all agree is the destination, more attractive liveable cities. We have addressed this issue of plurality by allowing our contributors as thinkers and practitioners to freely express their thoughts of what they see as the central issues and how they would like to see urban design developing. We believe that this is the right time to produce such a book. Urban design theory is at a point where debate is essential. This book contributes to the debate and presents some avenues of future development that all those involved in reshaping urban areas should be considering.

We decided upon the form of this book by choosing broad themes and a list of potential contributors to address them in their own terms. The contributors include talented urban designers that we know well and have co-operated with on projects, as well as those whose work and writing we have admired, to whom we wrote asking for a contribution. We have been fortunate in receiving stimulating and original work from all our twenty-two contributors and are grateful to them for their time and energy, but mostly for their ideas. Not surprisingly, we have learnt a great deal from the interchange of views that has greatly expanded our own knowledge and opinions on how to move urban design forward.

OVERVIEW OF THE BOOK

The book is structured around four themes with introductory and concluding contributions from the editors:

Part 1 Overviews of the key objectives that urban design addresses and the role and territories of the urban designer.

Part 2 The heart of urban design, the public realm and those for whom it is designed.

Part 3 The big issue of sustainability and how technology could be a means to achieve it through new building typologies.

Part 4 New forms of urbanism that are being created from the cross fertilisation of urban design with contemporary forces such as networking, branding, rapid change and uncertainty.

In the prologue to the book, Bernard O'Donoghue speaks of the layers of human occupation of the fragile land and the responsibility of those who build over but never totally erase earlier settlement patterns.

In the Introduction, Malcolm Moor sets the scene of where urban design is at the moment and how it arrived at the present situation, then signposts the themes and ideas set out by the different contributors.

In **PART 1**, **'Urban Design Comes of Age: The Bigger Picture'**, six contributors present overviews of urban design and development patterns. What are the central issues that urban design sets out to tackle and what are the trends taking place in society that are reflected in the form of the built environment?

Chapter 1, **Alex Krieger** gives a number of definitions of urban design and sets out ten spheres of urbanistic action starting with the basic position of the bridge between planning and architecture.

The objectives of 'mainstream urban design' are becoming well recognised in the developed world but are these same objectives applicable to third world cities? **Tony Lloyd-Jones** in **Chapter 2** lists these objectives and asks whether in a global world any form of universal urban design is feasible or desirable.

Harriet Tregoning in **Chapter 3** describes how Americans are schizophrenic about the built environment. They want to preserve green space but don't see how that relates to their own house built on former farmland.

In his **Chapter 4**, **'Civitas'**, **Paul Murrain** begins by defining what we mean by the 'public realm' and 'urbanism' and how the word 'tradition' is usually misunderstood. This article is an edited version of the introduction for Civitas, an exhibition of traditional urbanism in contemporary practice. The original has now been published in the Civitas Catalogue.

How to both raise standards and ensure that design effort is properly channelled into projects that get built? In **Chapter 5**, **John Punter** points to the recent experience in Europe and the USA that can teach us how to create more effective mechanisms for design control.

Endeavouring to revive 'the slow art of urban design' and make it exciting and memorable forms the core of **David Rudlin**'s **Chapter 6**. He is concerned that now urban design is finding acceptance it could be in danger of becoming boring and predictable.

PART 2, **'Connecting Social Spaces: Creating the Public Realm'**, shows how achieving an exciting yet safe public realm with a good balance between order and surprise is at the heart of urban design. Contributors cover all aspects of the design of the public realm and how we should set about its successful creation.

'The major attraction of any city is its people, its life and vitality.' This is how **Jan Gehl** begins his **Chapter 7**, **'Life, Spaces, Buildings – and in Said Order Please'**. The title aptly sums up his argument.

Tim Stonor uses his chapter 8 **'The Insecurity of Urbanism'** to express his concern that urban design methods are currently less secure than they should be. The answer, he says, is to study the link between space and activity using space syntax as a tool to create better urban places.

The public realm is the setting for everyday activities as well as civic and cultural events. **Chapter 9**, by **Adriaan Geuze**, shows how the street is an effective regulator of human activity.

The rapidly growing cities of Asia have embraced modern architecture as the embodiment of economic progress but in the process have rejected much of their own built heritage and traditional street-life. **Alex Lui** tells of a rare conservation success story in Hong Kong in **Chapter 10**.

In **Chapter 11, Ken Worpole** reinforces the view that urban designers need to pay attention to the fine detail of human needs and aspirations to create places that enlarge people's capacity for self-confidence and sociability.

That male-oriented perceptions continue to dominate the conceptualisation of space is the theme of **Mardie Townsend**'s **Chapter 12**. Townsend states that women's role as both carers and professionals has been ignored.

In **Chapter 13, Alain Cousseran** gives an account of how the Modern Movement rejected the idea of external space as something sculpted from the built volume and he criticises this ignorance of what has constituted public space.

Lucien Kroll passionately attacks the hypocrisy of modern architecture. In **Chapter 14**, he shows how through trial and error all the modernist diversions have been called into question. He illustrates his viewpoint with his own humanistic designs.

PART 3, 'Sustainability Through Technology: Creating New Typologies', states that the challenge of the sustainable agenda is to rewrite the way we do things. Reducing environmental impacts can range from refining existing building forms to making them more energy-efficient, to the creation of new building typologies that can totally change our perception of what constitutes the building blocks of urbanism.

In **Chapter 15, Bill Dunster** argues against carbon complacency and asks 'What is the new ordinary?' His BedZED project in Sutton sets a challenge for the building industry to mass-produce zero-energy housing as well as redefining what is considered good urban design.

The intensification of built form to maximise use of land is another route to increased sustainability, which means getting to grips with the high rise and redefining its role in the city. **Ken Yeang** has pioneered the green skyscraper and now puts forward his vertical theory of urban design in **Chapter 16**.

PART 4, 'Networks Expand Choice: New Frameworks for Urbanism' shows how powerful economic forces descend on cities, defy the street patterns and move the urban life blood, core retail and office space, into new shopping and commercial typologies. Business and industrial parks, airports and the complex networks of linkages of networked cities: are these the new urban dynamics?

Richard Rees of architects BDP has been involved in many major urban design projects with large retail elements. In **Chapter 17**, he reports that 'The Brand New Authentic Retail Experience' is all around us and is developing new forms of architecture which have a retail component at their core.

The networks that link economic and industrial activity are becoming increasingly complex. In **Chapter 18, Andrew Cross** looks at this phenomenon and asks, 'Can place be an experience defined more easily by movement?'

In **Chapter 19, Jason Prior** illustrates how the London Olympics is based on the dynamics of movement and the flexibility of specialised buildings to being adapted to post-Olympic urbanism.

Other forms of urban growth could be patterns for sustainable urban growth. **John Worthington**, in **Chapter 20**, takes us through the networked cities based on information technology where a new typology of places is beginning to emerge with overlapping functions and a synergy of complementary uses.

In the **penultimate chapter, Thom Mayne** succinctly describes his Morphosis competition entry for the World Trade Center site and how they rethought the concept of the tower.

In the **Conclusion, Jon Rowland** explores the various approaches with some thoughts of new directions that have emerged from the polemical views of the contributors. The future of urban design is still evolving and we hope that this book may guide its further development.

ACKNOWLEDGEMENTS

Our thanks go to Caroline Mallinder for her encouragement to edit this book and her determination to produce a final product of which we can all be proud.

We wish to express our unswerving appreciation to our assistant Nicole West who helped maintain the project momentum and kept us focused on the task with efficiency and humour. We also greatly appreciate the work put in by our contributors' support staff.

Thanks also to Annie and Marie-José for their support and patience, which have now been rewarded with seeing more of us at weekends.

This Introduction sets out the factors that have led to the current situation where urban design is at the forefront of the drive to improve our urban areas and achieve an urban renaissance. The past few years have seen real improvements in many urban areas. Regeneration is taking place on a broad front and at different scales of intervention from major developments to small-scale interventions of new buildings, changes in the nature of streets, refurbishment and renewal. An urban design vision provides the focus for these changes and acts as the point of communication for the increasingly broad range of disciplines of the modern design team of transport and traffic engineers, town planners, ecologists, landscape architects, property surveyors, civil engineers and sustainability specialists.

0.1 **Davygate, York. Well-designed modern infill, makes positive contribution to historic street while providing needed deep-plan shopping floorspace.**
Source: Panter Hudspith Architects

INTRODUCTION

MALCOLM MOOR

0.2 Vandalised garage court, Marsh Farm Estate, Luton. Isolated garage courts that are not supervised by housing are little used and become targets for vandalism.

0.3 Residential towers in park, Rochdale Road, Manchester, reflect Le Corbusier's view of the park integrated into the high-rise city but these flats are still due to be demolished.

0.4 Ring road severance, Bury. Shoppers prefer to negotiate the road at the grade crossing rather than the forbidding underpass to reach the new superstore.

0.5 Retail boxes along inner ring road, Telford, present blank façades to drivers negotiating Telford town centre one-way box road.

HOW DID WE GET HERE?

Urban design has evolved into its present form by learning from both the good and the bad examples of the past and through tapping into exciting ideas and innovation taking place in the built environment throughout the world. It is both these positive and negative forces that are driving the enthusiasm to produce exciting urbanism for the future. The book draws on the ideas and experience of thinkers and practitioners throughout the world in order to set the context. This Introduction first looks at the way past events have formed our views in the UK before giving a brief overview of the environmental and social forces for change that we must respond to now. It then sets out some potential future directions, most of which are applicable internationally.

'THOSE WHO CANNOT REMEMBER THE PAST ARE CONDEMNED TO REPEAT IT'

This quote from the philosopher George Santayana[1] is his interpretation of Darwin's evolution of species. Santayana's view was that we will get better at dealing with the ever changing world if we are both retentive and flexible; conscious of the past and yet adaptable. This describes the way urban design is driven by our determination not to repeat the mistakes of the past as well as responding to changes in the way we live now and could be living in the immediate future. Urban planning has progressed in a series of cycles that usually begin well and end badly. New urban theories gestate to a level of intellectual acceptance. Funds are then found through enthusiastic promoters to build a model scheme. The resulting seminal project is then praised by the critics and copied uncritically by other professionals, often in inappropriate loca tions. For example, Le Corbusier's Unité a Marseilles is an inspired design, but has been th inspiration for thousands of drab and usuall poor quality high-rise housing projects world wide. Clarence Stein's housing at Radburn, Nev Jersey, was an interesting concept of how the ca could be safely segregated from the pedestrian. Ir certain communities it works but it was copiec indiscriminately and became the standard rubbe stamp layout for soulless suburban housin estates where cars seldom park in vandalisec garage courts and residents prefer to park on th grass verges.

The cycle continues as time usually reveals th original concept to be flawed or used inappropri ately. A period of disillusionment and stagnatio follows as professionals wonder why problem were not spotted earlier, before another nev theory comes into vogue, gains a sufficient leve of acceptance to be built and the cycle is under way once more. This cyclical situation is ofte aggravated by abrupt changes of policy directio in line with the prevailing political climate an the demands of the most pressing issues of th moment. Viewed from this historical perspective it is not surprising that so little real progress ha been made in improving the quality of urban life

IT IS NOT ENOUGH TO HAVE GOOD INTENTIONS

Moving forwards while looking backwards wit only a vague idea of the route ahead, both plan ning and rowing progress in a similar fashio Looking backwards to Ebenezer Howard's bol concept of the Town-Country Magnet[2] is still th

0.6 Deck access housing, Gospel Oak, North London. Dramatic entrance ramp probably looked better on the architect's sketch than it does in stark reality.

most evocative expression of the peculiarly English desire to make a fresh start away from the pollution and constrictions of the industrial city. Clean air, a job down the road, kids in the local school and a cow looking over the back fence was the poster image of the perfect family life. Britain has exported this new town model world-wide with varying degrees of success and quite a few cases of 'new town blues'. The new town exemplar in the UK was Milton Keynes, where the planners, fresh from their US studies, boldly gridded up the fields, made a shopping mall serve as a town centre, and then, as if embarrassed by their boldness, hid the whole enterprise behind belts of shrubs and trees.

People at the time of Howard's book and today believe that the new town approach is a distraction from the crucial issue of making the best of our existing cities.[3] Modernism took the opposite premise of bringing the countryside into the city. The Modern Movement dismissed the new town's picturesque ethos, the industrial city was the place to build a better world for the future. This new city would of course require a new man, one who would evolve to fit this modern utopia.

THE MODERN MOVEMENT

The discoveries of science and the theories of Darwin, Marx, Freud and Einstein, together with the traumas caused by the Great War and the Depression, had set in motion the spirit of modernism that a new generation of artists and architects embraced. Gone were the shackles of conventional multi-purpose streets lined with houses, corner shops and the municipal park.

Architects were the protagonists of the new, free of the stifling brick overcoat of the nineteenth-century industrial city and free to create the ideal city in the park, the best of town and country on everyone's doorstep, a choice within easy reach of society or solitude. Every new building was a step towards re-engineering the human soul.

In Chapter 13 Alain Cousseran explains how the Modern Movement eliminated the idea of the clearly defined 'inscribed space' in favour of more fluid 'open space' and split the complex function of public space into separate areas. Colin Rowe has traced the schism that this view of space represented between the old and new worlds to the CIAM Congress of 1923. In his introduction to Rob Krier's *Urban Space*, he speaks of modernism as 'the architect Pied Pipers who charmed and seduced only to leave us in a wilderness far from home'.[4] Modernism required people to fit the architect's vision but many residents clearly did not adapt as there was a fundamental mismatch between the way architects intended people to behave in their new environments and how they actually did behave when living there. In the worse cases, tenants were marooned in high rises with no contact with the ground or had to negotiate scary labyrinthine deck access ways to their front door. The result was alienation and trashed estates set on a downward spiral of decay where few people wanted to live.

Not wanting to be left behind, traffic engineers argued that towns would not work without allowing unrestricted use of the car. Town centres were sliced up with inner ring roads and strict traffic segregation forced pedestrians off the streets into grim forbidding subways. The Labour Government of 1967 was determined to clear the slums and set a target of 300,000 new houses a

0.7 Hammersmith flyover, West London illustrates the wasted spaces left by large-scale highway engineering.

year (twice as many as were built in 2003). The building industry needed to build quicker and cheaper and pre-fabricated concrete building systems were the only way to achieve the production targets. Originally designed for only five floors, the systems were extended ever upwards for high-rise housing. The Ronan Point flats collapse in 1968 sent shock waves through the building industry and marked the end of pre-fabrication and an aversion to both high rise and pre-fabrication that lasted for decades. America was also experiencing problems with bold housing experiments. Pruitt-Igoe was a progressive racially mixed public housing project built in St Louis in 1950. Despite improvements to the notorious access galleries and barren stretches of public open space between the rows of blocks, the project became so run-down and unsafe that it was spectacularly demolished in 1972.

PLANNING IN CRISIS

This was the turning point, away from high density back to low rise, away from bold architectural statements and back to building conventional housing. Now public money was channelled through housing associations to rehabilitate whole streets of workers' terraces. There was a spirit of antagonism to all forms of planning. The result was a crisis of confidence of the town planning profession who appeared powerless to resist the anti-planning bias of the Thatcher Government that came to power in 1979. The Conservative market-driven philosophy led to a presumption in favour of development. Planners were instructed to grant permission to planning applications with little regard for design quality. The shoddy retail sheds and drive-thru fast food outlets that were thrown up then still blight towns throughout the UK.

Car-borne shoppers jammed the new ring roads to the fast-spreading 'out of town' centres that stole trade from traditional shopping streets. Commercial developers argued that the only way to save existing centres from further decline was to permit comprehensive redevelopment of the High Street. The resulting indoor malls have effectively privatised much of the public realm in city centres. Town councils wishing to rejuvenate central areas and diversify the retail offer now have little choice but to agree to the developers' remedy of paying for the improvement of run-down 'tired' malls by permitting their further expansion.

The property crash of the early 1990s halted all development and led to a period of stagnation. Town planners who felt aggrieved at being blamed for the sorry state of many towns reinvented themselves as conservationists with an anti-urban slant inclined to say no to any planning applications that looked contentious or modern. Architects were also suffering for their mistakes but shrugged off criticism by pretending to be ironic with post modernism and reflective façades.

New planning theories are periodically interpreted by law and become planning policies. These policies are blindingly obviously right to the profession at the time and equally obviously wrong to the following generation. For example, conservation is always considered a 'good thing' and conservation of the old City of London was writ in stone. Protect views of St Paul's and definitely no relenting to the market pressure to allow big floorplate corporate office redevelopment. Then, in 1985, Canary Wharf exploited a loophole in the Isle of Dogs Enterprise Zone to build a million square metres of deep-plan offices.

Fearing that Canary Wharf was going to poach the 'big players' from the Square Mile, the City responded by permitting the mega schemes to be built that it had earlier rejected. Further relaxations followed and, despite the early reaction against highrise following 9/11, there are now skyscrapers muscling their way up throughout the City and Central London as London chases economic growth. The view that if we don't allow the financial sector to have the new high rises that they deem necessary to be competitive in our 'winner takes all society', then they will decamp to Frankfurt or New York prevails over the planners' inherent need to keep a lid on things, and have some limits that they can defend. So when planning policies can be righteously defended one day, then relaxed the next, is it any wonder that developers believe they can bully planners into acceding to their demands? At its heart, planning is politics tempered with social concern and politics is business with a veneer of public accountability.

The recognition that mistakes have been made has had a profound influence on a generation of architects and planners. They were largely mistakes of being too interventionist. They experimented with a way we were to live in the future that the rest of society hadn't signed up to. That we may be making mistakes now that will be obvious to future generations should occupy our quieter moments. Architecture has failed due to a combination of poor quality, of both design and

0.8 Field analysis of Central London's Georgian estates. Completed at Cornell University, NY, in 1971, this thesis anticipated some of the issues of set piece interventions within an existing urban pattern further developed in *Collage City* of 1975 by C. Rowe and F. Koetter.
Source: Grahame Shane

construction, and misunderstanding the needs of their real clients, the users. Rather than providing for their needs of house, garden and parking space, enthusiastic architects gave public tenants much more, they shared with them their dreams of a new way of living. Brave housing experiments using public sector tenants as guinea pigs were applauded by the architectural magazines of the time and then quietly forgotten when they went wrong. Architects of the 1960s, creating their seminal works during the summer of love, could not envisage the abuse that their beloved creations would eventually be subjected to by 'ungrateful' tenants who, after all, had only wanted a home.

The failure of planning to bring about its lofty utopian ideals can be attributed to several factors. First, it was sucked into the intricacies and political machinations of the planning process so deeply that it forgot what its primary purpose was, *the art and science of town planning*. Sitting at a desk preparing plans seemed somehow arbitrary and wilful compared to the rigours of system analysis and the science of statistics. Planning felt it needed the certainty of a solid foundation of data for it to proceed logically from 'survey to analysis to plan'. By adopting a 'scientific approach' planning believed that if the process were followed correctly, then the resulting plan would inevitably be correct. The scientific philosopher Karl Popper[5] has taken issue with the very basis of the *scientific method* as the way science really operates. He contended that actually scientists postulate hypotheses that must survive experimentation to have validity, rather than evolving them as a result of the analysis of empirical evidence. So if planning assumed analysing masses of data would scientifically produce a good environment, then how different is the basis of urban design? Urban design takes as its starting point, 'let us design what we would like to see built, and then find the process and means to achieve it.'

THE ORIGINS OF URBAN DESIGN

Learning from the successes and failures of planning and architecture is one of a number of separate strands that have coalesced to become what is now generally understood to be 'mainstream' urban design. North America never developed a comprehensive planning system of land use controls, as the UK had done. Instead US planners relied on simple zoning ordnances to physically prescribe the overall massing of buildings and the cross-section of streets. Alex Krieger stakes his claim to Harvard being the birthplace of urban design in Chapter 1. He reports how a group of eminent architects and social thinkers gathered at Harvard in 1956 to inaugurate the first urban design conference. After a lifetime of study Krieger concludes that urban design is less a technical discipline and more a mindset of those determined to 'enhance urbanism'.

Bringing life to dull cities and the rejection of suburbia was the stimulus for the founders of British urban design in the same period. Ian Nairn criticised the spread of the suburbs or '*subtopia*' in 'Outrage' articles in the *Architectural Review* magazine.[6] Nairn was probably the first journalist and later TV commentator who treated the contemporary city as worthy of study as a

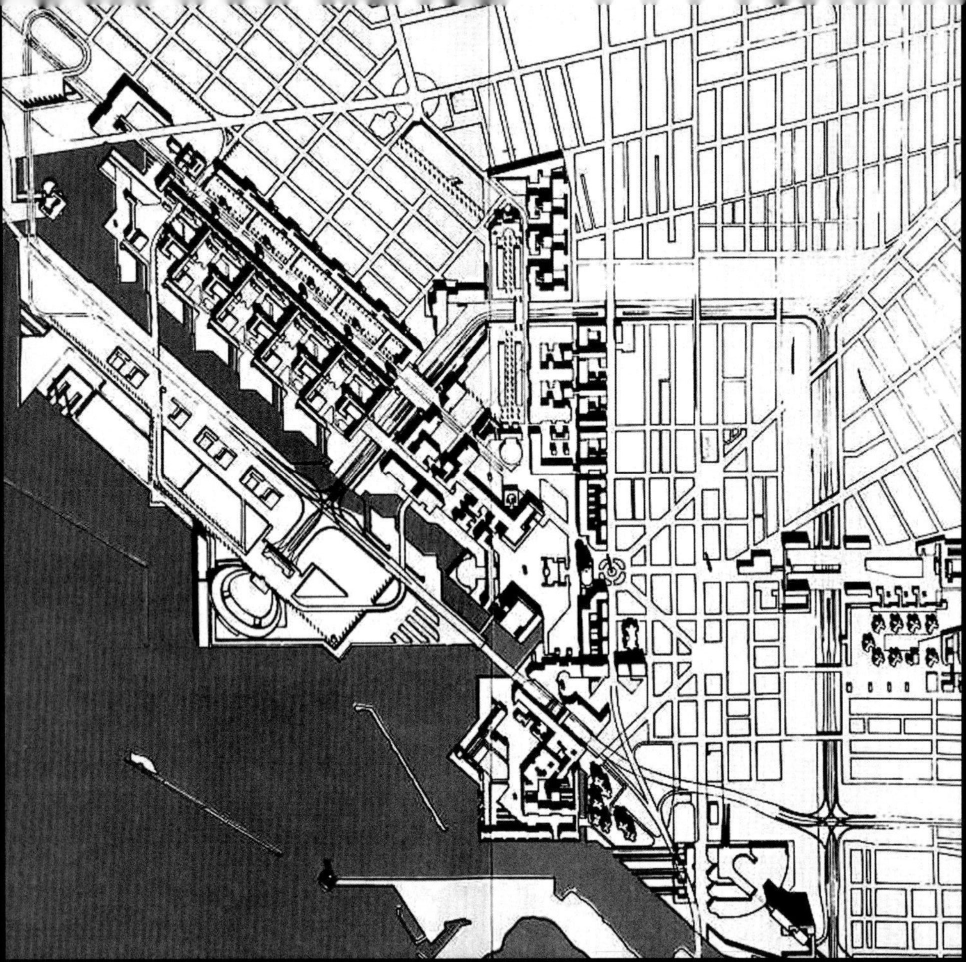

0.9 **Waterside development proposals, Buffalo, NY, Cornell Urban Design Team, 1969. This class project demonstrated how the intersection of a number of street grids can create exciting urban design opportunities.**
Source: Albright-Knox Art Gallery, Buffalo, NY

0.10 **Town Square, Poundbury. Sentimental attachment to traditional housing models in an era of rapid change.**

social and cultural entity that could be improved by good design. The 'townscape group' criticised the appalling low standards of the public domain and showed how introducing design into everyday streets and spaces could lift the greyness of post-war Britain. Gordon Cullen[7] and Kenneth Browne illustrated in simple sketches the benefits of designing the whole environment and learning from the best examples from the Continent. They also gave timely warnings of the result of the overprovision of space for roads, verges and building setbacks that resulted in wide open spaces between buildings and prevented any sense of urbanity in new developments. An article in *Counter-Attack* of 1956 by Walter Manthorpe demonstrated how 'Rules of thumb, planning controls, byelaws and general prejudice have now so combined that it is practically impossible to build towns: only garden suburbs are permitted.'[8]

Manthorpe goes on to criticise the approach of laying down the street grid first, then filling the space between with buildings rather than designing the best building relationship and then evolving a road pattern to suit. SLOAP, 'Space Left Over After Planning', resulted from this approach of laying out the road network first and leaving odd pieces of land behind that did not conveniently fit within the street grid. These become neglected wastelands cut off from the surrounding existing street patterns with no function but to collect rubbish.

If only these prescient thinkers had been heeded, many of the hundreds of housing estates that blight Britain now would have not have been so bleak and hostile to pedestrians, with wide expanses of grass between buildings that allowed for the second carriageway that was never built and over-engineered roundabouts that serve to separate rather than unite communities. Urban design is now seen as the means to regenerate these estates but at the time its role was limited to enlivening dull town planning reports with sketches of happy shoppers and children holding balloons in 'futuristic precincts'. Alternative views to the modernist agenda were heresy to the architectural establishment and anti-urban policies dominated town planning. To study urban design meant travelling to the universities of the United States. Here European *émigrés* rediscovered their urban heritage and made it relevant to the modern American city through the organisational rigour of the grid, the vibrant street culture of the city block and the dynamism of the high rise.

AMERICA TAKES THE LEAD

The writings of Kevin Lynch at MIT and Colin Rowe at Cornell University laid the philosophical foundations for this new approach to designing the modern city. *Image of the City*[9] provided the analytical tools of the path, edge, node, landmark and district that urban designers still use to understand urban areas. In *Collage City*[10] Colin Rowe and Fred Koetter asked, 'Why should we have to prefer nostalgia for the future to a nostalgia for the past?' They wanted the best of both worlds; the dynamism of modern architecture with the richness and variety of medieval and Renaissance cities; respecting the street pattern while still creating exciting new urban spaces. They suggested that 'a collage approach in which objects are conscripted or seduced out of their context, is the only way of dealing with the ultimate problems of either or both, utopia and tradition.'

Historical precedents were found in traditional villages, Renaissance set pieces and Georgian squares, no matter whether examples were from the twentieth or the fifteen century. A seminal work at Cornell was Grahame Shane's 'Field analysis of Central London' of 1971 showing how the Georgian 'great estates' were laid out in the lands between the main routes that followed the lines of the tributaries that flowed south to the River Thames (see figure 0.8).

Laid out with the grandest houses fronting the square at the heart of the estate to attract the wealthy early buyers and to set the market for the secondary street grid of more modest terraces behind this pattern well illustrated Rowe's philosophy of creating new urban set pieces while pragmatically working with the existing constraints and linking into the prevailing street pattern. This contextual approach was capable of phased implementation in step with market demand and available funding, in contrast to the grand avenues and places of Haussmann's Paris, later echoed by Le Corbusier's radical Plan Voisin of 1925, that would require the full unyielding might of the state to implement.

Away from the well-intentioned socialist myopia of Britain and the peer pressure to be up with the latest design fad aspiring ex-pat urban designers were freed to realise that the city is an act of creation by many hands rather than the by-product of bye-law streets, space standards and planning legislation. It was ironic how studying within an American environment opened the eyes of so many European students to the fantastic urban design models that had been created by their own culture.

BRITAIN LEARNS FROM AMERICA AND EUROPE

Made concrete by the gifted pragmatism of America, urban design then re-crossed the pond and set up base in the UK where raiding parties of enthusiastic recruits made forays into Europe to pillage ideas and plagiarise good examples to bring home. *Responsive Environments*,[11] produced by the Joint Centre for Urban Design at Oxford Polytechnic, introduced the practical concepts of 'permeability, legibility and robustness' to help designers create a democratic setting and maximise choice for users of the built environment. More recently *By Design*[12] and *The Urban Design Compendium*[13] have codified the issues and objectives of what has evolved to become 'mainstream urban design' that is taught as gospel to urban design students and tattooed on the perceptive faculties of practising consultants. Tony Lloyd-Jones expands on urban design theory in Chapter 2 and asks whether this western concept is a luxury for affluent societies or has any applicability to the developing world.

The replacement of the conservation-minded Royal Fine Art Commission by the more forward-looking Commission for the Built Environment (CABE) in 1999 has put urban design at the forefront of the drive to improve design standards. Design Review committees, discussed by John Punter in Chapter 5, suggest ways that projects can be improved and CABE technical publications and Summer Schools are raising skill levels. Richard Rogers has encouraged the Mayor of London to move design up the agenda of the Greater London Authority and the forthcoming Planning Act will require developers to prepare design statements with their planning applications.

OUR RESPONSE TO EARLIER MISTAKES

It is said that some of the places in which many people feel most comfortable appear to have evolved naturally over time rather than been consciously designed, so why can't natural processes be allowed to give individuality to our towns now as they did in the past? Why should towns need to be designed at all? The answer is that towns have never been designed for arbitrary reasons but have always been laid out for the functions and styles that prevailed at the time. Streets followed paths that were based on ancient field patterns, which in turn had historical, cultural or topographical reasons for their apparent randomness. But if the public appear to be more comfortable with the legacy of the past then why not give them traditional-looking buildings?

WHAT PLACE FOR TRADITION?

But what does tradition really mean? Is it a question of architectural style, a set of immutable principles, an aesthetic pattern book or an evolutionary process of re-using what has been found to work well while replacing that found lacking or redundant? The modernist view that the Victorian era left nothing of value has now been completely revised as we realise the bold ingenuity of engineers and architects of that dynamic era. Victorian architects skilfully planned their buildings with frontages to all sides, corners emphasized by turrets and exciting roof profiles to capture the sky.

The rediscovery of the modest street as more than a simple thoroughfare but a clearly defined and readily understood set of rules of where everything needed should be placed is a major achievement of urban design that Adriaan Geuze celebrates in Chapter 9 while Paul Murrain argues for the respect of tradition in Chapter 4. We appear to be in a period of rediscovery. History is recreated nightly on TV and old film classics are remade, yet we have never had more creative individuals. Have we lost hope in the future? When does respect for the past become too reverential, when does admiration of traditional forms lead to the creative cul de sac of reproducing facsimiles? We feel free to plunder the past to create the future but if the future is a copy of the past, then will all future environments be reproductions of some era of idealised market town Englishness or will the reference point be a rolling past so that at some point we will be copying the present?

Accepting the difficulty of side-stepping the

0.11 Covent Garden fruit and vegetable market, Central London, 1968. The market was a vibrant source of activity in the city centre for three hundred years but planners felt that too much lorry traffic was causing congestion, so the market was relocated to a bleak site in Vauxhall, south of the Thames.

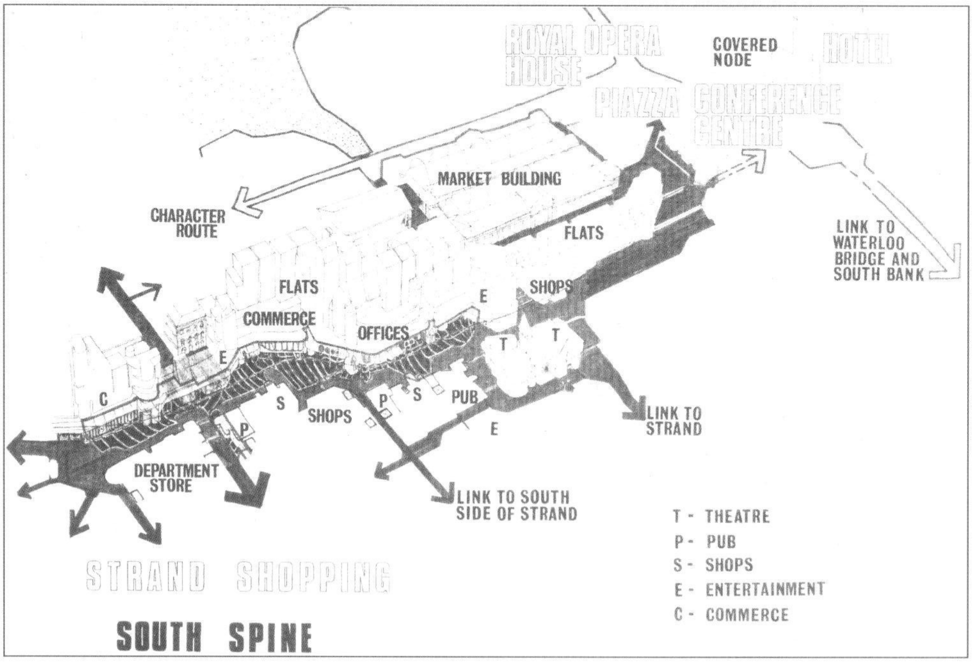

0.12 Proposed development of Covent Garden Market, Central London, 1968. Radical plans to redevelop 80 acres around the market caused widespread opposition that eventually led to the whole area being retained and now becoming part of the London tourist trail.
Source: Covent Garden Area Draft Plan 1968 Consortium of the GLC, City of Westminster, LB Camden

prickly issues of taste and tradition, urban designers need to prioritise their central task of improving all public aspects of urban life. Jan Gehl reminds us in Chapter 7 that the order should be 'Life, Spaces, Buildings: and in said order, please'. A view confirmed by Ken Worpole in Chapter 11 who goes on to emphasise the social dimension of public space. These pieces remind us not to be pessimistic about human nature. Despite the vandalism of estates, graffiti-tagged walls and chewing gum-spattered pavements, it is an article of faith for urban designers that attractive and stimulating environments can bring out the best in all of us as citizens and as neighbours. We should also accept that people have certain fundamental characteristics, foibles and weaknesses that a new environment is not going to change overnight. Rather, we should aspire to initiate a series of incremental improvements in order that residents can realise the mutual benefits of looking after and cherishing their surroundings. The aim is to initiate a virtuous circle where everyone gains from the improvements made by them and their neighbours to the collective environment.

Principally, urban design should not repeat the modernist mistakes of expecting the population to change to suit the designers' vision. The exercise of the creative ego is inevitable in every designer, otherwise there would be no innovation, but creative solutions should be used to encourage people to be open to new ideas and not to intimidate them. As Les Spark summed up at the 2004 CABE Summer School, 'We don't do urban design *to* people but *with* people.'[14]

FACTORS INFLUENCING THE FUTURE OF URBAN DESIGN

In addition to the issues raised by Krieger and Lloyd-Jones, a number of factors can be identified that have been significant agents for change. These include providing more housing while making better use of land and reconciling the emerging power of the consumer-driven market with the rising awareness of green issues and sustainability. Other contributors take up many of these points so the following is a brief review of the most significant issues of the day.

A NEW AWARENESS

In the past twenty years many organisations and pressure groups have been at work to raise awareness of the problems facing urban society. Until recently the decision-makers responsible for the built environment had dismissed many groups as marginal with little worthwhile to contribute to the central question of how we should build. That these 'soft issues' are now central to the government's agenda shows the foresight of many original thinkers, prepared to poke their heads above the parapet and speak out against the orthodoxy of the day. A conjunction of circumstances within a short period of time have raised the profile of 'quality of life issues' and kick-started the debate about what sort of urban environment we should be creating. Not least was a change of government in the UK to one that is less theologically opposed to the principle of planning.

CONSERVATION, THE GREEN MOVEMENT AND SUSTAINABILITY

Joni Mitchell's 'They paved paradise and put up a parking lot'[15] captured the feelings of impending loss of a more aware generation as did Rachel Carson's cataloguing of environmental damage in *The Silent Spring*[16] and *Small is Beautiful* by Schumacher.[17] Meanwhile opposition to the bulldozer of universal 'comprehensive redevelopment' found a *cause célèbre* over the battle for the future of Covent Garden in London's West End. Anticipating the planned relocation of the

0.13 BedZED frontage to public realm, Sutton. Strict north–south solar orientation of blocks can lead to interface difficulties with gable walls facing the public realm.

0.14 New Bank Headquarters, Central, Hong Kong. Always ready to accept more dramatic and prestigious new architecture, Hong Kong has only relatively recently accepted that its traditional built heritage has any value.

raditional vegetable market out of Covent Garden n 1971 the three newly formed Central London uthorities set up a consortium in 1965 to study the wider area's future'.[18]

he planning team produced a report in 1968 that ought 'to protect and enhance the historic, archiectural and social qualities of the area', but to esidents the images in the report of streets being eplaced by mega-structures prompted organised esistance. A very effective and widely supported ampaign forced a change of policy to one conerving virtually the whole district. The built abric has largely been retained but little by little he character has changed as the area has ecome ever more popular. Specialised theatre hops and real London pubs have been replaced y ever more expensive boutiques and cafés until ow, nearing the height of the real estate cycle of highest and best use', the chain stores are taking ver the prime spots. Covent Garden is now on he tourist trail and being invaded by Leicester quare souvenir shops. To many, Covent Garden s seen as a success story but it should act as a esson demonstrating how the preservation of uildings does not result in retaining the special haracter of a district nor the resident community s rising rents drive out local people.

CONSERVATION IS AN ALIEN CONCEPT IN THE DEVELOPING WORLD

Explosive economic growth and the desire to catch up with the West have led to even more wholesale redevelopment in Third World countries. Most have little regard for the value of their built heritage until it is almost all gone. The Tiger Economies of Asia have embraced both modern technology and modern architecture and reject traditional forms like the Chinese shop-house and the 'hutongs' of Beijing. Singapore redeveloped most of its old China Town but fortunately saved its Marina Quay, now a popular evening entertainment district albeit heavily gentrified, and Hong Kong saved Lan Kwai Fong while managing to keep aspects of its traditional street life. In a city that has been known to replace buildings with larger structures even before they are finished conservation is considered a radical idea. In Chapter 10 Alex Lui shows how the unpromising collection of streets up the hill from Central District on Hong Kong Island became a thriving entertainment centre. The steepness of the site and the ease of adapting the buildings to bars and clubs on lower floors allowed some residents to stay in place above. A well-organised local traders group and a ready supply of thirsty office workers in the nearby commercial towers have created a model of catering for change while keeping some of the old character that is applicable to other edge-of-CBD sites.

CONTEXT: AN END TO THE TABULA RASA

This raised awareness of the need to conside new buildings in the context of everything tha already exists, not only as buildings of architectural or historic interest, was the beginning of the end for the modernist view of city planning. The view that planning is an exercise to be conducted on a blank sheet of paper has been replaced by respect for existing street patterns and by creating a spirit of continuity with the past. While few would disagree with this axiom, the quote from Rem Koolhaas, however, leads one to wonder how deep his commitment is to respecting context. Can a yearning for 'the good old days be detected?

But the notion of a new beginning – starting from scratch, the tabula rasa – had been taboo ever since Le Corbusier's brutal attempt with the Plan Voisin to scrape everything away at once. The harshness, the shock, the incredible insanity – but at the same time the incredible eloquence – of his operation closed the book on the question of a new beginning for generations to come.[19]

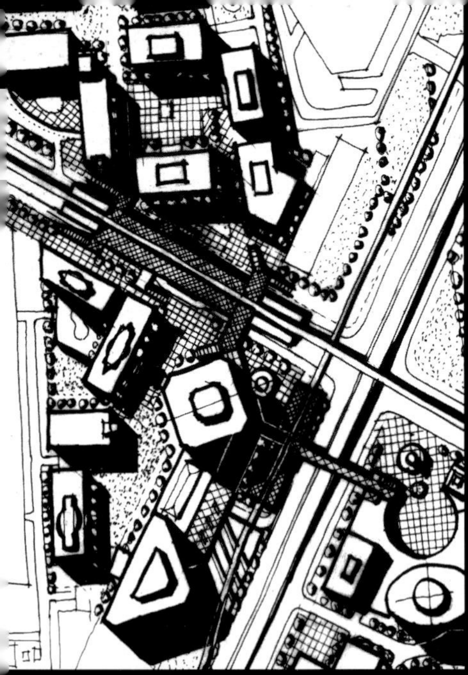

0.15 **Transport Development Zone Concept Sketch for concentration of high-density development in zone accessible to interchange stations between two elevated transit lines**
Source: Bangkok Transit System Corporation

0.16 **Place de l'Homme de Fer, Strasbourg. A quiet local square as it was before the tram and the associated renovation of the entire area**
Source: Jan Gehl

0.17 **Renovation of Place de l'Homme de Fer. A dramatic circular tram station and an underground car park are inspiration for the new pedestrian environment**
Source: Jan Gehl

0.18 **Circular tram station roof, Place de l'Homme de Fer. The huge floating glass roof accentuates the high priority of the main tram station and the importance of the tram line in the cityscape**
Source: Jan Gehl

Time, however, is now on our side. Many of the unloved buildings of the 1960s and 1970s have thankfully come to the end of their useful lives. Without guilt or regret they can be replaced with new buildings that relate better to their neighbours. This replacement process provides many opportunities to kick start regeneration which can be seen recently when the modernists lost the conservation battle in Portsmouth as crowds cheered the demolition of the brutalist concrete Tricorn Centre of the 1960s to make way for new development.

GREEN HAS BECOME THE NEW GOD, 'SUSTAINABILITY'

The Green movement has been the other great influence on this generation of designers. The campaign over decades to raise awareness of ecology and biodiversity, the benefits of walkable cities and the minimisation of waste have brought the issue of how to create sustainable communities to the fore. Sustainability is the potent issue of the moment, and possibly the most misused. It is a rallying point on which everyone can agree. Students are enthused by it, politicians quote it to support their green credentials, it is the coolest badge to wear for our brand-obsessed society. Everyone claims to support sustainable objectives, but do they have a good grasp of what they really are? Built evidence is thin on the ground, particularly in the mainstream building industry. Bill Dunster has been an ardent promoter and practitioner with his seminal BedZED zero-energy housing at Sutton, which he describes in Chapter 15. Rather than being a way to just save on electricity bills, Dunster is arguing for a radical restructuring of the building industry that could deliver higher environmental standards at little extra cost. Urban design supports sustainable objectives by improving pedestrian and cycle access and in saving land and sensitive areas by building at more efficient densities. But there is an inherent point of conflict. In order to maximise solar gain, efficient building orientation can result in regimented rows of south-facing façades that are at odds with urban design objectives of buildings fronting onto streets and enclosing private open space.

The converse is that the Prince's Foundation 'New Urbanist'-inspired design codes favouring traditional design at places like Upton 'are so rigid tha they make it impossible to harness wind and solar power', according to Bill Dunster.[20] This is an issue that deserves much more attention from both urban designers and sustainability promoters so that a situation does not develop where it is necessary to choose to support either sustainable techniques or practise good urban design principles, to promote modern buildings and technology or draw up coded traditionalism. There must be some middle ground.

THE NEED FOR MORE HOUSING, AND AT A HIGHER DENSITY

The single factor that has had the most profound effect on UK government policy in the past decade has been the demographic projections of how many more homes are needed to cope with the social changes taking place in society. Stating that lifestyles constantly change is a platitude but the realisation that millions of individual lifestyles changes could result in such an explosion of housing demand has been a profound shock to politicians worried by the unpopularity of more housing estates and a source of warm anticipation of increased profits by the housebuilders.

More divorces and separations, more older people living alone, more young people leaving home earlier and marrying later means that 80 per cent of the 4 million new homes needed over the next twenty-five years will be for single person households, according to Peter Hall.[21] This situation is exacerbated by the particular British attitude that housing is primarily an investment and larger houses appreciate in value more than small units. The likely result is that most of these homes will be larger than needed to house single people, so a vast amount of new housing has to be built and land for it has to be found. Cities have to be the answer if yet more precious countryside is not to be lost for this scale of residential development. The effectiveness of rural anti-development lobbies delaying the granting of planning permissions for greenfield sites has been an additional push factor towards targeting urban areas. The realisation of the enormity of these forces led to the government setting up the Urban Task Force and the publication of *Toward an*

Urban Renaissance in 1999.[22] This recommended that much more than the present target of 60 per cent of new development should be on previously used 'brownfield' sites at higher densities and regeneration has to be design-led. A similar debate is underway in the USA to fight urban sprawl with the snappily entitled 'Smart Growth Movement', which is examined by Harriet Tregoning in Chapter 3.

URBAN DESIGN OF MOVEMENT

The London Jubilee Line is noted for its distinctive Underground stations designed by different architects. The involvement of talented architects has not, however, extended to urban design as opportunities for using stations as catalysts for major urban regeneration are sadly lacking. Access to public transport and the clustering of development around stops are key sustainability objectives and are at the core of Transit Oriented Development that has been championed by advocates ranging from Peter Calthorpe[23] in the USA to the RICS[24] in this country. The symbiotic relationship between the transport infrastructure and urban design needs to be better exploited. Urban design helps in the creation of a better pedestrian environment with clear routes to stations that increase transit ridership and thus improves the economic viability of the system. Transit stops provide structuring elements for public space and increase activity levels that benefit supporting facilities. Densities can be increased, car use can be reduced and urbanity can be enhanced. Then why in Britain have we not had more success in integrating transport and urban design?

Trams and trolleybuses have formed the principal movement systems for cities since the nineteenth century. First, horse-drawn and then motorised, trams were the backbone of British cities. Even the Los Angeles conurbation was laid out for the tram before the motor lobby got State legislation changed to benefit the automobile and encourage freeway construction, according to Mike Davis.[25]

Europe has provided recent models of good integration of trams into the street system, demonstrating how new lines can be catalysts for improving the public realm. Strasbourg, Bordeaux, Lisbon and Amsterdam demonstrate how the tram is an integral and vital part of the street environment. The tram has made a comeback in the UK with seven systems running and twenty-five more planned, but a recent review by the National Audit Office[26] reports that existing systems have been dogged by low passenger numbers and high building costs, leading to financial losses for operating companies. The split between the engineering of systems and the planning of their surroundings has also hindered an integrated approach. Opportunities for 'joined-up thinking' are lost due to the mismatch in the shorter timescales of building development and the lengthy and often uncertain planning and implementation of transit systems. Extensive teams of specialist engineers and financial consultants are assembled to implement transit networks with architects and landscape consultants brought in at the end of the process to design the public areas and tidy up the streetscape. Considering urban design at an early stage is essential to maximise opportunities for integrated planning.

Enlarging the consultant team will inevitably complicate an already complex process but means must be found for all the disciplines to work together or yet more opportunities will be lost.

THE ECONOMIC VALUE OF URBAN DESIGN

This is an issue that has been given a preliminary airing by CABE[27] but deserves far more attention and detailed analysis and feedback from completed schemes to inform clients and investors. The extent to which public investment in urban design and the public realm improvements can bring forth increased levels of private investment and to what extent regeneration projects have achieved their stated aims are areas that need long-term studies to feed results back to urban design consultancies and decision-makers to guide future actions. The multiplier effect of new infrastructure and public realm investment is the basis for public capital investment to kick-start private initiatives but presently relies more on hope value than any quantifiable economic calculation.

THE RIGHT TIME FOR URBAN DESIGN

While people are increasingly mobile, cities of course are not. Urban areas are stuck with the baggage of their heritage and their image, and towns perceived to offer a better living and working environment are attracting more investment. Towns are in head-to-head competition to attract businesses as well as the best shops and the most financially liquid consumers. Tired and down-at-heel town centres must improve or they will

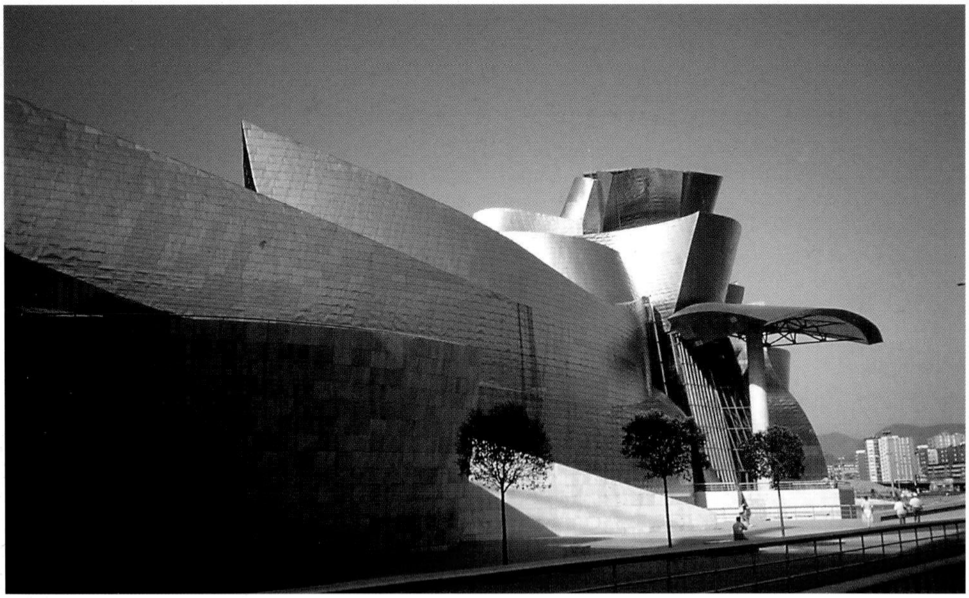

0.19 Guggenheim Museum, Bilbao, Spain. This iconic titanium-clad museum, designed by Frank Gehry, put the largest city of the Basque country on the tourist map and is now the model for every city wanting to raise its profile using the 'Bilbao effect'.

decline yet further. More local councils are coming to the conclusion that the 'cheap and cheerful' drive-in retail sheds have to go in order to attract more entertainment venues and designer stores back to town centres. Towns with a poor image need to be repackaged through new investment and renewal projects to stem the outflow of the young and able. Councils want 'to put our town on the map' and have been told that an urban design vision is the way to achieve it. Economic regeneration means attracting the 1 per cent winners to live and invest locally. This group have high expectations of a better environment and the designer lifestyle that councils are striving to provide.

ICONIC BUILDINGS, HYPER ARCHITECTURE, THE NEXT BIG THING

The success of the Bilbao Guggenheim Art Gallery demonstrated how the 'wow!' factor of exciting photogenic buildings can attract a good press that in turn attracts visitors. Further icons followed. The gleaming form of the Selfridges store landed in drab Birmingham and demonstrated with panache that galleries are good but the prestigious department store is still the ultimate urban draw. Richard Rees brings this out in his piece 'The Brand New Authentic Retail Experience' in Chapter 17. Other cities are contemplating building their own iconic buildings in a race to gain competitive advantage. Comparisons can be made with the Renaissance city-states vying to attract the best architects, artists and craftsmen to raise the prestige of the city. Those like Venice, 'the city in love with itself'[28] with the most famous monuments and artworks also prospered commercially.

But if one iconic building is a draw, then surely a whole bunch of them will be an even bigger attraction to put a town on the map. 'Big architecture' inevitably attracts more attention in the press than more visually restrained projects and, the client hopes, more publicity that can be translated into solid investment. Several high profile architects noted for their distinctive architecture are now chasing urban design projects and attracting commissions from councils who believe that these bold design statements send out a clear message to potential investors that they mean business and are committed to radical change. The 'mainstream urban design' community appear perplexed as to how to respond to these upstarts. Having advocated pluralism and a diversity of ideas, it would be hypocritical to now caution restraint on some of the bold concepts now emerging and, having eschewed questions of architectural style in the debate about traditional architecture, it would be churlish for mainstream urban design to pour cold water on avant-garde design.

BUT IS IT URBAN DESIGN?

But questions do have to be asked. Can these projects be implemented as shown, can whole layouts designed by one distinctive hand be split into packages designed by different architects or does the lead architect have to design it all? What about the cherished urban design objectives of promoting active frontages that enclose space and pedestrian-friendly ground planes in schemes comprising strange building forms balanced on piloti, 'blobs on sticks' to some critics? Is so much iconic architecture in such confined areas indigestible? Is there enough demand and funds for the special uses for so many special buildings in regeneration areas where only limited new retail floorspace is feasible and Millennium projects have already mopped up much of the arts and community budgets? The accepted design wisdom of setting a few special jewel buildings against a well-mannered background is being replaced by a kaleidoscope of 'look at me' buildings. What about the ethics of this individualistic approach translated to the larger scale of the masterplan? Should the plan be a broad framework flexible enough to accommodate many styles of built contributions or be a bold vision for how every part of a district should be built?

Until some of these projects are implemented and the built situation on the ground appraised, the jury will still be out on whether this is real progress in taking urban design to its next stage of growth or another 1960s-type diversion into

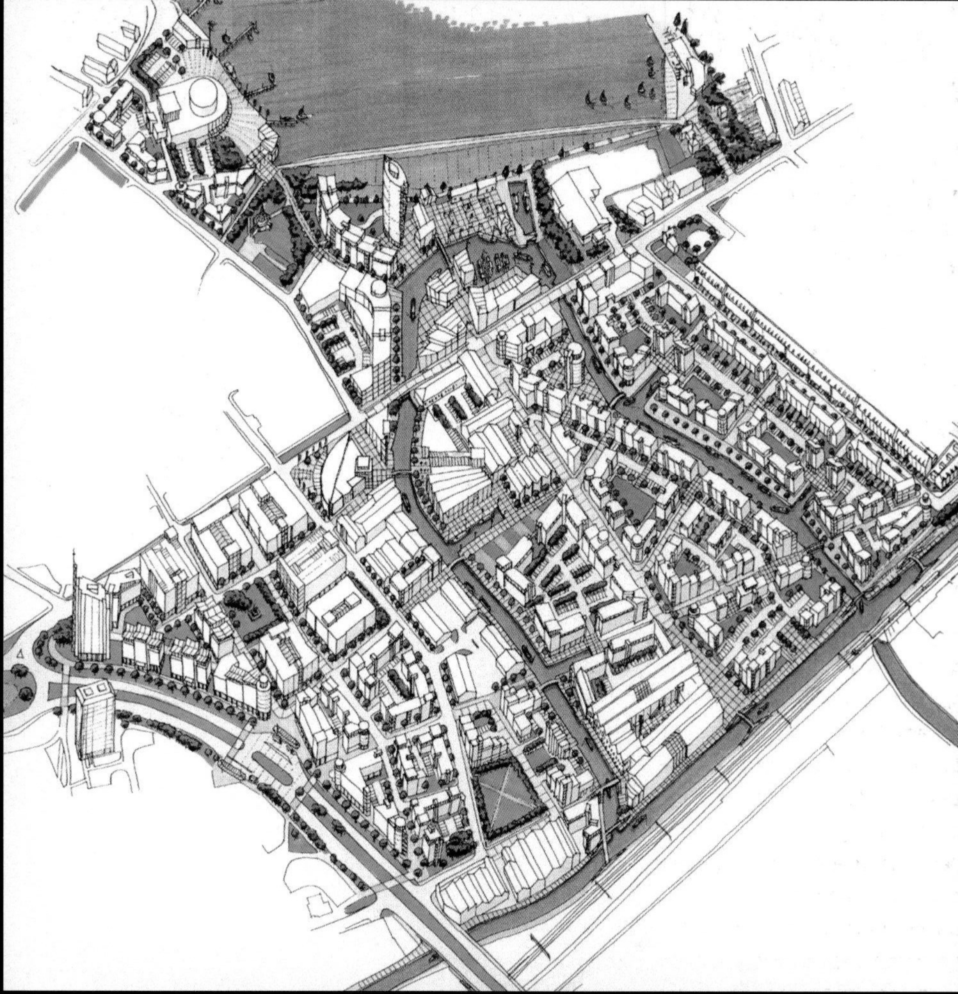

0.20 Icknield Loop Masterplan, Birmingham. A partnership of Birmingham City Council, Advantage Midlands and British Waterways is promoting the Birmingham West Side as part of the city's regeneration. This new mixed-use vision by JRUD is centred around Brunel's Canal Basin and old canal side warehouse and will link the outer suburbs to the centre.

object building that will cancel out many of the gains that urban design has painfully achieved in the past twenty years. Experience tells us that every new generation of designers reject the views of the previous generation and seeks to make their own mark on the built environment. Perhaps the current exponents of mainstream urban design have taken things as far as they are able and should give way to a new generation of talented designers who do not work with the spectre of past mistakes looking over their shoulders and can unself-consciously view the future as an exciting destination.

INVOLVING THE USERS

As well as being open to new ideas, urban design should encourage a wider and more representative cross-section of society to participate. There is a tendency for the views of white, middle-aged and middle-class men to prevail as these groups predominate in the active ranks of the design professionals. Mardie Townsend explains the female perspective on urban design in Chapter 12. However thorough in their analysis of the place and the problems, and however well-intentioned their desire to achieve the best result, they cannot see and experience the environment through the eyes of others. The public realm is the principal meeting place for different age, cultural and ethnic groups, so these groups need to be better represented within the design professions to influence the built product.

The public certainly want to have their say in what is built, as deference to those in authority making the decisions on how and where people should live has vanished. Sullen resentment was the response to the former paternalistic city fathers, recent converts to 'modernisation', who dragged their towns 'kicking and screaming' into the twentieth century with high-rise estates, inner ring roads and modern precincts. Almost every town and city has suffered at the hands of the 'modernisers' and now urgently deserves a better environment. Public consultation is one way to redress the balance towards the users but is often limited to asking the neighbours of a planned development to exercise their prejudices to decide the layout for future occupants unknown. Without the ability to identify the residents in good time the sort of positive involvement described by Lucien Kroll in Chapter 14 will not be possible.

COLONISING THE URBAN REALM

The perceived success of the public realm will be the main criterion by which the success of urban design will be judged. It is ironic that at a time when most private houses are more spacious and well equipped than at any time in history, we are making such efforts to entice people to spend more time outside.

In the eighteenth century keeping people out of the public realm was the objective. In *The London Mob*,[29] Robert Shoemaker describes how Georgian London was almost engulfed by the mob as riotous events and insurrections kept the city in a ferment of unease. Shoemaker's explanation for this eighteenth-century 'culture of open-air dissent' was the speed of growth of London and the squalid housing conditions that

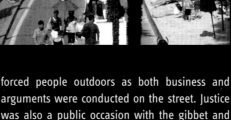

0.21 Paris Plage, right bank of the Seine. A range of activities along two miles of Paris's man-made beach are popular annual attractions.

0.22 Paris Plage, Hôtel de Ville to Pont Neuf. Palm trees and white sand transform a busy riverside boulevard into the Riviera for Parisians spending summer in the city.

0.23 Shopping street, Brisbane. Active pedestrian street scene includes weather protection canopies and island kiosks incorporating entrances to the bus station at the lower level.

forced people outdoors as both business and arguments were conducted on the street. Justice was also a public occasion with the gibbet and the pillories the focal points of public spaces.

Feeling safe in public spaces is an abiding concern with 'secure by design' principles dictating housing layouts and the threat of street crime and terrorism in public places leading to more CCTV cameras and other security measures. Bill Mitchell warns that 'the next big thing in 21st century civics is the anti-agora, a place defended against the theatrics of terror, but consequently no longer available for free assembly and expression'.[30] The invasion of the centre of cities by weekend binge drinking is another reason for some to stay at home and watch the TV in comfort and security.

A happier model is the Mediterranean lifestyle where shady piazzas are cooler than stuffy houses in the evening and families decamp outside to eat, socialise and debate. The hope is that this publicly conducted social life will not be killed off by air conditioning and Italian TV's answer to *Big Brother*. We must ensure that the public realm can offer things that the super-equipped home can never provide. The Campo in Venice devoted to debate where you are always sure of an argument in the morning and 'Speakers Corner' in London are unique places, but what chance of reproducing something of these traditions in new urban places? An interesting outcome of the ban on smoking in pubs in Ireland has led to a new spirit of camaraderie among the smokers gathered outside pub entrances.

As well as improving the use of the public realm for the activities of daily life, every opportunity should be taken to expropriate public spaces for special events. Traditional street fairs and Christmas and farmers' markets are still the main ways to colonise public space but sport is quickly catching up in importance. For centuries the Pallio has been a terrifying fast horse race in the centre of Siena and for a hundred years the Tour de France has brought sporting drama to town centres throughout France. Many major cities have attracted tens of thousands of runners onto the streets, copying the success of the London Marathon, and motor races bring hordes of petrol heads and celebrities to Monaco, Brisbane, Macao, and even London could one day host a Grand Prix. Paris Plage brings a taste of the glamorous Côte d'Azure beach life to stifling Paris in the summer. Occupying a usually busy traffic boulevard Parisians can bask in sun-loungers on trucked-in sand and pretend that the River Seine is really the Mediterranean.

Participation in the public realm can also be encouraged with responsive street furniture, lighting and art works, but mostly it is people themselves who are the biggest draw. The tables in a Paris café face out onto the street, the better to people watch, and our tribal origins are evident in the way people usually gravitate to busy rather than empty spaces. The mass body sculpture of artist photographer Spencer Tunick has clothed public spaces throughout the world with thousands of prone naked volunteers that literally humanise space. The places, ranging from the reflecting pools of the Washington Monument to the escalators of the Selfridges store in London,

0.24 Student demo, Oxford Street, London. The city streets are not just for traffic and shopping but also provide a venue for community events ranging from marathon races to student demonstrations.

0.25 Pompidou Centre, Paris. The building by architects Renzo Piano and Richard Rogers in 1977 promotes activity in the Place Georges Pompidou due to the dramatic architecture as well as its public function as an art gallery.

can never feel the same afterwards as the image still lingers after the participants have dressed and gone home. Artist Christo achieves this disorientation with his wrapped buildings by hiding the familiar, a trick now achievable by projected laser lights, as seen on Buckingham Palace at the Golden Jubilee concert.

IDENTITY NOT HOMOGENEITY

As we make advances in the understanding of urban design a new set of issues comes into focus. These include the big one, what gives places identity and how can we foster it? A law of physics states that there is a tendency of structures to homogenise over time[31]. There is a tendency for this process to also happen at the urban level where the distinctive character of places is being eroded as towns and cities compete to offer the same range of outlets that the public appear to want. The signs of identical retail and bars chains are prominent in every high street, developer standard house types and supermarkets grace the suburbs and similarly bland PFI hospitals and schools care for our needs. Urban design must respond to the aspiration of councils to raise standards and provide better facilities for residents whilst not contributing to making the problem worse. While many urban areas suffer from similar problems, solutions based on a too literal interpretation of the urban design toolkit could perversely produce places that 'work well' but look remarkably similar. The Law of Unintended Consequences could result in regenerated towns having a common, but rather too tasteful, look. Making distinctive places that people will want to live in because they feel they belong and will want to visit to experience their special-ness may entail designers taking risks. They may have to force themselves not to play safe. The too familiar low-fat design solution may need to be beefed up with something to give it more bite; an injection of protein to grow character.

As we hone the craft of the art of urban design and the basic principles of urban regeneration become more widely understood and disseminated priority now needs to be directed towards researching what are those factors that contribute to identity and how can design go the extra mile to reinforce it so that every town can feel proud to be unique. This will certainly require more quality design time but demands on urban designers' time are increasing from all quarters.

IS SPECIALISATION INEVITABLE?

Planning for higher standards in all aspects of urban living means that the process of preparing plans is being constantly stretched to address a wider range of issues. This will expand further as we peel away the layers to find what is at the core of sustainability. Is it humanely possible to manage them all? Will design skills atrophy as we get bogged down in ticking off the tasks on ever more check boxes? We have to be careful that urban design does not follow town planning into the process-driven netherworld that led to its disengagement from the design process.

Many postgraduate students enter urban design courses to pursue particular interests as well as learning the urban design core skills. While there is a shortage of graduates with traditional place-making skills there are plenty who are building up valuable knowledge in 'hot topics' such as green issues and sustainability. Those that wish to pursue these interests after graduation could specialise in a range of complementary disciples extending their core urban design training to effectively contribute in areas such as sustainability auditing, assisting with design coding, running community consultation exercises and preparing commercial 'value' assessments of the benefits of urban design. This could free up designers' time to get to grips with those elusive qualities that make places unique.

Many will say that only by continuing to cover the whole spectrum of issues can urban designers do a proper job. But practitioners have to honestly ask themselves if they can competently handle them all whilst maintaining standards? If not, increasing specialisation may be inevitable even at the cost of even bigger design teams requiring more time to co-ordinate all their inputs.

THE RIGHT TIME FOR URBAN DESIGN

Bernard O'Donoghue's poem in the prologue to this book touches on the audacity of those who take it upon themselves to determine how cities will be shaped and the environment formed in which people will spend their lives. It is an awesome responsibility but 'somebody has to do it', and that somebody has emerged as the urban designer. Urban design cannot complain of this onerous responsibility thrust onto its shoulders. Urban designers have been proselytizing and pamphleteering to champion their cause for thirty years. They have been demanding from the sidelines to be given a chance to show what they can do, so now the time has come 'to put up or shut up'. Recently the Urban Design Group celebrated twenty-five years as the main focus and driving force for urban design in the UK. CABE is encouraging local councils and private developers to raise their standards and to expect more from their designers and increase staff training in the principles of good urban design and public space.

In trying to maintain the validity of the present approach, practitioners need to be aware of the danger that urban design could become satisfied with what has been achieved so far or, even worse, hidebound with too rigid a set of objectives or be restricted to a tried and tested typology of forms. Nor should it be typecast by responding with the same answer whatever the context or issues, nor become constrained by historical precedents or stylistic architectural forms. It should avoid becoming too proscriptive or obsessed with making places tidy and avoid the lure of gentrification. Rather, it needs to achieve a balance between order and surprise, creating clear frameworks while allowing elements of ordinariness, even chaos, to create an exciting yet safe public realm. This is an over-simplification of the incredible complexities of life. Somehow it does not seem enough, there must be more to it!

This Introduction has set the scene for how the present mainstream 'urban design' paradigm has evolved and been systematically improved. The big question is whether it is capable of substantial further development or whether it will need to be superseded in a radical overthrow of current conventions. This book recognizes what has been achieved so far and endeavours to explore, through the voices of its twenty-two contributors, where urban design could be going from here.

Notes

1 M. Macrone, *A Little Knowledge*, London: Ebury Press, 1994, p. 237.

2 E. Howard, *Garden Cities of To-morrow*, Preface by F.J. Osborn, Cambridge, MA: MIT Press, 1965.

3 *Fabian News*, Dec. 1898.

4 R. Krier, *Urban Space*, Foreword by Colin Rowe, New York: Academy Editions, 1979.

5 K. Popper, *The Poverty of Historicism*, London: Routledge & Kegan Paul, 1957.

6 I. Nairn, *Outrage*, London: The Architectural Press, 1955.

7 G. Cullen, *Townscape*, London: The Architectural Press, 1961.

8 W. Manthorpe, *Counter Attack*, London: The Architectural Press, 1956.

9 K. Lynch, *Image of the City*, Cambridge, MA: MIT Press, 1960.

10 C. Rowe and F. Koetter, *Collage City*, Cambridge, MA: MIT Press, 1982.

11 I. Bentley et al., *Responsive Environments*, Oxford: Butterworth, 1985.

12 DETR and CABE, *By Design: Urban Design in the Planning System*, London: Thomas Telford Publishing, 2000.

13 Llewelyn Davies, *An Urban Design Compendium*, London: The Housing Consortium and English Heritage, 2000.

14 L. Sparks 2004 CABE *Summer School*, Ashford, Kent.

15 J. Mitchell (1969) *Big Yellow Taxi* (They Paved Paradise), Siquomb Publishing Co.

16 R. Carson, *Silent Spring*, London: Hamish Hamilton, 1963.

17 E.F. Schumacher, *Small is Beautiful: Economics As If People Mattered*, London: Sphere, 1973.

18 Consortium of GLC, Westminster and Camden, *Covent Garden's Moving, Planning Report*, London, 1968.

19 R. Koolhaas, *S, M, L, XL*, New York: The Monacelli Press, 1995.

20 *Building Design*, 5 Nov. 2004, p. 3.

21 P. Hall, *Urban Villages and the Making of Communities*, London: Spon Press, 2000.

22 DETR, *Toward an Urban Renaissance*, London: Urban Task Force, 1999.

23 P. Calthorpe, *The Regional City*, London: Island Press, 2000.

24 RICS Transport Development Areas, Sept. 2002.

25 M. Davis, *City of Quartz*, London: The Haymarket Series, 2004.

26 Auditor General, *Improving Public Transport in England Through Light Rail*, MMSO, 2004.

27 CABE, *The Value of Urban Design*, London: Thomas Telford Publishing, 2001.

28 F. Mosto (2004) *Venice*, BBC2.

29 R. Shoemaker, *The London Mob*, London: Hambledon Ltd, 2004.

30 B. Mitchell, *RIBA Journal*, 2004.

31 M.Rees, *The Big Bang* , p32 *New Scientist* 17.8.2005

1

URBAN DESIGN COMES OF AGE

THE BIGGER PICTURE

In 1956 an international conference took place at Harvard's Graduate School of Design determined to assemble evidence on behalf of a discipline called urban design. An impressive number of people then engaged in thinking about the future of cities participated in the conference. Among them were a not-yet famous Jane Jacobs, an already prominent Edmund Bacon, the Olympian figure of Lewis Mumford, several leaders of the soon-to-be-formed Team 10, prominent landscape architects such as Hideo Sasaki and Derek Eckbo, urban-renewal-empowered mayors such as David Lawrence of Pittsburgh, and innovators such as Victor Gruen, the oft-cited creator of the shopping mall.

As a group the participants concurred that the widening mid-century intellectual split between the 'art of building' and the 'systemic nature of planning' was not helpful to city building, or re-building as the post-WWII era still demanded. Hopes and ideas for a new discipline dedicated to city design were in the air, both in the USA and in Europe, with CIAM focusing more attention on matters of urbanization since the early 1940s. The conference participants were determined to share and further such thinking, hopeful that a new discipline could bridge this perceived split between design and planning. Indeed, within several years Harvard would commence one of the very first formal degree-granting curricula focused on urban design, and through that institution's prestige lend weight to the idea that educating an urban design professional was essential for a still rapidly urbanizing world.

CHAPTER 1

TERRITORIES OF URBAN DESIGN

ALEX KRIEGER

The proceedings of the 1956 conference reveal two working definitions for urban design, both articulated by José Luis Sert, who organized and presided over the conference. Urban design, he stated at one point, 'is that part of city planning which deals with the physical form of the city'. Here is the idea of urban design as a sub-set of planning, a specialization that he described as 'the most creative phase of city planning, in which imagination and artistic capacities play the important part.' At the beginning of the conference he identified a yet more ambitious goal 'to find the common basis for the joint work of the Architect, the Landscape Architect and the City Planner . . . Urban Design [being] wider than the scope of these three professions'. Here is the notion of a new overarching design discipline to be practised by all those who were, in Sert's phrase, 'urban-minded'.

Half a century later these two conceptualizations are still much in play, and a precise definition for urban design has not yet been achieved. Whether urban design has become a distinct professional specialization, or a general outlook that can be embodied in the work of several of the design disciplines dedicated to city-making remains a point to consider. However elusive a precise definition has been, few argue about the need for something called urban design.

In a world producing unprecedented kinds and sizes of settlement, it is an increasingly sought-after expertise, though not always well recognized. There are myriad expectations that society (rightly) has of those presuming to know how to design cities, and there is skepticism about how much such know-how exists. At the same time, it seems presumptuous to claim overview knowledge of something as immensely complex as urbanism. So it seems prudent to track several territories, spatial and conceptual, along which urban designers operate. Indeed, scanning the definitions of the word 'territory' in a good dictionary eventually gets you past geography to 'sphere of action'. This I find to be a particularly useful way of thinking about urban design – as *spheres of urbanistic action.* I will sketch out several such spheres of urbanistic action, for I do not believe that there is one general or over-arching way to describe what constitutes the urban design enterprise.

Before proceeding, it is important to acknowledge that while 'urban design' is a term first popularized during the twentieth century, cities have, of course, been the subject of design theory and design action for centuries. It is the notion of urban design as an activity distinct from architecture, planning, or even military or civil engineering, that is relatively new – as is the label of 'urban designer'.

Though Pope Sixtus V's impact on the physicality of sixteenth-century Rome was profound, contemporaries would not have thought him to be an urban designer. Spain's Philip II, who promulgated one of the most precise codes for laying out our cities – the Laws of the Indies – was, well, king. Haussmann was Napoleon III's Prefect of the Seine, an administrator, closer in point of view and responsibilities to Robert Moses, an engineer and civil servant, than to Raymond Unwin or Daniel Burnham, both architects acting as city planners. Ebenezer Howard, who truly had a new theory for urbanism, was an economist. Camillo Sitte was an art historian. Frederick Law

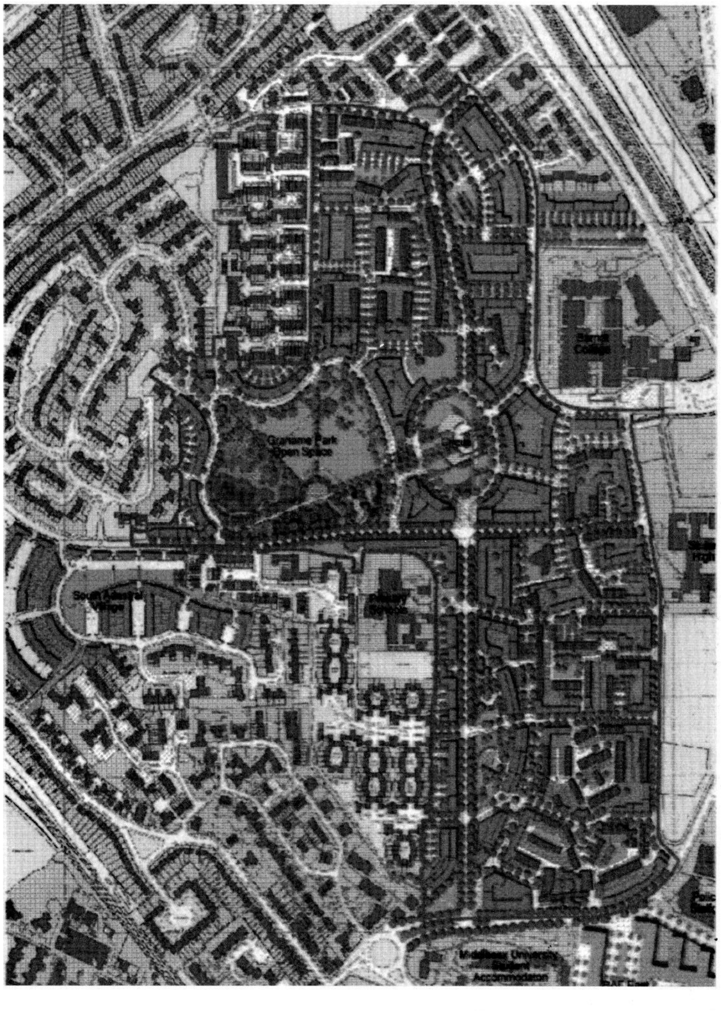

1.1 The axis of the Champs Elysées seen from the Louvre. Napoleon III's masterplanner Baron Haussmann was instructed to transform Paris, yet was not a professional designer but an administrator.

1.2 Grahame Park masterplan, Barnet, North London. Regeneration of the 1970s 'Radburn' estate with 2,900 new homes on tree-lined boulevards and traditional street patterns.
Source: Joint Masterplanners Levitt Bernstein Associates with Pollard Thomas & Edwards Architects: © Choices for Grahame Park

Olmsted, who influenced American cities more than any of his nineteenth-century contemporaries, was a landscape architect and earlier still a social activist. Lewis Mumford was a philosopher and author. The foremost Renaissance urban theorists were architects and artists, as was Le Corbusier. During much of the history of city-making an architect's expertise was assumed to extend to matters of town layout, and popes, prefects and utopian economists quite naturally turned to their architect to carry out their urban visions. Many of the 1956 conference participants were also architects, and an architectural point of view has tended to prevail in most efforts to describe what urban design is – prevail, but not encapsulate.

Below are ten spheres of urbanistic action which people calling themselves urban designers have assumed to be their professional domain, though obviously not all at once, nor even with unanimity about the list overall. The list begins with a foundational idea of urban design, at least as identified at the 1956 Harvard conference: that urban design occupies a hypothetical intersection between planning and architecture, and thus fills any perceived gaps between them. Urban design, many continue to believe, is necessarily and unavoidably:

1 THE BRIDGE BETWEEN PLANNING AND ARCHITECTURE

The most frequently offered response to what urban designers do is that they mediate between plans and projects. Their role is to somehow translate the objectives of planning regarding space, settlement patterns and even the allocation of resources, into (mostly) physical strategies to guide the work of architects, developers and other implementers. For example, many public planning agencies now incorporate an urban design staffer-or-two whose role is to establish criteria for development beyond basic zoning, and then help review, evaluate and approve the work of project proponents as they advance their projects through design and into construction. Such a design review process is an increasingly common component of a city's regulatory framework, allowing traditionally controversial issues such as aesthetics to become factors discussed during project review and approval. It is the urban designer's presumed insights on good or appropriate urban form that are seen as crucial in the translation of policy or program objectives into architectural concepts, or to recognize the urbanistic potential in an emerging architectural design and thus advocate for its realization.

A subtlety within this process is, however, often misunderstood. The translation of plans into designs is not meant to be a linear process – always emanating from planning to affect design – but interactive. The urban designer's own expertise in architectural thinking should inform the formulation of plans so that these are not fixed prior to consideration of physical implications. This design version of shuttle diplomacy, between plan formulators and translators is important, to be sure, but cannot rely only on mediation or persuasion to be effective. Urban designers must visualize, and make others see, the desired effects of planning. This requires specific techniques by which goals and policies are converted into potent design guidelines. It leads to the idea of urban design as a special nuance of public policy, an improvement on traditional land use regulations that shy away from qualitative assessments of form. So shouldn't urban design then be considered:

1.3 **Grahame Park, North London, Southern Square. The new square terminates a north–south route with twin social hubs containing retail and community centres, emphasising that this is a 'public' place for the wider area.**

2 A FORM-BASED CATEGORY OF PUBLIC POLICY

A book entitled *Urban Design as Public Policy*, published in the mid-1970s by Jonathan Barnett,[1] argued this very point and became highly influential. If one could agree on specific attributes of good urbanism (at least in a particular setting, as Barnett's book attempted to do with New York City), then one should be able to mandate or incentivize the incorporation of these through additional regulatory requirements. The radicalism embedded in this self-described pragmatic approach was to incorporate many more formal and aesthetic judgements – indeed *much* more judgement, period – into a standard zoning ordinance, and especially into the permitting and evaluative process. Restrictions on height or massing that in pioneering zoning codes (such as New York's own landmark 1916 code) were ostensibly determined through measurable criteria such as access to sunlight, could now be introduced as commonly held good form-based values. The mandating of continuous block-length cornice heights, for example, gained the equivalency of a lot-coverage restriction, though the former could not as easily be considered a matter of 'health, safety and public welfare' as the latter.

But why shouldn't public policy, as it pertains to the settled environment, not aspire to quality and even beauty? More recently, a New York disciple of Barnett's, Michael Kwartler, expressed this via the poetic notion of regulating the good that you can't think of, or, one may infer, seeking to achieve through regulation *what is not* normally provided by conventional real estate

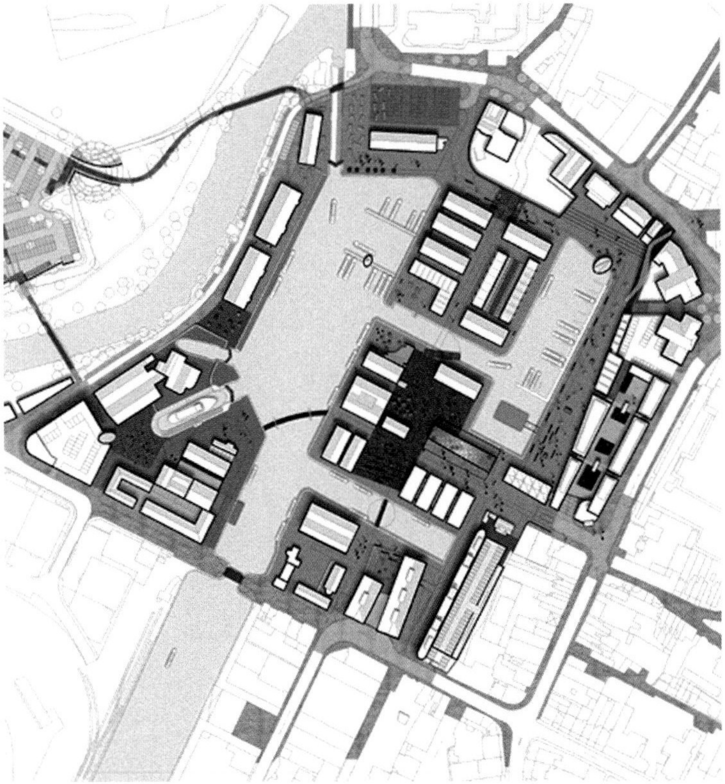

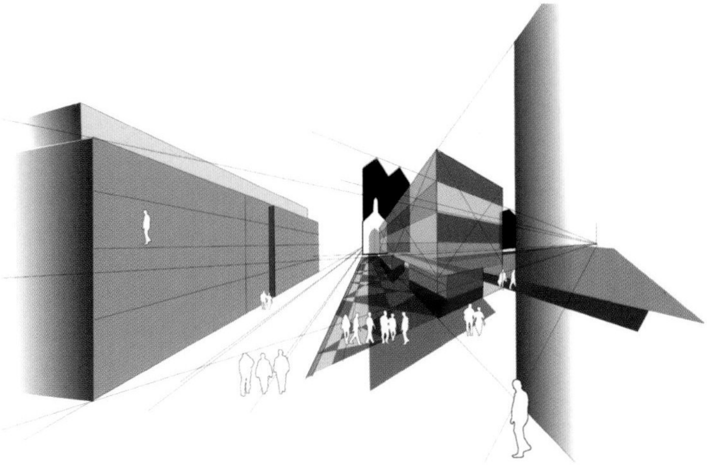

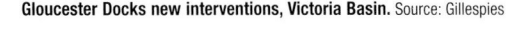

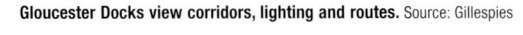

1.4 Gloucester Docks masterplan by Gillespies, JRUD, Fielden Clegg Bradley is a public/private joint venture that re-uses parts of this historic city to create a contemporary environment that reflects traditional components such as squares and streets. New interpretations of existing templates, in this case eighteenth- and nineteenth-century industrial warehouses, help create a synergy with other areas of industrial redundancy to catalyse regeneration. The new public realm now has to be useable day and night Source: Gillespies

1.5 Gloucester Docks new interventions, Victoria Basin. Source: Gillespies

1.6 Gloucester Docks view corridors, lighting and routes. Source: Gillespies

practices. Since American planning is often accused of being reactive to real estate interests, interests that do not always prioritize public benefit, here would be a way to push developer-initiated projects to higher qualitative standards. So, again, given the presumption that what constitutes good urban form (or desirable uses, or amenities such as ground-level retail, or open space) can be agreed upon by a community, these should be legislated upon. And the natural champion for this is the urban designer. The appeal behind this interpretation of urban design is two-fold. It maintains lofty ideals by arguing on behalf of codifiable design qualities, while at the same time operates at the pragmatic level of the real estate industry, facilitating better development.

This may all be well and good, but such mediating and regulating is not sufficiently rewarding for those who believe that less creativity is involved in establishing guidelines for others to interpret than to design oneself. It seems too administrative and passive a role for urban design. Is not urban design about giving shape to urbanism? Isn't it about:

3 THE ARCHITECTURE OF THE CITY

This conception of urban design is at once more ambitious yet more narrow than the idea of urban design as public policy. The roots of this view may be traced earlier in the twentieth century to the American City Beautiful movement, and further into the nineteenth century to the European Beaux

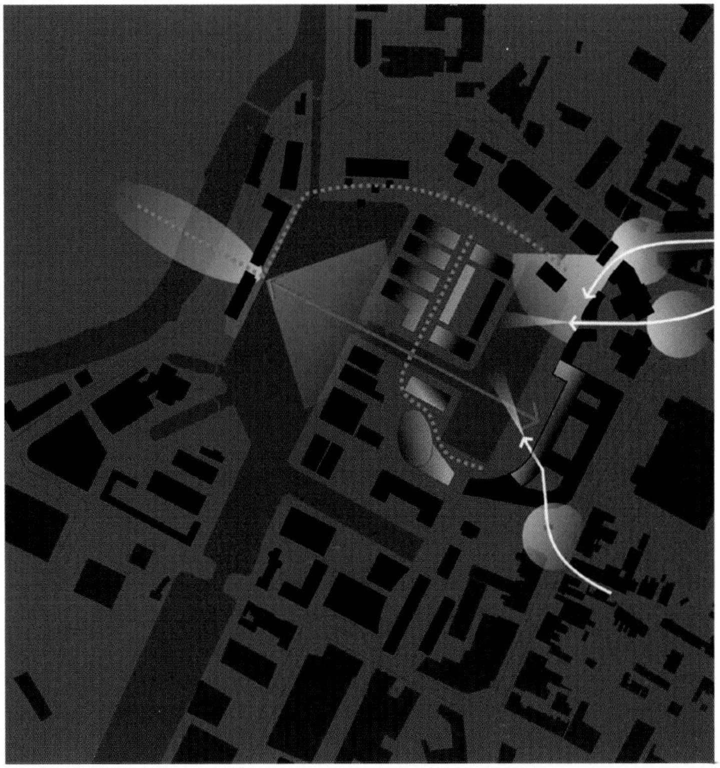

1.7 New Traditionalism, Poundbury Estate, Dorchester. A good example of the benefits of traditional street patterns espoused by the masterplanner Leon Krier with clear frontage to the public realm, but it is a pity that the architecture resorted to historicist pastiche.

1.8 Public realm, Buchanan Street, Glasgow. The completion of the Buchanan Galleries precipitated the creation of a whole new public realm designed by Gillespies and turned Buchanan Street into an exceptional place. The concentration of activities into key locations means that 'place-making' is becoming an increasingly important aspect of the urban designer's role.
Source: Gillespies

Arts tradition. Its proponents seek above all to regulate the shaping of those areas of the city which are public and, therefore, of common concern. It is a sphere mainly populated by architect-urbanists, but it makes kindred spirits of diverse figures such as Colin Rowe, Camilo Sitte, and William H. Whyte.

Shaping public space is considered the first order of urbanism by the architect/urbanist. Thus the primary role of urban design is to develop methods for doing so. Done with authority and artistry (and proper programming/furnishing which was Whyte's contribution) allows the rest of the city, all that is private, to distribute itself logically and properly in relationship to this public realm. During the 1970s and the 1980s, particularly in Europe, a related theory of the 'Urban Project' emerged. This entailed the programming, financing and design of a catalytic development, often a joint public/private venture, which would stimulate or revive an urban district. This notion of urban design is best embodied by a stable and stabilizing form, one that anchors its part of the city with unique characteristics that are expected to endure and influence future neighbors.

The idea of urban design as the architecture of the city is often conceptualized in terms of the ideal of Rome as portrayed in the Nolli Map, or in Piranesi's more fantastical description of Imperial Rome in his *Compo Marzio* engraving. Or, it is simply absorbed via our touristic encounters with the pre-industrial portions of the European city in which the emphasis on the public realm – at least in the places that we regularly visit – seems so clear. Not a particularly large conceptual leap from this formulation of urban design leads to the idea of:

4 URBAN DESIGN AS RESTORATIVE URBANISM

The form of the pre-industrial Western city – compact, dense, layered and slow-changing – holds immense power over city dreaming among both urbanists and the public. The traditional city seems at once so clearly organized, humanely sized, manageable and beautiful. Such virtues seems absent in the modern metropolis. Why not mobilize to regain these? At present, the New Urbanists are most closely associated with this sphere, but are part of a long tradition of those guarding or extolling the advantages of traditional urban typologies. As did the polemicists of the City Beautiful movement in America a century earlier, the New Urbanists advocate a return to what they consider time-honored principles of urbanism, now as often appealing to a disillusioned suburban culture as to those still facing the full onslaught of urban modernization.

Americans today seem particularly sympathetic to these ideas for two reasons. They hunger for a 'taste' of urbanity, pre-assembled and sanitized perhaps – 'lite urbanism' in Rem Koolhaas's wry phrase – having for several generations disengaged from (and still being unsure about) the real thing. And, assaulted by the new and the next, they seek comfort in the familiar. Traditionally, homes and neighborhoods have offered respite from the drumbeat of change. Thus, it is understandable how an era of seemingly unending innovation in business, technology and life-style marketing engenders a sentimental recall of the places we used to live in, Though we may demand the conveniences of modern kitchens and attached garages, many prefer to package these in shapes and façades reminiscent of earlier, (assumed to be) slower and pleasanter paces of life.

The walkable city, the city of public streets and public squares, the low-rise high-density city, the city of defined neighborhoods gathered around valued institutions, the city of intricate layers of uses free of auto-induced congestion are characteristics that remain appealing. Americans are not alone in pining for such qualities. In today's Berlin, to refer to one European example, the city planning administration's highly conservative architectural design guidelines for the reunified centre are but another manifestation of this instinct to slow the pace of change – at least as it pertains to the physical, if not the social or political, environment. Many urban designers believe that it is their discipline's responsibility to retard or undo change, resist unwarranted newness, or at least advocate for such old-fashioned notions as 'human scale' and 'place making'. Then shouldn't we think of:

5 URBAN DESIGN AS 'PLACE-MAKING'

A corollary to restorative urbanism is the rise of the term 'place-making.' There are actually architecture and urban design firms in the USA who advertise themselves as 'place-makers'. It is easy to express cynicism, So many ordinary developments advertise their placeless environments with catchy names ending in 'place,' among the most common, if absurd, of these being 'Center Place', a moniker promising the two things often missing in new subdivisions. There are times when a marketing slogan reveals the absence of something more readily than it delivers on its promise to achieve more of that very same thing.

Yet, creating exceptional places to serve human purpose has always been central to the design professions. We've just never called ourselves 'place-makers' before, or have been so self-conscious about the task. Economists often remind society that it is the rare commodity that gains value over time. As more contemporary urban development acquires generic qualities, or is merely repetitive, the distinctive urban place, old or new, is harder to find. This alone will continue to fuel preservation movements across the urban world. But in a world that adds 60 million more people to urban populations each year, preservation cannot be the answer to place-making. More urban designers should devote their attention to making new places as worthy as their time-honored predecessors. Again, it is the American New Urbanists who have articulated this goal most clearly, but with mixed results. Their rhetoric extols intimate scale, texture, the mixing of uses, connectivity, continuity, the privileging of what is shared, and other such characteristics of great urban places, but their designs tend to focus on familiar old forms and traditional aesthetic detailing.

The obvious merits of preserving venerable old urban places aside, or the wisdom of treading lightly in the midst of historic districts, doubts remain about how successfully we might organize and 'clothe' the complexities of modern life in familiar iconography. What if one places less faith in the dressing up of new development with emblems of urbanity, and devotes more effort to wiser distribution of resources or better land management? Your call to action becomes:

1.9 Exchange Square, Millennium Quarter, Manchester. EDAW's masterplan included a new square between Marks and Spencer and the renovated Corn Exchange with dynamic hard landscape designed by Martha Schwartz.

6 URBAN DESIGN AS 'SMART GROWTH'

While there has been a strong association of urban design with 'downtowns', demand for suburban growth management and reinvestment strategies for the older rings around city centers have collected many advocates. Indeed, to protect urbanism, not to mention minimizing environmental harm and needless land consumption, it is imperative, many argue, to control sprawl and to make environmental stewardship a more overt part of urban thinking. Expressed opportunistically, it is also where the action is. Since 90 per cent of development takes place at the periphery of existing urbanization, the urban designer should be operating there, and, if present, advocate 'smarter' planning and urban design. Conversely, ignoring the metropolitan periphery as if it were unworthy of a true urbanist, or merely limiting one's efforts to urban 'infill,' may simply be a form of problem avoidance.

That the twenty-first century will be more conservation-minded is little in doubt. That the world overall must be smarter about managing resources and land is also clear. Therefore, the traditional close allegiance of urban design to an architectural and development perspective must be broadened. Exposure to the natural sciences, to ecology, to energy management, to systems analysis, to the economics of land development, to land use law and to issues of public health have not been fundamental to an urbanist's training, but are becoming more so. Urban designers who are advocating a 'smart growth' agenda today generally do so out of an ideological conviction that sprawl abatement or open-space conservation is necessary. But as they enter this territory they quickly realize that acquiring additional skills and partners in planning are equally necessary.

To actually manage metropolitan growth requires dealing with systems that cut across jurisdictional boundaries, such as land conservation, water

1.10 **Gare du Nord Metro interchange entrance, Paris. Integrating city form and transportation also includes bringing daylight and the public realm into the station to enhance the travelling experience.**

1.11 **Stratford City is the new metropolitan centre for London at one of the high-speed Channel Tunnel Rail Link (CTRL) stations that will carry passengers to the 2012 Olympic site. The project was fundamentally enabled by the CTRL, which created a single land ownership and reinforced the accessibility and connectivity of the site.**
Image: Arup Urban Design
Design Team: Arup Urban Design, Fletcher Priest Architects and West 8

management and transportation. Therefore, and increasingly for many, urban design must be about:

7 THE INFRASTRUCTURE OF THE CITY

The arrangement of streets and blocks, the distribution of open and public spaces, the alignment of transit and highway corridors, and the provision of municipal services certainly constitute essential components of urbanism. Indeed, to focus on just one category of urban infrastructure, few things are more important to cities, or virtually any form of contemporary settlement, than well-functioning transportation systems. Yet, the optimization of mobility pursued as an independent variable, separate from the complex and overlapping web of other urban systems, ultimately works against healthy communities. Engineering criteria, we have learned, while important, are not sufficient city-producing tools.

Apart from the occasional efforts to 'architecturalize' infrastructure, as in the various megastructure proposals of the 1960s (a source of fascination again today), neither planners nor designers have played a significant role in the realm of transportation or other urban infrastructure planning. It has become another sphere for someone called an 'urban designer' to engage, at both the pragmatic level of calibrating demands for mobility with other social needs, and in advancing new ways in which city form and transportation systems may be integrated.

In a way, the twentieth-century love affair with the car – still considered the ideal personal mobility system – has reduced the range of conceptualizing

1.12 Landscape urbanism, Der Strype, The Hague. Houses back onto a series of landscaped ponds as part of the neighbourhood drainage system.

1.13 Woonerf (home zone), Der Strype, The Hague. An informal layout provides for pedestrians, planting, play areas and cars in a relaxed manner.

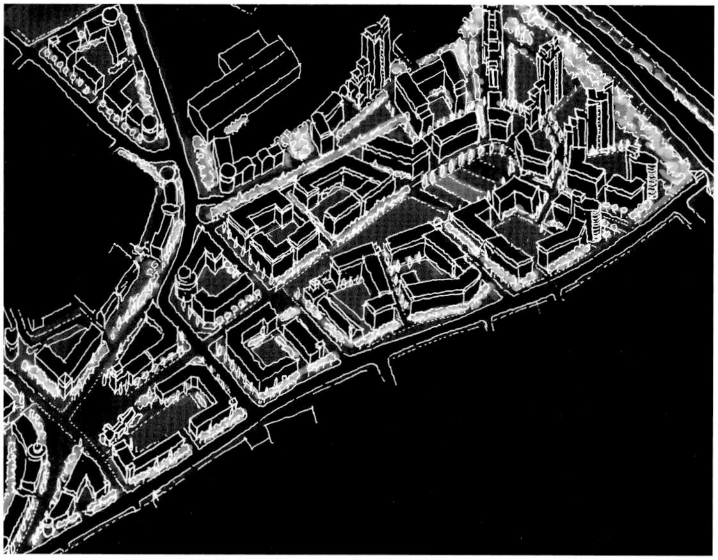

1.14 Visionary urbanism can help regenerate Colindale, North London. The urban design framework for this suburban development mediated between low-rise 1930s' suburban development and the new market demands for high-density housing. The diagram by JRUD demonstrates how bold design united a series of individual projects to create a focus for the wider neighbourhood.
Source: JRUD

1.15 Community participation, Cirencester, Gloucestershire This community event was part of Commission for Architecture and the Built Environment (CABE) research project in design coding which the UK government hopes will help raise the quality of housing design. Such a process fosters citizen's participation at an early stage of design.

about urban form and transportation. We were too mesmerized by the magic of Sant'Elia's Italian Futurist renderings and those of Le Corbusier's *Ville Radieuse*. An entire century later we are rediscovering that integrating urban form and mobility depends on more sophisticated umbilical cords than the open road. This is especially so since the engineering world is shifting emphasis from hardware to systems design, from adding lanes, for example, to traffic management technology. It is their acknowledgment that factors such as livability, sustainability, economic and cultural growth, in other words, good urban design, are the real goals of infrastructure optimization.

Agreeing with such a sensibility, the leaders of the field of landscape architecture, a field that has generally pursued a more humanistic perspective on planning, have recently advanced another perspective on urbanistic action:

8 URBAN DESIGN AS 'LANDSCAPE URBANISM'

In the past few years a new rallying point called *Landscape Urbanism* has emerged. Its proponents seek to incorporate ecology, landscape architecture and infrastructure into the discourse of urbanism. The movement's intellectual lineage may encompass Ian McHarg, Patrick Geddes and even Frederick Law Olmsted, though its polemical point of departure seems to be that landscape space, not architecture any longer, is the generative force in the modern metropolis.

To return to the 1956 conference for a moment, there was a good deal of rhetoric about how landscape architecture was to be an integral part of the urban design process. Quickly this aspect was subsumed under the architecture vs. planning dichotomy in which urban design would occupy the mediating middle. Momentarily there was no conceptual space left for landscape architecture. Ironically, more areas of settlement in North America have been designed by landscape architects then anyone else. However, there has persisted an accusation (sometimes accurate) that landscape-architect-directed urban design favors low densities, exhibits little formal sensibility, and contains too much open space; in other words, it produces sub-urban environments.

Landscape urbanists challenge such a cliché, instead insisting that the conception of the solid, 'man-made' city of historic imagination perpetuates the oppositional – and no longer pertinent – view that nature and human artifice are opposites. Landscape urbanism projects purport to overcome this opposition, holding neither a narrow ecological agenda nor mainstream (read architectual) city-making techniques as primary. Valuable urban design, landscape urbanists insist, is to be found at the intersection of ecology, engineering, design and social policy.

In one regard, the movement may be a reaction to the Nolli-Map view of urbanism: that is, of a binary conception of cities as made up of buildings and the absence of buildings, where the white of the map – the voids – are the result of, built from, the black of the map. Maybe this was a useful interpretation of the pre-industrial city – of the Italian piazza as space carved out of the solidity of 'built' fabric. Outside the pre-industrial walled city were certainly landscapes and undesignated space, but within the city, space resulted from built form. Any careful perusal of a pre-industrial-era city map proves this assertion false, and surely the 'white' of the Nolli plan comes in many hues and nuances of meaning. Besides, the landscape urbanists ask, isn't the landscape the modern glue that holds the modern metropolis together?

The radicalism inherent in conceptualizing landscape as the central component of urban design – where Nolli's white, as it were, becomes today's green – brings us at last to the territory of:

9 URBAN DESIGN AS VISIONARY URBANISM

I have saved, nearly for the end, this long-standing expectation of urban design; that its practitioners – or rather, in this instance, its *theorists* – provide insight and models about the way we ought to organize spatially in communities, not simply accept the ways we do. The prospect of hypothesizing about the future of urbanism surely attracts more students to urban design programs than any other. Being engaged in transforming urbanism is a sphere of action associated with the great figures of modern urban change, from (depending on one's heroes) Baron Haussmann to Daniel Burnham, to Ebenezer Howard, to Raymond Unwin, to Le Corbusier, and maybe even Rem Koolhaas and Andres Duany today. But such deliverers of bold saber strokes (to borrow a phrase from Giedeon) are rarer today than they were at the turn of the twentieth century, or we heed their visions less often. A new generation of visionary designers may arise in China or other parts of the world rapidly urbanizing today, but have yet to do so.

In the relative absence of contemporary visionaries, others have stepped forward to explore the nature of urban culture today. The urban sociologist/theorist – from Louis Wirth, to Henri Lefebvre, to Richard Sennett, Edward Soja or David Harvey – is not normally considered an urban designer but in a sense has become so, having supplanted in our own time the great urban transformers of the past, not in deeds but in pondering urban culture.

The heroic form-giving tradition may be in decline. After all, the twentieth century witnessed immense urban harm caused by those who offered a singular or universal idea of what a city is, or what urbanization should produce. But our cultural observers remind us that pragmatism and technique cannot be a sufficient substitute, nor can design professionals be mere *absorbers* of public opinion waiting for consensus to build. One must think and offer ideas as well. Still, there is the perennial conundrum about how directly engaged urban design must be with the 'real world'. Maybe, after all, urban design is about community assistance:

10 URBAN DESIGN AS COMMUNITY ADVOCACY (OR DOING NO HARM)

Mostly since 1956, and in academia largely still, urban design evokes notions of large-scale thinking: either the consideration of substantial areas of settlement, or theorizing at a grand scale about the nature of urbanism. But among contemporary dwellers of urban neighborhoods – the ostensible beneficiaries of this broad thinking – the term urban design is increasingly coming to be associated with local, immediate concerns such as improving neighborhoods, calming traffic, minimizing negative impacts of new development, expanding housing choices while keeping housing affordable, maintaining open space, improving streetscapes, and creating more humane environments in general.

In this newer almost colloquial usage of the term, urban design approximates what used to be called 'community planning'. A young Jane Jacobs' prescient comment during the 1956 conference comes to mind. 'A store is also a storekeeper', she said, with the implication that her designer colleagues at the conference better remember that a storekeeper is also a citizen, and that citizens have a stake in decisions being made about their environment. Not much follow-up of her point was recorded in the proceedings. It would take another generation to bring this view to the foreground.

The association of urban design and citizen participation was finally the result of the gradual bureaucratization of the planning profession itself. Sometime following the social unrest of the 1960s and a growing consensus about the failures of urban renewal, the focus of planning began to shift dramatically from physical planning to process and policy formulation. If the architect and urban designer were hell-bent on producing visions of a better tomorrow, the theory went, then the role of the planner must be dedicated to determining need and rational process, not seeking (the often dubious) vision. Indeed, a fear of producing more top-down, failed plans before an increasingly demanding, less patient public led the planning profession to embrace broad participatory techniques and community advocacy. But ironically, the concurrent disengagement from spatial concerns on the part of the planner began to distance the activities of planning from the stuff the beneficiaries of planning wish for most; nicer neighborhoods, access to better places of work and commerce, and special environments to periodically escape everyday pressures related to life or work.

As the planning profession continued to operate in the broader spheres of policy formulation, the focus of planning increasingly appears to the public as abstract, even indifferent to immediate concerns or daily needs. The urban designer who addresses these immediate, often spatially-related concerns, has come to be seen as the professional most attuned to tangible urban problem solving, but not as the agent of bold urban transformation. In citizens' minds those who practise urban design are not the 'shapers of cities', in large part because such shapers, if they do exist, are mistrusted. They are instead custodians of the qualities valued by a community; qualities which the urban designer is asked to protect. Today, it is the urban designer, not the planner, who has emerged as the place-centered professional, with 'urban design' often assuming a friendlier, more accessible popular connotation than 'planning'.

URBAN DESIGN AS A FRAME OF MIND

The above list is not intended to be exhaustive and other perspectives can surely be added. For example, in the parts of the world that are modernizing rapidly, urban design has emerged as an important tool of managing this modernization. Nor is the point of identifying – and even caricaturing – the above spheres of urban design to lay claim to vast jurisdictional territory for the discipline. On the contrary, it is to suggest, rather strongly, that instead of moving towards professional specificity, urban design has come to represent – and its varied practitioners have come to be aligned with – distinct avenues for engaging and facilitating urbanism. Rodolfo Machado, a colleague at Harvard, offers an appealing (if somewhat rhetorical) definition of urban design as the process of design that produces or enhances urbanity. Is this but an amiable generality?

Perhaps José Luis Sert would be disappointed that half a century following his first conference that no more precise a definition for urban design has emerged. Around the third or fourth of the near-annual urban design conferences that he hosted at Harvard throughout the 1960s and early 1970s, he expressed concern about the 'fog of amiable generalities' that the conversations had so far produced. He hoped to move past such, but they have persisted.

My own conclusion following a quarter of a century of practising and teaching urban design is the following. Urban design is less a technical discipline and more a mindset among those, of varying disciplinary foundations, seeking, sharing and advocating insights about forms of community. What binds different urban designers are their commitment to city life, the enterprise of urban maintenance, and the determination to enhance urbanism. The need for a narrow definition for such a constellation of interests is not self-evident. Because of this commitment to urbanism, urban designers distinguish among mandates; realizing that to renew the centers of cities, build new cities, restore the parts of old cities worthy of preservation, and construct equitable growth-management programs on the periphery require vastly different strategies, theories and design actions. There are, indeed, many spheres of urbanistic action for those who are urban-minded to dedicate themselves and their work to.

Notes

1 J. Barnett, *Urban Design as Public Policy*, New York: McGraw Hill, 1974

Is urban design equipped to address the global issues in urban development today? Or is it too narrowly concerned with the cities of Europe and North America (and, more specifically, only with small parts of those cities)?

By and large, urban designers subscribe to a common set of values that have emerged in post-war Europe and North America. These have been in response to some perceived failures of the modernist approach in planning and architecture, and latterly, in response to the impacts of globalisation, continued economic growth and the related environmental impacts on our towns and cities. These values, and the principles on which they are based, are recognizable as 'mainstream' urban design.

CHAPTER 2
GLOBALISING URBAN DESIGN

TONY LLOYD-JONES

Urban design, however, can also be viewed in the sense of any decision-making activity that has a physical impact on the shared built environment. In this larger sense, most urban design takes place as a result of decisions made about individual development with little conscious thought as to its impact on its surroundings, on the public realm and experience of place, and on city form as a whole.

This chapter juxtaposes these two views of urban design with the aim of exploring how the scope of mainstream urban design might be widened to address the concerns of the wider urban development process, and give a sense of purpose and direction to what is currently mainly 'unconscious urban design'.

It argues that mainstream urban design principles are derived from, and adaptable to, a particular urban morphology – mainly small footprint, small plot, densely developed, usually low or medium-rise areas – that makes up a small proportion of the urbanised area of the world today.

Even within this limited type of morphological development, a large proportion is to be found in high-density, low-income neighbourhoods in developing-world cities. Until now, this type of development has occurred without any conscious urban design direction, but offers the opportunity for urban design principles to be adapted and applied post-hoc, in slum upgrading and the spatial integration of irregular settlements into the formal public realm of the city.

The current constraints in the scope and application of mainstream urban design suggest, therefore, that its conventions need to be reviewed. We need to develop a broader set of principles, performance criteria and a body of good practice that can be applied to urban development of whatever form. This includes the majority of lower-density new development that is occurring on the urban periphery and in the areas around our cities in every part of the world. It also applies to the informal low-income residential and largely unplanned, often high-rise commercial development of the mushrooming towns and cities of the developing world.

PRINCIPLES OF 'GOOD URBAN DESIGN'

Many readers will be familiar with the broad principles of the contemporary mainstream approach to urban design. Their recent genealogy is in the contribution of a number of European and American academics, theorists and practitioners from the 1950s onwards.[1] In the USA, the foundations were laid by Kevin Lynch, Donald Appleyard and others operating out of MIT. Later contributions included those from David Crane and his colleagues at Harvard, from Christopher Alexander in Berkeley and more recently from the 'New Urbanist' movement. Of particular significance is the work of a non-designer, Jane Jacobs, who gave an economic and anthropological justification to the post-war urban design movement.

In Europe, a townscape approach was promoted by Gordon Cullen and others in the UK, while a more rationalist, morphological approach developed in continental Europe through the work of Aldo Rossi, Rob Krier and others. Rob Krier's brother, Leon, also had a strong influence, in particular through the urban villages movement in the UK, contrasting with the more rationalist and analytical 'Space Syntax' approach to the design of the pedestrian environment, developed by Bill Hillier and his colleagues at University College London.

By the mid-1980s, these various, often contrasting and conflicting strands of urban design thinking had been synthesized into a set of working principles published in the first working 'manual' of the contemporary approach to urban design, *Responsive Environments* produced by Ian Bentley and his colleagues at Oxford Brookes University.[2] John Punter in his 'Ten Commandments of Architecture and Urban Design'[3] later showed how these principles were echoed in one form or another across a whole range of influential pronouncements on urban design.

By the end of the 1990s, the mainstream approach to urban design had become part of the mainstream in urban planning in several countries. The UK Government commissioned, and eventually published, *By Design*,[4] a guidance manual for local authority planners incorporating the conventional approach to good urban design. *By Design* defines urban design as:

the art of making places for people . . . It concerns the connections between people and places, movement and urban form, nature and the built fabric, and the processes for ensuring successful villages, towns and cities. Urban design is a key to creating sustainable developments and the conditions for a flourishing economic life, for the prudent use of natural resources and for social progress. Good design can help create lively places with distinctive character; streets and public spaces that are safe, accessible, pleasant to use and human in scale.

By Design sets out the following objectives of urban design:

Character and identity: To promote character in townscape and landscape by responding to and reinforcing locally distinctive patterns of development, landscape and culture.

Continuity and enclosure: To promote the continuity of street frontages and the enclosure of space by development that clearly defines private and public areas.

Quality of the public realm: To promote public spaces and routes that are attractive, safe, uncluttered and work effectively for all in society, including disabled and elderly people.

Ease of movement: To promote accessibility and local permeability by making places that connect with each other and are easy to move through, putting people before traffic and integrating land uses and transport.

Legibility: To promote legibility through development that provides recognisable routes, intersections and landmarks to help people find their way around.

Adaptability: To promote adaptability through development that can respond to changing social, technological and economic conditions.

Diversity: To promote diversity and choice through a mix of compatible developments and uses that work together to create viable places that respond to local needs.

EMERGING CONSENSUS IN THE POST-WAR PERIOD

From the 1950s onwards, an urban design consensus began to emerge in response to a number of large-scale trends and influences on urban development and form in European and North American cities:

The impacts of motorisation on the physical form of the city: the primacy of traffic management over the pedestrian public realm and the fragmentation and suburbanisation of the city.

The functionalist 'masterplan' approach to town planning: single use zoning and the loss of vitality and efficiency that arises out of a mix of uses in an area; the perceived failures of other conventional modernist approaches to urban planning.

The impact of modernist building types, in particular, 'pavilion' architecture and stand-alone buildings; the loss in continuity of street frontages and the perception of streets and other public spaces as contained and meaningful places.

The emergence of an anonymous, international style of architecture, as a result of fashion, common construction methods and economies of scale and the loss of regional identity and diversity; the dominance of corporate-style buildings; public buildings losing their symbolic importance in the urban landscape.

The perceived failure of large-scale, planned, public sector-led and commercial development: the comprehensive redevelopment of central and inner-city areas, characterless city centres and monotonous public housing estates creating islands of social exclusion in both inner-city and suburban locations.

The associated loss of valuable historical heritage and social diversity: 'slum' clearance and the destruction of poorer historic and run-down neighbourhoods to make way for new infrastructure and commercial redevelopment.

The response to these trends drew on the experience of the pre-modernist urban form of historic and nineteenth-century cities and urban quarters.[5] The emphasis lay on contextualising new development, reasserting the place of the pedestrian in the public realm, increasing pedestrian accessibility generally and restoring the multi-functional character of the traditional street. The value of the mixed-use, high-density neighbourhood over a single-use, low-density approach was asserted.

The aim was to re-establish a strong urban structure through a legible network of enclosed streets and urban spaces based on formal grid layouts or (as in the more picturesque townscape approaches) on the more organic layouts drawing on earlier European historic precedents. Urban forms such as the perimeter block and mid-rise buildings with a regulated height and continuous frontages were promoted, giving substance to a strengthened urban structure.

This approach to urban design ultimately derives from, and is applicable to, a particular type of urban morphology – mainly small footprint, small plot, densely developed, usually low or medium-rise permeable areas arranged in manageably-sized city blocks.

In this first phase, urban design was fairly narrowly concerned with issues of urban form and focused on existing inner and central city neighbourhoods. In Europe and North America, the major phase of new town and city development in the post-war period was largely over and the major problems were occurring as a result of large-scale urban renewal programmes and the imposition of modernist solutions on existing pre-modernist urban forms.

Writers like Jane Jacobs, however, also emphasised the social and economic values associated with the new urban design approach, including vitality and community, safety and security, as well as the economic opportunities offered by a permeable network of city streets and a mix of uses and buildings.

Alarmingly, urban renewal, following the same purely commercially-led modernist trajectory, is ongoing on a vast scale throughout the developing world. Historic and culturally valuable areas are being torn down, low-income neighbourhoods destroyed and communities broken up to make way for urban motorways, high-rise apartment and office blocks, shopping malls and the other paraphernalia of the 'modern' city, craved by ambitious mayors and avaricious developers. In this context, the perceived wisdom of conventional urban design holds no sway, and all the lessons of the past will have to be learned anew.

EMERGING MEGA-TRENDS

In the later decades of the twentieth century, the broadly drawn, if narrowly focused, principles of the urban design consensus had to be adapted to an increasingly complex urban agenda. New, emerging large-scale concerns and trends included:

Urban sustainability: patterns of movement, energy and resource use, and waste and pollution in and around cities, increasingly perceived to have adverse global as well as local environmental impacts.

The erosion of the public realm through the privatisation of collective spaces in shopping malls, gated communities and inward-looking mega developments of various kinds; economies of scale; loss of permeability; the increasing dominance of private over public space.

Innovations in communications and information technology: the physical movement and mobility of people and goods facilitated by ever more sophisticated telecommunication; advances in information processing and economies of scale in management impacting on land use development, e.g. 'back-office' development in peripheral locations.

The emergence of the 'edge city': the dispersal of key industrial, institutional and commercial functions to the periphery – characterless, shed-type developments along arterial and orbital roads and in industrial estates, retail, leisure, business and technology parks huge shopping malls; a car-based suburban lifestyle predominating over traditional non car-based urban lifestyles.

The threat to existing town centres and the 'urban renaissance': the adaptation of existing city centres to a more specialised role as centres of leisure and finance, 'creative industries' and producer services and reserves of high-value uses; the renewed popularity of metropolitan living.

Decentralisation and 'disurbanisation' leading to metropolitanisation, the emergence of polycentric city regions and networks of cities; the urbanisation of the countryside with mixed

2.1 Unconscious urban design. Informal development in a small-town setting, Piraí, Rio de Janeiro State, Brazil.

2.2 Jakarta: commercial towers and informal squatter settlements. Challenges to conventions of mainstream urban design.

2. 3 Shedland?, Washington, DC. Characterless, shed-type developments along arterial and orbital roads and in industrial estates.

urban–rural areas, the growing role of smaller settlements as dormitories and centres of retirement and/or tourism.

The increased consumption of land: arising out of growing prosperity and increasing demands for an improved quality of life, ageing populations in many high-income countries and the growth of smaller and single person households adding to the demands for new housing.

The need for urban regeneration arising out of structural economic change: industrial decline in many cities and failure to compete in the global economy in new industries and services; the need to invest in declining inner-city neighbourhoods and redevelopment of large, brownfield sites, outdated port and railway lands.

Affordable housing: the shortage and ever-increasing prices of housing in accessible locations putting it out of reach of large sections of the population.

Regional and global economic imbalances and mass migration: associated with the increasing international flows of goods, information and finance; the concentration of migrants in poor and overcrowded neighbourhoods; ethnic and cultural identity and conflict.

These trends are discernible in and around most cities in the more developed world. Through globalisation, they are also emerging in the truncated development trajectory of cities and metropolitan areas of the developing world, overlaying the earlier phase of central city development and redevelopment, as outlined above.

In the developed world these trends have been in place since the 1980s and it is only fairly recently, if at all, that urban designers have begun to address them. However, as on the whole the new trends served only to continue and reinforce those of previous decades, the principles promulgated by mainstream urban design have proved relatively robust in addressing them.

URBAN DESIGN IN A WIDENING CONTEXT

Increasingly, urban designers are being called upon to address development issues in all types of context, greenfield, suburban and inner-city and brownfield regeneration, as well as the city centres. 'Compact city' models of sustainable, higher-density, mixed-use, permeable neighbourhoods and centres with well-structured, pedestrian and public-transport orientated features have been developed for most, if not all these contexts.

In the EU countries, in particular, the urban design agenda had been given considerable weight in government policy through the growing emphasis on environmentally sustainable development.[6] Conventional urban design contributes greatly to the policies required to achieve the sustainable development of rich world cities, most of which are not growing very much in population but most of which continue to eat up land and natural resources.

The model of high-density, mixed-use, compact cities with well-developed pedestrian-friendly, public infrastructure, reduced car use and vital, thriving centres is the one that the accepted tenets of urban design addresses. It provides the tools for planners and others to help counter the pressures of commercial development economics, with its demands for ever-increasing scale and standardisation.

The established urban design principles have also proved quite robust in addressing other aspects of sustainable development in the cities of the developed world, including quality of life, social inclusion and social integration and identity issues.

Nevertheless, it is true to say that most urban development flies in the face of mainstream good practice in urban design. A strong emphasis on economic-led development invariably undermines the role that urban designers can play. The commercial pressures for large-scale monolithic developments for many different types of land use and for low-density residential development are intense and show no sign of weakening, and, without strong planning constraints, the influence of urban designers in influencing this type of development is minimal.

Most urban development in towns and cities everywhere, perhaps 75 per cent, consists of residential, or mixed-use development in which the residential element dominates, and/or where the building plot and building footprints are generally small. The proportion of the existing residential development that is open to the broad application of urban design principles, however, depends on the context.

In general, without major redevelopment, it is difficult to apply mainstream urban design and compact city principles to low-density suburban sprawl which, in area terms, occupies a much larger proportion of the total urban extent of the world than the higher density inner-city areas (which may overall accommodate more people). The same constraints often apply to large-scale exclusively residential development. One possible urban design strategy, in these instances, is to retrofit higher-density, mixed-use nuclei. This has been proposed by some of the New Urbanists in the USA, for example but, as yet, is little tried.

A relatively small proportion of the remaining urbanised area consists of central area commercial development, where building footprints can be quite large, but where very high land costs lead to intensive land development and the need for public infrastructure to be tightly organised and planned along mainstream urban design principles.

The remainder falls into the category of large footprint, mainly low-rise, mainly vehicular-accessed, stand-alone buildings – offices, factories, warehouses, transport and utility-related buildings, retail sheds, shopping and leisure centres and institutional buildings of various kinds. Some of this development occurs in central areas, though it is increasingly confined to suburban and peri-urban locations where land prices are cheaper. There is little opportunity to apply mainstream urban design principles in this environment as the pedestrian environment counts for very little, streets do not exist and uses tend to be zoned.

Putting these factors together, in an admittedly less than scientific manner, probably between 60 and 80 per cent of the world's urban extent is currently inappropriate for the application of mainstream urban design and represents the primary challenge for urban designers in the twenty-first century.

THE DEVELOPING WORLD CONTEXT

Do the accepted urban design principles as they have been developed in the West have any place in the rest of the world, where the emphasis is less on sustainable development, and more on economic development and survival in a globalising world? The key factor is global urbanisation. Nearly all of the world's predicted population growth of 3 billion in the next fifty years will be added to the existing 2 billion living in urban areas in developing countries. Unchecked, the nearly 1 billion currently estimated to live in slums will rise to 3 billion, equal to the total urban population of the world today.[7] This process, called the urbanisation of poverty. has little to say about the way one-third of the people of the world currently live in cities, and, as this proportion grows, becomes even less relevant to their needs. Is this a question of developing new principles or adapting existing principles to new situations?

This figure of 1 billion slum dwellers includes those in the developed world, although these make up a small proportion of the total. Of the rest, a significant number live in formal settlements, but in dwellings that lack basic services or durable forms of construction. Maybe two-thirds, around 650 million, live in what we imagine as the slums of the Third World, informal settlements lacking infrastructure and services but also legal forms of tenure.

Most informal settlements fit within the urban morphological category where mainstream urban design principles might apply. Plots and building footprints are small, often very small. Streets usually exist, more often than not formed by continuous frontages. Properties fronting the main streets usually serve a commercial as well as residential purpose. Other mixed uses such as small-scale manufacture combined with residential uses are commonplace.

The public realm, although seldom 'safe, attractive and uncluttered' is often more friendly to pedestrians than vehicles. There is relative ease of movement, adaptability and diversity. A network of streets normally exists, though whether it is legible or not depends on the context. Above all, these settlements have their own identity and a natural vitality that originates from emphasis on the multiple use of common space, from the density of settlement, and the fact that most movement is on foot.

We tend to think of informal settlements as crowded shanty-towns and squatter settlements, with makeshift shacks built on tiny plots fronting onto warrens of ill-planned, unpaved narrow lanes. Many slum dwellers live in such conditions, particularly in the inner areas of developing world cities, but a greater number live in consolidated settlements, where shacks have been replaced with more robust structures of one, two or more stories, where the streets are often paved and where there are rudimentary services. Drainage, sanitation, water and power supply are usually inadequate, and the nominal owners will usually lack legal title to their property but many of such 'popular neighbourhoods' in Asia, Africa and Latin America are on their way to becoming, or are already, recognised city districts.

While such neighbourhoods are often well located in terms of access to employment and services, they are socially excluded and usually still carry the stigma of slums. The residents are mainly poor and the neighbourhoods are characterised by deprivation, including high levels of unemployment and crime. Physically, they remain ghettoes, isolated from the public realm of the formal city.

On this basis, major upgrading programmes for such neighbourhoods are sometimes urban-design-led, such as the 'Favela Bairro' programme in Rio de Janeiro. In this programme, local architects have planned interventions that are designed to integrate the neighbourhoods within the public infrastructure of the city, providing the public spaces that are normally lacking, for the communities to meet in parallel with formalisation of property ownership.

Mainstream urban design practice, then, does have some relevance to inner-city slum dwellers in developing-world cities. However, although upgrading of existing slums is now widely accepted as the best approach to low-income urban development, commercial land pressures mean that many local authorities routinely evict inner-city slum dwellers or relocate them to peripheral sites and large public housing schemes with the inevitable break-up of communities, loss of livelihood opportunities and new urban developments with little or no potential for mainstream urban design solutions.

It is also the case that the very rapid expansion of cities in the developing world, including the development of the road infrastructure around the cities, has meant that the growth in informal settlements is increasingly concentrated on the urban periphery. The form that this development takes depends on the geographical and cultural context.

URBAN TYPOLOGIES IN DEVELOPING COUNTRIES

In Latin America, much of the informal development on the urban periphery takes the form of illegal land divisions or planned invasions of public land by organized groups of existing low-income city residents. The resulting development tends to take a similar form – narrow plots, generally larger than are found in inner-city areas, but often completely built over and forming continuous frontages to reasonably well laid out networks of streets. Such settlements, then, given the limitations of their suburban location, are often planned along mainstream urban design lines.

As long ago as the late 1950s, John Turner described how such settlements were being created in the deserts around Lima in Peru, and tended to accommodate the consolidating low-income households of the city, while the inner-city slums attracted the newly-arrived, poorer migrant 'bridgeheaders'. This dynamic process of city creation is still going on.

Right:

2.4 Edge City? Dulles Airport, Washington, DC. Peripheral development as featureless tarmac.

Below, clockwise from left:

2.5 Back-office-land, Washington, DC. Streetless peri-urban development.

2.6 Perilous shacks in Tucunduba, Belem, Brazil. A stereotypical informal settlement.

2.7 Megacity downtown, Avenida Paulista, São Paulo, Brazil. A modernist avenue.

2.8 Illegal land divisions in São Paulo, Brazil. A common, more planned form of informal settlement.

2.9 Tucunduba, Belem, Brazil

In Africa and parts of Asia, informal settlements on the urban periphery sometimes take the form of very low-density randomly scattered dwellings, with residents combining city employment with small-scale farming. This type of development eats up huge amounts of often valuable agricultural land, is extremely expensive to service and is impervious to mainstream urban design principles, in the same way that most high-income, low-density suburban development is. The only way that this type of development could be contained and directed is through the imposition of planning controls that currently simply do not exist.

Beyond this variety of forms of informal settlement, developing-world cities are characterised by a large variety of urban typologies. There are quarters that have been laid out by colonial powers and reproduce European typologies, dense commercial downtown areas that follow the narrow and organic street patterns of traditional urban settlements as in many Islamic cities, or are laid out on a modern grid, more characteristic of the cities of North America.

As in the higher-income countries, the particular morphologies reflect the period during which the formative development occurred. Where the central city is mainly nineteenth century or early twentieth century, a high-density, highly structured legible grid/street network/block form is characteristic. In later developments, the road infrastructure becomes more dominant and more destructive of the pedestrian public realm.

Latin American, North African and West Asian cities tend to be higher density than cities in Sub-Saharan Africa, where suburban settlements (which can be high net density) are loosely grouped around a relatively small central business district. South Asian and East Asian cities also generally tend to be high-density but some are similar in form to the Sub-Saharan African ones.

While high-income, low-density suburbs are increasingly found around the periphery of developing-world cities in the same way as they are in the high-income countries, the middle and upper classes make up a smaller proportion of the population, and probably a smaller proportion of them live in this way. While the better-off, certainly in the UK and North America, are the majority of inhabitants on the urban periphery, in the developing world, the greatest proportion of its inhabitants are low-income.

The 60 per cent or so of the population in developing-world cities who live in formal settlements then, by and large live in more secure neighbourhoods within the city proper. Medium-rise and high-rise concrete apartment buildings are ubiquitous, normally thrown up with little relation to their neighbours or context, alongside neighbourhoods of high-walled town houses and compounds. (Defensive condominiums and gated communities are seen by the middle classes as a form of collective refuge from violent crime and the perceived anarchy of the streets in cities characterised by extreme inequalities.)

Developing-world cities, although usually of higher density than those in the developed world, are also characterised by the domination of motorised traffic, by scattered, low-density peri-urban development, whether high or low-income, and consequent high land take. This peri-urban development forms an urban-rural continuum – a patchwork of land uses with elements of agriculture/horticulture, industry/shed development, suburbia – high income and low income, formal/informal, institutional development, incorporation of existing villages, towns, and so on.

This development, whether central or peripheral, is largely of poor architectural quality and uncontrolled by planning laws. Any yet, many of the cities thus formed are highly dynamic and full of vitality. Little thought is given to the application of the conventional principles of urban design, but higher densities of living, and the fact that most people are poor and walk or use public transport rather than private vehicles, means that lively, pedestrian-orientated streets emerge of their own accord, despite the priority given to keeping the mainly middle-class traffic on the move.

To summarise, it is probably safe to say that a higher proportion of urban areas in developing-world countries is open to a more mainstream urban design approach than in the richer countries, by virtue of their poorer population, urban morphology, generally higher densities, and less extensive urban sprawl. The main concern is rather to develop effective forms of development control that impose order on the urban chaos, and within which urban design guidance could be incorporated. However, most new development is occurring on the urban fringe, much of it along the lines of peri-urban development in the higher-income countries, combined with particular forms of low-income informal settlement characteristic of developing countries in different regions of the world, and most of this outside the remit of mainstream urban design principles.

ADAPTING URBAN DESIGN PRINCIPLES

How should urban design principles be adapted to the wider development agenda globally? It is clear that the belated attempt to apply a purely 'compact city', based on mainstream urban design principles to the spatial planning and development of cities, is unlikely to succeed in Europe, let alone in the rest of the world. The scale of sprawl and the relentless pressures for its increase are too great. One strategy is to try to focus development in the wider urban regions around high-density sub-centres, designed according to 'compact city', mainstream urban design principles and linked together within a wider regional public transport network (as in the 'New Urbanist' model in the US or 'decentralised concentration' approach in Europe). These could form the nuclei of rather better planned low-density developments of sheds and single family-housing suburbs.

But the latter will continue to proliferate and will never be high-density, mixed-use, street-based or pedestrian-orientated. It means we have to give greater prominence to basic principles of good layout and planning for stand-alone buildings, how these relate to one another, to the landscape and the road infrastructure. This is partly about recasting the art of site planning within a larger framework of urban landscape design, and reflecting how well-designed sites can relate to the perception of a larger urban whole.

It is also about addressing good practice in the design of a range of building types that do not fit within the normal gambit of conventional urban design, with its excessive focus on the perimeter block. How can shed developments be organized into a coherent approach to the public realm that rises above purely pragmatic concerns of vehicle accessibility? What is a good urban design approach to the planning of towers, whether as clusters, or in relation to podia, streets and other public spaces?

Certainly there should be greater attention given to sustainable development and the needs of pedestrians and cyclists and to improve public transport links (as, for example, is the case the suburban developments found in cities in Scandinavia). But there should also be greater recognition given to the fact that most experience of the landscape on the urban periphery (and indeed a considerable amount of the experience of inner-city users) is in movement, mostly car, but also public transport-based.

Many decades ago, pioneering work was done in this field at MIT and Donald Appleyard wrote a book, together with Kevin Lynch and J.R. Myer, called *The View from the Road*.[8] It seems that, apart from the later influential essay by Robert Venturi on the street as a system of signs, *Learning from Las Vegas*,[9] little work has been done to follow up on this important starting point on a wider approach to urban design.

Arrive in almost any city in the world these days at the airport or from the motorway junction and your journey to the city centre is likely to involve driving through a familiar landscape of ill-planned sprawling industrial, commercial and residential development. If urban design is to have any impact at all on this type of development, it needs to look to a wider landscape understanding of character and identity, to relationships between built form that are not exclusively focused on continuity and enclosure; to consider pedestrian accessibility and legibility beyond the street environment, in relation to the natural environment, roads and public transport interchanges; and to give much greater concern to the legibility of the urban and suburban landscape as experienced as 'place in movement'.

Notes

1 The brief historical review outlined here is described in greater detail in my chapter 'The scope of urban design', in Clara Greed and Marion Roberts (eds), *Introducing Urban Design*, Harlow: Pearson Education, 1998.

2 Ian Bently, *et al.*, *Responsive Environments: A Manual for Designers*, Oxford: Butterworth, 1985.

3 *The Planner*, 76(39), 1990: 10-14.

4 *By Design: Urban Design in the Planning System*, 2003 – available from the UK government Office of the Deputy Prime Minister website: http://www.odpm.gov.uk/stellent/groups/odpm_planning/documents/page/odpm_plan_605981.hcsp

5 Hence, the common perception of mainstream urban design consensus as backward-looking.

6 See *Report of the Working Group of Urban Design for Sustainability* DG Environment Commission of the European Communities, Brussels (http://europa.eu.int/comm/environment/urban/sustainable_urban_design.htm)

7 UN-Habitat, *Guide to Monitoring MDG Target 11*, New York: UN, 2003.

8 D. Appleyard, K. Lynch and J.R. Myer, *The View from the Road*, Cambridge, MA: MIT Press, 1964.

9 R. Venturi, *Learning from Las Vegas*, Cambridge, MA: MIT Press, 1977.

Over the past decade or more, the term 'sprawl' has become popular pejorative, shorthand for poorly planned growth that consumes precious open space and mars the landscape with development that is too often large-scale, anonymous, and ugly. It is blamed for constant traffic jams, crowded schools and a host of other ills that afflict fast-growing communities. It is also castigated for accelerating, if not causing, widespread disinvestment and flight from center cities and older suburbs.[1] As former US Supreme Court Justice Potter Stewart said of pornography, most people would be hard pressed to define urban sprawl, but they know it when they see it.

For some, the word sprawl conjures images of interminable traffic jams, bulldozers wrecking farmland, cookie-cutter shopping centers, and endless suburban tract housing. Others have tried to be more quantitative and specific. In one recent study, researchers identified sprawl as the process in which the spread of development across the region far outpaces population growth. They describe the landscape created by sprawl as having four dimensions: (1) a population that is widely dispersed in low-density development; (2) clearly separated homes, shops, and workplaces; (3) a network of roads marked by very large blocks and poor access; and (4) a lack of well-defined activity centers, such as downtowns and town centers. Most of the other features usually associated with sprawl – the lack of transportation choices, relative uniformity of housing options or the difficulty of walking – can be seen as a result of these conditions.[2]

CHAPTER 3

IT'S SPRAWL, BUT IT'S MY SPRAWL

HARRIET TREGONING

Applying an index of sprawl that includes measures of residential density; neighborhood mix of homes, jobs, and services; strength of activity centers and downtowns; and the accessibility of the street network, showed some of the major metropolitan areas examined in the United States to sprawl badly in all dimensions. Visitors to the communities of Atlanta, Raleigh and Greensboro, North Carolina would not be surprised to find these places high on any sprawl index. The researchers found that some American cities sprawled substantially less; among them are San Francisco, Boston and Portland, Oregon.

Atlanta is in many ways a typical large American city. Its population has reached 3.5 million, and urban sprawl is such a problem that each citizen is obliged to travel an average of 34 miles per day by car – the highest figure in the country.

But the point of measuring sprawl is less to vilify particular metropolitan regions and more to understand the impacts differences in form and pattern have on people's lives. An objective index of sprawl may only tell us what we already know – that since the 1960s American cities and their suburbs have been spreading further and further out, converting land to urbanizing uses at two to ten times the rate of population growth.[3] As a result, we now spend much more on motorized transportation. Between 1969 and 1995, the number of private vehicles per household increased more than 50 per cent to more than one vehicle per licensed driver.[4] Cars have become so essential to working, shopping, and living in American cities that most people find a way to pay the more than $7,500 per year necessary to own, maintain, insure and operate a car.[5] Since 1970, the US population has increased 37 per cent, but the distance traveled by our vehicles, including SUVs, trucks, cars and motorcycles, rose 143 per cent.[6] This growing reliance on private vehicle transportation necessitated by low-density, sprawling land use has important implications – people living in more sprawling regions tend to drive greater distances, own more cars, breathe more polluted air, face a greater risk of traffic fatalities and walk and use transit less.[7] And a barrage of recent studies has suggested that traffic injuries, air pollution and an increasingly sedentary lifestyle have contributed to an epidemic rise in obesity. Today 31 per cent of Americans are obese and 65 per cent are overweight or obese.[8, 9, 10]

The cost of automobile ownership

In 1980, according to the American Automobile Association (AAA), the total cost of owning a typical car was $3,176 a year. That works out to 21.2 cents a mile if you drive 15,000 miles a year. Of that amount, 5.9 cents a mile went for gas and oil, 27.9 percent of the cost of driving. Last year, the total cost of owning a typical car was $7,533. That works out to 50.2 cents a mile. Of that amount, the same 5.9 cents a mile went for gas and oil. Gas and oil are now only 11.8 percent of the cost of driving.

YES, IT'S SPRAWL, BUT IT'S MY SPRAWL

Although many Americans have rising concerns about traffic, rapid growth, health and other consequences of current growth patterns, they remain largely and persistently happy with the quality of their immediate neighborhoods.[11] They are particularly sanguine about the quality of their housing and with the system that delivers that housing. And it is no wonder: a combination of government-backed enterprise, generous tax incentives, federal insurance and a robust network of property-rights protections have produced a housing-production system that is unrivaled around the world. One-quarter to one-third of America's tangible wealth (around $12 trillion) is in residential real estate.[12] Moreover, wealth in the form of the housing that homeowners occupy is the cornerstone of net wealth for most American households. Half of homeowners hold more than 41 per cent of their household net wealth in the form of home equity. Home-ownership has long been perceived as the main path for upward economic mobility particularly by the poor, immigrant families, and newly formed households.[13, 14]

In fact, Americans are schizophrenic about the built environment. They want to preserve green space, but don't necessarily see how that relates to their choice of a house built on former farmland. They push for new roads to relieve traffic and provide better access for new development on those former farms, but are surprised and frustrated by the growth that often follows. Or they embrace the notion of reinvestment in their neighborhood, but find reasons to protest a dense new development down the block, thus shifting that development to a further-flung, more land-consumptive location in the region.

For planners, designers, and architects who hope to counteract the societal forces behind sprawl, it is imperative to keep this perspective in mind. When immediate self-interest is pitted against some future public good, it is rare for self-interest to lose, especially in the context of a homeowner's 'investment'. Thus, for most people, landuse decisions that are intended to affect the greater good will only be supported if the homeowner impact can be shown to be at least neutral if not beneficial. And yet when the topic is not a specific and imminent development proposal, many citizens think about different facets of planning and development as isolated abstractions, not as decisions that will influence the nature and quality of their interaction with their neighbors, their mobility, the economic competitiveness of their community or, ultimately, the value of their investment in a home.

So, on the one hand, we have great dissatisfaction with the public realm, with the environment beyond our front yard; on the other, we have great complacency with our own homes, both as investments and as our own manifest realization of the American Dream. The housing-production system in the United States, together with strong incentives for Americans to become homeowners, and the naturally conservative attitudes of householders whose primary asset and wealth-creation potential are tied up in their owner-occupied home, have helped to create this dichotomy. Any attempt to do something about it must walk a knife's edge, simultaneously giving voice to dissatisfaction with the public realm; protecting and enhancing the inviolate notion of 'home'; addressing and reforming an entire interlocked finance, regulatory, and policy system whose default product is sprawl; and inspiring citizens with a new and improved vision of the good life.

In the United States, the 'smart growth' movement has emerged as the most promising attempt yet to deal with these contradictions. Advocates share many of the same goals of earlier environmental efforts – with a key difference. It has been observed that environmental attitudes in the United States are widely, but not deeply, held. Many Americans dissipate their environmental leanings by recycling their (ever-increasing) garbage and driving the Eddie Bauer edition of their SUV. The effectiveness of an appeal for self-sacrifice on behalf of the environment has steadily waned since the 1970s. The smart growth movement has adopted language and methods that are consciously more pragmatic and inclusive. Instead of appealing to environmental sensibilities, or otherwise asking for self-sacrifice, they have asked what issues ordinary citizens are most concerned about. Increasingly they wrap the discussion around basic quality-of-life issues.

By shifting the focus from self-sacrifice to self-interest, the champions of smart growth have tried to reframe the debate over sprawl and broaden the audience. These days, it's not at all surprising to see environmentalists sitting at the same table as farmers and suburbanites, developers and builders, public health advocates and fiscally conservative elected officials. In the process, they have opened up new opportunities to build consensus among once disparate groups and to attempt to resolve the contradiction between complacency with our large, auto-accessible, increasingly distant housing and our growing disaffection with the public realm. Which is not to say that smart growth advocates have figured out the way to relegate sprawl to the history books – far from it. There is a long road ahead. But more so than ever, there are a lot more people looking at the same road map.

SMART GROWTH: A REACTION TO MODERNISM?

Some have described the burgeoning anti-sprawl movement as a reaction to modernism. But that rationale gives both too much credit and too much blame to modernism, and indeed to architecture in general. The vast majority of building that goes on in the world is not the product of architects. Even in the developed world, the skills of the architect are primarily sought for complex buildings or those seen as cultural and political symbols. Many modernist architects – Le Corbusier, Frank Lloyd Wright – accurately foretold the transformation of cities and suburbs in the twentieth century. Sigfried Giedeon, writing in the bible of modern architecture, *Space, Time and Architecture* about Robert Moses, the New York planner and empire-builder, captured the spirit of the century.

> **As with many of the creations born out of the spirit of this age, the meaning and beauty of the parkway cannot be grasped from a single point of observation, as was possible from a window in the chateau of Versailles. It can be revealed only by movement, by going along in a steady flow, as the traffic rules prescribe. The space-time feeling of our period can seldom be felt so keenly as when driving.**[15]

The conjoining of machine travel and aesthetics, the seduction of automobile advertising, the tyranny of traffic engineering and the consequent ubiquity of the automobile, dwarf the contribution of any architectural style to the enormous changes in the form, pattern, and appearance of our communities in the past sixty years.

Yet in one sense, the mass production and standardization that became the hallmark of housing production in the post-World War II years, and later a dominant characteristic of housing and other real estate finance was first modeled by the Modern Movement in architecture, as a new and exciting aesthetic foundation. These architects of an earlier generation sought to replace dense and unhealthy tenements with high rises and open spaces to improve light, air and health. But even architecture's most compelling modernist vision of the re-built city failed to capture the imagination of America in the way their planning contemporaries did. These planners and designers, driven by more romantic, almost anti-urban dreams, developed ideas of how to build idyllic communities in more country-like settings. Forest Hills Gardens, a 142-acre planned community in Queens, designed by Fredrick Law Olmsted Jr., was a pioneering commuter suburb that gave the country a vision of suburban living like a 'modern Arcadia'.[16] Few new suburban communities were able to match the visionary planning of this first Garden City, but the public imagination was kindled. The gentrifying prospect of an escape to a suburban 'country estate' was increasingly assisted by major government subsidies, sophisticated mass production techniques, a burgeoning industrial lobby, and a uniquely supportive housing finance system.

SMART GROWTH: ATTEMPTING A SAVVIER SUSTAINABILITY

Smart growth has evolved rapidly from its mid-1990s' origins as an effort to recast the policy debate over sprawl in a way that more directly links the environment, the economy and daily life concerns. In 1996, the US Environmental Protection Agency launched a series of meetings with hundreds of individuals and organizations, trying to build consensus on land-use issues and figure out how to get better information and tools into the hands of local officials, designers, planners, developers, preservationists, environmentalists and others who were battling sprawl. That year, a broad coalition formally joined hands as the Smart Growth Network (SGN), with members spanning design, planning, real estate, advocacy and policy-making circles. In the effort to define what up until that time had been a little more than a new and catchy phrase, they came up with ten smart growth principles:

1. Mix land uses.
2. Take advantage of compact building design.
3. Create housing opportunities and choices.
4. Create walkable communities.
5. Foster distinctive, attractive communities with a strong sense of place.
6. Preserve open space, farmland, natural beauty, and critical environmental areas.
7. Strengthen and direct development toward existing communities.
8. Provide a variety of transportation choices.
9. Make development decisions predictable, fair, and cost-effective.
10. Encourage community and stakeholder collaboration in development decisions.

At the same time, Maryland Governor Parris N. Glendening was preparing to bring the concept into the realm of government policy with his Smart Growth and Neighborhood Conservation Initiative (passed in early 1997).[17] This ground-breaking proposal created a new framework for development decisions, turning to fiscal policy and incentives, rather than land-use regulations, to direct growth. Other partnerships were being formed to produce model regulations, planning guidelines, publications and other tools, and in October 1997, the SGN launched a monthly speaker series. Little by little, smart growth was becoming a recognized 'brand', if not a household term, that conveyed a new sense of balance and energy in the fight against sprawl.

Even earlier, a group of architects and designers articulated a philosophy of architecture and urban planning – the New Urbanism – that calls for the construction and reconstruction of communities around the pedestrian and the neighborhood, rather than the automobile. Architects Peter Calthorpe,

Andres Duany, Elizabeth Moule, Stefanos Polyzoides, Elizabeth Plater-Zyberk, and Daniel Solomon, along with organizer Peter Katz, founded the Congress as a non-profit organization to promote and disseminate information about the New Urbanism.[18] The first Congress of the New Urbanism, held in 1993, was a meeting of 170 designers organized to compare works-in-progress and exchange ideas about urban and suburban places; subsequent Congresses have been held in North American cities every year, attracting hundreds of architects, designers, developers, and city leaders to exchange ideas about enhancing our communities.[19] According to Professor Vincent Scully, an architectural historian at Yale University, New Urbanism is about a renewed focus on the pedestrian:

> It's important that people are within walking distance of the center of town. That streets are narrow and connected. And that the street is a place for people – not just automobiles . . . We started thinking about architecture as the structure of human habitation. The origins of New Urbanism are basically in the New England town.[20]

By the late 1990s, Maryland was using its $20+ billion budget to steer development to established communities and designated growth areas. If local officials and developers wanted to build in outlying areas, they would miss out on state funding for roads, water and sewer and other growth-related needs. On the other hand, they were rewarded with grants, tax breaks and infrastructure support for building in what are called Priority Funding Areas. Governor Glendening drew a clear connection between a healthy economy and a healthy environment, a link that had often been missed in the past. He also made a compelling case for the public benefits derived from revitalizing older cities and towns, though he is probably best known for his efforts in land preservation. Today, in Maryland, Massachusetts, Michigan, Utah, California and in many other states, 'smart growth' is widely recognized as a trend that is equally relevant – and important – to rural, suburban and urban areas. In joining the issues of community design and quality of life with transportation, housing, health, the environment and economics, its early advocates created a better understanding of sprawl and its consequences.

THE BRASS RING: ECONOMIC COMPETITIVENESS

A central premise of smart growth that is getting increasing attention today is that smart growth policies direct development toward existing communities already served by roads, sewer systems and other infrastructure. Robert Burchell of Rutgers University examined the effects of sprawl, or conventional development, versus managed (or 'smart') growth on land and infrastructure consumption as well as on real estate development and public service costs in the United States. In one recent national study Burchell concluded that sprawl produces a 21 per cent increase in the amount of undeveloped land converted to developed land and approximately a 10 per cent increase in local road lane-miles, compared to smart growth. Furthermore, sprawl causes about 10 per cent more annual public service (fiscal) deficits and 8 per cent higher housing occupancy costs.[21]

Because of the difficult economic and fiscal environments in which states and localities increasingly find themselves, the imperative of controlling costs is making reform of uncontrolled, unplanned and wasteful growth patterns unavoidable. Sprawl and urban decline are each burdening taxpayers. Low-density sprawl is raising tax bills because it frequently costs more to provide infrastructure and services to far-flung communities where longer distances separate houses and businesses. Urban decay, meanwhile, imposes even more painful costs, as decline depresses property values, and therefore tax revenues. Such trends place heavy pressure on older communities to set their property tax rates higher than developing outer areas, weakening their capacity to compete for new residents and investments. Moreover, many communities are in the ludicrous position of experiencing no net growth, but spreading out over more land and paying for substantial new infrastructure to accommodate a shrinking jobs and housing base.

At the same time, many of a region's most critical assets – colleges and universities, hospitals and medical centers, and cultural institutions – are found in its older communities. Regional growth strategies that foster continued outward growth at the expense of the center risk failing to capitalize on these assets at best and isolating or stranding them at worst. These dynamics also exacerbate the loss of young talent, worsening a region's workforce problems. Many older communities badly need to attract and retain more highly educated younger workers, including the enviable flow of top students who often *pass through* a region's institutions of higher learning. However, sprawl, on the one hand, and urban decline, on the other, each hinder a region's ability to create the kinds of places that attract critical human capital, and reverse a serious brain drain. In many older US communities, rarely do young mobile educated workers find the lively downtowns, healthy urban neighborhoods, wilderness recreation and vibrant close-in job markets to which they gravitate. That makes it harder to build and maintain the skilled and educated workforce necessary to spawn high-paying knowledge jobs and cultivate entrepreneurism.

Moreover, current trends are also isolating many regions' growing numbers of low-income and minority residents from opportunity. Most notably, the movement of jobs and middle-class families away from cities, towns, and older suburbs and into the outer suburbs means that low-income and minority workers have become spatially separated from economic opportunities. This physical isolation, compounded by serious skills shortfalls among these isolated workers, represents a serious drag on a region's productivity. Specifically, these growing disparities in economic opportunity, in educational achievement, and societal engagement mean that entire portions of a region are not just unengaged in the economic life of the region. In many cases, they are a dead-weight loss, requiring federal, state, and local subsidies, resources, and assistance simply to tread water in the same impoverished conditions.[22]

PERSUADING THE PUBLIC

Architects of the Renaissance were painters, sculptors, mathematicians, and draftsmen, as well as the designers of buildings. They were masters of the entire built environment. Today's architects may design textiles, tools, teapots and tables, but they rarely have the opportunity to affect an entire landscape, although many are increasingly concerned about its deterioration. Architects, particularly those that want to work at a scale larger than that of a single building, must share the undertaking with civil engineers, planners, landscape architects, economic development specialists, urban designers, retailing experts, traffic engineers and, increasingly, members of the public.

Momentum for finding more sensible and sensitive approaches to growth continues to build as elected officials in geographically and politically diverse areas offer initiatives touching on everything from land preservation and brownfields clean-up to economic development and transportation.

The American Planning Association documented 533 state or local ballot initiatives in the 2000 elections that focused on planning or smart growth issues – with an approval rate topping 70 per cent. Land preservation, in particular, has been popular. Since 1998, voters have supported more than $19 billion in open-space funding, passing 529 referenda. Even in 2002, in an off-year election, voters in 24 states and close to 200 local communities approved 137 out of 196 ballot measures to raise $1.7 billion for parks and open space.[23] There is plenty of other evidence that Americans are more worried than ever about the pace and form of growth in their communities – and receptive to new thinking. In 2000, the Pew Center for Civic Journalism released a poll in which people ranked sprawl alongside crime as their top local concerns.[24] At the same time, recent media coverage indicates that smart growth is becoming much more familiar. In 1996, there were fewer than 100 stories in newspapers and other print media that referred to smart growth. In 2001, there were more than 4,600 stories.

As more state and local politicians embrace at least some of the tenets of smart growth, they're starting to level the playing field between ex-urban development opportunities and urban infill and redevelopment by making the former more difficult and costly and the latter easier and more profitable.

But even as progress is made in expanding the 'supply' of smart growth, there's a lot of work left to do in cultivating 'demand.' Talking to developers gives the impression that it's getting easier, but not easy enough, to design and build communities that deserve the appellation. They still face the same skittishness from lenders and often overwhelming NIMBY (Not-In-My-Back-Yard) opposition at public hearings. A big part of the problem is simply public attitudes, and what is shaping them. Most Americans have never known a lifestyle that does not revolve around driving, and the auto industry spends billions telling them, 'You are what you drive.' Who will ever spend that kind of money promoting more compact, walkable neighborhoods and transit? That doesn't mean, however, that sentiment can't be tipped in a new direction. Consider how much attitudes have changed toward smoking since the 1980s. Look at all the cell phones and beepers people wear today to keep in constant communication. Human beings – and Americans, in particular – are constantly adapting to a changing world.

So what will it take for smart growth to become more than an encouraging trend? At this point, what is needed most is hands-on involvement by policy-makers, advocates and opinion leaders at the level of day-to-day decisions. It is time to step out of the ivory tower of theory and concepts and start paying attention to what's happening on the ground. It's time to start showing up at community meetings and working directly with more developers and builders, even if that means pushing a top-to-bottom remake of a bad project.

Policy-makers need to start cultivating YIMBYs, the 'Yes-In-My-Back-Yard' crowd, and enlisting them to turn up at public hearings to counteract angry neighbors. Such support can make all the difference, as it did in a recent vote on development around Takoma Park Metro station, in Washington, DC, next to the Maryland line. Advocates were outnumbered three-to-one, but there were enough of them to nudge elected officials to back high-density development that will boost transit ridership.

Opportunities to link development patterns with issues that resonate with the public at large must also be sought out and developed. A good example is the growing consensus among public health professionals that an obesity epidemic in the United States – where one out of five people is obese today – is due partly to sprawl. It's easy enough to get people to see that they would be a lot more active – without having to join a gym – if they lived in communities that were built for walking and biking, and not just for automobiles. To get the attention of parents, this same discussion of community design needs to be couched in terms of long commutes that eat up family time and the stress of having to juggle chauffeur duties until the kids are old enough to drive. Car dependence also eats up a growing chunk of the household budget, ranking only slightly behind housing costs for most Americans.[25]

REDEFINING 'THE GOOD LIFE'

These are the kind of issues that need to be tapped, and talked about in a way that redefines the vocabulary of architecture, planning, urban design and development. For example, experience has taught people in the United States to associate words like 'multi-family' and 'density' with sprawling, featureless compounds of renters who pack the roads and schools, then move on in a couple of years. Design professionals and policy-makers need to do a better job of showing what densely built neighborhoods look like in some of the world's best-loved cities and towns such as Annapolis, London, Saratoga Springs or Amsterdam, and figure out how to elevate expectations and standards for design. The same holds true for mixing land uses. After half a century of segregated zoning, most people can't envision how homes, shopping and offices could be compatible in close proximity.

In essence, what needs to happen is a redefinition of what constitutes 'the good life' in our times. The 'real-world' orientation of smart growth has given it a sense of immediate relevance that was lacking in earlier discussions of sustainability. What has happened is that the debate over sprawl and its consequences have been made to matter right now, not just to future generations. To give it staying power, architects, designers, policy-makers and advocates must offer more tangible examples of it in a variety of settings. And perhaps this new beginning means that we have to widen the range of problems studied in an architectural or design education, while throwing open the door to a broader participation in both the educational process and in practice. Craig Whitaker is one of a growing cadre of architects and planners who suggest that if we invite back into the drafting room the civil engineers, landscape architects, the historic preservationists as well as traffic planners and developers – we might start to bring these differing perspectives together again and collectively participate more successfully in shaping the built environment.[26]

In *The Tipping Point*, author Malcolm Gladwell outlines a simple and compelling theory, that 'ideas and products and messages and behaviors spread just like viruses do'.[27] That same thinking could be applied here. Not everyone has to be convinced that smarter patterns of growth offer better living in order to bring about meaningful change in development patterns and community design. Maryland's efforts got as far as they have largely as a result of the governor's success in getting people to think about sprawl differently. He was able to win broad support for the state's smart growth initiative, at least in part, by tying it to the goals of fiscal responsibility and a healthy economy. Clearly, that's not the only way to win support for smarter growth. But there's a lesson in it: policy-makers and smart growth's advocates need to become a little more subversive in how change is sold. You can only get so far by telling people to live differently for the good of the planet. They need to be shown how they benefit right now, in their waistlines, their wallets and their own backyard.

Notes

1 Harriet Tregoning, 'Sprawl, Smart Growth and sustainability', *North American Cities and Smart Growth*, Special Edition of Local Environment, 7 (4) November 1, 2002.

2 Reid Ewing, Rolf Pendall, and Don Chen, 'Measuring sprawl and its impact: the character and consequences of metropolitan expansion,' Washington, DC: Smart Growth America, 2002.

3 Don Chen and Kaid Benfield, *Once There Were Greenfields: How Urban Sprawl is Undermining America's Environment, Economy, and Social Fabric*, Washington, DC: Natural Resources Defense Council and the Surface Transportation Policy Project, March 1999.

4 'Summary of Travel Trends: 1995 National Personal Transportation Survey,' US Department of Transportation, Federal Highway Administration, Washington, DC, December 1999.

5 *Your Driving Costs 2003*, Washington, DC: American Automobile Association, 2003.

6 *National Transportation Statistics 2002*, Washington, DC: US Department of Transportation, Bureau of Transportation Statistics; December 2002, Publication BTS02-08.

7 Ewing *et al.*, 'Measuring sprawl and its impact'.

8 Centers for Disease Control and Prevention, US Department of Health and Human Services, Obesity Trends, 1985-2002, Atlanta, GA.

9 Shobha Srinivasan, Liam R. O'Fallon, and Allen Dearry, 'Creating healthy communities, healthy homes, healthy people: initiating a research agenda on the built environment and public health', *American Journal of Public Health*, Sept. 2003 93: 1446–50.

10 Andrew L. Dannenberg, Richard J. Jackson, Howard Frumkin, Richard A. Schieber, Michael Pratt, Chris Kochtitzky and Hugh H. Tilson, 'The impact of community design and land-use choices on public health: a scientific research agenda', *American Journal of Public Health*, Sept. 2003, 93: 1500–8.

11 Consumer Survey 2003, Washington, DC, National Association of Homebuilders and National Association of Realtors, 2003.

12 Federal Reserve Statistical Release, *Flow of Funds Accounts of the United States: Flows and Outstandings, Third Quarter 2003*, Washington, DC: Federal Reserve Bank, January 2004.

13 A. Holloway, 'The role of homeownership and home price appreciation in the accumulation and distribution of household sector wealth', *Business Economics*, April 1991: 38-44; Melvin L. Oliver and Thomas M. Shapiro, *Black Wealth, White Wealth*, London: Routledge, 1997, p. 57.

14 Zhu Xiao Di, *The Role of Housing as a Component of Household Wealth*, Cambridge, MA: Joint Center for Housing Studies at Harvard University, Working Paper Series, W01-6, July 2001.

15 Sigfried Giedeon, *Space, Time and Architecture: The Growth of a New Tradition*, 5th edn, Cambridge, MA: Harvard University Press, 1982, p. 826.

16 Susan L. Klaus, *A Modern Arcadia: Fredrick Law Olmsted Jr. and the Plan of Forest Hills Gardens*, Cambridge, MA: University of Massachusetts Press, 2002, pp. 4, 147.

17 Governor's Office of Smart Growth, 'Smart Growth in Maryland', July 2001.

18 Alex Marshall, 'Teaching New Urbanism', *Metropolis*, October 1997.

19 Andres Duany, Elizabeth Plater-Zyberk, and Jeff Speck, *Suburban Nation: The Rise of Sprawl and the Decline of the American Dream*, Appendix B, New York: North Point Press, 2000.

20 Noel C. Paul, 'Interview with Vincent Scully, "Putting people back into architecture"', *The Christian Science Monitor*, 5 April 2001.

21 Robert Burchell and Sahan Mukherji, 'Conventional development versus managed growth: the costs of sprawl,' *American Journal of Public Health*, 2003, 93: 1534-40.

22 Bruce Katz, *Back to Prosperity: A Competitive Agenda for Renewing Pennsylvania*, Washington, DC: The Brookings Institution Center on Urban and Metropolitan Policy, 2003.

23 *Planning for Smart Growth: 2002 State of the States*, Chicago: American Planning Association, 2002.

24 'Straight Talk from Americans', Pew Center for Civic Journalism, Sept. 2002, http://www.pewcenter.org/doingcj/research/

25 US Department of Transportation, *Summary of Travel Trends: 1995 National Personal Transportation Survey*, Washington, DC.

26 Craig Whitaker, *Architecture and the American Dream*, New York: Clarkson N. Potter, Publisher, 1996, p. 274.

27 Malcolm Gladwell, *The Tipping Point*, New York: Little, Brown and Company, 2000.

This is not the first essay that begins by seeking precision in language. If professions such as medicine were as sloppy with their language and terminology as we are in urban design, the mortuaries would be full. And yet, as designers, when we draw a line on a piece of paper it is the ultimate in precision once it is built because it is concrete, material, no longer abstract or theoretical.

'Public life' and the 'public realm' are terms used frequently by urban designers and are almost synonymous with the existence of urban design as a field of study and practice. So what are we attempting to communicate when we place that degree of emphasis on these terms, and how precise can we be about achieving success? In many ways it is the same as our current obsession and assumption that 'mixed use' is *automatically* a good thing rather than being precise about when mixed use is good and when it isn't.

CHAPTER 4

TRADITIONAL URBANISM IN CONTEMPORARY PRACTICE

PAUL MURRAIN

So what does the *Oxford English Dictionary* tell us about public life and the public realm?

PUBLIC: As an adjective, 'of, concerning, or open to people as a whole'. As a noun 'ordinary people in general'; 'the community'. As a phrase, such as *in public*, 'in view of other people'; 'when others are present'.

The word **LIFE** is explained as 'a particular aspect of people's existence'.

REALM is a 'field or domain of interest'.

From that it is reasonable to assume that by 'public life', we mean something particular at the core of our existence, namely that of being together, a collective will and collective conscience, the opposite of being *private* and clearly distinct from that other vital aspect of our existence. As long ago as the *polis*, the city-state of ancient Greece, this distinction was important, the private household and the public 'civitas', the clarification of the relationship between private matters and civic responsibility.

For urban designers the 'public realm' is the tangible physical space where public life takes place. One of the most important 'lines' we draw as urban designers is the one that defines the clear distinction and it does so for the benefit of both realms. Put simply, the street wall. For you cannot have one realm without the other and they have to be as close as possible to allow a civic society to thrive. As Roger Scruton points out, lacking a boundary lacks the character of publicness.[1] Space does not become public merely by ceasing to be private. When we look back and learn from traditional places we discover the clarity of this relationship time and again. The places that are old and still loved all exhibit this fundamental relationship that is then layered by the rich cultural differences between those places.

Codes and pattern books are ways of operationalising the products of traditional urbanism, in that they are the common language of town building, decided and sanctioned by as democratic a decision-making process as an urban designer can muster. Alexandria, Virginia, is one of the most desirable places to live in the Washington, DC, area. It is a simple orthogonal grid plan and an eighteenth-century town of immense beauty. It is very expensive to live there and it functions perfectly well 250 years after the plan was drawn. What is also telling in terms of a town code is the fact that the town leaders got together and made a code that required a 'street wall type of residence, essentially terraced houses, because some of the first houses were located on private property in a disparate fashion so that the town realised that if this continued, they would not have a town in the true sense of the word. They would simply have houses.

Criticism of design codes primarily comes from architects who fear that the guidelines restrict their creative abilities. To some extent, this can be true. But there is enough evidence in the urban world, and enough agreement too, that an underlying unity within individual interpretation is welcomed in the essence of great urbanism. Of course, all the architects engaged in New Urbanism either create codes or respond to them. There is intense debate within that paradigm, but no debate about their worth because those wishing to code for towns tend to argue for collective citizenship and empowerment via a coherent public realm and acknowledge that mediation is the way to achieve these goals. One code interpreted by many hands: the essence of great towns and cities for centuries.

But all too often in the modern city the public realm is no more than just space which is not private. In 1958 Hannah Arendt wrote an extraordinary book entitled *The Human Condition*[2] in which she explained that the term 'public' signifies the world itself, in so far as it is common to us all and distinguished from our privately owned place in it.

To live together in the world means essentially that a world of things is between those who have it in common, as a table is located between those who sit around it; the world, like every 'in-between', relates and separates us at the same time.' She adds, 'if that table is taken away, the people sitting opposite each other are no longer separated but neither are they related by anything tangible.[3]

Take those remarkable words and transfer them to the so-called public spaces we have all too often produced in the past sixty years. What a lamentable effort we have made.

Arendt also reminds us that 'through many ages before us – but not anymore – we entered the public realm because we wanted something of our own, or something we had in common with others to be more permanent than our earthly lives'.[4] When a public realm is designed to allow us to come together we still do it in droves when nobody is forcing us to do so. And there is often little reason to be there than to be there. It is not nostalgia that has us looking to the past for lessons. It is by observing, recording and measuring these spaces, realising that they have so much in common and that their local success is because they are part of something bigger. This is the essence of the remarkable work of Bill Hillier and his thorough understanding and demonstration of how traditional places work.[5] But he also warns traditional urbanists of romanticism in that successful streets and squares cannot be created purely as local places without understanding the realities of scale, space and function that cause them to exist in the first place and thrive thereafter.

In their excellent book *The Public Face of Architecture*, editors Nathan Glazer and Mark Lilla suggest that 'whatever other maladies we may suffer from, we are also in the grip of a deep intellectual confusion about the nature of public life.'[6] They go on to urge that we need a kind of civic education that emphasises the distinctive nature of these public questions.

That was never clearer to me than when attending a workshop at a National Urban Summit sponsored and hosted by the Deputy Prime Minister in November 2002. The workshop was supposedly focusing on good urban design principles. One of the keynote speakers uttered the following: 'Planning cities around an accepted set of principles equals painting by numbers. The results are barely acceptable and the products lack soul.' The combination of ignorance and arrogance in that statement beggars belief. To dismiss the time-honoured principles of good urbanism that have been duplicated by different communities, even with little or no knowledge of what each other was doing, is extraordinary and smacks of failure or an unwillingness to understand the difference between creativity and self-conscious originality. William Westfall refers to this phenomenon when he laments the modern conviction, that 'Man' lacks a fixed nature. 'Therefore there is no intrinsic justification for any attempt to describe universal or permanent norms or principles to guide any field of human endeavour, including the making of buildings.'[7]

G.K. Chesterton is more cutting in his criticism of this attitude:

Tradition may be defined as an extension of the franchise: **Tradition** means giving votes to the most obscure of all classes, our ancestors . . . **Tradition** refuses to submit to the small and arrogant oligarchy of those who merely happen to be walking about. All democrats object to men being disqualified by the accident of birth; tradition objects to their being disqualified by accident of death. Democracy tells us not to neglect a good man's opinion, even if he is our groom; tradition asks us not to neglect a good man's opinion, even if he is our father.[8]

At the most pragmatic example of tradition, how significant is 'High Street' in our culture? Why have we named it so, and when did we last build one; a real one, as opposed to giving that name to the main drag of a private internal shopping centre? Let us dip into the dictionary again to learn why we attribute this name to the place where communities gather and where locals and passers-by unite:

HIGH: 'Great in amount, size, value or intensity; Great in rank or status, culturally superior'.

STREET: 'A public road in the heart of a city, town or village'.

So the title High Street that has been with us for centuries suggests it is the highest order of street in whole neighbourhood or town. It has been given that attribute because of what it was built for and what it signifies, namely the focus of public life and interaction.

In the USA, the High Street is known as Main Street, more literal perhaps, but of the same significance. Here is what Carole Rifkind said in a book entirely dedicated to these essential spaces:

It was called Towne Street when it was a single wilderness road in New England, High Street in a southern New Jersey town, Broad Street in Pennsylvania, Market Street in Ohio, Grand Street in a brash Wyoming city, Broadway in California. But as Main Street it was uniquely American, a powerful symbol of shared experience, of common memory, of the challenge and struggle of building a civilisation. Through history, the name embraced a variety of urban forms – the thickened spine of a New England township, the central street in a neat grid, the city centre at the junction of diagonal boulevards . . . Yet Main Street was always familiar, always recognisable as the heart and soul of village, town or city.

These days it is called a 'collector road' – or is it 'distributor road'? – en route to a 'local centre'. Language reveals so much.

But we must also attempt to define 'urbanism'. Again, William Westfall does this concisely as 'the design and construction of a setting meant to support a civic realm'.[10] In this sense, it is perfectly understandable that the term 'New Urbanism' was deemed appropriate for this refocus of design effort in the USA in the past twenty years. The one thing that has been singularly lacking from (sub)urbanisation in the USA has been the setting to support a civic realm. They have been building all the individual components of urbanism but they have not been building true urbanism because the glue of a public realm has been completely absent. Many regard the term New Urbanism as being inappropriate for Europe because we did not destroy our old urbanism to anything like the same degree. But we must be careful of complacency, for we too have lost the ability to delivery that unifying public realm in so many of our new built environments. What is more alarming is that so much of our regeneration also fails to bring with it a coherent, legible and connected public realm. Instead we are all too often importing a suburban mentality into our existing cities and simply making them more dense.

There are different kinds of urbanism from different parts of the world. They vary markedly in their architecture. Criticisms can be levelled at elements of each of them perhaps. Doubtless there will be those who will limit their judgement to issues of style because that is the limit of their willingness to engage in this complex subject. Sadly, one of the biggest challenges to urbanists in the UK is to get so many of our architectural fraternity beyond 'style' as the sole or, at best, main criterion of debate on these complex matters.

Despite global differences and the different geographical locations in the city, the creation and response to a public realm are more important than any individual component. Good examples embody traditional urbanism. They learn from the past and from generations of refinement and experience because urbanism and locale mattered more and were more in the collective consciousness than they are today, certainly when contrasted with those who produce and sanction our contemporary built environment. For those who consume it however, true urbanism never really went away even though it disappeared. It is remarkably successful when offered because it reconnects us with the idea of being public. As Hannah Arendt warned us in 1958:

The public realm, as the common world, gathers us together and yet prevents us from falling apart. What makes mass society so difficult to bear is not the number of people involved but rather the world between them has lost its power to gather them together, to relate and separate them at one and at the same time.[11]

This polemic is about reclaiming that public realm. I hope it inspires you to do the same.

Notes

1 R. Scruton, 'Public Space and The Classical Vernacular', in N Glazer and M Lilla (eds.) *The Public Face of Architecture Civic Culture and Public Spaces*, New York: Collier Macmillan, 1987

2 H. Arendt, *The Human Condition*, Chicago: University of Chicago Press, 1958.

3 Ibid.

4 Ibid.

5 B. Hillier, *Space is the Machine: A Configurational Theory of Architecture*, Cambridge: Cambridge University Press, 1996.

6 N. Glazer and M. Lilla (eds.) *The Public Face of Architecture*, Boston: Free Press, 1987

7 R.J.Y. Van Pole and C.W. Westfall, *Architectural Principles in the Age of Historicism*, New Haven, CT: Yale University Press, 1991.

8 G.K. Chesterton, *Orthodoxy*, Ignatius Press, 1908

9 C. Rifkind, *Main Street: The Face of Urban America*, New York: Harper & Row, 1977.

10 C.W. Westfall, *The Classical American City*, Architectural Review at the University of Virginia, 1995

11 H. Arendt, *The Human Condition*, Chicago: University of Chicago Press, 1958

INTRODUCTION There is no doubt that the British planning system has become vastly more design-aware in the past decade in contrast to the dark, deregulatory days of the 1980s when design interventionism was actively discouraged by a Thatcherite view of planning. Much more positive central government advice has driven this revival, removing one of the major constraints on proactive design at the local level. More design-aware Planning Policy Guidance Notes and supporting manuals have been reinforced by documents like *Towards an Urban Renaissance*, the progenitor of the Sustainable Communities Initiative, bringing urban design into mainstream urban policy and planning programmes. There has been an outpouring of design guidance from such diverse bodies as the Commission for Architecture and the Built Environment (CABE), English Heritage, the Urban Design Group and the RTPI, much of which has received semi-official endorsement.

CHAPTER 5

THE PLANNING SYSTEM AND THE DELIVERY OF DESIGN QUALITY

JOHN PUNTER

Massive challenges remain to the routine achievement of design quality, and these are clearly evident in the agenda and initiatives of CABE. It recognises that the drive for better urban design has to be taken forward on many fronts – more research of design matters, better patronage and procurement (especially in public building), better public education, better design skills in planning/regeneration/development, and much more sophisticated design review. It has explored the design dimension of development control, recognising that planning authorities are under-resourced, under-skilled and too pressured for rapid decisions, but arguing for planning authorities to be proactive and much more design vigilant particularly as regards outline applications, planning conditions, post-permission amendments and enforcement. It notes failures of monitoring and review, and regrets the inability of the system to routinely add value to development, both literally and metaphorically, for developers (and householders) and the wider public. These are the issues discussed in this chapter, which is concerned to establish how the British planning system can contribute to the delivery of better urban design. It adopts an international perspective to assess how British practices and proposed reforms compare with those in other Western countries, in the hope of sharpening our agenda and aspirations for improved practice.

INTERNATIONAL EXPERIENCES WITH DESIGN REVIEW

British planning and design review remains very insular, not least because our discretionary planning system, based on rather vague land use plans, is so different from the administratively driven Western European and North American systems, where planning decisions are based upon legal rights to development enshrined in a development plan (and its regulations) or in a zoning code. However, the recent experience of these countries has much to teach us about how we might create more effective mechanisms for design control (just as our ultimately flexible, market-responsive system may have some lessons for them). Across Western Europe there has been a strong drive for de-regulation of development controls, and a search for new instruments to ensure design quality. There has been a cross-European adoption of aesthetic advisory committees (a Dutch tradition) as a way of injecting more skills and flexibility to the control process, and interest in more closely integrating development and conservation controls. There are new kinds of plans emerging at different spatial scales with a specific design component, and new roles being created for architectural supervisors and project managers. Similarly, North American practices of design regulation and review (review is a preferable term to our self-deceptive misnomer of 'control') have much to teach us. The exponential growth of design review over the past two decades has produced much innovation, and been rigorously scrutinised by development interests, design professionals and academics contesting both its legality and utility. These critiques of design review provide valuable pointers as to how the system might be better constructed to ensure a range of outcomes under four principal headings: **(1)** greater community assent; **(2)** better connection to wider planning goals; **(3)** use of a more meaningful set of design principles; and **(4)** fairer and more effective decision-making processes (see Box 5.A).

BOX 5.A
BETTER DESIGN PRINCIPLES

Community vision

1. Comprehensive, co-ordinated, community commitment to environmental beauty and design (Brennan's Law).
2. An urban design plan with community and development industry support periodically reviewed: a community design plan?

Design, planning and zoning

3. Harnessing the broadest range of actors and instruments to promote better design (tax, subsidy, acquisition, etc.).
4. Mitigating the exclusionary effects of control strategies and urban design regulation.
5. Addressing the limitations of zoning and integrating it into planning.

Broad, substantive design principles.

6. A commitment to urban design that goes well beyond elevations and aesthetics to embrace amenity, accessibility, community, vitality and sustainability.
7. Basing guidelines on generic design principles and contextual analysis and articulating desired and mandatory outcomes.
8. Not attempting to control all aspects of community design but accommodating organic spontaneity, vitality, innovation, pluralism: not over-prescriptive.

Due process

9. Clear *a priori* roles for urban design intervention.
10. Proper administrative procedures with written opinions to manage administrative discretion, and appropriate appeal mechanisms.
11. An efficient, constructive and effective permitting process.
12. The provision of appropriate design skills and expertise to support the process.

These guidelines provide a framework with which to interrogate current British debates about future planning reforms, and the new planning system emerging as the Planning and Land Compensation Bill goes through both Houses of Parliament.

COMMUNITY VISION AND CORPORATE COMMITMENT TO DESIGN

The **first two principles** relate to the necessity for the drive for better urban design to be firmly rooted in a community vision that drives local governance. Both emanate from an American Supreme Court decision known as 'Brennan's Law' which requires any local authority wishing to impose design review on private individuals to demonstrate a comprehensive, co-ordinated community commitment to environmental design quality. A pre-requisite is a real political commitment to good design by the local council, and effective corporate working, especially on the enhancement of the public realm and all public estate management activities. Portland, Oregon, remains an exemplar of both in the past three decades, while Copenhagen, Barcelona and Melbourne have outstanding public realm achievements.

The **second principle** suggests that the focus and policy frame for this commitment to design should be provided by some kind of urban design plan which can act as a synthesis of community values and provide a policy framework for council decisions. It emphasises that development industry support is a necessary component of community support, and implies that any plan must provide adequate opportunities for development, commensurate with local demand, while also providing acceptable rules for regulating the quality of urban design. Exemplars would include two of the City of Vancouver's many innovations – City Plan (1996) was a deeply participative, city-wide visioning that harnessed an astonishing 80 per cent community support, and is now being translated into neighbourhood plans through the same participative processes. Meanwhile a set of masterplans, covering much of Vancouver's waterfront, has been created by a 'co-operative planning process', based on early public consultation and political inputs translated into a detailed 3-D plan, subsequently implemented by zoning controls and design guidelines that guarantee delivery, with the permitting process dealing with matters of detail. This is masterplanning in its true sense, and a reminder of the persistent abuse of the term in British practice, though charrette-based projects like West Stevenage or landowner-driven masterplans like Harlow East are positive signs.

Community Strategies have recently been introduced into British local government (2000) to promote the economic, social and environmental well-being of areas through sustainable development but few have a strong design dimension. Now such strategies have to inform the new local development schemes which are replacing and extending the existing Urban Development Plans, the best of which did have a clear design commitment. It is still an open question as to how design policy will be enshrined in the new local development frameworks. Lessons (positive and negative) might be learned from the way the 1987 Highbury Initiative and its tightly focused (limited participation) visioning exercise underpinned the urban design renaissance in Birmingham, and were subsequently expressed in centre-wide movement and design guides, and the inner-city Quarters Studies.

DESIGN, SOCIAL INCLUSION AND THE PROVISION OF INFRASTRUCTURE

Principles 3–5 relate to how to link planning, design and development regulation to ensure that quality development is delivered, and that quality is measured in terms of public facility/amenity and affordable accommodation provision, as well as in terms of detailed design quality or environmental sustainability credentials. American critics of design review focus on the necessity to link planning and zoning into a positive relationship (planning seeks to manage change; zoning so often seeks to prevent it), the necessity to mitigate the exclusionary effects of urban design strategies and regula-

tions, and to harness a wide range of actors and instruments (particularly impact fees or gap funding/grant mechanisms) to the design agenda. The key instrument is undoubtedly a variant of development impact fees/cost levies/planning obligations designed to provide funds for public facilities/amenities and particularly for traffic management. In Britain, while engineering services, education, and open space requirements are well established, the question of wider planning obligations has never been satisfactorily resolved. The latest government proposals (November 2003) suggest locally set tariffs as alternatives to the negotiation of Section 106 agreements, which would be a step forward from the current system. Many American cities have undertaken thoroughgoing exercises in calculating the costs of financing growth and maintaining existing levels of facility/amenity provision. Vancouver has built this into its masterplans (including day-care facilities and public realm requirements), while city-wide it is seeking to recoup more than the one-third of the costs of development that it currently collects.

Closely related are matters of fixing proportions of housing type, tenure, and affordability which help to reduce the gentrification and social exclusion in new development and regeneration. As with the issue of planning obligations, it is important to set out local authority expectations as policy, so that the cost of such provision can be factored into land prices, rather than being squeezed out of design costs. Levels of affordable housing provision are still not a standard requirement across the UK (compare with a 20 per cent standard in Orange County!), and the regulation of unit mixes is repeatedly sacrificed to developers' perceptions of market demand. Such provisions are critical to place-making and sustainable communities. The same is, of course, true of conventional infrastructure, some of it, such as park space, having a potentially determinate effect on development quality.

Principle 5 is the challenge of connecting planning and zoning into a set of effective controls that can positively regulate urban form. This is very much an American and European problem, but, despite zoning's bad press,

5.1 Java Island, Amsterdam. Redeveloped wharves masterplanned by the project's 'architectural supervisor' deliver continuous street façades and a mid-block walkway/landscaped corridor that connects the entire social infrastructure. Each block is designed by a separate architect, nineteen in all, with different unit types and social mix.

5.2 Ira Keller Foundation Park, Portland, USA. Built in the 1960s, this swimmable 'fountain' remains as popular as ever, and Portland has gone on to create a public realm of a quality that can stand comparison with any city in the world. Strong political commitment to quality design has been a key factor in Portland's achievements.

5.3 False Creek North, Vancouver, Canada. The collaborative planning process that underpins the masterplanning of these mega projects ensures the community and the developer sign up to an 'official development plan' that provides certainty as to both permitted floor space and public amenities. Affordable housing, careful massing and site planning deliver attractive streets and excellent private open space match parks, and a quality public realm.

5.4 Chillingworth Road, Islington, North London. Altruistic architect developers have achieved a 50 per cent social housing content (the Mayor of London's target) on this site at a density of 150 dwelling units per hectare. Such ground-oriented, high-density housing provides the key to making residential intensification acceptable to local communities in many Western cities.

5.5 The City of Sydney Model, Australia. The Sydney's city model is a long-standing design tool still used to assess development proposals that have to be modelled and inserted into their context. The city's design excellence programme requires all major development projects to go through a competitive design process based on a detailed planning brief.

it remains a valuable tool for implementing masterplans, encouraging intensification and land use change, and creating predictable urban forms. North American experimentation with different forms of zoning has seen design guidelines and design codes added to encourage more sophisticated and consistent responses. In some instances additional floor space is only allowed if the guidelines are adhered to, creating a simple but extremely effective form of incentive zoning (e.g. Sydney, Vancouver). In other cases, the resolution of detailed design within the zoning entitlement is left to neighbourhood committees with support from planners (Seattle).

SUBSTANTIVE DESIGN PRINCIPLES FOR DESIGN REVIEW

Principles 6–8 relate to the question of substantive design principles. There are three overarching concerns. First, urban design needs to ground itself in a set of design principles that are not solely preoccupied with the way things look but tackle the whole range of environmental experience, embracing access, safety, health, comfort, vitality/sociability, and community with the context of substantiality in the immediate, but also the longer term. Many would regard the codification of British urban design principles into the seven Responsive Environments' urban design principles as a major step forward, but there ought to be more concern to extend these principles into wider sustainability principles (bio-diversity, energy efficiency, self-cleansing) and to refine them for particular development situations, particularly in suburbia. There are dangers of a design orthodoxy stifling the development of urban design thinking.

Second, there is the important proviso that all generic design principles have to be varied accordingly to the local context and site characteristics, and that the careful appraisal of a locality is a necessary first step to respecting local distinctiveness. Included in this principle is the view that design principles need to be expressed as a set of mandatory requirements and desired outcomes (guidance) so that it is clear what are the absolutes (a long-standing issue in British practice). Principle 8 emphasises the dangers of over-prescription and the way that any form of planning and design regulation constitute innovation, originality, spontaneity and diversity. Much of this trap can be avoided by not getting too embroiled in matters of detail, which remains an apparently irresistible temptation for amenity and neighbourhood groups and less experienced development controllers. Overall, the best British practice has made good progress on these issues.

There is much discussion in the Office of the Deputy Prime Minister (ODPM) responsible for the Built Environment in England of the value of design codes and CABE have begun to think about their application, suggesting the adoption of certain key development parameters (the Building for Life criteria?) as the mandatory elements, and allowing contemporary or traditional architectural interpretations according to context and market. They recognise that such codes need an enlightened landowner or strong public sector involvement to be delivered and that the whole question of the legal force of such new kinds of guidance needs to be re-thought.

DUE PROCESS IN DESIGN REVIEW

This is the fourth area where there has been significant debate in American and European design circles, partly because mechanisms for design review have had to be grafted on to established forms of plan-checking, permitting or zoning variances (rather than being integral as in Britain). The requirement to establish clear *a priori* rules for design intervention is the biggest challenge, especially to a discretionary system that has always relied upon professional judgement, even within its appeal system.

Appropriate administrative procedures and appeal mechanisms remain relatively unproblematic in the British context, but there are deep concerns about public consultation being subverted by an emphasis upon the speed of decisions, and the absence of third party rights and appeals (included in the Labour Manifesto but excluded from current planning reforms). Principle 10 concerns the development of an efficient, constructive, and effective development control process. The great danger is that efficiency interpreted solely as the speed of decision generally eclipses all other issues under this banner, and this will continue until broader performance indicators are introduced. The government has recently suggested new Best Value performance indicators (January 2004) that attempt to address these issues, but they still measure inputs rather than outputs; though they do address some key issues (the existence of advice, pre-application negotiations, skilled design/conservation officers, special teams for major applications). Cambridge City Council's range of consultation/conflict resolution techniques provides a positive example. One valuable lesson learned from Europe and North America is the benefit of integrating building, planning and conservation controls into a single permitting process, helping to improve adherence to plans and enforcement while also reducing bureaucracy.

Finally, there is the requirement for appropriate design skills and expertise to support the design review process, an issue that goes back to the roots of planning and architectural education. The short-term solution lies in the establishment of design panels to offer advice to developers and local authorities. CABE has revamped its design review procedures and made them much more constructive and considered, and is busy extending this service into the regions, as are the Regional Development Agencies. Some local authorities have established new design panels, while others have continued to use Architectural Advisory Panels. All these panels are second-best solutions because their inputs are infrequent, and they are simply another consultee in the system. The alternative is to give them a statutory role, as has recently been done in the Netherlands with the long-standing Aesthetic Advisory Committees, or fully embed them in the control process so that their influence is assured. Vancouver's Urban Design Panel has become so respected it now operates as a peer review system as much as a stepping stone to a development permit.

The issue of design skills is being addressed on a wide variety of fronts. These include the research and lobbying of CABE and the Urban Design Group, and the Royal Town Planning Institute's (RTPI) New Vision for Planning and its education reforms. The dearth of design skills remains a major barrier to a more effective design review processes, though the time to exercise these skills, and political support are equally critical. The best control systems rely upon a high level of design expertise: Vancouver, for example, has six development planners, each an architect trained with five years of private sector experience, available to negotiate on all the major or controversial development applications. Could British development control attract such people?

CONCLUSION

Arguably the most important work that CABE has commissioned has been that focused on the value of urban design to developers, consumers, communities and government. While not always offering convincing evidence, this research argues that good design can create win-win situations for developers/investors, occupiers and communities, adding value to both the development and locality, increasing its longevity and reducing life cycle costs. Until both developers (including householders) and local politicians are convinced of these arguments, there will be limited progress towards a general raising of urban design standards across the country. The job to be done on local politicians is particularly acute, both in the most prosperous areas where good design can help to reduce NIMBYism, and in the less prosperous regions where good design can improve regeneration prospects and performance. It is worth reminding all politicians that recent research argues that for European cities quality urban design has become a prerequisite for, and not a consequence of, economic development. Among many other examples, Sydney's recent conversion to design excellence (forcing all major developers to hold limited design competitions for their developments) is instructive.

Four broad issues have been reviewed in this chapter, and each issue and its constituent principles are central to any programme to make British planning practice more capable of routinely delivering quality urban design. The following seem to be the most pressing issues.

1. How to develop anything approximating to an urban design plan, at regional, district and neighbourhood scale, that has clear community and political support, and is useful to developers and decision-makers? The models here would seem to be American Comprehensive Plans (Seattle) or European City Structure Plans (Berlin's Flächennutzungsplan): at the district neighbourhood level, Birmingham's Quarter Studies are a step in the right direction, with adopted masterplans for major brownfield or greenfield developments (Brindley Place or West Stevenage, respectively).
2. How to create a system of planning obligations, or development levies/impact fees, that embraces the key elements of physical and social infrastructure to create the conditions for the provision of appropriate amenities and mixes of development? Such issues ought to be part of the debate on Council Tax reforms because public funds will either have to come from residents or developers, and must be shared according to ability to pay.
3. How to clearly extend design principles into the arena of sustainable development, and articulate mandatory and desired outcomes in design policy and advice that can impact positively on design quality? Huw Barton's work points the way here but there remains insufficient concern with landscape/ecology in all urban development. The opportunity to link urban design (planning) and sustainable building (building control) in a single evaluative and regulatory process, as they do elsewhere in Europe and North America, must be seized.
4. How to provide high levels of design skill in the control process that embrace facilitation and conflict resolution as well as design sensitivity and creativity? This is both a political and educational task. Local political leaders have to believe in the value of good design, literally and metaphorically, to create the basis for job satisfaction, and a new generation of design-literate planners has to be educated and supported through lifelong learning by the professions working collaboratively.

The good news is that, however haltingly, many of these issues are being addressed in current British reforms and consultation documents, though powerful vested interests continue to resist innovations that would restrict speculative gain and short-term profit-making in development and help pay for better design. International exemplars offer us lessons of principle and practice. Meanwhile, closer to home, the achievements of the Beacon Councils demonstrate how local planning authorities can achieve high standards of design, even if (in the words of the Chair of the RTPI Urban Design Panel), the key task is not to celebrate the achievements of the best, but to raise standards across the board.

The past fifteen years have been a good time to be an urbanist in the UK. Arguments that seemed lost have held the day and urbanism has become established in public policy and largely accepted by the development industry. Now, however, is no time to be complacent. If this were to happen, our generation of urbanists would become the establishment that the next generation kicks against. Urbanism will become little more that a passing fashion like post-modernism or progressive rock – sorry, that was unfair! This is already happening. Architects of the present generation, let alone the next, are already finding urbanism too restrictive, too stylistically prescribed, too boring! If urbanism is to survive – as it must, if the recovery of our cities is to continue – it must be embedded more deeply beneath the vagaries of style. This task is now urgent if urbanists are to secure the territory that has been won in recent years.

Over the past ten years my practice, **URBED**, has been wrestling with these ideas. We have slowly built up an urban design practice from a background in urban regeneration and planning rather than architecture. We therefore know (or believe we know) what it is that makes urban areas work in terms of their social, economic and environmental sustainability. Our masterplanning is grounded in this knowledge but our hope is that it is also interesting and challenging as a piece of creative design. This has made us realise that there are two types of urban design taking place in the UK, and indeed the USA, at present. The first is the work of urban designers that is in danger of becoming boring and historicist. The second is the work of architects that is much more interesting and challenging but often fails to recognise the basic principles on which urban design is based. **URBED** has been trying to chart a middle course between these positions – endeavouring to create challenging work without breaking the 'rules' of urban design. This has prompted the thoughts that I explore in this chapter and led to the design work that I use to illustrate the piece.

CHAPTER 6

THE ART OF CITY BUILDING

DAVID RUDLIN

PUSHING AGAINST AN OPEN DOOR

For someone accustomed to being a voice in the wilderness, the way in which principles of urbanism have been adopted as part of national policy comes as a pleasant surprise. Back in the early 1990s, working on the redevelopment of Hulme in Manchester, those of us arguing for urban design principles which are now enshrined in national policy, were dismissed as hopelessly naïve and irresponsible. An alliance of highways engineers, developers, housing associations, planning officers, police architectural liaison officers and even architects were lining up to scoff at urbanism and the situation seemed hopeless.

Now the principles of urbanism are embedded in all manner of public policy from the Urban White Paper to the Communities Plan through a wide range of planning policy. There are also signs that the development world is changing, albeit slowly. The quality of development in town and city centres is immeasurably better that it was ten years ago and the rapid growth of urban housing is transforming our cities. Even the volume housebuilders are gradually evolving, replacing their low-density detached catalogues with Georgian terraces and flats.

These changes – which in the UK have become known as the Urban Renaissance and in the USA a combination of 'Smart Growth' and 'New Urbanism' – have not happened because we urbanists made a good case (although of course we did!). We were fortunate reformers because we were pushing against an opening door. In the mid-1990s there was a confluence of pressures pointing towards the importance of urban development. From the political right came the Countryside Lobby and the feeling that England's green and pleasant lands were being concreted over. At the same time there was a realisation[1] that twenty years of urban policy and billions of pounds of public spending had only seen conditions in the inner cities worsen. It was finally realised that the flight of investment to the urban edge – that was putting such pressure on the countryside – was also responsible for the decline of inner areas struggling to deal with industrial restructuring, crime, poor housing and poverty. At around the same time there was concern about the decline of retailing in town and city centres[2] in face of competition from out-of-town development and links were also being made to

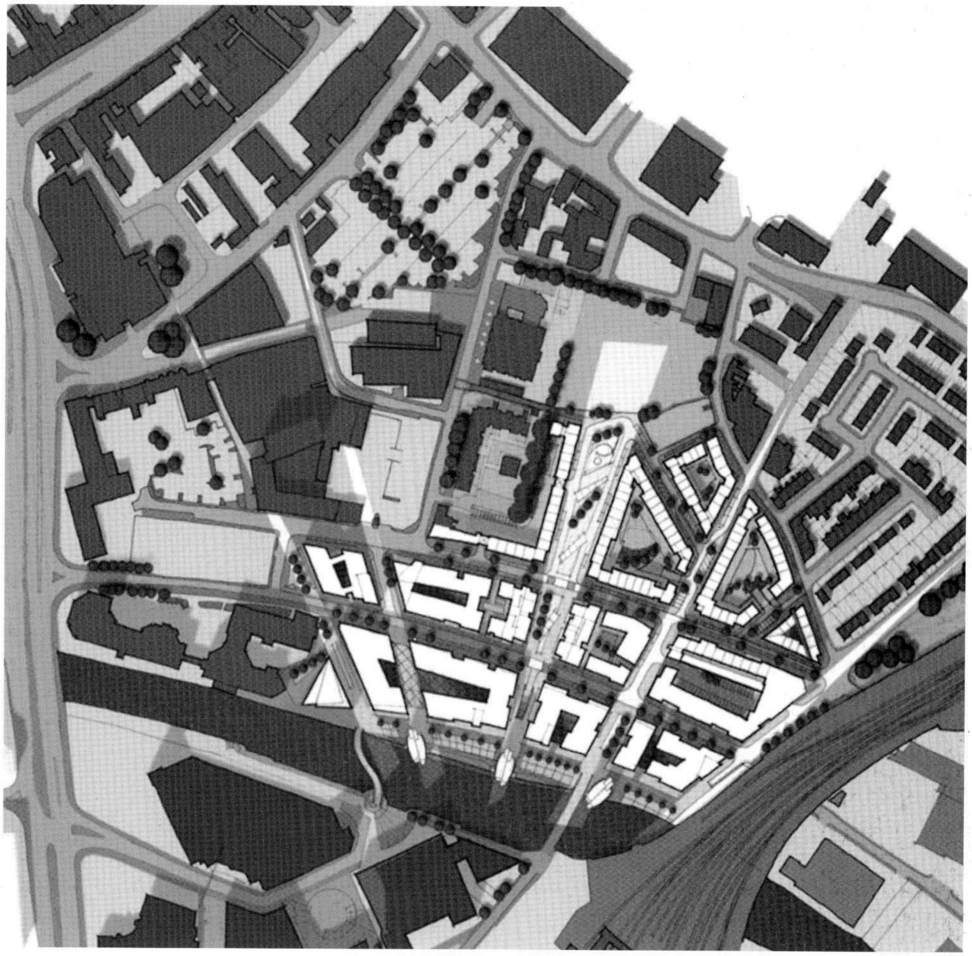

environmental issues and the relationship of development patterns to resource consumption especially with regard to transport. Policy-makers started to link these issues in the early 1990s, first the Conservative Government and then with gusto by John Prescott under the new Labour Government. This was one of those rare political agendas with the potential to please the shire counties, the Labour heartlands and the environmental lobby. It is set out most clearly in the Communities Plan[3] with its mirrored concern to deal with over-demand for housing in the South-East and the collapse of housing markets in parts of the North.

However, even this powerful confluence of political issues might not have succeeded had wider trends in society not been pointing in the same direction. Prime among these was the changing demography of childless households. This fed into the policy agenda through the panic over where to accommodate the projected 4 million or so extra households. However, it has also had a profound effect on the housing market by undermining the hegemony of family-based suburban development. The development industry was slow to catch on and some housebuilders continue to argue that even single people want a three-bedroom semi with front and back garden. No doubt many do; however, as developers like Urban Splash have shown, there is a huge market for something very different and much more urban. This is part of a wider economic change that has seen the replacement of manufacturing industry with knowledge and service industries. This initially contributed to the decline

6.1 **Temple Quay 2, Bristol, historic view of site.**

6.2 **Temple Quay 2, Bristol, aerial view.**

6.3 **Temple Quay 2, Bristol, masterplan.**

6.4 **Bristol context figure-ground plan.**

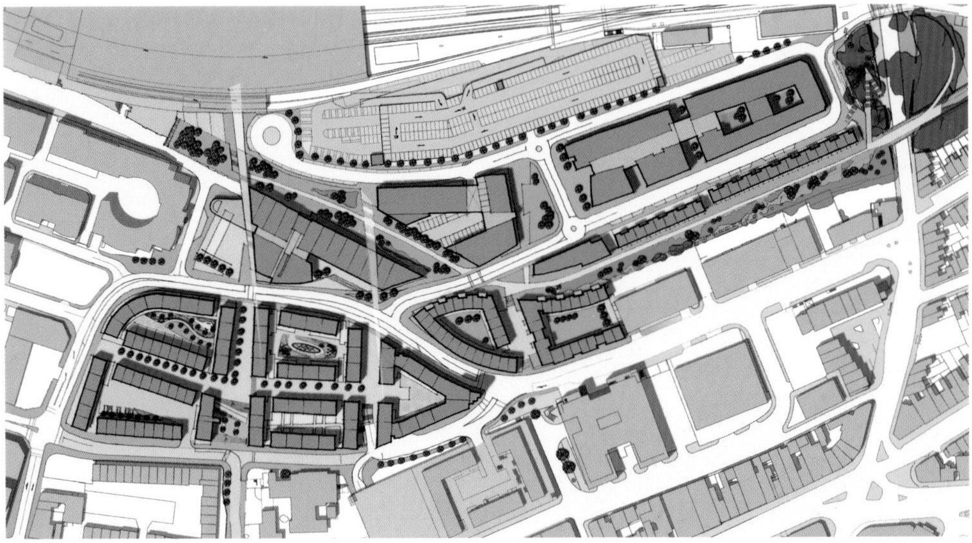

6.5 New England Quarter, Brighton, aerial view.

6.6 New England Quarter, Brighton, housing above Sainsbury's store.

6.7 New England Quarter, Brighton, masterplan.

6.8 Brighton context figure-ground plan.

of traditional urban areas through industrial closures. However, the growth of the knowledge and creative industries swayed the pendulum back in favour of cities. For all the early talk about the suburban dream of California's Silicon Valley, the dot.com revolution has predominantly been an urban phenomenon. This is because it is only in cities that there are sufficient people to create the creative buzz sought by the new knowledge workers, not to mention the broadband infrastructure that they need to thrive.

This confluence of urban trends that in the past decade has overwhelmingly favoured London is growing at a rate not seen since the 1930s. What is more, for the first time in its history, under Mayor Ken Livingstone, this growth is being encouraged. It has also led to a renaissance of the provincial cities, led by Manchester, Leeds and Glasgow, and even to a resurgence in places like Liverpool, Sheffield and Bradford that some people had feared to be in terminal decline. These cities have stopped losing population and have become once more the economic drivers of their regions.

HOW DID URBAN DESIGN BECOME BORING?

These trends should make it a good time to be an urban designer. For the first time in many years a large amount of urban, mixed-use development is taking place and most of this is being masterplanned by architects and urban designers. The ground rules of urban design that caused such battles in Hulme are now an accepted part of public policy and urban designers are in such demand that there is a national skills shortage.

Yet, something is missing. True, we have improved the worst of the development that was taking

place. However, we somehow still have to produce anything that could be described as really good urbanism. National and local policy combined with changing attitudes has put a stop to the worst excesses of modernist and suburban planning that dominated the twentieth century. We have edged away from the mall, the grade-separated highway, the modernist object building and the sprawl of suburban semis on cul-de-sacs. However, the development that has resulted from these new policies and attitudes is yet to produce anything that approaches the sublime beauty and intricacy that can be found in even the most mundane market town.

It is, of course, difficult to create, on a plan, the qualities that have developed over hundreds of years in traditional places. We have not even come close to matching the achievements of urban designers in the past such as Edinburgh New Town, Grainger Town in Newcastle or Bloomsbury and Regent Street in London. The best recent examples that we have of master-planned urban areas include Brindley Place in Birmingham, Silvertown in London, Hulme in Manchester or Crown Street in Glasgow. This is becoming a tired and over-used list. All these places are a huge improvement on what preceded them. But will they be looked back on in fifty years time as classic designs? Of course, it takes a long time to build a neighbourhood and there are, no doubt, many better examples of masterplans that are being realised at the moment. Despite all the progress of the past 15 years, it is still not possible to point to an exceptional contemporary piece of realised urbanism. Prince Charles' question of the early 1990s is still relevant today: 'Why can we not

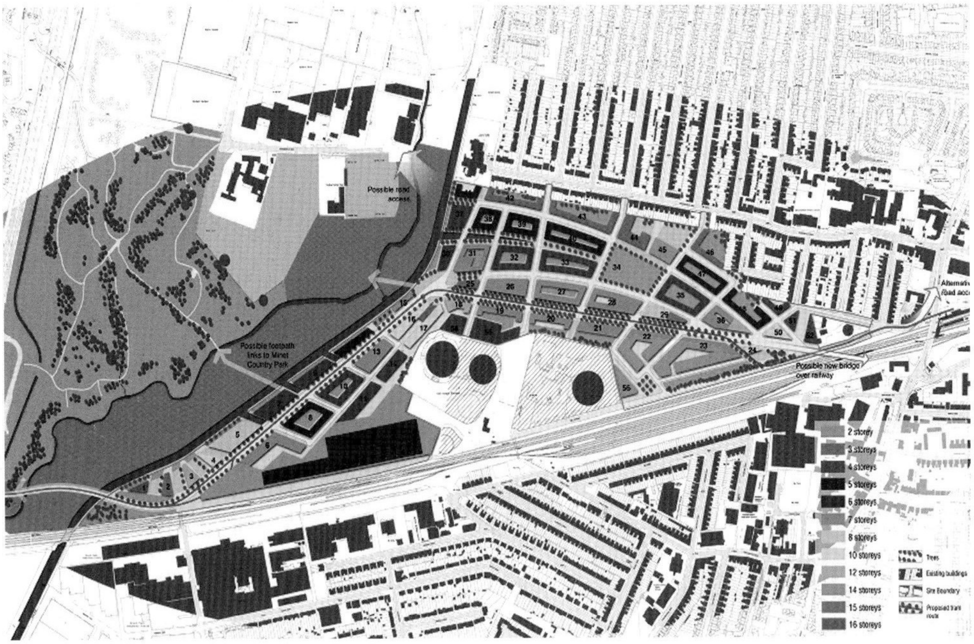

6.9 **Southall Gasworks, Ealing, London, aerial view of proposals**

6.10 **Southall Gasworks, Ealing, London, masterplan**

6.11 **Southall Gasworks, Ealing, London, aerial view**

build in the manner of our favourite places?' Urban designers are creating places that avoid the mistakes of the past, that are correct in terms of urban design, but which are, frankly, a boring a historicist mush of boulevards and crescents.

The masterplanning that is receiving the most attention and generating the most excitement is being developed by architects. These architect-designed masterplans may not be boring but they invariably ignore the hard-won principles of urbanism. This, after all, is how interesting architecture is produced, by testing boundaries and breaking rules. It surely cannot be the case that we must break the rules that urbanists have fought so hard to establish in order to create exciting urbanism. That, after all, is what got us into this mess in the first place.

There must be another path, which is what my practice, URBED, has been trying to find through our masterplanning work. Our aim is to create urbanism that is as bold and exciting as the great masterplanners of the past and yet is contemporary and of its time. This we are trying to do as urban designers, not architects. We therefore do not have recourse to the architectural fireworks that architects have at their disposal. Our inspiration must be realised with a limited set of tools; the massing and siting of buildings and the form of the public realm. Urban designers should be seeking to create magical places with these limited ingredients.

A PASSING FAD?

The danger is that urban design comes to be seen not as a fundamental change in the way that we develop, but rather as a passing style or fad. This danger is greatest in the USA where 'New Urbanism' has become synonymous with a particular style of architecture, the small-town America of Seaside, Celebration and Laguna West. This clapper-board vernacular with its front porches and Norman Rockwell styling has a huge nostalgic appeal to many Americans. It has become the house-style of US urbanists such as Duaney, Plater-Zyberk, Peter Calthorpe and Urban Design Associates.

In the UK we also have our backward-looking urban styles, be it the village vernacular of Poundbury or the neo-Georgian pastiche of places like Great Notley or Cambourne. People, it seems, will accept urban development, higher densities, streets (rather than cul-de-sacs) and even

back-of-pavement housing provided it is in historical fancy dress. All the character of a traditional English village but with double-glazing, a double garage and new white goods! It has been argued that this is a necessary first step and that the resulting housing areas are a huge improvement on the formless suburbia that was the norm only a few years ago. This is undoubtedly true. This, however, cannot be the end result of the Urban Renaissance. Surely there must be something more?

The danger of course is that what comes next is not a step forward but a backlash. This is what happens when a movement becomes too associated with a particular style – the way that modernism was supplanted by post-modernism. This too was seen as a fundamental change after a century of architectural theory. Yet post-modernism was to soon to be dismissed as lightweight and jokey and little more than a passing architectural fad. How do we ensure that New Urbanism does not suffer the same fate? An article in the Dutch magazine *Archis* in 2003[4] was already predicting that the post-September 11th America would turn away from urbanism to more defensible and dispersed forms of gated-development. At the same time Bruce Katz, one of the founders of New Urbanism was railing, in a lecture in London, against the 'virus of ideas'. His concern was that one generation inevitably reacts against the ideas of their predecessors and that the quest for the new crowds out last year's ideas before they have been properly tested. He saw a generation of architects and planners growing up in America that no longer saw New Urbanism as a fresh alternative to conventional thinking but rather as the new establishment that needed to be challenged. He feared that New Urbanism would be jettisoned before it had the opportunity to put down roots and prove its worth.

The answer to this is not to try to halt the march of ideas – that would guarantee us being written off as reactionaries. The only response is to embed the core principles of urbanism at a deeper level of the urban debate. Urbanism must be a sufficiently broad church to accommodate and evolve with changing architectural ideologies. The imagination of architects and designers – including the young turks of the next generation – should be realisable within an urban framework. This is not a huge thing to ask because it has been happening for years in existing cities. No architect feels hidebound by the constraints (for which read urban structure) of an infill site in downtown New York, Tokyo or London. Yet somehow, when faced with a large empty site, these same urban principles are regarded as an onerous stylistic fad.

Urbanism must be more than a vessel that can accommodate changing architectural movements. It needs to diversify and evolve and develop its own critical debate. It should be possible to have traditional urbanism, organic urbanism, modernist urbanism, fractured urbanism, etc. . . . In this way the inspiration of the masterplan and excitement of the architecture can reinforce and play off each other to create truly exceptional places.

URBAN/QUALITY

One of the problems with the urban renaissance debate in the UK is that the words 'urban' and 'quality' have become interchangeable. This was a useful rhetorical device when the argument for urbanism was not yet won. It is difficult to argue against the idea of 'quality' development whereas there were many prepared to argue against the idea of 'urban' development. Yet these words are not at all the same. It is possible to have quality suburban or even out-of-town

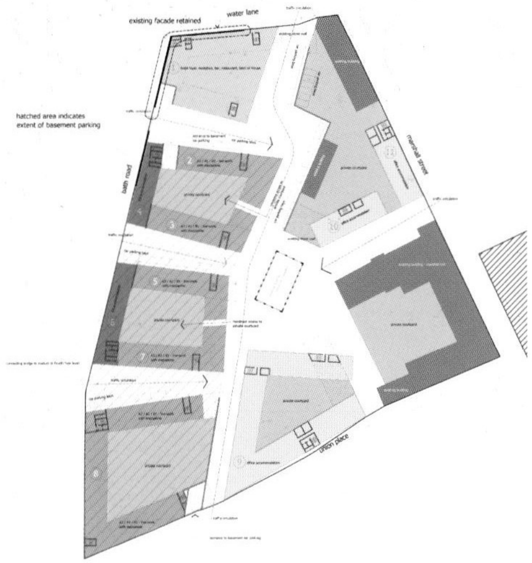

6.12 **Marshall Mills, Leeds, new square.**

6.13 **Marshall Mills, Leeds, masterplan.**

6.14 **Marshall Mills, Leeds, aerial view.**

development just as there is a great deal of poor-quality urban development. The Stockley Park business park in West London is a good example of the difference between these words – a development of exceptional quality but profoundly anti-urban in its form, layout and density.

This confusion lies behind Richard Rogers' view that the first and perhaps the only step needed to produce good urbanism is to appoint a good architect. That way you get design quality – ergo you have a scheme that contributes to the urban renaissance – masterplanning is something that only really architects can do. However, truth be told, many very good architects are terrible masterplanners. They see masterplanning as little more than large-scale architecture and approach the task with the same outlook that they use to create challenging buildings. This can produce extraordinary plans such as the masterplans of Michael Sorkin, Daniel Libeskind, Will Alsop and Zaha Hadid. We urbanists should not dismiss these plans, they are important because they expand the language of urban design and are undoubtedly plans of tremendous quality. However, quality design and urban design are not

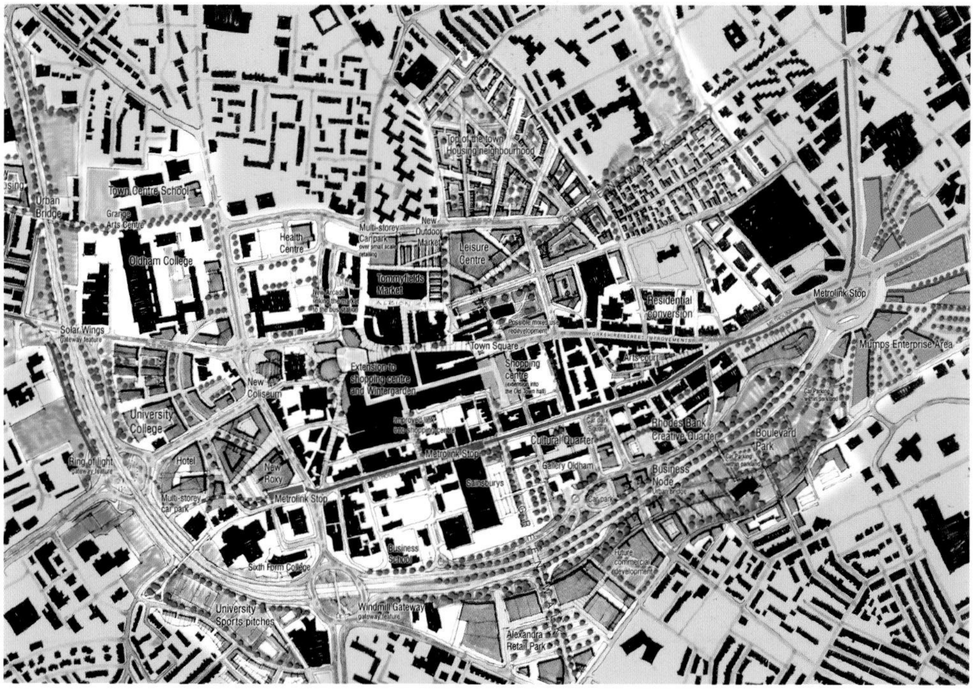

6.15 **Oldham Beyond, Oldham, UK, masterplan.**

6.16 **Proposed Oldham theatre.**
Source: S333 Architects

6.17 **Proposed new business quarter.**
Source: S333 Architects

the same thing. Many of these wonderful plans are profoundly flawed when it comes not just to the rules of urban design but also to the realities of living in a city. When designing an individual building within an existing urban context rules are there to be challenged. However, when this approach is applied to the masterplanning of a large section of a city, it can lead to ridiculous ideas – such as a masterplan for a difficult council estate with no ground-floor accommodation. It is only the idea of architectural 'quality' that somehow has a magic wand to solve urban problems that allows such ideas to go unchallenged.

A LIMITED PALETTE

One of the reasons for this is that the distinction between architecture and masterplanning has become blurred and confused. This is understandable because there is inevitably an overlap between the two activities and masterplanning is a process that has yet to be properly defined. A definition would include the fact that masterplanning covers a number of urban blocks and that it is concerned with the use, form, siting, orientation and massing of buildings and their effect on the scale, proportion and character of space. This is a relatively limited palette of elements. It does not include the architecture of the buildings, the design of the public realm or the quality of materials. Many of the worst masterplans hide their failings behind beautifully drawn trees and public realm or eye-catching architecture. These masterplans can be unmasked by removing the architecture and the public realm from the plan – rendering it as a figure-ground plan (a plan that shows just the buildings in black and no other detail) or a massing model and asking whether it still retains its strength. Then ask whether the masterplanner has control over the design of the public realm and the buildings. If they do not, it is legitimate to ask whether the plan can ever be realised as envisioned in the masterplan.

Instead of this, masterplanning should make the most of its limited palette of materials by using them and them alone to create exceptional plans. These plans should create the context for the inspiration of architects and public realm designers in the future. A really good masterplan should be strong enough to embrace a wide range of architectural styles. Indeed, the best plans retain their strength even when many of the buildings are mediocre. Berlin is a good example of this, a city where many of the buildings are of very little distinction but, because they follow the parameters set by the masterplan for the city, they do not undermine its quality. The ideal, the magic that created the best masterplans of the past, happens when the inspiration of the masterplan and the inspiration of the architecture combine and complement each other to create exceptional places. One of the best examples of this is the junction of Langham Place and Portland Place – part of Nash's Regents Park masterplan of 1811. This particular part of the plan terminates the grand vista of Portland Place and pivots around All Saints Church (that pre-dates the plan). The building that really makes the area memorable is, however, BBC's Broadcasting House, designed a century after Nash's death by George Val Myer.

THE LOST ART OF CITY BUILDING

There is a further problem with designing a masterplan as if it were a building. A building is designed, tendered and constructed by a contractor under the supervision of the architect (design-and-build aside). Most masterplans are very different in that they are realised over a number of years, often by different developers employing their own architects. Architect-designed masterplans rarely recognise this. Many are based on the assumption that the plans will be realised with the same level of control that the architect would have over a building. On occasion, this can happen such as the More London Bridge Masterplan by Norman Foster that includes the Mayor's building. However, this is rare, and it is common for masterplans to be undermined because the level of control assumed in the plan cannot be maintained for the years required to realise the vision. Inspiring as many of these plans are, without a mechanism for implementing them over the many years that are needed to realise the plan they are doomed to failure. This is one reason for the difficulty that we had earlier in naming successful recent masterplanned neighbourhoods. Many of the best plans are never realised or are corrupted in the building. The solution to this may be to increase the level of control over the way that plans are built. This lies behind attempts to prevent developers using trophy architects to win permission for a scheme and passing it on to lesser practices. A better approach might to be take account of the process of urban growth in the way that we masterplan. This is what the great masterplanners of the past did and what we are so poor at doing today.

Masterplanning today has become an attempt to create pieces of towns and cities on a drawing board (sorry, computer screen). The very work 'masterplanning' is perhaps unhelpful in this respect because it implies an immutable blueprint without flexibility or the capacity to evolve. This was not the way that Edinburgh New Town, Grainger Town, Regent Street or Bloomsbury were created. True, they were masterplanned, but the output of the plan was an infrastructure network including the streets that gave form to the area. The promoters of the plan often developed only a few key buildings themselves such as the church and civic buildings. While these were the buildings that created a sense of place, most of the buildings were erected by others. Just as important as the plan was therefore a set of rules for development that were enshrined in the deeds of development plots as they were sold. Some plots were sold to individuals to build their own home or business premises. Others were sold to small developers and artisans who would build four or five properties a year to standard designs that they bought in pattern books. This system was not infallible and some areas, such as the estates north of Euston Road, degenerated into a slum before they were complete. This is, however, the process that lies behind most successfully realised masterplans, be it Pope Sixtus's Rome, Haussmann's Paris or Cerdà Barcelona.

In a piece entitled 'The Art of Urban Generation and Regeneration'[5] we suggested that this way of implementing masterplans worked because it tapped into the natural process of urban growth. This we likened to the way that a vine grows on a trellis. If the city is a vine, the masterplanner is the person who designs the trellis upon which the vine grows. The urban designer is thus able to shape the structure and form of the city but not in a direct way and not always with predictable consequences. This is something that Christopher Alexander understood and described wonderfully in the series of books from the *Oregon Experiment* through *Pattern Language* and finally *A New Theory of Urban Design*.[6] Through this process, masterplanned urban areas grow and develop in much the same way as do unplanned urban areas. The masterplanner creates the initial form but the beauty that we find it so difficult to recreate is the result of decisions made by hundreds, even thousands, of people over decades and sometimes centuries. In this way the Tuscan towns of Italy, that have provided such inspiration to urban designers, were created by the people who lived there without the benefit of planning control or urban design qualifications. This collective process of design has somehow conspired to create places that are as complete and beautiful as any Renaissance painting.

A NEW PROCESS OF URBAN DESIGN

The way that a lot of masterplanning is done today is completely alien to this natural process of urban growth. We have lost our nerve when it comes to allowing urban areas to grow and evolve in a self-regulating way. There are many reasons for this, not least the dead hand of the planning system. It is also partly due to the nature of today's development industry that is larger and more corporate than it was in the past. Today the majority of housing is built, not by small artisans producing four or five units a year, but by volume housebuilders that produce thousands. Likewise commercial buildings are built, not by merchants for their own use (and self-aggrandisement) but by corporate developers. Even public buildings are procured through PFI rather than by aldermen and councillors with an eye to their place in posterity.

Masterplans must therefore be designed and coded to allow them to be implemented over a long period by unsympathetic developers. Many an excellent plan has been fatally compromised in the building through the ignorance, expediency or just pig-headedness of architects and developers who have seen no reason not to build over that central axis, to increase yields by removing that central square or by adding five storeys to that commercial block. Each of these decisions may seem sensible but they can easily undermine the masterplan.

URBED has therefore developed a process of masterplanning based on the techniques used in the past. The masterplans that URBED creates for developers and landowners are normally used as the basis for an outline planning application. This includes siting, massing, land use and means of access and so is ideally suited to the limited pallette of materials available to the masterplanner. While the masterplan normally includes illustrative material to sell the concept, the core of the application is a regulatory plan that sets out key parameters of siting and massing. This is enshrined in the planning consent and creates a three-dimensional envelope for the buildings of the masterplan. This allows individual buildings to be brought forward over time by a variety of developers and architects as reserved matters planning applications. This is not foolproof but does use the planning system to recreate the conditions that led to the best masterplans of the past and sets out a clear division between masterplanning and architecture.

A DISTINCTIVE LANGUAGE

URBED's masterplans as illustrated by the plans throughout this chapter are predicated on this natural process of growth both in the way that they are created and the way that they will be implemented. Our concern is to develop our own design language that makes our work recognisable, charting a middle course between the boring and the inspirationally flawed. Our design style stems in part from an approach to masterplanning based on, what we call, the 'Three Rs':

1 **RE-DISCOVERY** – the discovery of what was therefore before through use of historic maps.

2 **REPAIR** – fixing the damage done by recent planning and highways decisions.

3 **RENEWAL** – adding our own distinctive contribution to the area.

Our hope is that in 100 years time people will be able to uncover the layered history of the area, including the layers that have preceded us and those that followed our work. Our aim is to ensure that our layer will be seen as a positive contribution, sympathetic but of its time and something that was able to give coherence to the layers that followed.

This approach to masterplanning does not imply a historicist approach to design. On the contrary, rooting it in an understanding of an area's history frees us to add our own contemporary contribution. As urban designers we are not very good at describing our aesthetic, something that we should no doubt work harder on. However, I hope that URBED's aesthetic comes through in the schemes that illustrate this chapter. This is work that owes much to my friend and collaborator Charlie Baker and draws on influences as varied as Mirralles, Nash, Libeskind, Haussmann, Hadid, and Lenné. We draw on the forms that Charles Jenks described in his book *The Architecture of the Jumping Universe*,[7] 'a language of buildings and forms close to nature, of twists and folds and undulations, of crystalline forms and fracture planes'. These seem to sit easily with the forms of Lenné's Tiergarten or Haussmann's Paris. Our plans use acute angles, shallow curves and tapering vistas combined with the squares, rond points and boulevards of eighteenth- and nineteenth-century planning. Our hope is that our work is recognisably that of URBED and that we have started to develop a distinctive language and style. This language is our own and is not something that we would want to impose on anyone else. We would, however, hope that urban designers think more about the 'design' in urban design and that they too work on developing a distinctive aesthetic. Only in this way will urban design reinvigorate itself and avoid being written off as a fad while the task of designing our towns and cities is given exclusively to architects.

CONCLUSION

In this chapter I have argued that urban design is not big architecture in three important respects, The first is that urban design is underwritten by a set of rules that are fundamental to its success. These rules should be broad enough to encompass pretty much any architectural style. They can be broken occasionally and with care, but only by people who understand them implicitly. The second is the fact that urban design must work with a limited palette of materials – essentially the form, massing and siting of buildings and the space between them without reliance on architecture and detailed public realm design to disguise design failings. The third respect in which urban design is different from architecture is the fact that it is a slow art. Urban designers cannot directly impose their vision because the urban areas that they are creating are built over many years, decades or even centuries. Urban designers must therefore work one step removed to ensure that the work of architects and developers, some operating many years into future, will contribute to the plan.

These three aspects are part of the lost art of city-making, a subtle mix of craft, intuition and politics that created the great cities of the past. My colleague Nicholas Falk has suggested that this is more like gardening than architecture. The CABE commissioner Les Sparks suggested something similar; that architecture may be three-dimensional but that masterplanning had a fourth dimension, namely, time. This is a difficult and demanding challenge – one for which architects are ill suited to but to which urban designers are yet to rise. The past decade has been a good one for urban designers, but unless we rise to this challenge we risk losing the gains we have made.

Notes

1 *B Robson, The State of English Cities , DETR 2000*

2 *URBED, Vital and Viable Town Centres, HMSO 1995*

3 'Sustainable Communities', *Building for the Future*, ODPM, HMSO 2003

4 J. Inaba, *Urbanism without Urbanists*, Archis 2003

5 D. Rudlin, N. Falk, *Sustainable Urban Neighbourhood: Building the 21st Century Home*, The Architectural Press: Oxford, 1999

6 C. Alexander, *A New Theory of Urban Design*, New York: Oxford University Press, 1987

7 C Jenks, *The Architecture of the Jumping Universe*, Academy Editions: London, 1995

2

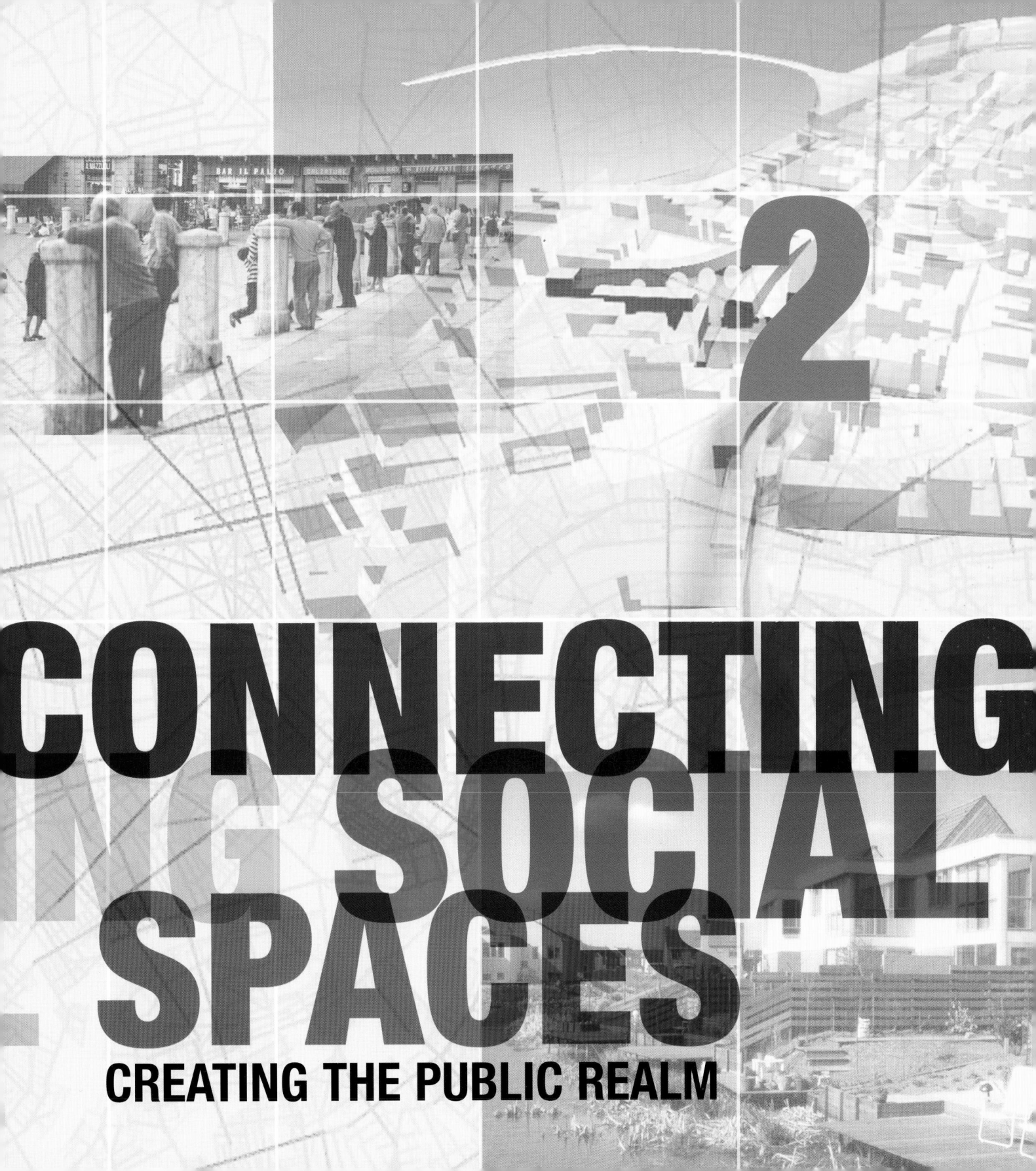

CONNECTING SOCIAL SPACES

CREATING THE PUBLIC REALM

The major attraction of any city is its people, its life and vitality. This is clear, as the benches with the best view of public life are always the first ones to be occupied; we can see this in the fact that the café chairs all over the world are oriented towards the pavement, towards the passers-by. The most essential quality of the street café is simply the opportunity to people-watch.

Cappuccino, fresh air and contact with others represent a combination that is hard to beat. The best of both worlds. And when choosing between walking in an empty, deserted street or in a busy street, most people by far choose to walk through the busy street, where there is a greater variation of experiences along the way and a greater sense of security.

CHAPTER 7

LIFE, SPACES, BUILDINGS

AND IN SAID ORDER, PLEASE

JAN GEHL

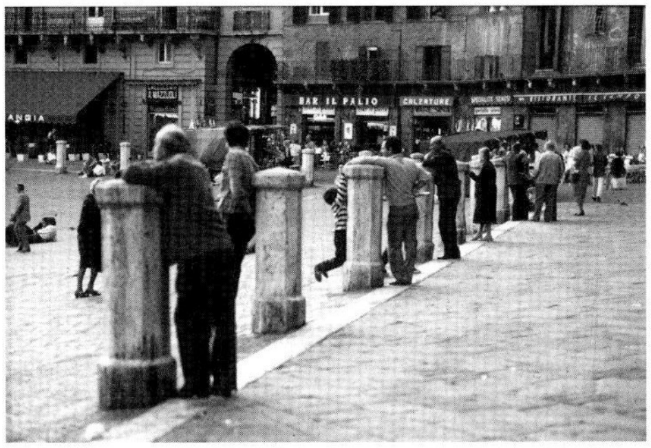

Street life is a much sought-after and essential quality in a city, even on a larger scale, where one is not concerned with just a single street but rather whole cities, towns and neighbourhoods. In this context, the discussions regarding the atmosphere and qualities of the built environment should to a much higher degree cater for the life and vitality of the 'spaces between'.

In city politics, planning guidelines and building programmes, the desire is for cities and neighbourhoods – new as well as existing – to be lively, attractive and safe. However, most of the recently developed neighbourhoods, with apartment blocks spaced far apart, are inherently boring and deserted, and have unfortunately become examples of what not to do. Equally so are the typical new office parks, where shiny, new business headquarters frame non descript parking lots, and where the few people who, despite the unwelcoming environment, travel through the spaces, experience first hand, that very little thought – if any – has gone into life, people and safety. Life between the buildings is – at best – a fleeting afterthought . . .

Thought-provoking scenarios are found in the completely deserted cities that have gradually evolved in the United States. In these cities, the automobile has completely taken over the city. Pedestrian traffic and all city life have vanished, transportation is undertaken solely by car. The city centre has become a large parking area; the buildings resemble unwelcoming fortresses made of steel and glass in a sea of asphalt. There are no pedestrians, no pavements and of course no bicycles. Fitness centres and home exercise equipment are the only way to get fit, unless you accept the invitation posted at many of the shopping centres, located at the periphery of the deserted cities: 'Walkers/joggers welcome between 8 and 10a.m'.

Many features of Western society today make our dreams of lively cities hard to accomplish or even imagine. Households are reducing in size, the density of the population is far less in modern city areas, and people are busy with an array of tasks demanding increasingly more of their time and attention. Through electronic media, people have the opportunity to contact each other – if not directly, then at least indirectly. The circumstances and possibilities for creating life in the city have changed dramatically. Changes in traffic patterns, principles of town planning, methods of construction and the scale of the building complexes themselves have furthermore changed the circumstances for life in the public spaces.

When these new circumstances combine, the lifeless neighbourhoods are created almost automatically every time new areas are developed, and in existing neighbourhoods we can observe how increased traffic congestion, together with changed shopping habits, arrogant, blank supermarket façades and dull, new buildings little by

7.1 **Public bench, Copenhagen. The bench is turned away from the public life but people find ways to make the location work.**

7.2 **Private moments, Copenhagen. Another bench is turned the wrong way but these ladies are determined to face the sun and the view.**

7.3 **Outdoor café in Strøget, Copenhagen. People-watching is an essential quality of the street café.**

7.4 **Bollards in Piazza del Campo, Sienna, Italy. The bollards create an edge for standing and watching life on the square.**

7.5 **Kalvebod Brygge waterfront, Copenhagen. New waterfront development which does not support any public life whatsoever.**

7.6 **Kalvebod Brygge, Copenhagen. Left-over green space between apartment blocks becomes a barrier rather than a place for gathering.**

7.7 The deserted street. The street has been created with no consideration for life between buildings.
7.8 Spokane, WA, USA. The city centre has become a parking lot with no place for people.
7.9 Clarksdale, MS, USA. Empty street scene, a waste of space and rather depressing.

7.10 A Sunlit Street, Copenhagen. Using the façade as a place to linger.
7.11 Karl Johann Gaten, Stockholm. The sunny side of the street is an inviting place for people-watching.
7.12 Aerial view of Aker Brygge, Oslo. This new waterfront district has been carefully planned around the concept of 'public life'.

little make it increasingly unattractive to use the public spaces. The life of the city is gradually disappearing. When it gets to a certain point, one will merely walk through the area as fast as possible – until the desire to walk through completely vanishes.

THE CITY AS
A MODERN MEETING PLACE

One reply to these features, that automatically reduce the life in the public spaces of the city, has gradually been to assemble experience and knowledge of how to support and encourage public life through planning measures. It has thus been shown that in places where careful attention has been given to invite people to use the public spaces, the city life will indeed increase, which emphasizes the fact that city dwellers – even in modern society – are very interested in actually walking in the city and seeking out the attractions of the lively, public spaces. The city as a place for meeting others even seems to have an increasingly important role in a society where people live at low densities and where a great deal of personal contact is indirect. The city provides the scene for random or chance meetings, informal gatherings, and thus has a new and important function. It is no coincidence that there can presently be found steadily increasing interest and demand for the life and vitality public spaces have to offer. These are qualities that everyone has experienced as meaningful and joyful – and that we, as social human beings, continue to need and seek out.

A HEARTFELT INVITATION, PLEASE

It is certainly difficult to create a context in which public life is encouraged in today's society, but it is indeed possible to a much larger extent than is happening. First and foremost, we need to use the basic knowledge we have regarding factors that make places comfortable to be in or move through. We all use this knowledge every time we furnish our own spaces, or organize spaces for personal events and gatherings.

The basic requirements of human comfort are also used in the planning of commercial spaces that depend on their ability to attract people – such as shopping centres and amusement parks. It is simply the art of inviting people to come, to linger in and use the spaces, rather than more or less unintentionally ending up with public spaces that are uninviting. It is all about extending a heartfelt invitation.

EXTENDING AN INVITATION TO COME TO PUBLIC SPACES
– AND STAY FOR A WHILE . . .

Invitations are neither new nor unknown within the area of city planning. It has for years been a well-known fact that inviting cars by providing more roads and more parking places results in increased traffic. Henry Ford suggested to his employees at the Ford Motor Company, that they each in their local communities demanded more roads, in order to increase the sales of motorcars.

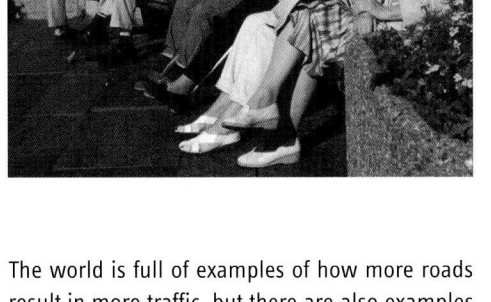

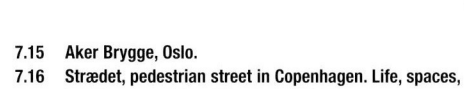

7.13 Aker Brygge, Oslo. The recipe for success is simple: high density, a great diversity of functions, well-proportioned outdoor spaces provide plenty of possibilities for sitting and watching the crowds passing by.
7.14 Aker Brygge, Oslo.

7.15 Aker Brygge, Oslo.
7.16 Strædet, pedestrian street in Copenhagen. Life, spaces, buildings – and in said order PLEASE!

The world is full of examples of how more roads result in more traffic, but there are also examples of how less roads can lead to less traffic and changes in traffic patterns.

The Embarcadero Freeway in San Francisco was one of the most important links to the city. Unfortunately it was an elevated freeway located between the city and the bay, cutting off the direct connection from the city to the water – but it was deemed indispensable for the functioning and vitality of the city. Then the earthquake happened in 1989. The Embarcadero Freeway cracked and had to be demolished. A committee was quickly put together to establish alternative options for replacing the freeway. Even before the committee had finished its work, it was found, that traffic in San Francisco was flowing fine without this once-crucial freeway. Some of the traffic had simply disappeared, other segments utilized alternative routes, or had shifted to public transportation. Today the Embarcadero is no longer an elevated freeway, but instead a tree-lined boulevard with an integrated light rail line running along the San Francisco Bay.

Other successful examples of invitations to new activities are the improved conditions for cyclists that have been implemented in many Danish cities and towns. Everywhere it has been a contributory factor in increased use of the bicycle for transportation. In Copenhagen bicycle traffic has increased by 65 per cent during the past twenty-five years. The latest subject for debate in local papers has been the overcrowding of the bicycle lanes! Just as more roads results in increased traffic and improved conditions for cyclists results in more cyclists, it has in recent years been established that improved conditions for pedestrians and public life invite more people to walk through and spend time in public spaces.

A classic example is the widening of the pavement areas of the Champs-Elysées in Paris. The 12-metre wide pavements were a few years ago widened to a total of 24 metres on either side of the avenue. Both new pavements are now well used. Better conditions for pedestrians have directly resulted in more city life.

Also the remarkable and well-documented development of life in the public spaces in the inner city of Copenhagen shows that better quality public spaces invites more life in the city. When 'Strøget' street was made into a pedestrian street in 1962, a total of 15,000 m^2 was reserved for pedestrians and city life. At present – forty years later – the city of Copenhagen has reserved 100,000 m^2 for city life, which in the meantime has become much more dense and diverse. Strolling through Copenhagen on a summer day you will meet five times as many people as you would have met twenty-five years ago.

When single public spaces are upgraded and care is taken to address basic measures of human comfort, surprising new patterns of public life arise. From cities all over the world we can find examples of the fact that whole-hearted invitations to utilize the public spaces within the city, result in a much richer and varied city life.

ATTENDING TO LIFE IN EXISTING CITY AREAS

Because of the difficult conditions for generating city life in most modern, sprawling cities, the aim of creating entire cities bursting with street life is an unreasonable – and certainly impossible – task. But in all cities, new or old, small or large, dense or sprawling, there is ample opportunity to create pleasant areas for walking, and wonderful squares and plazas that are inviting spaces in which to meet, linger and stay.

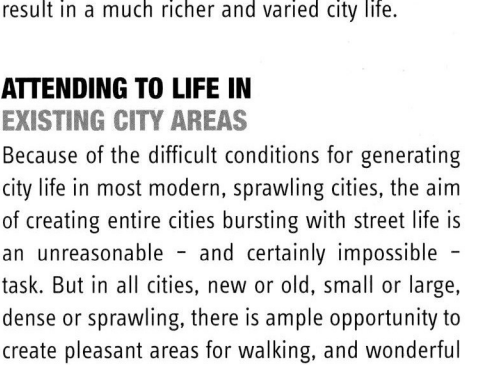

It is certainly a realistic proposition and should be included in any city's planning guidelines. It is difficult to argue against the desire for cities to become inviting places – places that encourage foot and bicycle traffic and invite people to use pedestrian-friendly paths and plazas in pivotal areas of the city.

The question is how to ensure that the life in the city is given the required attention and care in city planning. For inspiration we can turn to the well-established and well-functioning departments of traffic and transportation which exist in almost every city. These departments typically have thoughtful strategies and lofty visions for the future of traffic planning, based on diligent and continuous traffic analysis. Traffic and transportation are important issues, which are automatically considered in all future planning for the city. In short, traffic is an ever-present and very visible, integral part of city planning.

As for the life in the city, the situation is entirely different. Almost no city has staff or departments systematically looking after the interests of pedestrians and city life. Knowledge and data on the life that goes on within the public spaces – on how the public spaces and paths are utilized by locals, is most often missing. The people who actually use the city and the public spaces are thus an almost invisible factor, when it comes to city planning and city politics.

A logical step seems to be to utilize the same methods and policies already in place within other areas of planning. When a house is in need of repair, the state of the house is analysed and a plan for the upgrade put in place. In the traffic planning process, traffic patterns are analysed, and, based upon the analysis, new strategies are formed. In exactly the same way, life within the city should be studied and recorded as a basis for debate and decision-making, and as an important baseline for creating strategies regarding a given city's public space policy. It is encouraging to see that a number of cities in various areas of the world already have initiated comprehensive goals and strategies for developing public spaces and public life within the city, based on concrete analysis and knowledge of the use of existing public spaces. Life in these cities is thus, slowly but surely, becoming more and more visible, and the extent of this life within the public spaces of a city is, to a much higher degree, regarded as an important measure of quality for that city.

ATTENDING TO LIFE IN THE INDIVIDUAL PUBLIC SPACES

When a single public space is being created, the focus must be on careful attention to detail and to the people, who will be using this space in particular. In his book *Social Life in Small Urban Spaces* William H. Whyte introduces the concept of '100% places', i.e. places where most of the essential requirements for a comfortable, public space have been included.[1] The place must be protected from risk and uncomfortable situations, it should provide possibilities for most of the basic human needs such as strolling, standing, sitting, observing, listening, talking. And the places should carefully offer challenges and architectural and visual qualities, a sense of human scale and good climatic conditions. In connection with every upgrade of an existing public space, or the creation of new one, several questions must be answered in order to take full advantage of the space: What are the potential qualities of the space? What are the problems with the space? Who will be the users of the space? Which activities are likely to take place? Which qualities must be present in order for the users to get the most out of this space in particular?

CARING FOR THE LIFE IN NEW CITY DISTRICTS

Another area of concern are the public spaces and public life within entirely new neighbourhoods. 'Pedestrian traffic, bicycle traffic and public street life will be prioritised', are the often-stated goals in the visions and guidelines for the new areas. Despite good intentions, the vision falls apart in one project after another. One of the problems is the way in which the new neighbourhoods are developed, the size of the buildings themselves, the extremely large spaces that are often 'left over' between the buildings and the popular architectural styles with glassy, shining façades, that do not invite people to linger along them, and in general do not address the adjacent open spaces. Every building is built with great thought as to what goes on within the building itself, but apart from that, the buildings as such do not address their surroundings or the activities that take place around them – or could potentially take place – even though the overall visions for the areas typically include the desire for a wonderful atmosphere and lively public activities in adjoining public spaces.

AKER BRYGGE: A SUCCESSFUL NEW WATERFRONT DEVELOPMENT IN OSLO

That it is indeed possible to create modern, lively areas in newly created neighbourhoods can be seen in the example of Aker Brygge in Oslo, Norway. This new waterfront district has from day one been planned with careful thought and attention being given to issues of public life – not just within the buildings themselves, but even more so between the buildings – in the public spaces. The recipe for success as seen in Aker Brygge is simple: high density, a great diversity of functions, well-proportioned, good outdoor spaces, a good use of the inherent qualities that the site has to offer, in this case especially the view of the fjord, taking into consideration the orientation for optimal use of sun and wind, and, last but not least, active ground-floor façades along the main walkways and public plazas. Life within as well as outside of the building is thought of as one single entity. On a pleasant summer day, as many as 35,000 people from other areas of Oslo visit Aker Brygge – not because they necessarily have an errand there, but because it is a pleasant place to visit, to stroll. The invitation to come and spend some time here is whole-heartedly accepted.

Active ground-floor façades and a good connection between indoor and outdoor activities are crucial factors in the creation of attractive neighbourhoods, and thus also in the neighbourhood of Aker Brygge. This knowledge of the importance of the function and design of the ground floor has led to new strategies for future developments along other parts of the waterfront in Oslo, where investors are reducing the rent for commercial space on the ground-floor level, in order to attract desirable tenants. It will not be Mercedes Benz showrooms or McDonald's fast food restaurants occupying the spaces, but rather smaller entities, that will add to the public street life, such as cafés, boutique shops, galleries, convenience stores, etc. The investors are convinced that lower rents along the main paths of travel and along the edges of public plazas will attract people to the area, who in turn will ensure a lively, attractive neighbourhood, which is deemed to be a solid, long-term investment.

LIFE, SPACES, BUILDINGS – AND IN SAID ORDER, PLEASE

For a long time it has been common practice in the development of new neighbourhoods to prioritise the buildings themselves, then, if possible, the public life. The buildings themselves were the focus, the public spaces whatever happened to be left over in between, and the life at best a half-hearted afterthought. The results everywhere are dreadful, deserted neighbourhoods.

A much better strategy would be to consider initially the 'Life', then the 'Spaces', then the 'Buildings'. This planning method has been used in the new areas of Oslo harbour. First to be discussed is what kind of life is desirable along the waterfront, then which types of public spaces would support the desired activities and life in the area, and, finally, guidelines are created that the new buildings in the neighbourhood must adhere to, in order to create the desired public spaces and thus the life within the area as a whole.

The 'said order' is logical when considering the sensitivity of the life within the city. But the best strategy, however, would of course be to consider life, spaces and buildings in a holistic manner.

Better public spaces are not created solely by virtue of form, design and choice of materials. All aspects must be considered in order to ensure the creation of beautiful and useful public spaces.

This would be a worthwhile innovation.

NOTE

1 W.H. Whyte, *Social Life in Small Urban Spaces*, New York, Project for Public Spaces, 1980

Urbanity, the product of urbanism, derives from the synthesis of social, economic and environmental factors. The practice of urban design must engage fully with each of these if it is to be effective. A key challenge of urban design is that its practitioners successfully orchestrate diverse professional inputs. These inputs include (1) space/form issues such as layout and building orientation, typically the preserve of urban designers; (2) transportation issues, normally undertaken by transport planners; and (3) land use issues, generally the domain of property consultants. Urban design methodologies must be robust if they are to achieve intended outcomes.

Our contention, which we will set out in this chapter, is that urban design methods are currently less secure than they should be for two important reasons. First, the necessary synthesis between space/form, transport and land use is often hindered by ineffective communication between professionals in different disciplines. Second, design decisions are not subject to the same level of objective analysis enjoyed by transportation and land use decisions because the fundamental effects of space/form on urban outcomes are not well understood.

CHAPTER 8

THE INSECURITY OF URBANISM

TIM STONOR

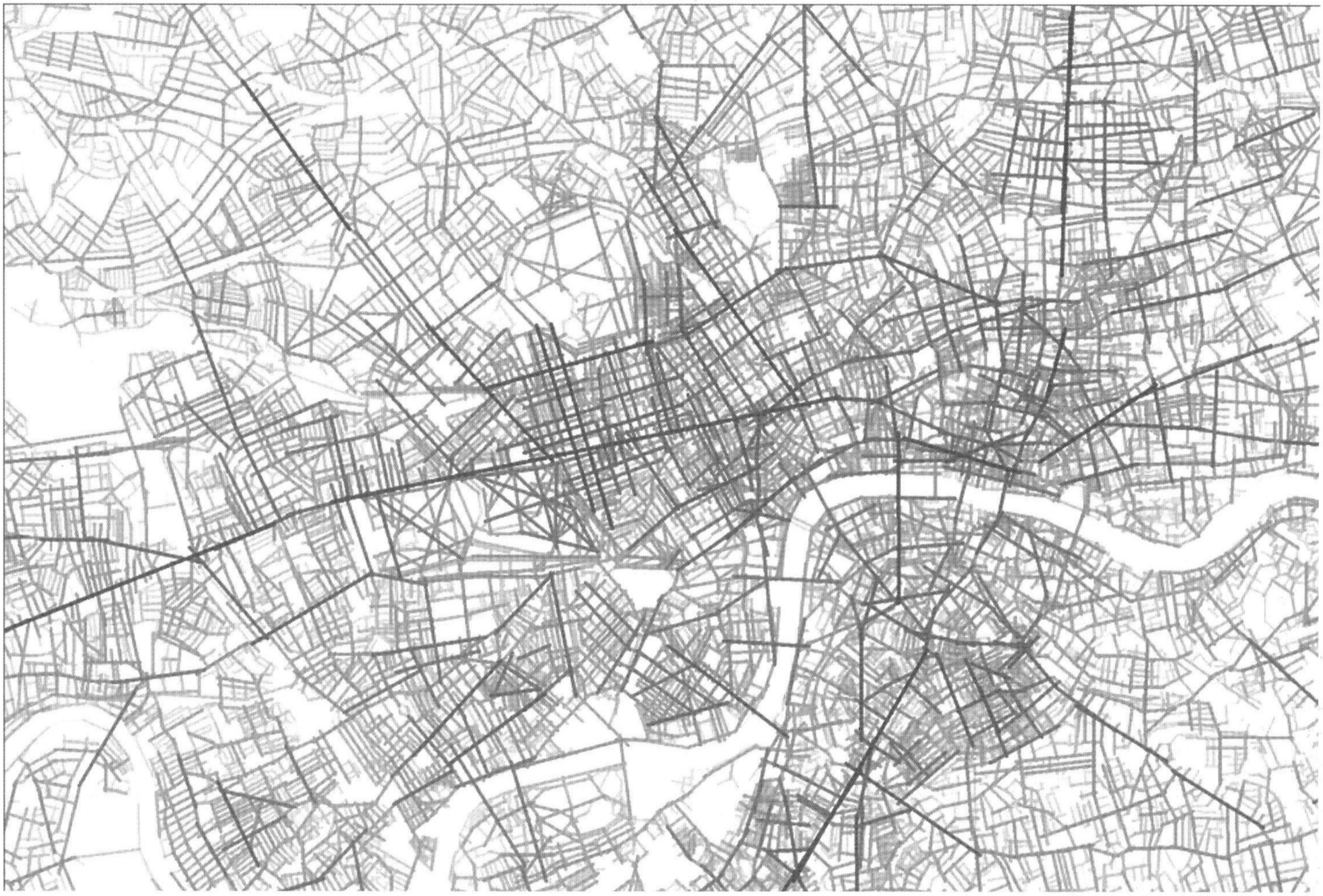

8.1 Spatial integration map of central London showing relative local spatial accessibility. Darker spaces are more accessible, lighter spaces less so.

8.2 New central staircase for Trafalgar Square, London. Part of the space-syntax-informed masterplan developed with Foster and Partners.

On the first point – the separation of the professions – our experience is that a critical divide exists between the various professional consultants charged with creating and evaluating urban schemes. In its simplest manifestation, the divide is technical – the deficiency of designers in understanding transport planners, property consultants understanding design, and transport planners understanding property. This springs from ignorance either of each participant's methodology (How do designers design? How do transport planners plan? How do property consultants measure value?) or of their nomenclature. (What is 'materiality', or 'free movement' or 'junction capacity' or 'yield' or 'juxtaposition'?) At a more complex level, and of greater concern, the divide is philosophical. One example relates to movement and the design of public space. The urban transport paradigm has been to keep traffic moving – including pedestrians – whereas the intention of the public realm designer is often to stop people moving by giving them somewhere to sit. Similarly, the property consultant is often looking to avoid 'leakage' in shopping centre designs whereas the urban designer is advocating 'permeability'.

One of the consequences of the divide is suspicion about the real agendas of other consultants. ('They're just in it to get a building' or 'They're just trying to build more roads' or 'They want to turn the town centre into a giant mall.') Another less obvious but potentially more damaging consequence of the divide is lack of interest, such as when one consultant tunes out in the middle of another's presentation. Ultimately, the results of such professional 'collaboration' are varied. Sometimes, surprisingly, an acceptable outcome is achieved. More frequently the places that result are mediocre, and all too often they quickly become little used and unsafe.

The second reason urban design methods are less secure than we might hope lies at the heart of the urban design process – inadequate analysis of the socio-economic impact of space/form decisions. Design evaluations are often cast in subjective terms that fail to connect design intentions with social and economic outcomes other than in a superficial way. This is especially so for conceptual design, which should hardly be surprising given that the conceptual design process is often described in emotional terms: as the designer's personal response to a situation, or as a feeling.

When designs are explained by designers in terms of their intended effects on human activity – e.g. 'this will be a vibrant public space' – the conviction behind the sentiment is normally derived from subjective appraisal, based on skill and experience. Unfortunately, skill and experience – combined with the innate compulsion of designers to innovate and ignore established, organic contexts – create a mix that has been shown to fail more often than succeed. For example, the intended social benefits of the twentieth-century housing programme went generally unrealised. This was not due to a lack of good intention, passion and positive emotion but instead, in large part, from the inability to foresee the likely outcomes of design inputs.

As a result, great social damage has occurred in the environments that were created. Responsibility for influencing that failure is rarely accepted by designers because the link between design and outcome has not been made. Indeed, the notion of a form-function relationship in architectural and urban design has troubled the profession for the best part of a century. On the one hand, designers are prepared to stand in front of artist's impressions that convey intended social and economic outcomes. On the other, professionals have been quick to play down the connection between design and social malaise when, so often, it has occurred.

The obscurity surrounding this connection is hardly surprising since urban design is only ever partly responsible – if at all – for any socio-economic outcome, positive or negative. But if there is a link between design and outcome, what is the nature of that link? And what might this mean for the practice of urban design?

One way of addressing these questions is to study the product of urban design in a very specific manner. First, identify the spatial and formal qualities of design, including the location and orientation of individual buildings and the assemblage of buildings and space layouts. Second, observe the patterns of human activity – such as movement and public space occupancy – that occur within these layouts. Finally, look for consistent relationships between patterns of space/form and patterns of activity.

This type of approach underpins 'space syntax' analysis, which was pioneered by Bill Hillier and his colleagues at University College London in the mid-1970s. Hillier's innovation was to describe buildings and places not only in terms of their formal substance (i.e. what they are made of and how they are put together) but also in terms of (1) the spaces that stand between buildings and link them together as layouts; and (2) the activities and potentialities for social interaction that are created by these layouts.[1]

The essential proposition behind space syntax is that the configuration of the urban grid exerts a powerful influence on the disposition of urban land uses and the patterns of movement that flow between them. Space syntax researchers have found that these processes can both be described and measured using analytical spatial models. Extensive, empirical testing in situations throughout the

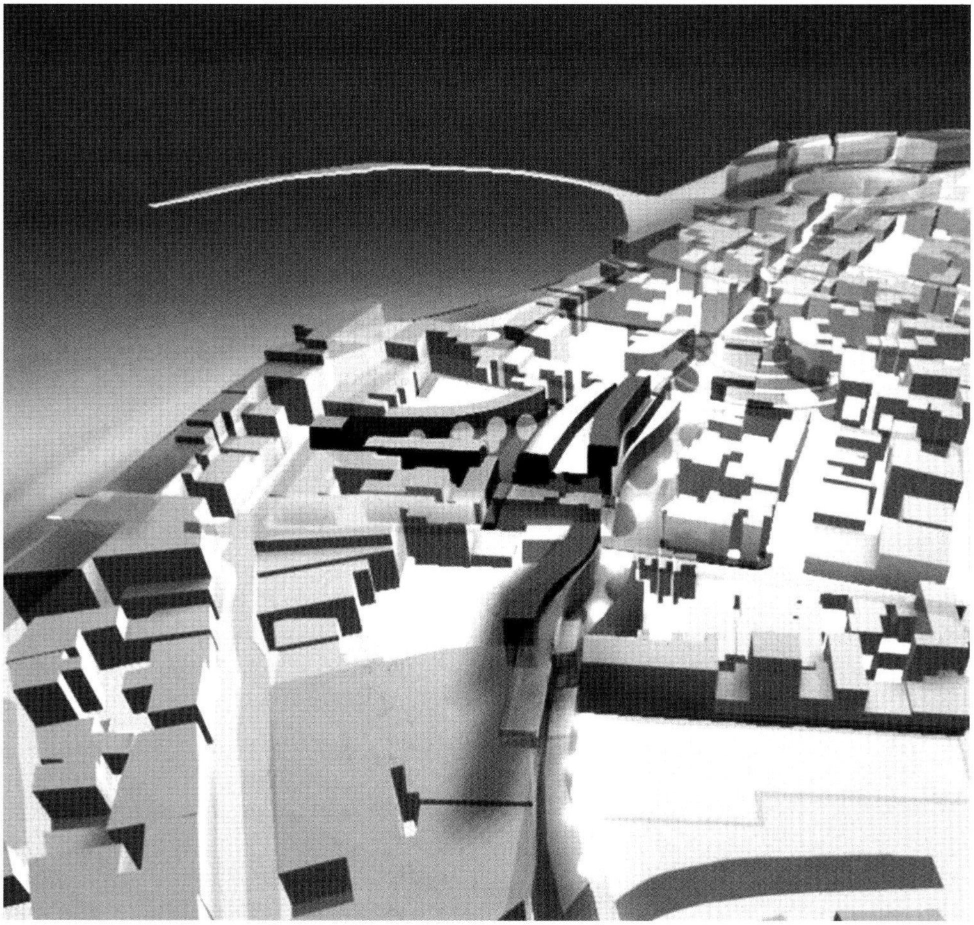

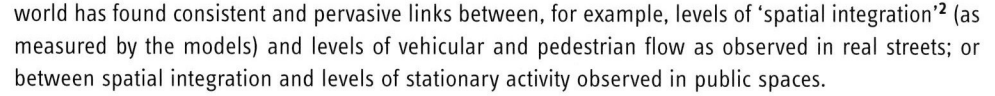

8.3 **Strategic design proposal for the historic core of Margate, UK. An example of the influence of design factors, such as footfall, natural surveillance and connectivity that encourage social and economic activities.**

8.4 **Margate, UK**

8.5 **Margate, UK**

world has found consistent and pervasive links between, for example, levels of 'spatial integration'[2] (as measured by the models) and levels of vehicular and pedestrian flow as observed in real streets; or between spatial integration and levels of stationary activity observed in public spaces.

Most importantly for urban design practice, the link between space and activity has been found to be able to be forecast in new developments by testing proposed designs within the spatial models. Originally intended as a means of *understanding* the connection between design and outcome, space syntax has evolved into a tool for *improving* designs and creating better urban places. As the influence of Hillier's work has grown in academic circles internationally – with centres of space syntax research in over fifty universities around the world – so has the demand to use the forecasting element of the techniques in design practice. Projects including the Millennium Footbridge and Trafalgar Square in London have been developed using the techniques to generate and test design options.

A growing number of practices – including design, transportation and planning consultants – now offer space syntax services in a wide range of applications, including conceptual design generation, master-planning, crime reduction and spatial policy development. After a decade of serious application, one conclusion is that we may well be seeing the emergence of a professional discipline of 'space syntax' or 'configurational studies'.

These objective space syntax methods raise an important issue for urban design. Previously, designers could avoid blame for the effects of bad design because it was not possible to directly relate design inputs to social and economic outputs. On the other hand, the limitations of a subjective approach to

evaluation have seen other disciplines stealing the lead from urban design, and none more so than transport planning with its quantitative methodologies. Faced with the choice between design subjectivity and transport objectivity, decision-makers have largely opted to go with the numbers.

In providing urban design with a quantitative approach that reveals something fundamental about human activity, space syntax has offered a means of demonstrating design's fundamental influence on value. Being able to identify the design factors that influence footfall, enhance natural surveillance and encourage the conditions for social co-presence has meant that more reliable decisions have been made on proposed designs. It has also meant that projects can be described not only in the obscure, subjective jargon of the design profession but also in a new vocabulary of particular space/form characteristics that illuminates their likely social and economic impacts. Although it has been criticised by some designers as a 'black art', 'smoke and mirrors' or 'pseudo-science', the experience from practice suggests that the way in which space syntax describes the link between design and outcome is appealing to non-designers, including members of the public.

The availability of a methodology that can effectively expose flaws in design proposals has been seen by many in the design profession as a threat. Others have taken a different view: that the techniques can help to generate and then substantiate a design idea. In other words, space syntax can be creatively used as a fundamental design 'tool'.[3] The list of names to draw on the input of space syntax practitioners – and to do so during the early, strategic phase of design generation – includes Foster, Rogers, Farrell, Grimshaw, Hopkins and Hadid.

In recent years, several space syntax practitioners have begun expanding their formerly design-focused methodology to include a number of transport and property factors. These practitioners have created

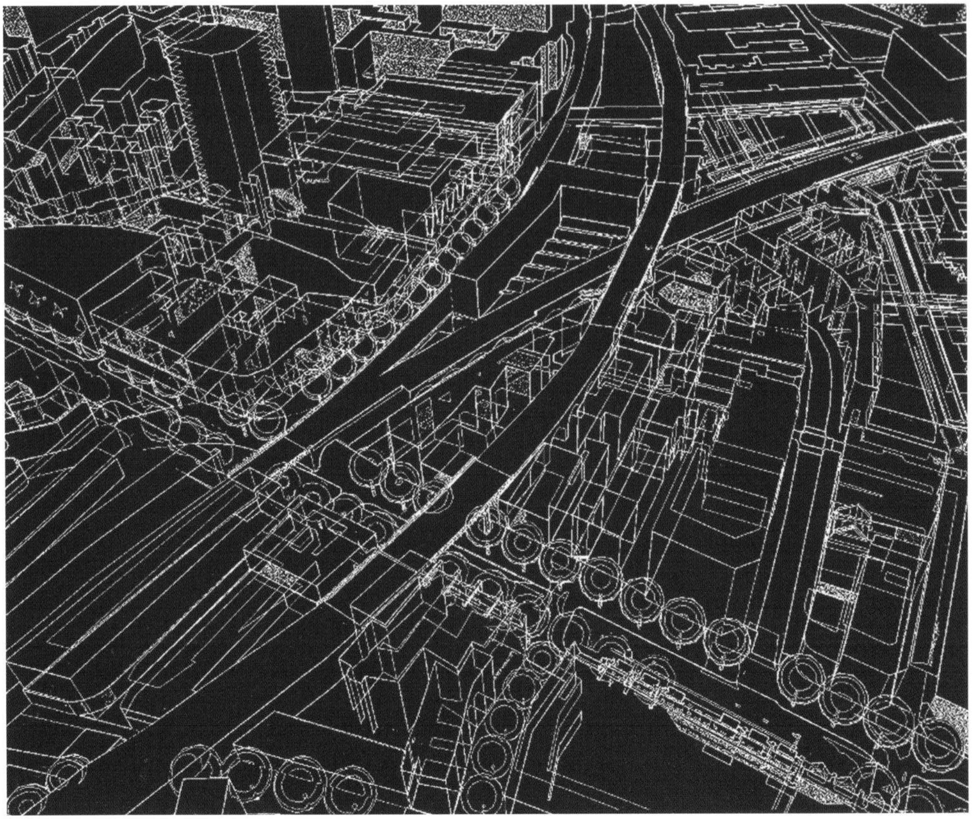

8.6 **A strategic design proposal for the Brixton Town Centre Interchange, London. The methodology has expanded to include a number of transport and property factors in this situation.**

8.7 Masterplan for historic St Botolph's Quarter, Colchester, UK. The aim of the plan is to re-establish direct links that had been severed by poorly planned transport infrastructure and development.

8.8 Sketch of proposal for a new public space at Princes Circus, London. Space syntax tools provide a partial solution for some of the challenges of urban design.

8.9 Princes Circus, London, sketch.

new analytic tools that engage not only with issues of layout, building location and orientation but also with the effects of local transport nodes and land use patterns on human activity.[4] In this way, they have taken an important step towards integrating design issues with the interests of transport planners and property consultants.

Thus, a tool designed to address our second problem, of knowing how design influences outcome, can also help to foster communication between professional disciplines (our first problem). Of course the mutual exposition of professionals can also be seen as a threat, this time to the territories of the individual disciplines themselves. However, if the new multi-disciplinary models make professional borders more permeable, they also appear, in our experience, to have created a more congenial and effective process for delivering urbanism. The new process not only allows the designer to make transport and land use recommendations: it also puts the designer's pen into the hands of the transport or property consultant.

Space syntax tools provide a partial solution for some of the challenges of urban design. Currently they place us on firm ground in forecasting generic patterns of human behaviour in urban space (moving, stopping, sitting) and some of the social conditions that arise from these (whether places are likely to be lively communities or dead zones people avoid if they can). These social conditions certainly have economic and financial effects – higher retail takings should accrue from higher passing foot traffic, for example. However, there is certainly room to investigate whether more precise methods of translating spatial factors into financial and economic outcomes can be developed. Which neighbourhood layout is likely to lead to higher property values? How much is likely to be saved in healthcare spending from a plan that encourages movement on foot? Will a physical regeneration scheme pay for itself by delivering enough people to a city centre to sustain new businesses and the jobs and tax revenue they generate? These are questions that should interest urban decision-makers. If they can be answered, it will be through interdisciplinary dialogue, objective analysis and – of course – a healthy dose of creativity and innovation.

ACKNOWLEDGEMENTS

The author wishes to acknowledge the help of Chris Stutz and Sacha Tan in preparing this chapter.

Notes

1 Readers wanting a full, technical discussion of space syntax theories and methods are directed to B. Hillier and J. Hanson's *The Social Logic of Space*, Cambridge: Cambridge University Press, 1984, and B. Hillier's *Space is the Machine*, Cambridge: Cambridge University Press, 1996.

2 'Spatial integration', a fundamental concept in space syntax, is a measure of the relative accessibility of spaces in an urban area. It is calculated by analysing the complexity of routes between a particular space and all the other spaces in the area.

3 Of course, like any tool, space syntax can also be misused. One way to do this is to pick a concept and employ it indiscriminately. Such has been the case with permeability, a frequent topic in discussions informed by space syntax. With permeability comes the need to animate every route at ground level with active frontages. Permeability without activation is a recipe for unsafe spaces, which provide unwatched access routes for anti-social users.

4 The Walkability Index makes use of the statistical technique of multiple regression to analyse the relationship between different spatial, social, and geographic variables. A full account is given in 'Towards a 'Walkability Index'', a paper presented at the third annual Walk21conference in 2002, and available for download from http://www.spacesyntax.com/news/WalkabilityIndex.pdf. See also D. Chang and A. Penn, 'Integrated multilevel circulation in dense urban areas: the effect of multiple interacting constraints on the use of complex urban areas', *Environment and Planning B: Planning and Design*, 1998, 25: 507–38, and J. Desyllas *et al.*, *Pedestrian Demand Modelling of Large Cities: An Applied Example from London*, CASA Working Paper #62, 2003, available for download from http://www.intelligentspace.com/download/Pedestrian%20Demand%20Modelling%20of%20Large%20Cities.pdf

Public space was not given by God, it was created by human desire.

European public space as we now know it crystallized in the eighteenth and nineteenth centuries in the form of parks, squares and boulevards, with the most fundamental element being the street. But what is so interesting about the street? What has it done to merit such praise? Well, imagine the complexity of human beings: our unpredictable behavior, our problems, obsessions and neuroses; our inclination toward random chaos, our individualism — the list goes on for another 10 kilometres. However, once we come out of our houses, our places of work or wherever we happen to be, and enter the street, we know exactly how to relate to one another and where to position ourselves. This is brought about by the street acting as a guidebook, an instruction manual with a simple and clearly defined set of rules. Yes, of course there are anomalies, people whose individuality is immune to regulation. But in general, we can look at the street as an amazing regulator of human activity.

The street appeared as result of collectively accepted – though unwritten – codes which have over time been absorbed and written into civil law. At first sight, the street is little more than a simple collection of kerbstones; a couple of pavements and the road in between, yet closer inspection reveals much more. The street determines where the trees are placed, the position of lamp-posts, rubbish bins and furniture, it decides where cars can and cannot park, where to walk, where to cross from one point to another, it even specifies where rainwater will pour into the gutter.

CHAPTER 9 THE STREET

ADRIAAN GEUZE

And there's more. The street also provides an address. Not merely a numerical tag on one's front door, this address is also a stage on which to show the world who we are. A display window for our identity and status.

Since the nineteenth century there has been an expansion of public realm, primarily driven by increasingly efficient transport systems: the train, the car, the airplane. Railroads and highways have given mass audiences access to entirely new public spaces. In turn, this has led to the colonization of lakesides, mountains, forests and woods, beaches.

In the late 1950s the highway reached its climax as the most important public space. Rock'n' roll music connected to the car, connected to Hollywood to produce a sublime combination of sex, rhythm and speed. That is where freedom is. The ability to move from point to point in your very own car-branded identity. The rules are simple, clear and easy to follow. There is also the pleasure of being hypnotized by the rhythms of the car engine backed up by radio music, news and other info; the scenic views, the gentle pull of gravity as we accelerate along the highway's sweeping curves.

Above, left to right

9.1 **Les Halles present entrances.**

9.2 **Les Halles roof-lights.**

9.3 **Les Halles landscape proposals.**

Below

9.4 **Les Halles, Paris. Cross-section of proposals. West 8's competition entry for the regeneration of the depressing underground shopping centre in central Paris exemplifies the need to design the street as both a public thoroughfare and a place of fun.**

Right

9.5 **Exciting night view of Les Halles proposals.**

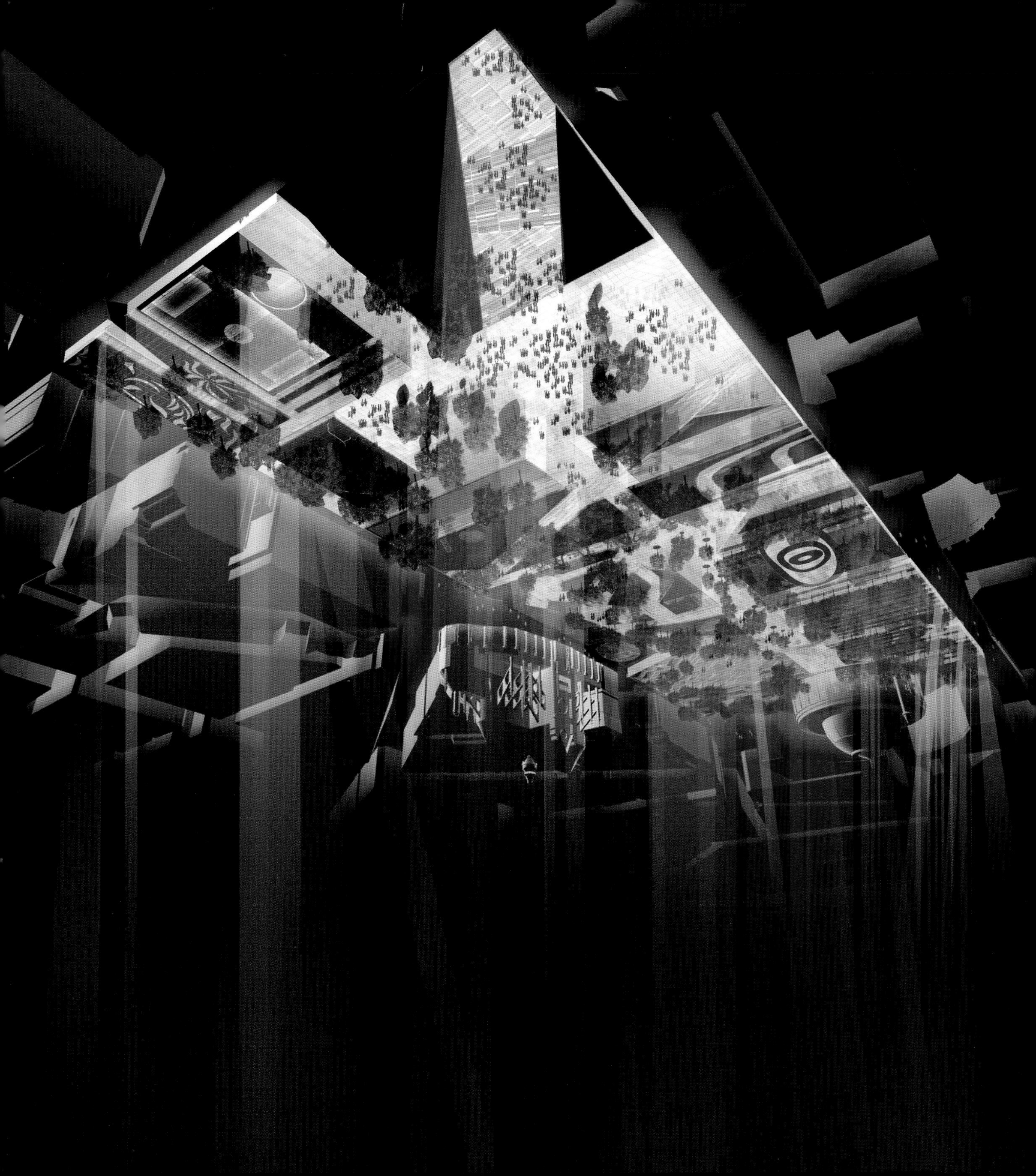

Meanwhile, within the urban fabric there has been an explosion of new facilities able to serve as public spaces: shopping malls, cinemas, theatres, fast food outlets, service stations, garages, commuter trains, transport hubs and sports centres.

As these new public spaces have grown exponentially, what has happened to the street? How has it been getting along? Not very well. The street has been kidnapped by traffic engineers, town planners, architects, local residents, shop owners and developers. The authentic street is hard to find, replaced by mongrel spaces. Purposefully deformed designer roads, buildings pulled back and lifted high above the ground, result in endless and undefined public voids. Modern architecture has simply ignored the street and chosen to hover and float above it all, preying on sites, hijacking the scene and leaving behind shadow, wind and anonymity. The boundary between public and private space has lost definition. Within the cities there is an excess of public space; urban planners feed the audience with numerous squares and parks and greenery. There is so much of it that is has become impossible to define and to maintain, which has brought about a permanent state of irritation.

These beautiful urban centres were captured by commercial enterprise, stripped of their public qualities and put to monofunctional use. This was followed by the rapid degradation into *Logo Cities* where the street level no longer welcomed the free spirit but instead gave itself over to the consumer. The visual bombardment of advertising billboards, traffic signs and commercial logos has turned the domain into an expanse of sameness. It was only logical for the graffiti artists to move in with their spray cans and tag everything in sight. A cry for identity. The last bastion of the individual?

Contemporary culture has increased the public realm to the point where it has evolved beyond physical space. This shift began with the radio and was followed by television. Now we have the Internet and high-velocity mobile communication systems becoming the dominant public realms: near-impenetrable jungles of information; hidden/confused/lost identities; abstract rules and high maintenance costs.

The street has lost its regulatory function and has become a battlefield through which we struggle. Is it possible that the original simplicity of the street has now been adopted and subsequently taken over by the highways? And are the new meeting grounds for people now found in new media: reality TV, Internet and mobile communication?

The recipe of the street has been lost. Even though we now have an abundance of public space, the primary need for the street has not diminished. It cannot be replaced by these new zones, which can be seen as additions and optional extras. The loss of the *street* has done one thing; it has given rise to a new and rather hysterical profession– the Public Space Designer, also known as the PSD. In the beginning, they were promoted by property developers craving the nostalgia of the authentic street and preoccupied with the resurrection of medieval and Renaissance market towns. This was necessary to brighten up their newly acquired territories: the shopping malls, leisure centres, exhibition halls, suburbs, waterfronts. The PSD's attempts to reinvent the street have resulted in generally friendly and pleasant streets, complete with beautifully safe paving, mosaic floors, soft sunshine filtering through prudish nursery trees, gaily designed lamp-posts and furniture. A rigid amalgam of colour and texture that precisely defines acceptable behaviour.

After a series of lawsuits in the Anglo-Saxon world, the PSD standardized and perfected public space design. They rejected everything slippery, dirty, uneven, rough, hot, low, wet, sharp, painful, open, sloping, busy. An endless reproduction of innocence. These spaces are so pleasant and convenient no aftertaste is ever left behind in the brain. The memories of having visited these spaces is vague, unclear and easily replaceable. Public space designed by PSDs on auto-pilot. Call it Junkspace.

And then there was Barcelona . . .

In the early 1980s, with the re-establishment of democracy and Catalonia's new-found autonomy, Spain was experiencing a renaissance. Entry into the EU, the honor of hosting the 1992 Olympic Games and FC Barcelona winning the European Football Championships led to an almost unprecedented flowering of national pride. Suddenly there was a new gateway into Europe.

Barcelona had no choice but to revitalize a dusty city in order to accommodate the influx of Olympic guests and other curious visitors. They transformed the city into a state-of-the-art city and welcomed an international audience into splendid new public spaces. Squares, boulevards, parks, markets, beachfronts were all designed from a heritage sharing the best of Catalonian spirit and international avant-garde. Nobody had ever seen public spaces like this before. A new style evolved from Gaudí, Dali, Miró and others, and represented a euphoric cry of freedom and pride. The most amazing thing of all was that these designs were created by artists and architects and not by engineers or PSDs. Barcelona created a new recipe for the street: styled mosaic floors, artistically designed furniture and sculptures, small-scale water and greenery.

In the mid-1980s the success of Barcelona's public space was quickly reproduced in Paris as Mitterand imposed his Grands Projets on the city. This became the starting shot for local governments all over Europe to begin a race to reclaim their public spaces. This was inspired by a new generation of PSDs now claiming professional avant-garde skills. Designed spaces spread over the rest of Europe. Even the coolly sophisticated less-is-more Danish school of design got in on the act and adopted the warm-blooded Catalonian vernacular. Who cared if it spent half the year under opaque layers of ice and snow? With Europe infected by the new Spanish *élan*, the PSDs claimed victory over the traffic engineers.

In the past twenty years too many European cities have received massive facelifts with questionable results. The fundamental problem of these new spaces is that they lack resilience. No physical staying power. Add to that inadequate maintenance budgets and poor urban management; there is nothing to keep these places smiling. It gets worse, even more disgraceful than their inbuilt fragility, is the fact that they do not always represent the culture of their cities and societies. Too many of these spaces are interchangeable from one city to another. So, no matter the amount of *artistic* input and over-design in these places, they still remain Junkspace.

Please, please, please– give us back our streets!

Of course, every city deserves at least one Barcelonesque square. But the other streets should be non-designed and left to their own devices. So we need less public space and what there is should be better designed. Simpler streets: road and pavement; straightforward kerbstones, trouble-free parking – if there is traffic congestion, then opt for one-way streets. Construct the street using local flavours with a strong identity: brick in Amsterdam, York stone in London, tarmac in Geneva, grey granite in Milan, plane trees lining Parisian boulevards. And because every city has a limit to the resources it can devote to public space maintenance, it is essential for the street to have a clear definition of its responsibilities, of where it begins and ends.

In order for the street to regain its guidebook function, it needs to regain clarity, and neutrality. It should abandon its attempts to please and pamper everyone and no one, and return to an openness that offers freedom and invites individual colonization. Bring back the meeting places as well as the space and opportunity for people to distinguish themselves in the street.

A proud city should identify its own textures and street sections and simply roll this as a carpet over the town without interference from PSDs. Perhaps it is time for the PSDs to leave the public domain alone and concentrate on designing decorative commercial spaces.

ACKNOWLEDGEMENTS

The author wishes to acknowledge the help of Chidi Onwuka in the production of this chapter.

'At the dawn of the twenty-first century, the global marketplace is a celebration in diversity. People differ no only among cultures, but within cultures.'[1] Hong Kong is a meeting place of eastern and western cultures. Th seed of diversity was sown in its early days as a British colony on Chinese soil. Cultural diversity is celebrat ed in the daily life of citizens and manifest in the physical forms of the urban fabric. Marketplace diversity i an outcome of the city's culture. In return, it drives human activities in every imaginable way, including th shaping of the city's physical environment.

CHAPTER 10

ASIAN COMMERCIALISM AND THE DISCOVERY OF PLACE

THE LAN KWAI FONG STORY

ALEX LU

GROWTH POWERHOUSE DRIVEN BY COMMERCIALISM

Hong Kong is a commercial city. Its freewheeling business environment has often been cited as a key factor in helping Hong Kong to make such impressive achievements. Ever since World War II, the government has adopted a *laissez-faire* policy in governing Hong Kong. Under this doctrine the government only becomes actively involved in essential matters such as safety, health, social stability and security. The government has tended to refrain from interfering in economic activities. During the past three decades the city has seen several cycles of rapid growth culminating in a vibrant economy prior to 1997. Year after year, Hong Kong has been named the world's most free economy by international organizations such as *The Wall Street Journal*, the Heritage Foundation, the Fraser Institute, the Cato Institute and the Economic Freedom Network. The *laissez-faire* policy has largely been extended into the post-1997 era, when Hong Kong returned to Chinese sovereignty.

Despite its success in promoting growth, this policy is not without its shortcomings. For instance, city planning in Hong Kong – serving a government function – has been passive and fragmented in guiding and controlling developments. Land-use zoning control was introduced in the 1960s, but this was only applied sporadically, and it took more than twenty years for this control to be extended to most urban areas. However, even today there are still no comprehensive policies regarding urban design and historic preservation. Co-ordination between public and private developments is lacking. Most of the city's infrastructure systems – such as roads, sewers, water, power and public transportation – are independent operating monopolies with their own plans and goals. The city's cultural and natural heritage is often ignored in the process of urban development. Old buildings, historic or not, have normally been demolished rather than preserved or recycled for other uses. During the years of rapid growth from the early 1970s to the late 1990s, hundreds of old buildings, including many historically significant ones, were bulldozed for new developments. An invaluable portion of the city's heritage was sacrificed in the name of progress. Hong Kong's cityscape has been transformed drastically, with large buildings replacing smaller ones in every corner of the city. With many old neighbourhoods gone, today there is generally a lack of historic representation in the city's urban fabric.

1 Victoria Harbour
2 Star Ferry
3 The HongKong Shanghai Banking Corporation
4 Jardine House
5 Exchange Square
6 Two International Finance Centre
7 The Landmark

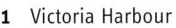

10.1 Hong Kong aerial view showing Lan Kwai Fong. The location of the niche area at the edge of Central office district is apparent from the reduction in size of building grain.

After years of economic growth, Central (the Central District) has evolved to become a high-density, highly valued, cosmopolitan, urban centre. Several strong forces have shaped Central into an office, retail and entertainment hub enriched by a mixed cultural flavour. These include the continuous displacement of residential uses by commercial functions, the creation of a large workforce representing local, Western and other ethnic backgrounds, and the effects of thousands of visiting tourists. Central is both an

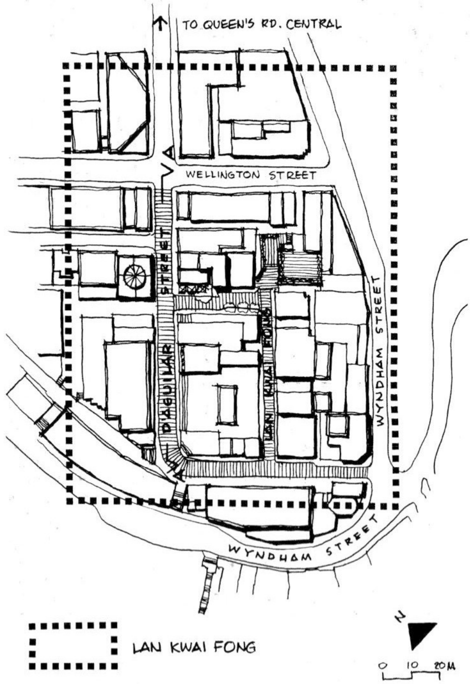

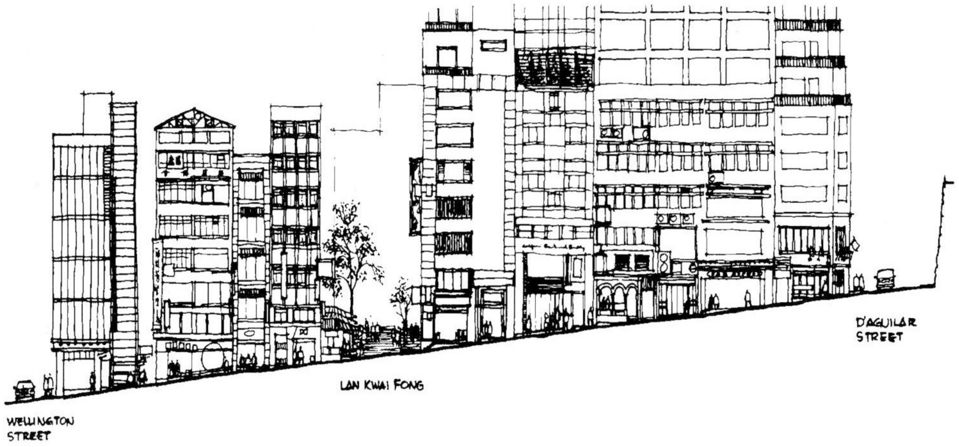

10.2 **Lan Kwai Fong location plan. Small block footprints create a dense urban enclave of streets suited to new service industry created by market forces rather than planning.**

10.3 **Elevation of D'Aguilar Street. Nondescript 1960s' office and apartment buildings have been found to be flexible for change of use and provide density of activity with street frontage of bars and restaurants.**

exciting and an extremely interesting place. As in most other major cities, Hong Kong's CBD (Central Business District) is characterized by an institutional front of grand corporate buildings that dominate the main streets. Fortunately, a secondary network of side streets still exists behind the shiny towers. In contrast to the principal streets, these smaller streets are pedestrian-oriented and they sustain a host of activities. Lined with moderate-sized buildings, shops and vendors' stalls, these secondary streets and alleys play an important role by nurturing the humane aspects of city life and forming a curious mix of interesting urban places.

Old and obsolete in the handling of modern vehicular traffic, these secondary streets have adapted for today's needs. Mainly they support the CBD's daily operation and provide much-needed urban spaces for human activities in the heavily developed downtown. Many have been transformed into unique places that sell various specialities such as photographic equipment, Chinese herbs, discount clothing, vegetables and flowers, and Chinese stamps. Some districts have concentrations of boutique restaurants featuring local and western cuisines, as well as herbal teashops, cafés, bars, curio shops and stalls, and locksmiths. The abundance of small urban niches like these in and around Central adds considerable delight to Hong Kong's city centre and, among these, Lan Kwai Fong stands out as one of the most significant.

Lan Kwai Fong (Orchid Laurel Court) is the name of a side street within a small urban enclave, which includes several clusters of old commercial buildings nestled at the fringes of the corporate CBD. During the 1970s and 1980s, while many old buildings in more strategic locations in Central were being torn down to make room for taller commercial buildings, the Mass Transit Railway, road widening and other amenities, these few blocks of old commercial buildings remained largely underutilized. One by one, they were recycled or redeveloped to become fashionable restaurants, bars and entertainment places – a new use much in demand in the CBD as Hong Kong emerged as a globally important financial and service centre. For both business and leisure, Lan Kwai Fong is now a favourite spot among business communities, locals and tourists – in part because the area brims with life around the clock. For more than twenty years this neighbourhood has gradually gathered strength to become an attraction reflecting a unique character.

THE RISE OF LAN KWAI FONG

Near the turn of the twentieth century Lan Kwai Fong was a market-place for flower vendors. Neighbouring D'Aguilar Street was a red-light district frequented by sailors, who used to buy flowers in Lan Kwai Fong to send to their favourite ladies. Today there are still a few flower stalls and they have been incorporated into a neighbourhood improvement programme. In the early twentieth century, this neighbourhood was predominantly occupied by densely packed timber buildings, three to four stories tall and situated on small lots.[2] They generally reflected a socially and financially modest community. In the early 1960s, some of these buildings were still being used as brothels and 'godowns'. At that time there was not the slightest hint of what the neighbourhood would become today.

During the 1960s and 1970s many of these old timber buildings were redeveloped into larger reinforced-concrete buildings varying from five to twenty stories for commercial and residential uses. They were rather nondescript buildings and many can still be seen in the district today. Other than flower and fruit vendors, other kinds of shops also found their way to Lan Kwai Fong: those selling rice, groceries and other produce, and carpets, as well as European-style tailors and offices. Today, when most areas in Central have been redeveloped and modernized, this neighbourhood has become ever more distinctive, not only because of its commercial activity but also because it arouses so many memories of a bygone Hong Kong.

Economic development brought new lifestyles and western forms of entertainment. The first discotheque in the area, 'Disco Disco', was opened in 1978 on D'Aguilar Street, followed in 1982 by two bars, 'California' and '97'.[3] As Hong Kong became more international, many residents became more affluent. During the 1980s Hong Kong's economy was booming, but at the same time it was undergoing a quiet but fundamental change. While light industry moved north to China because of lower costs, Hong Kong's service industry grew rapidly, bringing in large numbers of workers from western countries. Many of these newcomers, suddenly transplanted to an Asian city, longed for a meeting place they might identify with home where they could hang out with friends, entertain guests or find an attractive watering hole. Entrepreneurs who sought a place to establish new businesses identified Lan Kwai Fong as a location accessible to a large pool of expatriate workers in Central, and at the same time relatively affordable.

By the mid-1980s several famous bars, clubs and restaurants in Lan Kwai Fong had made the neighbourhood well known for its exotic European flavour, quality food and entertainment. The Lan Kwai Fong Association was set up in 1990, primarily to handle objections raised by nearby residents complaining about the noise and other disturbances caused by these operations that were usually active until early morning. The booming businesses lured even more restaurants and bars to open in this location and in turn they attracted even more patrons. By the end of the twentieth century this small urban enclave had become so busy that during holidays like Christmas and New Year, the narrow sloping streets were fully packed with celebrating crowds. According to police records, on New Year's Eve in 1992, almost 20,000 merrymakers gathered in this small neighbourhood. The tremendous success of this occasion inadvertently and regretfully brought about a great tragedy.

On New Year's Day 1993, city residents were shocked when they woke to the news that frolicking crowds in Lan Kwai Fong had tripped and had fallen over one another, leaving twenty people dead. The tragedy dealt a heavy blow to burgeoning business, and for a long time horror haunted the neighbourhood. An independent enquiry was held to review the incident and to recommend measures to avoid any recurrence. As business owners learned from past mistakes, they met to plan for improved activities in the neighbourhood. Through the Lan Kwai Fong Association, they worked with the government and other social groups, sometimes co-sponsoring activities. Their relentless efforts have been the main driving force in restoring vitality to the neighbourhood.

Although Lan Kwai Fong has undergone dramatic changes since the food and entertainment businesses began to operate in the late 1970s, the government has played only a passive role as a regulator. There have been few government-sponsored urban design improvements to make Lan Kwai Fong a special place. For example, street paving, lights and railings were all standard provisions in other areas in Hong Kong until 2003, when they were finally upgraded as a part of a neighbourhood improvement programme. Unfortunately, other improvements such as iconic gateways for a better neighbourhood identity, trees on all neighbourhood streets and alfresco dining were curtailed due to a variety of reasons such as underground utility restrictions, public-private ownership constraints and traffic circulation.

UNIQUE NEIGHBOURHOOD CHARACTERS

Successful urban places appeal to a wide range of people. In Lan Kwai Fong, this success has resulted largely from market forces rather than official planning or urban design. As a city neighbourhood, Lan Kwai Fong is small. The core area occupies less than two hectares of land, at the edge of the CDB and at the base of steep slopes that rise up to Victoria Peak. From the air, Lan Kwai Fong appears no different from other old urban neighbourhoods containing a mix of densely packed, small, low- to mid-rise buildings. While fun, food and entertainment businesses occupy most of the lower floors; the upper floors contain shops and offices, with a few buildings still housing residential flats. The streets are narrow and sloping; open space is limited. Overall, the physical character of the neighbourhood is anything but distinctive. Despite an ordinary urban setting and limited public support, Lan Kwai Fong thrives largely due to the following factors:

1 ***Superb location***. Within convenient walking distance of most parts of the CBD, the neighbourhood is within reach of a huge pool of potential patrons. On weekends and holidays, a different crowd often joins the activities, using roads, car parks and public transportation systems that serve Central to congregate

10.4 Daytime scene enables street refurbishment to be visible. New planting and paving part of 2003 neighbourhood improvement programme.

10.5 Night scene shows people, not buildings are the centre of attention. Office workers from nearby Central climb the hill for after-work recreation, but overcrowding is sometimes an issue.

10.6 **Neon signs are Hong Kong's aesthetic. Despite typhoons, flimsy signs proliferate and add to the atmosphere of vibrancy.**

in Lan Kwai Fong from all parts of Hong Kong. Street carnivals and festival celebrations are held mostly on holidays.

2 ***Critical mass***. Lan Kwai Fong consists of a group of independent entrepreneurs who are particularly sensitive to a special segment of market demands and who consciously choose to operate in the same close vicinity. Synergy among businesses broadens their appeal and heightens their attraction. The concentration and varieties serve the varied needs of customers coming from different cultural backgrounds and having broad personal desires. In 2003 the number of food and beverage operations, entertainment businesses and private clubs had grown to over 100, featuring a variety of national and cultural tastes and flavours.

3 ***Vision, persistence and recognition***. During the heyday of urban growth in the 1990s, many property owners and real estate developers in Hong Kong made huge profits quickly by redeveloping old neighbourhoods *en bloc*. However, the majority of business and property owners in Lan Kwai Fong chose to preserve their own neighbourhood. Eventually, several Lan Kwai Fong entrepreneurs redeveloped a few well-situated neighbourhood buildings. In contrast to wholesale neighbourhood redevelopment, these smaller projects are enhancements rather than hindrances. Their moderate scale, contemporary design and compatible uses blend with the neighbourhood's character and inject a modicum of modernity to the environment. The gradual, incremental replacement of older buildings with newer ones is a sign that Lan Kwai Fong is a healthy, lively neighbourhood. Lan Kwai Fong's visions and achievements are now recognized by the community at large, because the neighbourhood has enriched city life, regenerated an old neighbourhood, preserved urban heritage and promoted tourism. Lan Kwai Fong community members take pride in their neighbourhood and cherish the fruits of their achievements.

4 ***Lan Kwai Fong Association***. In the aftermath of the 1992–3 New Year's Eve tragedy, the Lan Kwai Fong Association was designated the *de facto* representative of local businesses. The Association actively deals with the government, utility companies, social and cultural organizations as well as commercial sponsors. It airs community concerns, monitors street improvement programmes and co-ordinates the use of private and public spaces. It also assumes the role of a neighbourhood manager, helping to formulate annual activity programmes, obtaining necessary permits, and planning events either on its own or in collaboration with other sponsoring organizations. Today community events and street carnivals – such as Hallowe'en, International Food and Drinks, Open Air Arts and Music, etc. – are regularly organized. The neighbourhood is renowned as a place for people to have fun and celebrate. Local patrons already outnumber expatriates and visitors. Lan Kwai Fong has become a household name. Due to the efforts of the Association, this unique place has received unprecedented recognition.

5 ***Interesting environmental settings***. After nightfall, the narrow and small open spaces effectively restrict the visual perception of Lan Kwai Fong to its streets, which are vibrant with the exciting ambience of an entertainment district, obscuring a relatively dark and quiet background beyond the celebrating patrons' perception. However, during the day, two very different environmental settings in close juxtaposition are clearly visible, creating a somewhat surreal and stimulating feeling. The unique experience of dining on the verandah of a lavishly furnished restaurant that provides not only every comfort of modernity but also a close-up view of old Hong Kong is an unusual novelty. The co-existence of two, drastically different environments intertwined in the same neighbourhood may only be possible in large cities possessing diverse characteristics. Hong Kong is certainly one such city. This juxtaposing of old and new may well persist for some time in Lan Kwai Fong, much to the delight of the local businesses, which see the existence of old buildings as helping to lend a unique character and identity to the neighbourhood. However, in the absence of any public programme, the redevelopment of these old buildings will probably occur as they have in the past, when market forces drove development.

FUTURE URBAN LANDSCAPE

As a major city in the world with an open economy, Hong Kong is in the mainstream of globalization. The evolution from an industrialized city to a corporate city has taken a much shorter time than in most western countries. The rise of Lan Kwai Fong has occurred in synchrony with Hong Kong's shift from an industrial economy to a service one. This crucial shift has resulted in dramatic changes to the city's demography, culture and built environment. Since the 1990s, Hong Kong has virtually been on a par, at least financially, with other major world cities such as New York, London or Tokyo. Preoccupied with 'growth' (or the creation of wealth for a rising number of residents) and yet simultaneously overshadowed by an uncertain political future, the city's social agenda was skewed against matters of long-term concerns. In the past few years of British rule, the colonial government primarily focused on continuous 'growth' (through massive public programmes to support development) as a way to secure social stability. With this backdrop, the emergence of Lan Kwai Fong as a prime food and entertainment centre exemplifies a remarkable success of old neighbourhood regeneration driven by commercialism.

However, a more active role on the part of government would have brought greater benefits. For instance, without forward planning for an inhabited downtown, Central (including Lan

Kwai Fong) has lost ever-increasing numbers of its residents, leaving most streets empty and most shops closed after work except for a few nightspots. Historically significant buildings at important urban nodes could have been preserved to reflect the city's rich cultural heritage. Old neighbourhoods targeted for regeneration could have gone through the challenging process of 'growth' with fewer pains and less confrontation. And generally, more open space and a better urban environment could have been provided in Central. The present systems relating to planning and urban development leave much room for improvement. Furthermore, urban design by its very nature involves multiple stakeholders in the public and private sectors of the community. In Hong Kong, urban design has lagged behind and this was mainly due to the government's passive attitude and highly compartmentalized institutions and policies, insufficient involvement of the community and business sector, and the general lack of awareness of potential damage to the urban environment by unscrupulous developments.

The strong economic outlook in Hong Kong took an about-face near the end of the twentieth century, following the devastating economic turmoil that affected (and continues to have an impact on) many Asian countries. This turnaround was followed by acute downward adjustments in information, technology, finance and other key industries in the global economy, causing a wide segment of economic activities in Hong Kong to come to an abrupt halt. In 2001 the accession of China into the World Trade Organization has redefined Hong Kong's relationship with China and with the rest of the world. The pace of urban development has slowed down, allowing many in Hong Kong to take a self-reflective moment to ponder the effects of several decades' rapid and sometimes hasty growth, and to deliberate on appropriate ways to move forward in the context of regional development of the Pearl River Delta (and indeed of development throughout China) in a new and ever-challenging era.

Hong Kong's strengths lie in the city's mixed and diversified culture as well as in its ability to integrate into the global economy. Hong Kong has been a window for China to reach the world. It can also be the world's window to reach China, as the Pearl River Delta is quickly becoming one of the world's pre-eminent factories. In order to regain its prominence, Hong Kong is on course to further integrate with China, its hinterland as well as the 'motherland'. The firm stance adopted by China to implement the 'one country two systems' approach has helped to remove political uncertainty from this former British colony. After reverting to Chinese rule in 1997, a shift in the community's social values has taken place, generally in favour of a distinct identity for the city, the preservation of Hong Kong's natural and cultural heritage, the improvement of the urban environment's quality and a more open, transparent policy-making process. A proactive attitude has begun to emerge in the community to influence many city development, planning and urban design policies, such as the creation of a new cultural district, harbor protection and harbour-front developments, often putting the government on the defensive. Because of today's fast-changing and complex urban environment, past government policies and attitudes will probably need to be adjusted from time to time so that different community aspirations can be aired and strategic social goals can be formulated and then realized. Urban development policies have to be reviewed and redressed to meet the new values related to time and place.

However, as public revenues shrink, public programmes are scaled back. Plausibly, urban development will increasingly rely on the motivating force of the private sector and probably commercialism will largely continue to shape Hong Kong's urban landscape. Those who help manage a free economy such as that characterizing Hong Kong will likely have no quarrel with market forces taking the lead in economic activities. However, both city planning and urban design encompass a broad matrix of public interest issues, which cannot and should not rely exclusively on the mechanisms of the private market. It is therefore essential that the government plays a larger role in defining the public interest and acts as both a facilitator and regulator in furthering those interests. What's more, it is essential to replace the current fragmented system with a more co-ordinated and effective institutional framework for planning, urban design and implementation. One of the challenges the government faces is to motivate private resources and to harness and guide market-driven forces towards fruitful ends for the mutual benefit of both private entities engaged in development activities and of the community at large. The Lan Kwai Fong story has been a useful lesson for Hong Kong, and perhaps also for other Asian cities, as the pace of economic activities picks up speed again.

Notes

1 Leon G. Schiffman, *Consumer Behavior*, Englewood Cliffs, NJ: Prentice Hall, 2000, 7th edition, p. 3.

2 Hal Empson, *Mapping Hong Kong: A Historical Atlas*, Hong Kong: Government Information Services, 1992, p. 166, plate 3-5a.

3 Ping-wa Leung, *Heritage of the Central and Western District, Hong Kong*. Hong Kong: Central and Western Provisional District Board, 1999, pp. 243-5.

In October 2003 the Danish architect and planner, Professor Jan Gehl, reminded a packed audience at Glasgow's Lighthouse architectural centre that in serving the cause of successful urban design and planning one should remember these priorities: 'First, the people, then the spaces, and then the buildings.' Such, he said had informed the programme of work designed to make a more convivial city of Copenhagen, which he and his colleagues have successfully undertaken over the past thirty years. In answering a question from the audience about values and design, Gehl reminded everybody of what architect Ralph Erskine had replied when asked what was the most important quality any architect needed to possess: 'Above all, you must love people.'

There is nothing ambiguous here. The key factor for two of the most accomplished architects and urban designers working in Europe has been the attention to the fine detail of human needs and aspirations, for spaces and places which enlarge the human capacity for self-confidence and sociability. This is easier said than done. Human happiness, it is often claimed, resists the art of the planner, as well as the builder or the engineer. Many writers would argue that one can no more plan for those occasions of townscape epiphany – cycling through the Fredericksburg district of Copenhagen on a crisp winter's morning, for example, or strolling through streets of Georgian terraces in Dublin or Liverpool – than one can plan for fine weather. This aesthetic pessimism has to be challenged.

CHAPTER 11

THE SOCIAL DIMENSION OF URBAN DESIGN

KEN WORPOLE

11.1 Waterloo Station, London. When urban design fails: the pedestrian obstacle course at the entrance to the station.

In fact, it is easier to argue about what results from an absence of planning, than what results from conscious design. When one considers what can arise from bad planning or design – say, driving out of a multi-storey car park at night into a narrow, poorly lit cul de sac, or trying to negotiate a pedestrian underpass pushing a pram – then one can begin to see how planning, design and the arts of human place-making can in fact make the difference between human happiness and human despair.

Nowhere in the built environment is this becoming more critical than in the design of public space, an area where Gehl and his colleagues in particular have managed to combine aesthetic quality with a commitment to human enjoyment and urban well-being.

Over the past decade, political interest in the UK in the quality of streets, parks and other public spaces – often described as the 'public realm' – has grown enormously. Yet to a large degree, this has been an overdue response to a genuine public concern that Britain's streets, parks and public areas have become less well maintained, dirtier, and more prone to graffiti and vandalism over the years. There is certainly evidence to support this assumption, particularly in relation to parks, where decline in facilities and budgets has been well documented.[1] The newly formed CABE Space project has already attracted national attention with its 'Wasted Space' campaign, drawing attention to the myriad bits and pieces of derelict, vandalised, fly-tipped land which disfigure so many neighbourhoods and inner-city communities.[2]

Furthermore, Britain's parks and public spaces now appear to lack the quality that many people see elsewhere in Europe – in city centres and in residential areas – as they travel on business or holiday abroad. It is frequently said that Britain's public realm lacks imaginative design and flair, as well as being less child-friendly.

As a result, there have been many reports and government initiatives in the UK on such issues in recent years, including *People, Parks and Cities* (1996), *Towards an Urban Renaissance* (1999), the Select Committee Report on *Town and Country Parks* (1999), *The Urban White Paper* (2001), *PPG 17: Public Spaces* (2002), the Urban Green Spaces Task Force Report *Green Spaces, Better Places* (2002), the ODPM report, *Living Places: Cleaner, Safer, Greener* (2002) and *Sustainable Communities: An Action Programme* (2003) among others. In addition, the Heritage Lottery Fund established an enormously popular Urban Parks Programme in 1997 (now the Public Parks Initiative), and other lottery boards have also targeted green spaces and play projects across the UK. A dedicated 'Space Unit' devoted to these issues, already mentioned, was established at CABE (Commission for Architecture and the Built Environment) in May 2003.

Every regeneration document, or urban design brief, now pays attention – even if it is only lip service – to the requirement to provide high-quality public space. *The Good Place Guide: Urban Design in Britain and Ireland*, by John Billingham and Richard Cole,[3] provides a tantalising glimpse of some of the more successful examples of townscaping and place-making in contemporary towns and cities. This guide has not been without its critics, who have variously described many of the schemes as representing 'a hard townscape for a hard society',[4] or as paying too little attention to the needs of children.[5] Nevertheless, some of the schemes have brought a new *élan* to particular waterfronts, town squares and shopping streets, and that is to be greatly welcomed.

The Good Place Guide, however, illustrates one of the formalistic problems which besets the theory and practice of urban design, in that it relies wholly on still photography to convey the messages of success or failure. Yet it is salutary to remember that one of the early exponents of good public space design, William H. Whyte, based many of his observations and lessons for

11.2 The Promenade Planté in Paris extends above the streets of Paris from the Bastille almost to the Bois de Vincennes, along a disused railway viaduct. The new park was created in 1988 by Philippe Mathieux and Jacques Vergeley and is hugely popular and well policed.

11.3 Norr Mälarstrand, Stockholm. Erik Glemme's linear park is a masterpiece of landscape design.

designers on the use of time-lapse photography. For Whyte, spaces and places can only be fully understood through the medium of time. Indeed, the opening image in Whyte's marvellous book, *City: Rediscovering the Center*, is a photograph of Whyte himself squatting behind some garbage cans filming passers-by.[6]

The social meaning of urban design has as much to learn from film (including popular feature films and the *mises en scène* they represent in street scenes, park meetings) as it does from computer graphics and artistic impressions. In the absence of film, a programme of observations at different times of day, week and season, on the use (and abuse) of public space, is crucial to learning the lessons on long-term use, appreciation and sustainability.

Furthermore, in modern urban design and regeneration initiatives, the new links with transport strategies mean that there will be an increasing emphasis on linear spaces, on the networks and flows of people in the public realm, rather than on formally self-contained or bordered places. For myself, two of the great pieces of urban design in Europe have been Erik Glemme's linear park at Norr Mälarstrand in Stockholm, developed between 1941 and 1943, and, much more recently, the Promenade Planté in Paris.[7]

This linear walk extends above the streets of Paris from the Bastille almost to the Bois de Vincennes, along a disused railway viaduct, and is one of the most remarkable new parks in Paris. The original elevated freight railway was closed in 1969 and in 1988 the new park was created by Philippe Mathieux and Jacques Vergeley. It is enormously popular with walkers, joggers, pram-pushers, and others, though the use of bicycles or skates is forbidden.

A number of government ministers, including the Prime Minister himself, have made street quality and safety a priority issue. Even television companies are now commissioning 'makeover' programmes about public spaces – turning unloved pedestrian or vegetated eyesores into glamorous arcadias with a flourish of a magic wand – following the success of similar formats with domestic interiors and private gardens. Channel 4 Television has already announced that it is to commission a series of five programmes which will detail a year spent 'making over' the town of Castleford, felt to be in need of physical regeneration and improvement.[8] A key premise of such initiatives is the belief that neglected and unattractive environments not only send messages to people that their quality of life does not count very much politically, but that they can also be breeding grounds for vandalism and anti-social behaviour, particularly among children and young people.

Yet what most of these initiatives, programmes and studies have in common is that they regard public space as primarily a physical matter, which good design (allied to a little bit of public consultation) can largely solve. Yet as a forthcoming study of new public spaces in Glasgow is likely to demonstrate,[9] design alone doesn't guarantee success. Of five commissions to design new public spaces, three were regarded as having failed within a year of completion, largely due to vandalism, misuse or sheer public indifference and neglect. Such problems can occur in the best of schemes, as the photographs of the rapid decline and eventual abandonment of the northern section of prestigious Museum Park in Rotterdam, designed by the Office of Metropolitan Architecture, between 1985 and 1993, show.

That lesson has been learnt in many other places also, where a mix of prettification schemes, token works of public art, and a few new planters and street benches, have often been vandalised within weeks, leaving the areas supposedly regenerated looking just as depressing and unloved as they did before.

Not only are there concerns that a bland approach to urban design is producing a standard repertoire of new townscape features – usually taking wholesale pedestrianisation as its starting point, and then throwing a random collection of catalogue street furniture into the mix – but commercial forces are also moving in as the other half of a kind of pincer movement, reducing many small towns' economic diversity to a handful of chain stores and themed pubs. This latter point certainly comes across in the CPRE's new report, *Lie of the Land*, whose author, Flora Gathorne-Hardy, writes:

> **Year by year, England is becoming less varied and more and more the same. High streets are becoming almost indistinguishable from one another. We are developing nowhere places, where the buildings and shops in one place are identical to those in the next town.**[10]

Good urban design can counteract this homogenisation of townscape to some extent, but poor or inappropriate design can exacerbate it, and in many places now does.

These arguments have of course been heard before, notably in the writings of French anthropologist, Marc Augé, whose book *Non-Places: Introduction to an Anthropology of Super-Modernity* (1995),[11] has had such an impact on the cultural geography of place in the past decade. It is increasingly evident that new paving, clean lines and public art alone will not bring about that elusive (possibly mythical?) urban conviviality and sense of place so earnestly sought by governments and citizens alike.

In order to explore fully what is meant by the concept of the public realm – which is surely necessary if we are to design appropriately for it – then the term should be broken down into its several constituent elements. To my mind, the public realm actually consists of at least three elements: **(1)** a physical realm; **(2)** a symbolic (or political) realm; and **(3)** a relational realm. Unless these three are somehow in concert, then sustainability is likely to be elusive.

The physical realm has already been discussed, and continues to remain the focus of most present regeneration activity. The symbolic realm is an altogether harder nut to crack. A quick way of understanding what it feels to inhabit a townscape with a high degree of symbolic authority, can be gained by a walk through the City of London. Every street sign, lamp-post, bollard, rubbish bin,

11.4 **The northern section of Museum Park in Rotterdam. Designed by the Office of Metropolitan Architecture, completed in 1993.**

11.5 **The same park in 2001, just after the bulldozers had finished their work. Lack of maintenance and vandalism reduced the park to an eyesore.**

11.6 **Victoria Square, Birmingham, UK. The pedestrianisation of the busy streets saw the creation of a great fountain and monumental steps, with clear links to New Street to the east and Centenary Square to the west. Designed by the Landscape Practice Group of Birmingham City Council, the Square acts as a gathering place.**

park gate, flower bed, is imprinted or adorned with the coat of arms of the Corporation of London (which also has its own police force). The symbolic message is clear: this is our territory, we manage and maintain it, and if there are any complaints it is clear where responsibility lies.

Compare this level of symbolic authority in the public realm with that of any of the city of London's neighbouring boroughs, where the streets signs today are now in a jumble of different styles, the lamp-posts are fly-posted daily, the rubbish bins are sponsored by McDonald's or some other fast food company, the streets are cleaned by a changing army of private contractors, and even street security is now in the hands of at least three different agencies, all tricked out in different shades of fluorescent vests or para-military uniforms. Who is in charge here? The answer is everybody and nobody. The public realm here has been stripped of all its civic – and indeed its political – associations, and is now just another market-place of contracted and sub-contracted services. Design coherence is simply not a factor in this mélange.

Of course, there are exceptions. Two of the most successful pieces of new urban design in the UK in recent years can be found in Birmingham and Sheffield, particularly in relation to the town halls and their immediate environs. The pedestrianisation of Birmingham's Victoria Square and the creation of a great fountain and monumental steps, with clear links to New Street to the east and Centenary Square to the west, are very impressive.

This was designed by the Landscape Practice Group of Birmingham City Council. Equally impressive, and the work of another local authority in-house design team, are the Sheffield Peace Gardens, immediately adjacent to Sheffield Town Hall. Both successfully restore that crucial notion of the town hall curtilage being of great symbolic importance spatially.

This will not come as a surprise to the French, for example, where the space in front of the Hôtel de Ville, is always immaculately maintained and used for weddings, festivals and even demonstrations, nor to the Dutch, where in the traditional genre of paintings of children's games (*kinderspelen*), many of these portray children at play in front of the town hall, emphasising the link between games, rules and citizenship.

The third element, the relational realm, is perhaps the most important of all. For it is in public spaces that many of us sustain our sense of physical contact and familiarity with other people, in the daily routines of setting out from home, waiting at the bus-stop or station, taking the children to the park,or going shopping. The late Katherine Shonfield, expressed this understanding beautifully when she wrote:

> [Another] principle behind the expansion of public space is the physical experience of democracy. Ideas of democracy are shifting and electronic media, like E-mail and the Net, bring new opportunities for chance meetings, and a sense of public membership. But they are no substitute for the bodily experience of democracy. This bodily experience of the random good will of the majority, unmediated by hardware, is as fundamental to the experience of humanity as the loving touch of the parent.[12]

The planner principally responsible for the excellent Public Realm Strategy produced in 2002 by Bath & North Somerset Council, Penelope Tollitt, wrote in her introduction:

> In legal terms the public realm can be used to 'pass and repass', allowing us to gain access to land and buildings and for the passage of goods and people. But the public realm gives benefits beyond 'just' access. It helps to structure our lives.[13]

This structuring of social life, and its daily replenishment, can either be supported by attractive design, careful management and maintenance (allied to a strong sense of stewardship and security), or it can be left to go to the dogs, sometimes literally.

11.7 The Peace Gardens, Sheffield, UK, immediately adjacent to the Town Hall were designed by the City Council's in-house team. A great success.

There is no doubt that increased car dependency, abetted by the pre-eminence of traffic engineering priorities around issues of street design, scale and management, has had a baleful effect on local relational intimacy, though in many places this is, thankfully, now being reversed. The private car has been an important instrument of freedom and mobility on the larger scale, but disastrous at neighbourhood level. The renewed interest in encouraging a return to walking, for health, ease of accessibility and environmental reasons, will require forms of urban design that are much more responsive to pavement flows, coherent lighting schemes, visibility and security, and the sense that a pedestrian network, like a chain, is only as strong as its weakest link.

The social relations of the town or city can also be improved by the re-allocation of space for temporary festivals and events, which also require new urban design skills. In Europe, the most spectacular piece of spatial engineering in recent years has been the annual recreation of a public beach in the heart of Paris, by the side of the Seine. Allied to this measure has been closing of the main freeway along the Seine to cars every Sunday, making the road available for cyclists, roller-bladers, joggers and walkers, a move that has been immensely popular and is now already part of the new Parisian urban calendar.

The debate about how to finance, manage and maintain a high quality public realm is not going to go away – in fact, it is only just starting. The appearance and quality of Britain's streets, parks, playgrounds, squares, precincts, railway stations and other public spaces are not only a matter of unsightliness and environmental hazard, but more importantly provide a barometer of how much we value and are prepared to support civic life and culture. The scale and quality of urban design are central to this debate, though design alone cannot solve many of the problems which are raised in modern market societies about civility and conduct in the public domain. For this, design has to be part of a new political vision as to how we live in cities once again.

Such a project is fraught with difficulty because we now have at least one generation of children – often denied the freedom of the streets by their anxious parents, and for whom the car is the principal aid to mobility – who no longer feel comfortable in their own environmental skin. The lack of knowledge of local townscape and local history among many is worrying. The kind of environmental education pioneered by Colin Ward and others at the Town and Country Planning Association in the 1960s and 1970s, involving school-children studying local streets, parks and the local built environment, through visits and interviews with residents, would now be frowned upon.[14] While Citizenship is to be a new subject on the National Curriculum, its remit is largely institutional and constitutional rather than geographical, topographical or urbane. How will future generations address the agenda of good place-making?

Here is a job for CABE, along with those in local government and the planning profession who want to grasp the nettle of civic design. A campaign to put environmental education (including matters of good urban design) back on to the school curriculum, and to make such knowledge an essential part of citizenship studies, is vital. By definition such an understanding of the art of place-making starts not in the abstract, but in the quality of the local environment itself. Exceptional projects such as the Hackney Building Exploratory, along with work by some local architecture centres, have shown the way. It is time to put environmental education once again at the heart of the relationship between school and the wider society.

11.8 The closing of the main freeway along the Seine to cars every Sunday has made the road available for cyclists, roller-bladders, joggers and walkers, It now plays a vital role in the new Parisian urban calendar. London may follow suit with proposals to pedestrianise the Victoria Embankment on Sundays.

Notes

1 Urban Parks Forum, *Public Parks Assessment*, May 2001. This survey estimated that some £1.3 billion in revenue expenditure had been lost to parks in the twenty years prior to the publication of the report.

2 Commission for Architecture and the Built Environment, *Wasted Space*, London: CABE, September, 2003.

3 John Billingham and Richard Cole, *The Good Place Guide: Urban Design in Britain and Ireland*, Batsford Books: London, 2002.

4 Judith Ryser, in *Urban Design Quarterly*, Autumn 2002, Issue 84, pp. 40-1.

5 Ken Worpole, *No Particular Place to Go? Children, Young People and Public Space*, Birmingham: Groundwork UK, 2003.

6 William H. Whyte, *City: Rediscovering the Center*, New York: Doubleday, 1990. It is interesting that one of the largest set of page references in the Index appears under the heading 'Schmoozing'.

7 For a fine essay on Glemme, see Thorbjörn Andersson, 'Erik Glemme and the Stockholm Park System', in *Modern Landscape Architecture*, edited by Marc Treib, Cambridge, MA: MIT Press, 1993.

8 'Channel 4 outlines more plans for town makeover', *Architects' Journal*, 24 April 2003.

9 Pauline Gallacher, *Looking Again at the Five Spaces*, NESTA Fellowship report, forthcoming.

10 Flora Gathorne-Hardy, *Lie of the Land*, London: CPRE, 2003.

11 Marc Augé, *Non-Places: Introduction to an Anthropology of Super-Modernity*, London: Verso, 1995.

12 Katherine Shonfield, 'At home with strangers: public space and the new urbanity', in *The Richness of Cities*, London: Comedia & Demos, 1998. The untimely death in 2003 of Katherine Vaughan Williams (Shonfield), has been a great loss to the world of humane architecture and design thinking.

13 *Life in the Public Realm*, Bath: Planning Services, Bath and North East Somerset Council, 2002.

14 For a brief history of this era of environmental education, see Eileen Adams, 'Education for participation: art and the built environment' in Ken Worpole (ed.), *Richer Futures: Fashioning a New Politics*, London: Earthscan Books, 1999.

Despite the advent of women's liberation in the 1970s, women's views continue to be ignored in a crucial area influencing social life: the planning of our cities. Whether or not male town planners have deliberately excluded women from having a say in the development of the physical infrastructure of society, or merely failed to recognise the potential women might have for making a positive contribution to the planning of our cities and social spaces, our cities and those who live in them (male and female) have suffered the consequences.

Women have traditionally been the 'carers' in society – those who attend to the needs of the young, the frail, the aged, the poor. This remains substantially true even in the context of the increasing role of women in the paid workforce. As well as their tacit knowledge of family and community needs acquired through their traditional caring role, in recent years women have acquired explicit knowledge through their participation in higher education and their involvement in professions, trades and delivery of community services. Yet, in the designing of housing and urban environments, the expertise arising from this combination of tacit and explicit knowledge has been largely ignored, resulting in houses and urban environments which alienate and divide.

CHAPTER 12

MEN SHOULDN'T DECIDE EVERYTHING

WOMEN AND THE PUBLIC REALM

MARDIE TOWNSEND

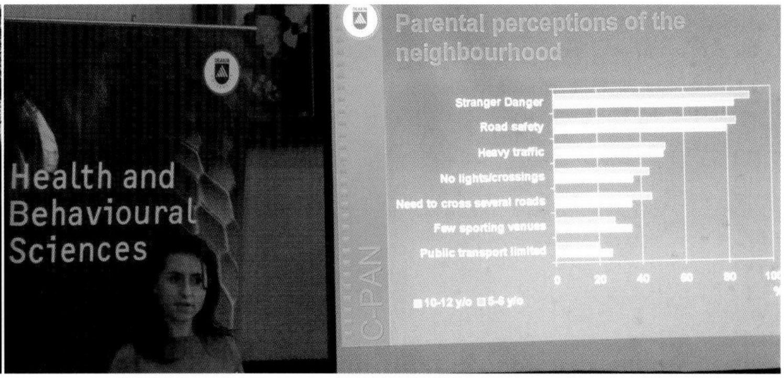

12.1 Putting women's views on the design and planning agenda. Despite women's liberation, their views on the planning of cities have been ignored.

12.2 Presentation on 'parental perceptions of the neighbourhood', including issues such as 'stranger danger' and road safety.

Having somewhere pleasant to live is important to all of us. But finding housing that meets our needs is often difficult. Family circumstances change, our incomes may fluctuate, neighbourhoods may become more or less congenial. Often we think of housing in terms of the physical structure: houses, roads, schools, shops and so on, yet what makes somewhere pleasant to live is often less tangible: the support of friends and neighbours in good times and bad, recognising familiar faces on the street and in the park, an open view at the end of the street, and feeling safe. Getting this mix of physical and social elements 'right' is a challenge that can be met only if city, town and country planners listen to the voices of local communities.[1]

The importance of housing for health and well-being was recognised in Article 25 of the United Nations Declaration on Human Rights, which states:

everyone has the right to a standard of living adequate for the health and wellbeing of himself and of his family, including food, clothing, housing, medical care and necessary social services.[2]

However, our expectations of housing that is 'adequate for . . . health and wellbeing' have changed since the Declaration on Human Rights was penned. For many families, the idea of children sharing a room is anathema, and the thought of having to cope with just one bathroom is incomprehensible.

Changes have also occurred in the ways household members perceive and relate to their local community. In the past, people expected to be part of a community to which they would feel a sense of belonging, and which would meet their needs for services and social engagement. Like the right to housing, the sense of community and the opportunity for people to have their needs for services and social engagement largely met within their own community have been (until recently) taken for granted by many people. Recently, however, for many, the picture of neighbourhoods filled with people who know and care for one another, and who share in one another's joys and sorrows, has been replaced by the reality of dormitory suburbs where people no longer know their neighbours, let alone fulfil a mutual support role.

Despite major changes in the factors influencing household and community life, the legacy of the past remains with us: in the physical infrastructure which surrounds us; and in the psychosocial paradigms which influence our expectations and our planning. The need to take account of changes in demographic, economic, environmental, technological, political and social aspects of modern life, at the same time as recognising the constraints and opportunities posed by the physical and psychosocial legacies of the past, creates a challenge for urban designers, planners, developers and policy-makers.

Of particular relevance in this situation are the outcomes of two studies exploring women's views on housing and neighbourhoods for the future: an initial project undertaken in the UK in 1999,[3] and a follow-up study completed in 2001.[4] The studies were designed to explore women's aspirations for housing and neighbourhoods by the year 2020, and to benchmark against those aspirations in assessing a particular urban extension proposal.

TRADITIONAL APPROACHES TO URBAN DESIGN

Jonathon Porritt, in his Foreword to the report on the follow-up study, said:

It is quite astonishing how rarely developers stop to ask ... questions [about whether or not people will want to live there] before starting work on the blueprints. And the construction industry as a whole has been slow to learn from other sectors that have already discovered the real value of consulting their customers, over and above a basic market approval of their products.[5]

Women in particular have come to expect that their needs and views will be, to a large extent, overlooked, ignored or misinterpreted by designers and developers. Wendy Saunderson observes that 'it is only within the past 15 to 20 years . . . that British town planning has acknowledged its failure to consider women's position in the production and consumption of urban planning and design'.[6] Yet, despite recognition of this problem,[7] male-orientated perceptions and expectations continue to dominate the conceptualisation of space and place, including within the planning and design professions.

Sheila Scraton and Beccy Watson note: 'Traditionally, urban geography located men in the public city spaces and women in the private, domestic spaces, usually on the outskirts or in suburbia.'[8] However, in the context of recent economic and social changes, including women's increased participation in the workforce, such a dichotomy is no longer appropriate. Day notes that '[the] assumption that women will stay home in the suburbs, caring for children and home' and the 'separation of home from jobs, retail, public transit, etc. decreases women's public space opportunities and increases the burden of care-giving'.[9] Even when women do adopt the traditional care-giving role, Kettel observes: 'Women's particular housing needs, such as adequate space, play areas for children, access to shopping and transportation, and security, are rarely taken into consideration in the design of urban structures and neighbourhoods'.[10]

Why is this so? The feminist movement has been influential since the early 1970s, yet still urban planners do not take adequate heed of the voices of women when planning our cities. Could this be because men as urban planners are not only clinging to past realities and outdated paradigms of the roles of men and women in society, but also that women see spaces and places differently from men? Evidence from a recent Australian study indicates that there are gender-related differences in the ways people interact within social spaces,[11] so it seems likely that there may be corresponding gender-related differences in perceptions of social spaces. Lefebvre notes that 'social space is neither object nor subject, but appears as the intangible outcome of history, society and culture'.[12] In light of the differences between the social and cultural experiences of women and men over the past century, it would not be surprising if there were gender differences in perceptions of social spaces.

Catherine Hakim proposes another explanation for the failure of those in authority to listen to the views of women. She says: 'The main reason is that they want to treat women as a single-issue constituency.'[13]

Whatever the cause, the reality of the mismatch between the views of so-called 'ordinary women' and the views of planning and urban design 'experts' was plainly evident in the first of the 'Women and Housing Towards 2020' studies.[14] Interestingly, in the 'Women and Housing Towards 2020' studies, diversity of views within the group has been seen as a strength rather than a problem. While there were diverse views expressed, the participants demonstrated an amazing capacity to come to a consensus view which reflected the experiences of them all.

PUTTING WOMEN'S VIEWS ON THE DESIGN AND PLANNING AGENDA

A review of the literature and consultations with 'experts' as part of the first of the 'Women and Housing Towards 2020' studies indicated two main drivers for future change in respect of housing: the rapid development of information and communications technology,[15] and the change in social structures related to increased life expectancy and changes in household size and composition, marriage and divorce rates.[16]

Most 'experts' argued that lifestyles reflecting the knowledge-based economy would account for the majority of households by 2020, and some considered that this would be the case much sooner – by perhaps 2005. In general, experts' views of future homes implied a concept of home as a multifunctional space, providing:

- an office for home-based working;
- a substitute for short-term hospital and long-stay care;
- a centre for learning and substitute school room;
- a virtual global shopping mall;
- a virtual community centre;
- a venue for technology-based home entertainment.[17]

The women in this study, in contrast to the 'technological determinism' view put forward by the 'experts', defined housing issues and the drivers for future change much more broadly. Though they acknowledged the importance of developments in technology and of changing demographic profiles and household structures, they also highlighted the influence of:

- pressures to achieve 'ecological sustainability';
- growing Europeanisation of Britain;
- changes in employment patterns and arrangements;
- the nature and condition of existing housing stock;
- government policies in the areas of housing, health, education, welfare/social security;
- changing community attitudes and expectations.

In contrast to the views put forward in the literature and through many of the key informant interviews, women in our focus groups argued for a rather different concept of home and neighbourhood. From their perspective, many of the homes we will live in by 2020 are not well suited for multi-functioning. Moreover, even where they are suitable, the women in this study questioned whether or not living, working, caring or being cared for, shopping, being educated and entertained in the same space would be a congenial lifestyle for many. Rather than having multi-functional houses, the women involved in this program expressed a preference for housing within multi-functional neighbourhoods.

Ideally, in the view of women in this study, homes would be set in neighbourhoods characterised by community cohesion, social inclusion, equity, safety and security. They would possess the physical infrastructure to support community-oriented lifestyles, and would provide:

- places for 'home' working;
- centres for local shopping and markets;
- facilities for childcare and other services;
- alternative 'public' transport options;

12.3 Focus group discussion. Why is there such a gulf between the aspirations of women and proposals for new planning development?

- a wide range of leisure opportunities;
- access to non-monetary exchange market-places.

These would be vibrant, mixed use, multifunctional neighbourhoods where the focus would be on social capital, human capital, physical capital and natural capital, rather than on financial capital.

Increasingly, in industrialised nations, we have moved to a more privatised and individualised lifestyle, and this is reflected in the 'expert' views on housing for the future. Yet this is the opposite of what the women in these studies wanted – a greater sense community. They wanted a future in which the loneliness and isolation experienced by many at present are replaced by a greater sense of community and social cohesion, and by better links between those within the community in different age groups. In contrast to the recent trend towards viewing public open space as 'a waste of potential development opportunities', these women recognised the need both for community facilities and for public open space within residential areas. Without these features, they considered that it would be difficult to promote the community-oriented lifestyles which underpin community cohesion and create a sense of safety and security, which they saw as a very high priority.

The literature suggests that the path we are taking currently is one that undermines civil society and social capital, and that has detrimentaleffects on individual and community health and well-being. Moreover, it is a downward spiral: as we reduce activities in the public realm (by encouraging 'virtual' rather than 'real' communities), we reduce people's sense of safety and comfort in public spaces, and this leads to a further reduction in the use of public open spaces.

According to Brian Furnass, well-being includes: satisfactory human relationships, meaningful occupation, opportunities for contact with nature, creative expression, and making a positive contribution to human society.[18] Well-designed public spaces will facilitate and encourage these features, and if they are designed in an inclusive manner, they will be meeting the fifth of these requirements before they are even physically in place. The 'Women and Housing Towards 2020' Stage 1 study indicates that those in charge of urban planning and design need to adopt a more inclusive approach by listening to the voices of the people concerned and understanding what makes a place livable to them. This includes the views of women, who make up more than 50 per cent of the population, live longer than their male counterparts, and play a major role in the care and nurture of the young, elderly and those with disabilities (i.e. those who may not be able to speak for themselves). Only by engaging women in the 'public process' of planning both 'public' and 'private' spaces can we ensure that the vision of housing and neighbourhoods expressed in the introduction to this chapter is realized.

ENGAGING WOMEN IN THE PLANNING PROCESS

A follow-up study was undertaken during 2001 involving women from the Stage 1 study in a series of structured focus groups to consider proposals for a large urban extension in north Swindon (UK). The Stage 2 focus groups compared the aspirations of women in the Stage 1 study with the proposals for the development, to identify the extent to which the proposals (if enacted) would fulfil or fall short of those aspirations. The key research questions for the Stage 2 study were:

- Is the layout likely to result in the kind of neighbourhood envisaged for 2020?
- Do the proposed facilities and services match the requirements anticipated for 2020?
- Are the designs for the homes like those expected for 2020?

The Stage 2 study found important gaps between the women's aspirations and the proposals for these new neighbourhoods. Given that the women involved in this study were 'ordinary' women, drawn from a range of different contexts, it is reasonable to assume that the views they were expressing would be similar to the views held by many women. Likewise, given that the

12.4 Low and high-rise housing, Raleigh Park, USA. Home as a haven from the outside world.

12.5 Community tree planting encourages grass-roots participation in green projects.

plans for the developments being reviewed comply with current planning guidance and reflect current 'good practice', it is likely that they also are fairly typical. Why, then, is there such a gulf between the aspirations of women and the proposals for new planning developments?

UNDERSTANDING AND ADDRESSING THE PROBLEM

The explanation for this disjunction can be found in a combination of legacies of the past and expectations of the future. Recent decades have seen changes in the aspirations and expectations of many people in terms of their housing and their neighbourhoods which have not been matched by the reality. We have, in effect, a situation of 'past', 'present' and 'future', both in terms of the physical structures of housing and neighbourhoods and of the psychosocial lenses through which we look at them.

Existing housing stock (a legacy of the past) is often inadequate to meet the demands of the present, with inappropriate space standards, a high level of inflexibility, and infrastructure inadequate to support the technologies of the modern era. New housing is often modelled on former housing styles, and while it may have more up-to-date features such as multiple living spaces, it still often fails to meet the needs of modern lifestyles, let alone those of the future. As one woman in the first UK study put it: 'I have a broom cupboard in my house; they call it a bedroom!' Imagine how different it would be if houses were designed with in-built flexibility: modular construction with some walls that could be moved as household needs change! The women involved in the first study expressed a strong view that appropriate flexible housing designs would be more likely to occur if women were involved in the design process. Instead of women's experience as the housekeepers, cleaners, counsellors and social organisers in households being something which consigns them to a position of limited influence, planners and designers should use them as 'expert consultants'. After all, where would most households be without 'Mum – the problem solver'?

Also, we need to do away with the idealised vision of 'home as a haven from the outside world', which remains dominant in the minds of planners and designers, as well as those who live in those homes. This vision was based in the 1950s when the workforce was predominantly male, and where women stayed home to care for children and to 'keep the home fires burning'. It does not take account of the modern realities of family structures, with an increasing proportion of single-parent households, and of economic participation, with many households now dual income. For many women especially, home is simply another work setting imposed at the beginning and end of every day. Unless people revise the psychosocial lenses through which they view the functioning of their homes, the gulf between the legacy of the idealised vision and the modern reality will undermine their sense of well-being. The women in this study recognised that new visions of home are needed – visions that incorporate relevant elements of the vision of the past but which also take account of the realities of daily life. Recognition of the increasing role of women in the workforce and the need for community-based systems for meeting some of the needs previously met by stay-at-home Mums would be a good start. Perhaps planners could facilitate the establishment of community non-monetary exchange schemes in neighbourhoods, through which skills could be exchanged (for example, where the supervision of and help with children's homework, which normally forms yet another pressure point for working single parents at the end of a long day, could be taken on by another community member with the appropriate skills).

In the neighbourhoods in which people live, the legacy of the past remains with us too. The physical layouts and service provision of many existing and emerging housing developments are designed on the assumption that every household will have at least one car, so that those without vehicles are isolated from schools, shops and services. Moreover, the idealised notion of cohesive, self-sustaining communities, which contrasts starkly with the reality in many neighbourhoods, has become a myth that fosters a sense of insecurity and dissatisfaction with modern spatial aggregations. Again, it is obvious that the inappropriateness of past physical layouts and service provision that are evident in the face of present needs will be even more problematic in the future. While there is no way that the clock can be turned back to retrieve the cohesive communities of the past, and to dream of such is foolhardy, our focus groups recognised the need and the opportunity for developing new notions and models of community which reflect cohesiveness built around the realities of modern life. The establishment of non-monetary exchange schemes noted above is one way of building community cohesion.

Perhaps even more crucially in terms of future housing and neighbourhoods, the legacies of traditionalism and specialism among planners, developers and policy-makers are ensuring that the present is constrained by the past, and that the future is approached through incremental change rather than a radical new vision. Many planners see themselves as regulators rather than facilitators of change. With some notable exceptions (for example, the Beddington Zero Energy Development – BedZED – and the Sherwood Energy Village), this results in an inappropriate and unsustainable approach to addressing the needs for housing and neighbourhoods of the future. The Women and Housing Stage 1 project identified energy-efficient housing, alternative energy sources and recycling of water and household waste as strong preferences for future housing. Yet the Stage 2 project found that, apart from meeting basic building regulations, energy efficiency and sustainability issues had not been taken into account in the proposed development. Imagine if the views of the so-called 'ordinary women' involved in the Women and Housing Towards 2020 studies were taken seriously by planners and developers – perhaps quality of life would not only be improved for this generation but for generations to come, through averting potential disasters such as climate change.

The Women and Housing Stage 2 project, by contrast to the majority of housing developments, engaged 'grassroots' people in the process of visioning for the future and has provided a forum for such people to interact with the planners, developers and policy-makers in charge of a large urban redevelopment project. Perhaps because of the 'naïvité' of the women involved, the planners, developers and policy-makers were confronted with questions about the rationale for adopting particular strategies or approaches to the development. In the discussion that ensued, new possibilities for overcoming the legacies of the past and for addressing the needs of the future were developed. Judging by the reactions of all involved, it was a process that merits more widespread use.

Notes

1 C.L. Andrews and M. Townsend, *Women @ 2020.Living: Perspectives on Housing and Neighbourhoods of the Future*, UK Housing Corporation Report, Abingdon: Northcourt Press, 2000, p.4.

2 United Nations, *Universal Declaration of Human Rights*, New York: UN, 1948. Part 1.

3 Andrews and Townsend, *Women @ 2020.Living.*

4 C.L. Andrews, W. Reardon-Smith and M. Townsend, *But Will We Want To Live There? Planning for People and Neighbourhoods in 2020*, UK Housing Corporation Report, Abingdon: Northcourt Press, 2002.

5 Ibid., p. 3.

6 W. Saunderson, 'Issues of women's fear in urban space: the case of Belfast', *Women and Environments*, 28–30, Spring/Summer 2001, p. 28.

7 For example, see K. Day, 'The ethic of care and women's experiences of public space', *Journal of Environmental Psychology*, 20: 103–24, 2000; D. Massey, *Space, Place and Gender*, Cambridge: Polity Press, 1994; and S. Scraton and B. Watson, 'Gendered cities: women and public leisure space in the postmodern city', *Leisure Studies*, 1998, 17: 123–37.

8 Scraton and Watson 'Gendered cities: Women and public leisure space in the postmodern city', *Leisure Studies*, 17: 135.

9 Day, 'The ethic of care', p. 109.

10 B. Kettel, 'Women, health and the environment', *Social Science and Medicine*, 1996, 42(10), 1374.

11 J. Hughes and W. Stone, 'Family and community life', *Family Matters*, 2003, 65: 40–7.

12 H. Lefebvre, *The Production of Space*, trans. D. Nicholson-Smith, Oxford: Blackwell, 1991, p. 92.

13 C. Hakim, 'Competing family models, competing social policies', *Family Matters*, 2003, 64: 52–61, (p. 52).

14 See Andrews and Townsend, *Women @ 2020.Living.*

15 For example, see John D. Arras (ed.), *Bringing the Hospital Home*, Baltimore, MD: Johns Hopkins University, 1995; Daniel Fox and Carol Raphael, *Home Based Care for a New Century*, Oxford: Blackwell, 1997; Penny Gurstein, *Planning for Telework and Home-Based Employment: A Canadian Survey on Integrating Work into Residential Environments*, Vancouver: Centre for Future Studies, University of British Colombia, 1995; Geoff Mulgan (ed.), *Life after Politics: New Thinking for the 21st Century*, London: HarperCollins, 1997; Liza

Provenzano, *Telecommuting: A Trend towards the Hoffice*, Kingston, ON: IRC Press, 1994; and Marjorie Scott, *Telematics for Health: The Role of Telehealth and Telemedicine in Homes and Community*, Oxford: Radcliffe Medical Press, 1995.

16 For example, see Robin Ellison (ed.), *Family Breakdown and Pensions*, Oxford: Butterworth, 1997; Lisa Harker, *A Secure Future? Social Security and the Family in a Changing World*, London: CPAG, 1996; Irene Hoskins (ed.), *Combining Work and Elder Care: A Challenge for Now and the Future*, Geneva: International Labour Office, 1996; Carolyn M. Morell, *Unwomanly Conduct: The Challenges of Intentional Childlessness*, London: Routledge, 1994; and Jane Wheelock and Åge Mariussen (eds.), *Households, Work and Economic Change: A Comparative Institutional Perspective*, Boston, MA: Kluwer Academic Publishers, 1997.

17 Andrews and Townsend, *Women @ 2020.Living*, p. 9.

18 B. Furnass, 'Introduction', in *Survival, Health and Wellbeing into the Twenty First Century*, proceedings of a conference held November 30–December 1, 1995 at the Australian National University, Canberra.

PART ONE: THE MODERN MOVEMENT

The twentieth century was characterized, first of all, by its rejection of the idea of external space as something sculpted from the built volume, that is to say 'recessed' or 'inscribed' space. This was accompanied by an ignorance of what constitutes public space and the fact that scale alone is not adequate to give it meaning, and was followed, in the latter part of the century, by a gradual return to traditional ways of thought, albeit through lack of a suitable alternative to established theories. These events began in a climate where the needs of the human body were often disregarded and the extreme position of the Modern Movement held sway, as in Germany with the Bauhaus and in France with Le Corbusier. Their theories were promulgated and exercised on a large scale as an answer to post-war reconstruction and the housing shortage in cities and New Towns.

CHAPTER 13

POST MODERN MOVEMENT

THE 'INSCRIBED' CITY

ALAIN COUSSERAN

The Modern Movement was, in part, an answer to the failure of urban planning in the great industrial sprawls of the nineteenth-century metropolises, and also a manifestation of a new-found freedom born of the reconciliation between art and science since the eighteenth century. The resultant abstract rationalization of space was backed up by three convincing, yet totally unfounded, arguments. The first concerned zoning and the belief that the confining of commercial activity to separate areas was the only way to preserve the residential districts. The second supported the craving for open space with the increasing trend towards low-density construction on greenfield sites. The third argument was based on the belief that the old town centres were archaic and necessarily beyond improvement, so that the only solution was to start afresh outside the existing boundaries, employing new ideas.

The consequences for urban space were to be profound. The compartmentalization of towns led to a dramatic simplification of the urban plan, whereby the sole issue of any considered importance in the design of whole urban districts resided in the provision of a spacious and hygienic environment. Mass production brought about by the new 'alliance' of art and technical practice led to the transformation of houses into mere objects. The infinitely reproducible housing unit was viewed as representative of the basic building block in the efficient production line leading to the construction of the new cities. This production line would result inevitably in the breaking down of the process of fabrication into many separate and smaller processes which, in turn, led to a need for pre-organization of the whole sequence of construction. Predominantly flat and isolated sites were chosen in order to further simplify this process.

The Modern Movement, it can be argued, eliminated the idea of the 'inscribed' space in favour of the 'open' space, and split the function of complex public space into separate areas of specialization. The 'open' space opened the way for the 'green' space which has, unfortunately, become synonymous with 'empty' space.

The street, being the result of a random development, had no place in this new order. All new exterior space was necessarily, therefore, 'open' space, which would turn out to be catastrophic for the urban environment. The change of scale, inherent in an 'open' space, leads rapidly to a loss of visual and dimensional bearings, in contrast to the traditionally planned town where the scale of existing buildings and spaces corresponds with their range of uses. The size of new developments, as result, knew no natural limits.

The 'open' space was intended as a means of 'opening the dwelling to nature, to light and to fresh air' and, as such, was considered a hygienic environment. With the trend in urbanism towards the very ordered yet abstract arrangement of building objects on the site, the 'open' or 'hygienic' space became little more than a non-appropriable void between the volumes, and the distinction between public and private space was swept away. 'Open' space, reduced to little more than circulation space, was not an essential component of the town, but simply a specialized service. 'Public' space and its symbolism were disinherited.

Under the guise of an open attitude towards modernity and the machine age, the uniformly planned neighbourhood would constitute a barrier to progress The mass-produced constructions, while technically efficient and leaving little to chance, were often anchored in time and space, and incapable of adapting to change. With the rise in traffic in towns, the open 'public' space has become more akin to 'polluted' or 'uninhabitable' space, leading, paradoxically, to its introversion.

Our society, confronted as it is with the unprecedented social fracture between the older parts of towns and of those under construction, is still searching for an answer to this problem. Aldo Rossi, the Italian Modern Movement critic, shed some light, at the beginning of the 1990s, on the fact that certain urban forms have remained unchanged throughout time despite many changes in use. But Rossi's theory limits itself to an examination of the built form, whereas, as we have seen, it is the voids that structure towns.

The Krier brothers would discover the idea of 'sculpted' or 'inscribed' external space, which, for them, would be a way of organizing an urban quarter. However, through lack of awareness of the user and of the way in which urban forms come about, they locked themselves into a formal theoretical debate which paid little attention to human needs. Kevin Lynch examined the mental image that inhabitants construct in the course of journeys through the town and concluded that most people's perception of the built environment corresponded to the model of 'sculpted' or 'inscribed' space. Robert Venturi showed, through the study of a wide avenue linking Las Vegas Airport to 'the Strip', the extraordinary example of an urban space defined solely by the use of signs and advertising hoardings, the equivalent of which did not exist in traditional European towns. The analyses of each of these authors are based on the notion of urban space as a system of representation in the same vein as pictorial or language space, which, unfortunately, makes the mistake of disregarding the user. In effect, urban space is not a language but its foundation, and it is first and foremost a production, and not a representation.

13.1 Orchestration of changes in scale in the 'inscribed' space of the street. The passers-by orientate themselves with the axis of the street, not with the buildings on either side.

13.2 'Inscribed' space restructured by the 'service' space. Urban space can be defined as inscribed space, public space and service space.

13.3 Giving meaning to an open space through treatment as an avenue. The alignment of trees became an important element of city planning in the seventeenth century.

PART TWO: THE INSCRIBED CITY

If the city is, truly, a composition of solid and void, then it might more readily be defined as a diverse ensemble of these two opposites, and urban space, which would, then, become an entity in its own right, would, therefore, be perceived as a veritable landscape. The urban landscape has entertained throughout the ages many associations with the garden, its structure and its geometry and its composition has always kept pace with the evolution of garden artistry. In cities, the buildings are mostly grouped together in blocks and terraces, and are rarely free-standing, which, as a result, masks their three-dimensionality. Where blocks are constructed close together, which is usually the case in cities, the street comes to resemble a cleft or 'urban channel' contained between two parallel 'walls'. The passers-by orientate themselves with the axis of the street, and not with that of the buildings on either side, insofar as they have not yet reached their destination, and this is what, for the most part, will constitute their spatial experience of the street. In this example, the space could be said to take on the role of the 'figure', as opposed to the void which will be represented by the building volumes. Urban space is, therefore, an artificial creation, whose material form owes more to that of the human body, or being, and its needs, in terms of the organization of solid and void, materials, lighting, assortment of signs and moving objects, functions and pleasures, efficiency and comfort. Given its complexity, one of the main issues concerning urban space is the attention paid to rhythm.

Urban 'space' can be defined as a function of three notions. These are the 'sculpted' or 'inscribed' space, as described above, the 'public' space and the 'service' space. It is not sufficient to describe it as only that which is found between built volumes or as something that exists in the absence of buildings. It is also the extension of our own being, and of our own experience. As a totally artificial built creation, it follows that urban space has a direct and fundamental relationship with the human being. It will, therefore, necessarily be perceived from within and, at the same time, as within us. We are inscribed in space. Seen from this angle, the city can be thought of as a whole from which space has been 'sculpted' or 'inscribed'.

Urban space is one of the essential vectors for a dynamic urban landscape. As with any project, its formation is a creative process based on what is known of its previous evolution through archaeological research, history and literature. Characterized by 'public' space, the city is by nature social, but the term 'public' space is rather ambiguous signifying something different for user, sociologist, politician, geographer, architect and transport engineer. Its association with 'inscribed' space, as a projection, or extension, of the human being, instils it with a certain dynamism fundamental to its structure and form. It can be described as a space which progressively invents itself, rather than an application of formal archetypes such as the street, the square and the pavement.

Urban form is not something that can be deduced at the outset of a project. It is rather the result of the overlay of several processes at work at a particular moment. As with an analysis, the design and construction of the space only become evident in the multitude of small modifications which take place over the span of its successive states. The basic urban elements which, together, form 'inscribed' space, such as the building volume which encloses it, be it housing or a monument, can only be fully appreciated when viewed in relation to this space. Their understanding will make reference not only to intelligence, history and politics, but also to the experience of the human body, or being, to its displacement through the space, to the pleasure taken in one's passage through the city, and finally to different aspects of time.

The practice of urbanism requires that one take account of time. Projects of this nature rarely last less than ten years, and sometimes more. In this respect, it is difficult to embark on a project with a predetermined notion of what one will end up with, which leads one to the question of what it is about a particular process, or processes, that give rise to living, vibrant cities. These processes, rather than being sequential and accumulative in nature, have more to do with a confrontation between issues of community and individuality,

NOVOTEL

13.4 'Public' space can make up for the absence of a discernible streetscape. A new tram line animates the scene.

13.5 Landscaping as a means of restructuring open space. The urban landscape owes a lot to the presence of greenery and planting.

13.6 The 'service' space leaves its trace in the form of metal inserts.

of objectives and strategies, of unity and diversity, of a search for coherence and the preservation of heterogeneity.

'INSCRIBED' SPACE, A DYNAMIC PROCESS

The notion of 'inscribed' space is of most importance to us by virtue of the fundamental relationship which exists between it and the human body. It can be defined as a physical, three-dimensional space through which we pass. 'Inscribed' space is an idea that cannot be characterized by the use of certain forms such as the 'street', the 'square', or the 'courtyard', but is, instead, defined by the notion of limits. In modern-day cities, the limits are all too often too vaguely defined, using, for example, grilles or railings to separate public and private domains. It becomes little more than a residual space between buildings, a 'negative' of the architecture.

People possess a mental guide, a mind's eye perhaps, which anticipates their route and helps them to distinguish between obstacles and unrestricted passages. In this respect, the streetscape encountered must allow the user to anticipate his route in order to be sure that their choice corresponds with their intention. This idea of anticipation is essential, and is not achieved by the mere provision of the necessary practical information to make way-finding possible. It must also contain the necessary expressive qualities in order to elicit an emotional response in the user with regard to the street, whether it be the impression of ease or comfort, of clarity or precision in terms of well-defined limits, of hierarchy of signage and the use of texture or colour. Visually, the definition of the route is more than a simple way-marking on the ground. The city street is perceived as a three-dimensional channel formed by the ground plane and the building fronts. The horizontal constitutes the plane in which the user moves, while the vertical forms the primary dimension of their sight.

Similar to Petrarch's experience of climbing Mont Ventoux, the perception of landscape is characterized, primarily, by the sensation of envelopment whereby all our senses are called upon. There exists a profound relationship between our being and this space, with which we form an entity. 'The living body creates or produces space ... and space exists only as something experienced from inside.'[1] The perception of space is an existential process in which time plays an important role. It becomes apparent and tangible at the moment one begins to move through it, or through a sequence of spaces, and is not totally contained. Only an appreciation of the different processes at work, rather than a fixed consideration of suitable forms, will give an indication as to how to proceed in the construction of a city. 'Inscribed' space is a very particular kind of space, being artificial, anthropological, totally constructed by the human being, and progressively created.

'PUBLIC' SPACE, A MEETING PLACE?

'Inscribed' space and 'public' space are notions not to be confused with one another, as they occupy different areas of theory, namely that of the behaviour of the human body, and that of social behaviour. The relative autonomy of the one with regards to the other means that they cannot be totally superposed. Not all 'inscribed' space is public, and some 'public' space is open.

'Public' space is, by nature, social. The term refers to a social space defined by the activities which take place there and by its symbolism, and not necessarily by its form. 'Public' space is a particular kind of social space created specifically for the bringing together of people, and where locals and strangers, the familiar and the unusual, can mingle freely. It can be likened to a stage for the free expression of opinion and the organization of events. It is worth remembering that the idea of 'public' space was first developed, along with politics, by the Ancient Greeks and that it was set in concrete, as it were, with the advent of democracy. In Western civilization, this particular form of social behaviour bestowed certain places with symbolism, which became enrooted and more intensely felt though time, leading to an enhanced use of the space. The problem was that, in becoming more and more codified, subject to rules and charged with significance, it also became a prime target for disobedience and demonstration of discontent. It is essential that a political will establishes a public project as a powerful means of social identification. The successful creation of a city centre consists in the joining together of three elements, namely the social practices of the inhabitants, the progressive construction of a place and a factor, dynamic or symbolise which all the inhabitants can identify with. The paradox is that what will be created is in reality an empty space.

'SERVICE' SPACE, SERVICE INTERCONNECTION SPACE

The construction of 'inscribed' space is an existential process, the edification of 'public' space is a political act, and the putting in place of a service network is a question of technical know-how. If the service routes often correspond with the public domain, it is for practical reasons only. It is not the network of services itself, but rather the service provided which is complementary to 'public' space and which forms a principal part of public property. It can be said to amplify or reinforce the role of public space and is manifest in an array of objects such as vents and grilles, lighting poles, posts and panels, letter and telephone boxes. The proliferation of such clutter is, today, becoming overwhelming, particularly with the rise of traffic in towns, and it tends to produce a rupture rather than unity. Sometimes, however, the confrontation of 'public' and 'service' space can bring about beneficial effects, introducing new landmarks, or means of orientation, responding to certain needs, welcoming a new, more dynamic way of living and, in short, giving an enhanced sense of urban life.

In spite of the fact that analysis of urban space leads to three independent notions – namely 'inscribed', 'public', and 'service' space – they all form a dynamic whole, a single entity which forms the basis of urban space. The establishment of a hierarchy is crucial. The 'service' space depends somewhat on the arrangement of 'public' space which is, in turn, influenced by 'inscribed' space, which is often the easiest to recognize as it contains the greatest quantity of physical 'markings' on the ground.

The appreciation of 'inscribed' space as the primary element of a process has, logically, many consequences for the manner in which an urban project is conceived. It brings together in a single physical and symbolic entity all that surrounds it. In view of this, it cannot be over-stressed just how important is the proper approach to urban design, and that it can only take place as an integral part of a wider process.

'Inscribed' space remains, therefore one of the key issues facing the future of urbanism. The definition of the urban landscape, it can be seen, owes a lot to the presence of greenery and planting. So much so, in fact, that it leads one to the question of to what extent the idea of the garden generates the city, a paradoxical notion considering the organizational complexity of the city compared with the apparent simplicity of the garden. The formal arrangements of parks and garden have, however, always been closely associated with the composition of the city and have influenced it in a decisive way.

Gardens are often open on a permanent basis, offering to all the chance to daydream a little in pleasant surroundings. Far from being a luxury, they, in fact, provide the image of the city and impart to it a sense of availability, accessibility and elegance. Contrary to all expectations, it is the association of gardens with cities which provides the key to the understanding of the urban environment. In the Middle Ages, few trees were to be found in public places. On the other hand, at the centre of the urban 'islands', generated by the network of streets, were to be found a multitude of gardens and courtyards forming 'clearings' in the densely packed medieval urban structure.

In the seventeenth century, the city began to open up to the exterior and the row, or alignment, of trees became very important as a element of urban planning. The analogy between certain planned and planted interventions and contemporary gardens was clearly discernible in the layout of cities, one example being the Champs Elysées in Paris. This axis was designed by Le Nôtre as a visual extension of the Tuileries Gardens, opening them to the countryside to the west of the city.

During the eighteenth century, the use of geometrical forms, following the manner of the classical French garden, became widespread with its adoption for all remodelling schemes throughout the country. Towns and cities were to be changed permanently and even the later and altogether different aesthetical notions of the picturesque would not completely erode the regularity of their organization.

We are now witnessing the advent of the development of a new vocabulary of planting adapted to the needs of the city, including boulevards, promenades, avenues, walks and squares. The unifying role of the garden would seem to be gaining ground after the digression of the Modern Movement to the extent that, today, it can once again be considered a major constituent of urbanism. Nevertheless the simple matter of planting trees will not bring about an improvement in the urban environment, and this must take place within the framework of certain rules or theories. It may even be that, in some cases, planting is not a suitable option. Far from being uniform, it lends itself more to the design of spaces of a subtle nature occupying the boundary between the finite and the indeterminate. The garden represents the most elaborate and sophisticated form of the notion 'nature/illusion', all the more fascinating because it remains in constant change. In contrast to the built volume, planting offers an ever-changing display of transparency, luminosity and rhythm, creating limits or enhancing distant views.

13.7 The garden is, today, considered a major constituent of urbanism. The unifying role of the garden is gaining ground after the digression of the Modern Movement.

13.8 The garden creates an image of the city and imparts a sense of availability, accessibility and elegance.

13.9 The garden structures the streetscape: the analogy between planting and the planning of cities.

Note

1 H. Lefebvre, *The Production of Space*, trans. D. Nicholson-Smith, Oxford: Blackwell, 1991.

HOTEL
M

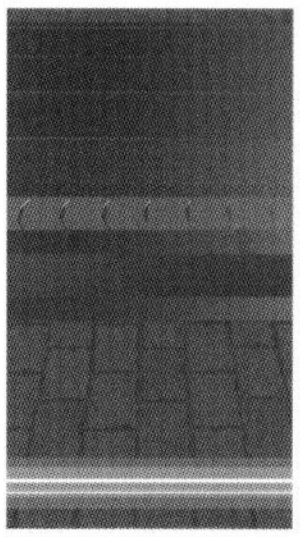

We are painfully tearing ourselves away from the last century's deep-rooted 'modernity'. When it was new, its freeing and its creativity delighted us, then due to its wear and tear and its violent nature it admitted its shameful fascination for eradication, artificialisation, negativism of culture or feeling; a *tabula rasa*?

We stopped following that theory in ready-made towns; the more functional it is, the less it functions! After that we were merely satisfied with cosmetics which helps to sell the same junk for a while. And slowly the artificialisation moved away from the social utopia to address itself to the 'market' to make us believe, together with the innocent Adam Smith (with his invisible hand) and the fascinating Friedrich Hayek, that modernism is the only tool to ensure universal equity. 'The sum total of selfishness is the real way to automatically ensure universal equity', they say in an outrageous and childish way, meaning, forget the raptors (wolves do not eat one another, do they?) and the well-dressed gangsters. Obviously, market freedom is guaranteed by Human Rights, but also by the simple right to life, and the weaklings are not left to fend for themselves without tribunals or policemen.

CHAPTER 14

ANIMAL URBANISM AND HOMEOPATHIC ARCHITECTURE

LUCIEN KROLL

This fairy tale is true only in a theoretical and ideological world but not in the real world that we know is hiding behind the alibi of a democracy where less than one ten-thousandth of the population makes all the others vote for the financial neo-colonialist tools which they themselves will fall prey to. Well done!

I am not talking about geo-economy but only a little about institutional analysis in order to find out in which theatre the architects perform and who wrote the play. Does this make a town?

> We begin to see modern times, as a whole, as a time when monstrosities have been produced by human actors, contractors, technicians, artists and consumers.[1]

SO, WHICH ARCHITECTURES AND WHICH URBANISMS?

The answer is ecological: by trial and error almost all the modernistic diversions have been called into question but without renouncing the knowledge that has been acquired. Difficult, despite the end of utopias, an absurd, anguished and inhuman monomania of tidying up remains rooted in the heads of the 'people responsible'.

The utopia of 'merchandising' survives as the last totalitarianism in current use. This utopia is hanging on but is being bravely shaken up (Seattle, Davos, Prague, Millau, etc.).

But what about architectures and urbanisms? They keep up very slowly: a dozen 'important' architects at the most put into practice ecology (neither decorative nor commercial). In order to understand this better, one has to unravel the inevitable distortions between the architects' thinking and the meaning of their architecture . . . Generally, they say one thing, carry out another one and do their best to make you believe, and sincerely try to believe it themselves, that their thinking can be found in the object. They are not even guilty of double-dealing: they are the last romantics and we need them . . .

The minimum level of ecology is the relationship with the user! We had to wait for the creation of Advocacy Planning by New Yorkers, which they taught us as they themselves forgot it, to encourage us to put into practice this participation by the inhabitants and to change the meaning of urban images: already research into this participation changes the meaning of the projected architecture.

EXOGENOUS PURPOSE

Which new image can the architect still express? Not his own: his *raison d'être* must be impartial for fear of complacency, narcissism or confinement (I am talking about the built object . . .). Ecology puts us in touch (this is its simple definition as expressed by Ernst Haeckel in 1866) with the Other, the unknown, the missing, the entitled. In this way the architect self-selects a new role and sometimes has the strange feeling of being useful . . .

There is no precise architecture that expresses ecology. Ecology is an attitude, not a style. However, some types of architecture are incompatible with ecology and a kind of committed obligation to make sure that all the 'primary' elements are present: earth, wood, stone, metal, air, fire, etc. is a prophylaxis, a rite, an incantation that prevents lapsing into this modern monoculture. Fortunately we meet some who continue to link the forms of their architecture to their immediate context.

HOMEOPATHIC ARCHITECTURE

Homeopathic architecture sets the minimum amount of directives (of potent medicine) in order to let the body find its own energies to sort out its own health . . . Because the more the architecture dictates, the more the users doze.

ANIMAL URBANISM

Le Corbusier admired the donkey that makes its path alone in the mountain. This winding shape is fully rational and is not produced by engineering but by an overall, spontaneous intuition. Urban design should only be that . . . Strangely enough, Le Corbusier himself drew all his roads in a nastily straight way.

BIO-DIVERSE ARCHITECTURE

Organised: has a natural ability compared with the organic ability of living bodies.

Organic Kingdom: group of all plant and animal living bodies.

Inorganic Kingdom: group of raw substances, with or without structure, that are called minerals. Substances that can only grow by juxtaposition.

INORGANIC

So the inorganic applies to minerals that are unconnected, the dead recurrences of identical and emaciated elements, the simple and mechanical systems, without any history, thus without any future. Here is a quick definition of modern urbanism and architecture.

The inorganic architecture is the one that is unaware of the users and their active life, that only shows techniques and frigid ways of doing things, that invents a model (of its technique or of its 'ego', it is equally schizoid) and keeps saying it like a deaf man as no one can be heard asking for something else: the users are eternally absent. Modern urbanism is a model of plumbing. Its only rule: hot water should not be mixed with gas (movements and areas).

ORGANIC

On the other hand, organic architecture is the empathic architecture that only follows the living shapes, first, the shapes of its users as individuals and as society (architects always sterilise), then the shapes of nature and of its image as a model of growth through complex internal laws. It is limited to only giving a motivating frame to 'inhabitants' movements' (we inhabit our train, our street, our office, our mountain, our dream, etc, and we have an effect on them). Then all the elements must take part, and a long way before the physical elements: the simplest form of ecology immediately requires the presence of the inhabitant (of the civil society).

The organic organism is the urbanism where human gestures (past, existing or future of the project) create the urban form. Someone walks: they create a street: this street is still a virtual street but it only needs to wrap up its action with façades and it exists. This pedestrian meets another and stops: together they immediately create a public place. This also only needs to protect itself by other built elements and it exists. There is also the courtyard and the garden and some details useful to the foundations of organic urbanism. Therefore the inhabitant creates the town: not the engineers, not the architects (a few of them dream of it sometimes) . . .

MODERN

Today I am not sure that there is a difference between Ceausescu and Le Corbusier of the Plan Voisin: both wiped out the valuable fabric of their town and rebuilt palaces for the people (Le Corbusier, less barbaric, contented himself with drawing it on paper!). If painted in green and the roof covered with grass and some photovoltaics, would Ceausescu's palace be an ecological masterpiece? That is what we call 'green stickers': a few gimmicks and some savings.

GPS

At the time each modernist inevitably embraced the ideas of the time and followed a general attitude of faith in problem solving (today this is called General Problem Solving, it is computerised and as distressing and fascist as before). Innocently everyone thought human matters could be solved artificially, rational solutions could be found to irrational problems (the habitat!) and everything could be worked out definitively: they never suggested an inceptive or homeopathic approach.

A LACK . . .

France (Europe, the world!) has perpetrated charitable 'inorganic' (the needy have to be housed), and democratic (all equal in the face of the prefab . . .). Now we know it: 'it was no good' . . . We have to revert back to organic. Well, no: the HLM are refurbished with the same attitudes and the same methods that were originally used . . . The architect, my friends, sterilises as much: simply it is sometimes more pretty or rather peculiar. The inhabitants are still tremendously absent. At best, the landscape is organised 'as if' they had decided themselves: and here we have the new urbanism.

RULES

In the immediate and tactile detail, schizophrenia is the same: outdated rationalities, nakedness, absences (Bauhaus is not dead) are still taught. For example, one material for various uses, identical orientations for all, same locations, one shape reproduced till exhaustion; only an ideology could impose such fanaticism.

The classical rule of the three unities: place, time and action are in the context of architecture a sort of self-mutilation! And the simplisms offered patriotically as morality are only shrinkages, narrow-mindedness, boredom. It must be white, smooth and square! To choose THE material is absurd: first of all, all available materials are to take part.

In the field of urbanism, the three unities create the zonings: each thing in its place, the order is restored, one no longer moves. But to survive in society (each family is already a district committee), contradictions are necessary, healthy.

The 'people' have never liked the 'modern': they have had to invent the 'kitsch' as self-defence, to survive in their culture: kitsch has never been nasty . . . To be rational it is best today to be emotional rather than rational. And also to be contemporary rather than modern . . .

VAULX-EN-VELIN, LYONS, FRANCE

Picture for a competition for the refurbishment of the Zup in Vaulx-en-Velin based on the need for mixed use (business, facilities, schools, etc.) and communication links (streets, junctions, commercial and activity boulevard), with the aim to add without demolition, build spaces around and on the existing 'blocks'.

As soon as the projects were submitted (urgent: in July 1992), it was once more nipped in the bud: the jury and the organisers were so scared to take action that they never dared inform anyone of the results of the competition.

We promised ourselves that we would deal with the (too) lively elements, to ask them as a whole to rebuild with us and to respect their untidiness: it is only a living and invisible order as long as it is not going into action.

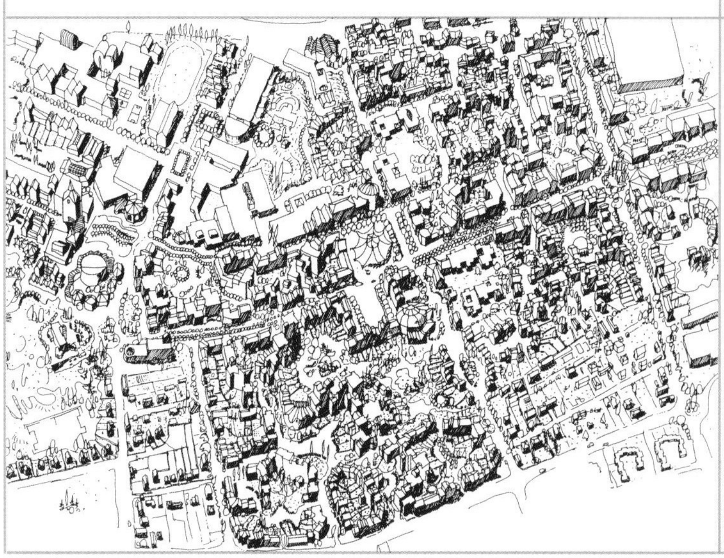

14.1 Vaulx-en-Velin, Lyons, France. Concept sketch plan for a competition for the refurbishment of ZUP, based on 'organic' pattern of additions to existing blocks without demolition.

ECOLONIA, ALPHA-AAN-DEN-RIJN, NETHERLANDS

A hundred houses; 'environment friendly' as the Dutch say. We have coordinated the nine local architects chosen on the basis of their environmental projects, i.e. we disorganised them in such a way that they had to meet, even without us, to match their projects. Unable to find a Dutch architect who would listen to this culture of disorder, the housing association (the Bouwfonds) assigned us this task.

Of course, Holland is full of neighbourhood committees. After very lively discussions, what happens is that an architect is chosen who then carefully ignores everything that could alter his 'concept' and conceives of a product whose image never quite reflects the abundance of the intentions.

We have drawn up a list of 'urban components' for elements covering 'une action d'habitant', then we let our feelings guide their arrangement where they could become active. Then only did we take care over the meetings, the vis-à-vis, the boundaries that link instead of separating. All the urban ecology themes have been raised and handed out.

How to re-invent a contemporary practice that will manage to escape from the pitfalls of modernism by leaving behind its mechanical procedures, to embrace other more living procedures: with each extra technical comfort, people say they are more unhappy than before. Each gesture, each decision mobilises our conditioned reflexes, our functional education, our aggressive competition, our pragmatic entertainment, etc. This search requires a strict close watch: we have to discipline ourselves against the rules so as to

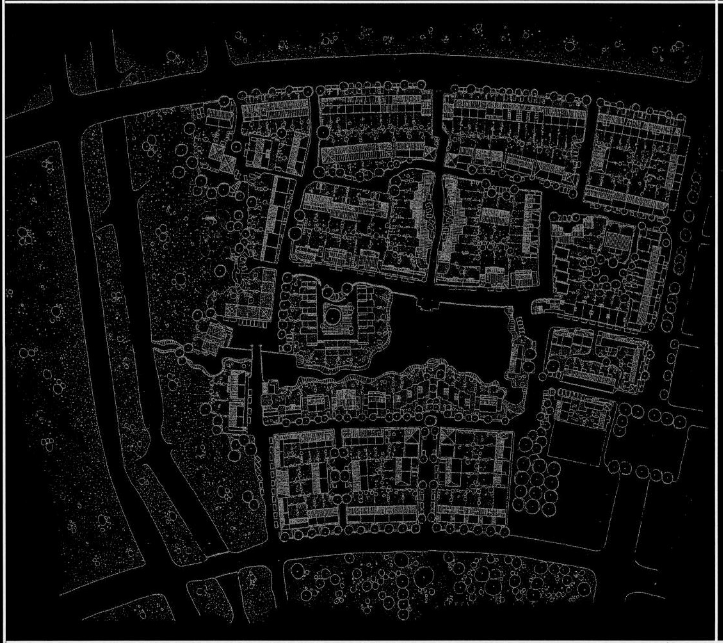

14.2 Ecolonia, Alpha-aan-den Rijn, the Netherlands. Masterplan showing structure of neighbourhood with lake and canal.

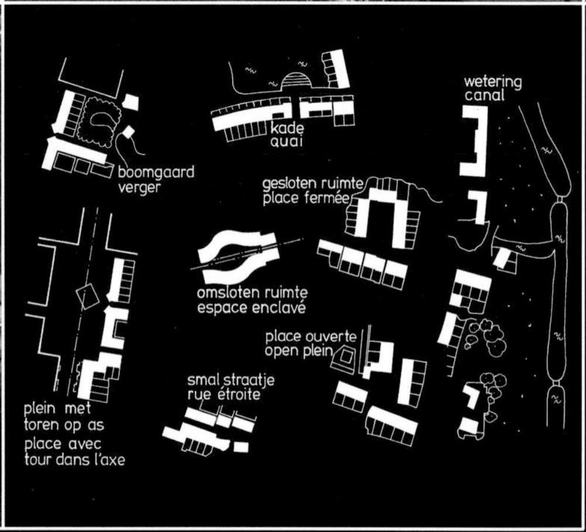

14.3 Ecolonia, public space. The main square lies on the visual axis to the lake, the square is a well-used social space for the two terraces of houses that face each other.

14.4 Ecolonia, private space. Gardens backing onto the lake; decks provide private space, which is visible within the early days of establishing lakeside planting. Privacy gives way to neighbourliness.

14.5 Ecolonia, built form. Informality and lack of symmetry are to encourage the inhabitants to manage themselves.

14.6 Ecolonia, context and ecology. This represents freedom of the individual within a society.

14.7 Ecolonia, urban components. The urban spaces that make up the community. No two dwellings or spaces are the same.

A FEW CLUES:

- Automatic urban writing (it is more conducive to habitability than the cold approach).
- Ecology that commands true connections.
- A certain voluntary poverty.
- Time, space in their role of forms and image creation.
- Disorder or casualness (risk/uncertainty).
- The reason for decisions taken between several independents.
- Human measure of time and space, etc. . . . accepting only what relates to 'here and now'.
- The village test (but then we want to build it).
- Voluntary disorder (more creative than planning).
- The obstinate involvement of uncertain users.
- The absolute respect of all that pre-exists: the context as regulatory plan; the exact opposite of 'Forget Context' of my friend Rem Koolhaas because context, it is others, the Other.
- Anything but this abstract creation of 'single objects' that make the 'inhabitants disillusioned'.

We then mix 'ordinary inhabitants', therefore with no knowledge of architecture: they have this instinct that has not yet been corrupted by education (architecture is not part of education: just as well!). And we ask them to conceive (always in a group) their own environment and to preserve, as if a treasure, all the differences, the blunders and the contradictions so as to rationalise the construction without losing anything. Insofar as this power over the environment taking shape eludes us, it becomes fertile and alive.

We want the image of a neighbourhood or architecture to be the image representing the freedom of elements in a society, allowing them to manage themselves and also to create unrestricted interdependence. In no way can this image be one of order or authority. There cannot be any symmetry or stupid repetition of elements (prefabricated or not).

We should remind you that the Technical Department of the town in charge of the realisation betrayed us very simply each time they failed to understand an idea. For example, the trees in the streets: instead of being disciplined in a straight line, we suggested that one tree should be planted in front of each house and to leave the choice of the species to each family. It seemed very logical to us: not to them. In this case, discipline prevailed.

We were not allowed to plan activity centres: in conjunction with one of the architects we organised the living room and a garage that could be converted into a business space: spontaneously a hairdressing salon was created and called 'ecohairdressing'.

14.8 Bethoncourt-Montbeliard, France. Better to rescue and refurbish this line of forty units rather than demolish.

14.9 Bethoncourt-Montbeliard, blocks remodelled. Rectangular blocks in poor state transformed to stepped profile with new roof forms.

14.10 Bethoncourt-Montbeliard, casualness replaces banality. Refurbishing was half the cost of new, and probably better.

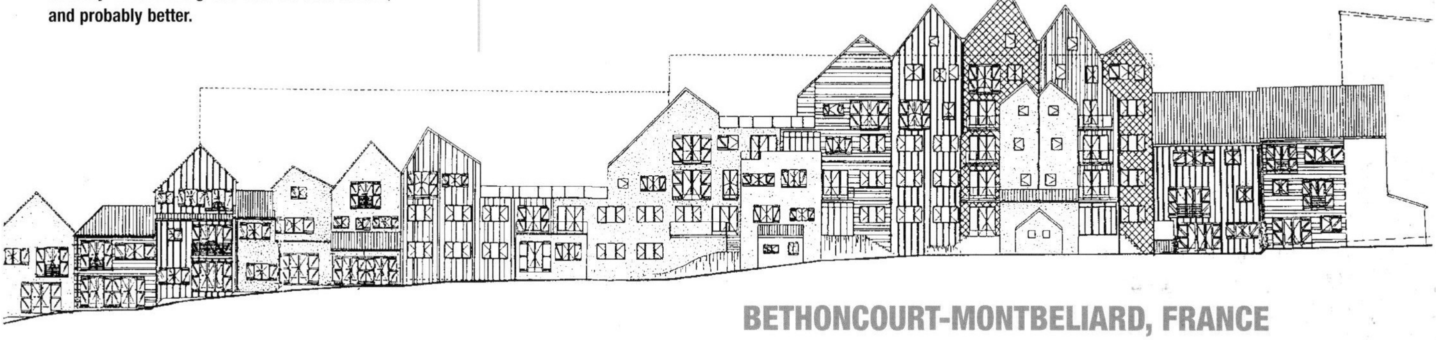

BETHONCOURT-MONTBELIARD, FRANCE

14.11 Bethoncourt-Montbeliard, elevation of block. No two dwellings are the same.

14.12 Bethoncourt-Montbeliard, sketch of tower.

A cursed district: almost empty, bricked-up windows, broken window panes on the upper floors, obviously with squatters. We had suggested 'rescuing' a line of forty units: to demolish it is too easy and too expensive (more than half the cost of new building) and a little bit shameful.

We planned a small square to adjoin it by breaking the fast street. Then we altered it deeply, made a hole in, inserted the necessary additions to conform to the new standards: it became untidy as its inhabitants are when you really look at them, and not only in the account books. There are no two dwellings the same . . . We adjusted it in minute detail to the programmes, the habitability, the budgets and the firms: within a month it was rented. Again. It was even a good deal: so we decided not to do it again.

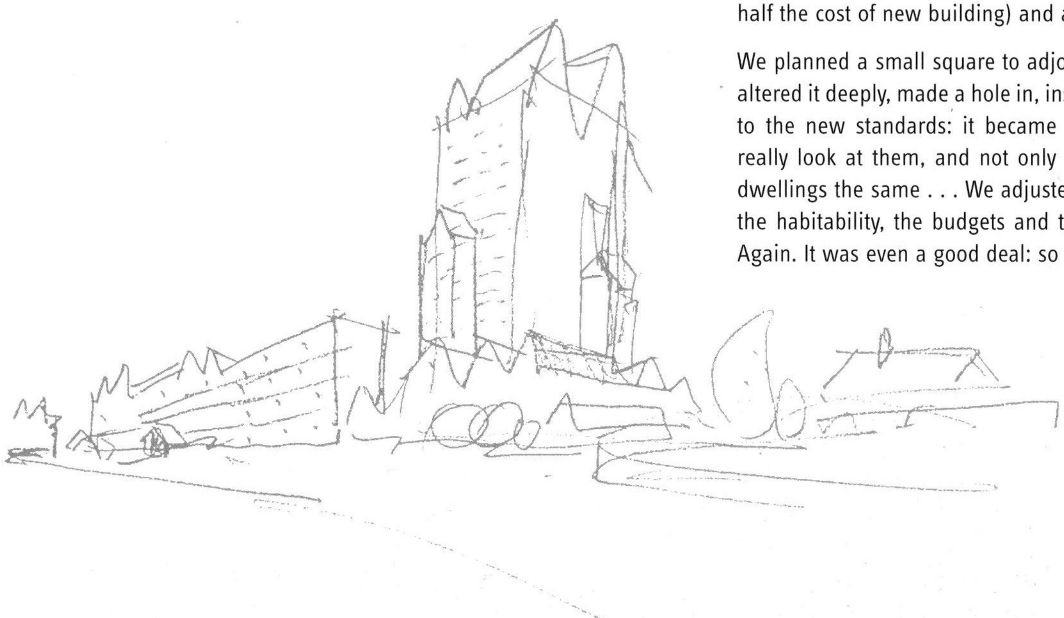

ALEA, ALENÇON, FRANCE

The inhabitants of the district of Perseigne rebelled against the project to double the number of social prefabs: at the next elections they voted for the other side and found themselves sitting in the Mayor's armchair. Let's refurbish! They had chosen me: rumour had it that I was not deaf and that I asked people how to do it . . .

Meetings elected inhabitants (sometimes the same people), discussions on all the suggestions and criticisms, proposals, no battle plan . . .

Then a primary school and an experimental building to refurbish.

Afterwards everybody was tired.

14.13 ALEA, Alençon, France. The inhabitants chose to refurbish this district of Perseigne.

14.14 ALEA, Alencon. Residents committee decided approach to provide new roofs, roof gardens and balconies. The forms are softened.

14.15 ALEA, informal pathways.

14.16 ALEA, social spaces.

14.17 ALEA. The transformation proves the point that bland buildings can be humanised.

3

SUSTAINABILITY THROUGH TECHNOLOGY

CREATING NEW TYPOLOGIES

Carbon complacency, urban design, cash, and modern methods of construction within the Sustainable Communities Programme – the need for joined-up thinking and a holistic industry 'Vision'.

At almost any point in the history of the UK construction industry there has been healthy debate between those proposing reduced environmental impact, and the majority of the developers, consultants and their supply chain who have just got used to the previous change in minimum legislative standards – and want to practise business as usual, undisturbed. This is only natural as predicting out-turn construction cost, minimising planning risk and minimising sales risk is how a volume house builder can guarantee profit on new developments. The truth that planners and developers refuse to admit is that ordinary affordable housing (whether private or public sector) cannot be specially designed for each site. To cut costs and deliver to tight margins, it is necessary to invest in a highly refined product with as much standardisation as possible between different sites. Only cladding materials and roof forms can really be changed from site to site, producing a formula capable of convincing local planners, but in reality achieving a monoculture of similar estates from Cheshire to Wiltshire.

CHAPTER 15

WHAT IS THE 'NEW ORDINARY'?

BILL DUNSTER

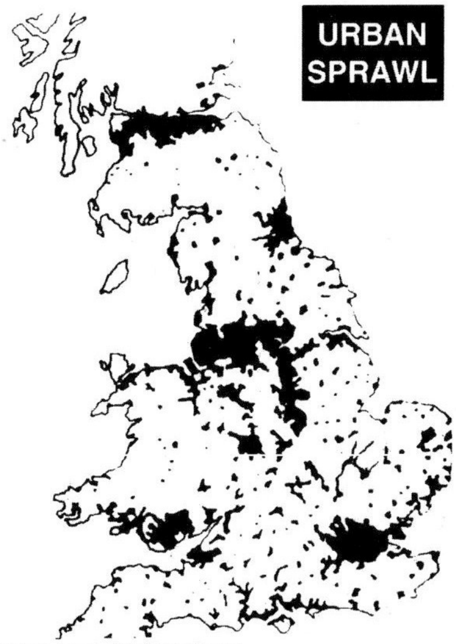

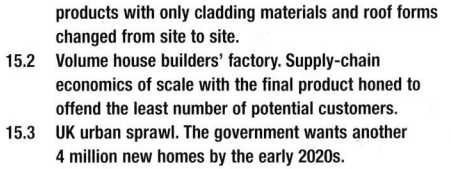

there has to be a limit to Urban Sprawl...

15.1 **Volume house builders' output. Houses are rarely designed for each location but are standardised products with only cladding materials and roof forms changed from site to site.**

15.2 **Volume house builders' factory. Supply-chain economics of scale with the final product honed to offend the least number of potential customers.**

15.3 **UK urban sprawl. The government wants another 4 million new homes by the early 2020s.**

This has produced a volume house building industry in the UK that works with a very limited number of standard house types, carefully engineered to skim through the building regulations' legal minimum construction standards, with standardisation of architectural form maximising the opportunities for supply chain economies of scale, and with the final product honed by marketing professionals to offend the least number of potential customers. Flying over almost all of our major cities, it becomes obvious that a very limited number of standard house types built in relatively short periods of time in the past 150 years account for most ordinary homes in the UK.

Each mass housing boom and its associated typologies have been derived from the prevalent social, economic and technological conditions of the period. The UK government is currently proposing an unprecedented expansion of our current housing stock – fuelled by increasing house prices, and a lack of affordable homes, especially for key workers. The current shortage of housing stock is generally attributed to increased lifespan, marital breakdown, and immigration, with little or no notable increase in the indigenous UK population. So before setting out on the next major housing boom and planning to build around 4 million new homes by the early 2020s, it is very important that we anticipate the major resource challenges awaiting UK society in the twenty-first century.

Accelerating climate change will mean summertime temperatures in the South-East will approximate to Marseilles sometime between 2050 and 2080. Affordable 'coolth' will become a bigger issue than affordable warmth, with many already dying from overheating in the urban heat islands of Paris and London in summer 2003. Any lightweight building without high levels of thermal storage will require carbon-intensive air conditioning to be habitable throughout a UK summer. Current government policy promotes lightweight prefabricated modern methods of construction with virtually no passive cooling qualities. There are no examples of lightweight homes or workspace in Mediterranean climatic zones.

Almost all timber-based lightweight construction concepts have originated in Northern America, Scandinavia or northern Europe, where overall average temperatures tend to be significantly cooler and summer overheating is rarely a problem. It is important that the UK construction industry plans for the worst-case scenario of the Scandinavian winter combined with the Mediterranean summer. The long-term scenario of climate change redirecting the Gulf Stream away from our shores could still take place, however; experts predict this is likely to start affecting the UK climate after around 150 years of intense warming, with the effects beginning to be felt over a 300-year period.[1] The challenge for the UK will be to combine the construction and urban response suitable for a Scandinavian winter with the searing heat of a Mediterranean summer. Simply meeting one or the other will either produce cold gloomy buildings in winter, or cause problematic overheating in summer. Addressing such a new bioclimatic challenge will inevitably lead to a new urban language for much of the UK, with summer shade and passive cooling strategies needing to be convincingly reconciled with the need to capture low-angle winter sun

15.4 **Internal view of BedZED living room. Houses need to capture low-angle winter sun for passive solar gain and maximise daylight in gloomy winter months.**

15.5 **Computer section through BedZED. Best value demonstration projects like BedZED are an essential part of a continuous innovation programme.**

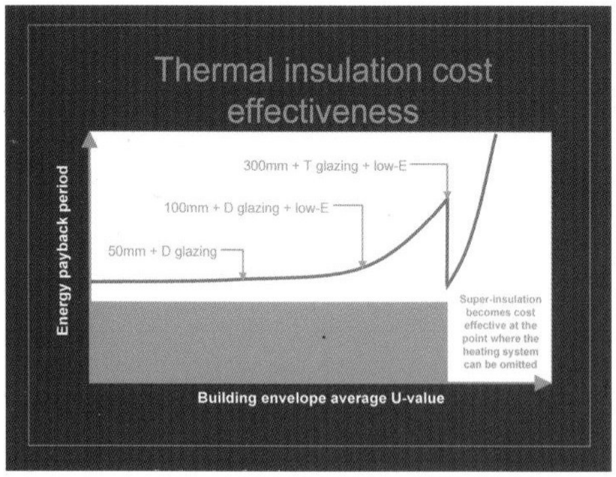

15.6 **Cost-effectiveness plotted against thermal performance. Super-insulation becomes cost-effective at the point where the heating system can be omitted.**

for passive solar gain and maximise daylight in the gloomy winter months. Perhaps the new government-sponsored urban design codes will champion the ordinary citizens' right to be both cool in summer and receive a third of their winter space-heating needs from passive solar gain?

Global agricultural production will be in crisis, as climate change creates winners and losers with desertification affecting areas of southern Europe. The UK imports 70 per cent of its food today, so losing agricultural land to housing may not be the most sensible strategy. With around 11 per cent of the surface area of the UK covered by urban sprawl, and with the average UK meal having travelled over 2,000 miles from farm to dinner plate, it may not be in the long-term national interest to plan a large percentage of the 4 million new homes required by 2020 on prime agricultural land. We would certainly struggle to provide a subsistence diet for the current UK population from food sourced within our national boundaries, and, with the human global population still expanding exponentially, it is likely to be increasingly difficult for the UK plc to find the resources to secure healthy low-cost food on the international markets. This may be one of the most important reasons why the UK cannot contemplate a secure future without almost total dependency on the European Union breadbasket.

The challenge here is to reconcile the densities found in the centre of a typical UK market town (100 to 120 homes/ha) with the amenities and private garden provision found in semi-detached 1930s' suburbia.

Meanwhile the UK government has a duty to be wise and far-sighted (we hope). It has a public duty to the electorate to consult the best experts and plan ahead. While future predictions about anything are notoriously fraught, just about the only thing that both experts and public awareness agree on is climate change and global warming. So achieving a democratic mandate to plan for climate change and the phased withdrawal from our near-total addiction to carbon-emitting fossil fuel is unquestionably realistic. It is this thinking that has produced the latest White Energy Paper, with its startling statement that North Sea gas will run out in five years and North Sea oil in ten, making UK plc totally dependent on fossil fuel imports from some of the most politically unstable countries in the world. Fortunately the UK government has accepted the connection between atmospheric carbon emissions and climate change and has signed up to an agenda that will deliver a 20 per cent reduction in carbon emissions by 2020 and a 60 per cent reduction by 2050. So even if we found new unlimited stocks of gas and oil, we couldn't really burn it!

As, collectively, we have democratically reached this conclusion, it becomes very important to debate the best way of deploying our limited natural resources to cope with an increasingly uncertain future. The billions of pounds spent on military intervention trying to secure political stability in the Middle East oilfields could have been spent on fast-tracking the UK's snail-like process towards a low or zero-carbon economy. So complacency about reducing carbon emissions is probably about the most anti-social, dangerous stance to adopt at this point in our island's history. We have to regard a low carbon diet as a cultural priority or fight and be prepared to die for our perceived right to contribute more than our

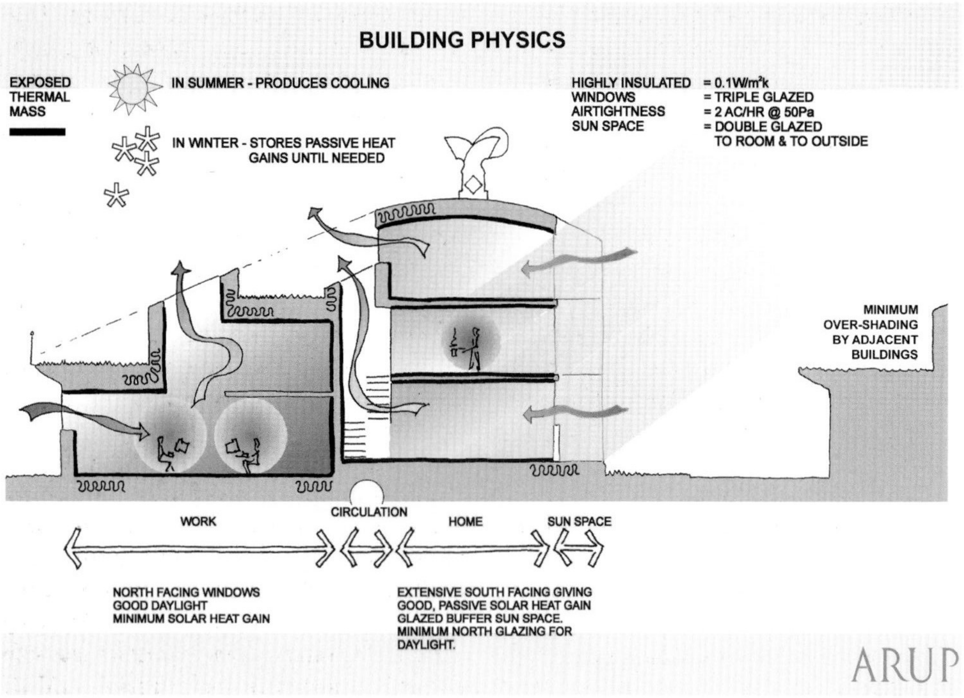

15.7 Cross-section of BedZED building physics strategy. This diagram shows how a combination of thermal mass and high levels of solar gain can reduce the need for a conventional heating system.

fair share of global warming. But the critics will say, 'Don't be ridiculous, we could never afford this whole-scale change of technology, cultural priorities and social change!' So the government consults the construction industry, suggests sensible targets for reducing environmental impact and always finds any chance of progress hindered by the industry lobby. Our experience indicates the following standard responses are encountered in most circumstances when consulting the key industry stakeholders:

PLANNERS SAY:

'We cannot move away from our formulaic design codes, with our preference for perimeter block layouts and courtyard parking. We find the technical requirements of daylight, solar access, airflow, acoustics and renewable energy integration within the urban fabric hard to integrate within conventional urban design priorities. We know what has worked in the past, so please use our design codes for masterplanning any new projects. In this case, social stability is perceived to come from continuity with our historic past. Most people find comfort in urban form and architectural expression derived from a rose-tinted view of our heritage. The danger is that this approach degenerates into sentimentality, reconciled to an orgy of material and resource consumption that rapes the present without restraint or joy.'

ARCHITECTS SAY:

'We cannot innovate easily, because there is no fee, time or client appetite for environmental innovation without coercive legislation. If left to our own devices, we really prefer maximising peer approval by building experimental artworks for wealthy clients, and avoiding unrewarding, high-constraint social housing, if at all possible. And, anyway, how can we integrate solar technologies if the master planner or urban designer has ignored solar access?'

VOLUME HOUSE BUILDERS SAY:

'The carbon emissions from new housing are relatively small, why not look at improving the existing building stock before making us change our product? Our standard house types have evolved from market demand, please leave us alone to get on with the job of increasing annual numbers of new stock.'[2]

DEVELOPERS SAY:

'Homes have a different market from workspace. Please let us build office parks near motorway junctions and keep housing on greenfield sites away from complex urban communities on problematic brownfield land.'

THE SUPPLY CHAIN SAYS:

'We can only tool up and invest in new low-environmental-impact technologies and products if we have sufficient demand. Go and buy from Germany if you want this specification now! If all the industry wants is the legal minimum specification, that is all we can realistically provide.'

THE LEGISLATORS SAY:

'We cannot persuade the market to embrace low-environmental-impact thinking without waiting for legislation, which will be unpopular and slow in coming. We have to treat the industry like a child being given some bad-tasting medicine that, though initially unpleasant, will provide a long-term cure. Here are some nice, easy-entry-level standards, that won't taste too bad, and will start the process of removing the national addiction to fossil fuel. We cannot push ahead with reducing environmental impact too fast without attracting a vociferous industry lobby.'

THE GOVERNMENT SAYS:

'Our short-term target is to build more affordable homes as soon as possible. Environmental innovation costs more. Let's just build as many homes as possible to the minimum plausible ecohomes standards. Speed and delivering the maximum number of affordable homes are far more important than carbon, so let's promote lightweight modern methods of construction to overcome perceived traditional skills shortages, and let's adopt non-controversial urban design codes to accelerate the planning process. Building traditional-looking homes is always populist, even if they are really made in factories using modern methods of construction.'

THE PUBLIC SAY:

'We want as many affordable homes as possible, while allowing the existing housing stock to increase in value, and without losing any green belt or agricultural land, and without creating higher density communities anywhere near my home. Just about the only politically expedient response to this challenge is building large numbers of new homes on unpopulated flood zone, preferably in the Thames Gateway. And if we must have new development, please make it look like something we are familiar and comfortable with – preferably Victorian or older.'

And the inevitable conclusion is – changes in the legal minimum standards regulating carbon emissions always seem to meet the predictable lobby against change from diverse organisations ranging from the Urban Villages Forum to the House Builders Federation, and those that stand to lose most from their physical or intellectual investment in the current status quo. Radical proposals such as zero-heating-spec homes are deemed unpalatable and before long we will be fighting our next war to ensure supplies of fossil fuel from outside our national boundaries. So if we know what the long-term carbon emission targets we have to meet are, and we also know roughly what it costs us in military intervention outside our national boundaries to ensure supplies of fossil fuel, it should be possible to agree a phased programme of progressive legislative carbon-reduction legislation, and this could be interpreted through a planned tightening of building regulations on minimum carbon emissions standards, or through planning legislation such as PPS22.[3] The proportion of renewable energy generated on site will become very important, as almost all the capacity provided by green tariff electricity will be required to support our historic urban quarters, where the heritage culture lobby requires preservation in the interests of historic continuity. Renewable energy only makes sense if the demand has been reduced by excellent passive design. It will simply not be possible to run UK plc on renewable energy sourced within our national boundaries without adopting zero-heating-specification building fabric – or ZED standards. Once these national environmental performance targets for any new urban fabric are agreed to be in the national interest, it becomes important to develop design codes that provide the planning system with an impartial assessment procedure for development control. Somehow environmental impact, ecological footprint analysis and carbon footprints need to be introduced into the government's current enthusiasm for design codes, currently designed to speed up planning approvals in the attempt to maximise the delivery of new affordable homes.

Publishing this long-term strategy of ever-increasing carbon reductions would do wonders for the UK development industry. The planning profession can familiarise itself with the new urban morphologies and aesthetics created by a low or zero-carbon cultural agenda. The supply chain could make long-term investments in tooling for the new standards, research and development would flood back into the industry – and the cost of this new planned innovation would drop dramatically. Better still, the government could recognise that best-practice demonstration projects are an essential part of this continuous innovation programme. The carbon threshold provided by minimum legal regulations can only be increased if the government is sure that workable affordable upgrade solutions can be delivered at a reasonable cost. Projects like BedZED are essential to show where the regulations and urban design codes could go over a five to ten-year period. Initially these pathfinder projects attract higher 'prototype' construction costs – just as a prototype car costs far more than a production-run model. The building regulations' minimum pass specification will always provide the cheapest out-turn construction cost simply because 99 per cent of the industry builds to these standards – achieving massive economies of scale. It is absurd for industry critics to point to such projects, comment on the increased construction costs, and then lobby against any upgrading of carbon reduction legislation, or the introduction of meaningful solar access into urban design codes. Providing that the same carbon-saving legislation applies to the entire industry, a 'level playing field' is achieved – and any associated increase in construction costs effectively reduces land value, anticipating that no developer will accept a reduction in profit. Only those industry players with large existing land banks will object to this approach, but then they shouldn't be hoarding such a precious resource anyway. An easy way to phase in any renewable obligation under the planning system would be to make the exact percentage of building-integrated renewables required on each site proportional to the rateable value or local council tax band. This would prevent the renewables obligation becoming a development tax, making regeneration unviable in low-value areas of the country.

Understanding that small runs of zero-heating-specification homes would always attract higher construction costs, ZEDfactory have now value engineered the BedZED prototype to create a range of standard house types and associated urban design codes that could be tendered to achieve similar supply chain economies of scale to that achieved by the volume house builders. This is important, as it is virtually impossible to distinguish their volume product by company or brand, resulting in spectacular rationalisation of the house building industry. This approach does not mean that all zero-heating-spec homes have

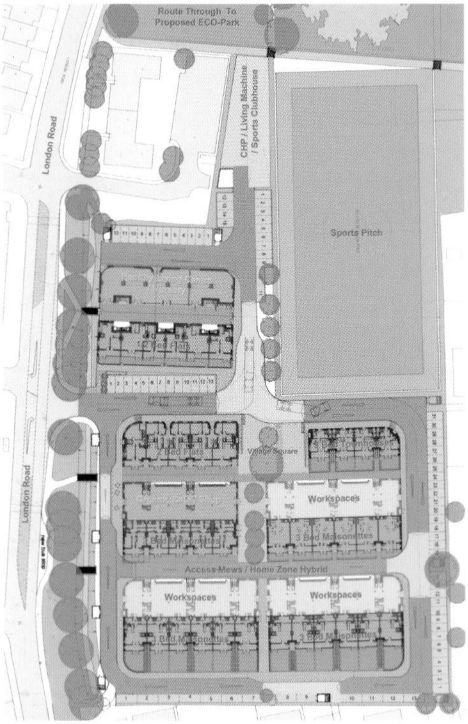

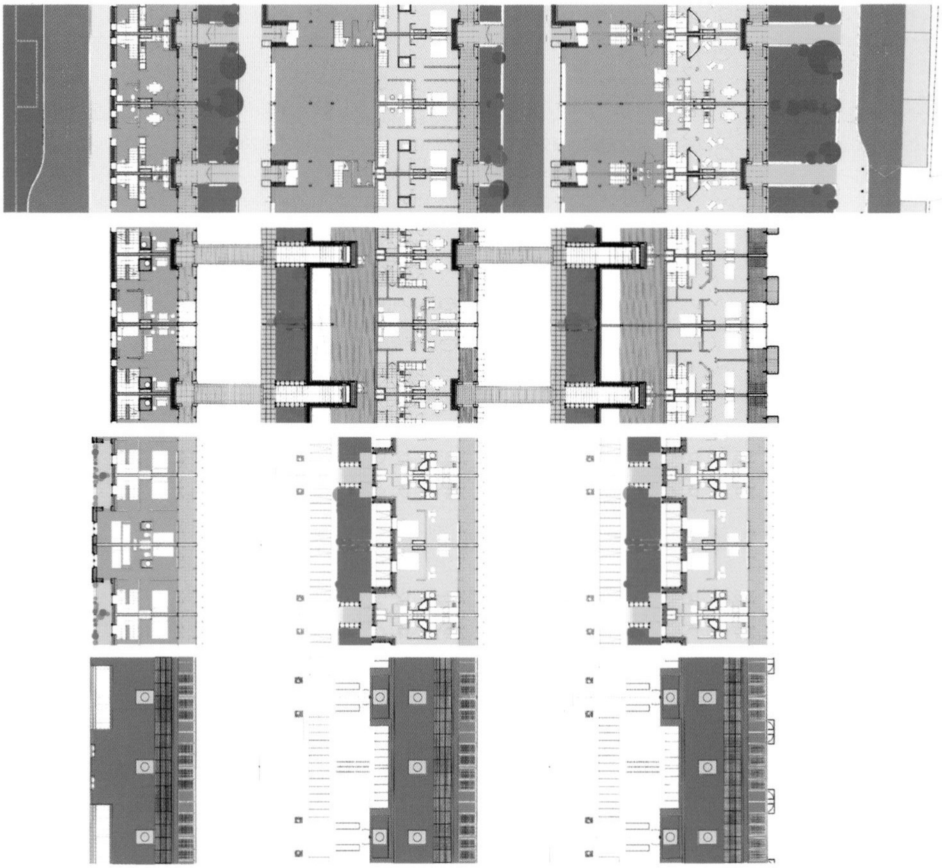

15.8 Site plan of BedZED. A series of live/work blocks with parking in perimeter home zone.
15.9 BedZED floor plan. A more sustainable urban lifestyle is not only practical but attractive and desirable.

to look like BedZED, but that the integrated supply chain defined in the ZEDproducts range can now be used to create a variety of different generic forms capable of supporting different architectural palates. The results of applying volume discounts to the ZED supply chain are spectacular, with 100 homes/year costing about 30 per cent above regulations minimum, 1000 homes/year costing around 15 per cent above regulations minimum, and 5,000 home/year providing no extra cost over regulations minimum. Once this volume throughput has been achieved, the omission of the central heating system pays for the additional fabric investment (super-insulation, triple glazing, heat recovery, etc.). Almost all of the ZED supply chain can be used to upgrade existing buildings, potentially increasing its carbon savings by application to our existing stock of homes and offices. Perhaps large regeneration projects could look at the potential of volume-discounted supply chains, ensuring a consistent standard of high-performance components and locally sourced building materials, but with a number of different professional teams including urban designers and architects to provide variety and different forms of architectural expression.

So why not use the government's Sustainable Communities Programme to pioneer some of these best-practice demonstration projects, and kick start the supply chain economies of scale? If only 5,000 of the 160,000 new homes built in the UK each year were built to ZED standards, there would be no additional premium for meeting this carbon-neutral specification for both homes and workspace. Instead the best we can hope for is the BRE ecohomes excellent pass specification – offering only 35 per cent carbon reductions over a building regulations minimum specification. This is the maximum green specification that the government will countenance, based on consulting the conservative volume house builders. Most new homes will be built to ecohomes 'very good standard' – offering an even lower carbon reduction performance. Equally worrying is the official promotion of lightweight prefabricated construction under the modern-methods-of-construction banner. With increasingly hot summers, it is likely that affordable 'coolth' will become as important as affordable warmth as contributors to fuel poverty in under-privileged households. The lack of internal radiant thermal mass in both timber-frame and steel-frame solutions virtually guarantees the need for air conditioning within a thirty-year period – again raising carbon emissions. And it is no use relying on ground source heat pumps – the electricity consumption still rises spectacularly, incurring carbon penalties far in excess of proven passive cooling strategies. It could be proposed that to

15.10 Helios Road balconies. Typical south-facing gardens with balcony at first-floor level.

15.11 Village square from south. Blocks clustered around a village square and centralised community meeting space.

build the sustainable communities programme to these mediocre specifications, ignoring climate change, would be an environmental liability, especially when the concept of creating new households without any increase in population is already a strategy virtually guaranteed to increase national carbon emissions.

It appears that English Partnerships, the government's regeneration agency, owns around 50 per cent of the land proposed for the Sustainable Communities Programme. It seems that many of the sites in Milton Keynes are being marketed with perimeter-block masterplan briefs requiring max densities of around 45 homes/ha. The ZEDinabox range of standard house types achieves between 80 to 90 homes/ha, with integral live/work workspace as required, and virtually every home having a private garden, and all family homes an integral conservatory. It looks possible to almost halve the amount of agricultural land lost to new housing, achieve more balanced mixed-use communities that encourage home working and shared facilities such as car pools, and still achieve the same financial receipt from the land sale, at the same time as building an aspirational carbon-neutral community. Until the necessary economies of scale are achieved, additional density or planning gain is the best way of offsetting the additional construction cost, and creating a level playing field for the ZED developer. All that is required is a little vision. If the 5,000 homes/year target was achieved over a three-year plan, then there would be no financial penalty for constructing to the ZED specifications, and most volume house builders would automatically adopt these standards without concern – as is beginning to happen in other parts of Europe – particularly Austria. This would achieve a step-change reduction in carbon emissions without any real investment. It is vital that we do not worry about the solar urban design breaking the rigid and out-dated design codes currently being promoted by the neo-conservatives from the Prince's Foundation – a new set of design criteria is bound to generate a fresh urban layout, a fresh aesthetic and a new ways of leading a *one planet lifestyle*. The UK replaced its homes and workspaces at around 1.5 per cent/year over much of the twentieth century, meaning national carbon neutrality could be achieved through the urban regeneration process alone – a target now possible before the start of the next century. So how does this potential reassignment of our cultural priorities translate into new urban form with carbon auditing and ecological footprint analysis beginning to inform fresh environmentally accountable urban interventions? The following examples show how the ZED supply chain and urban design approach can deliver different development solutions to match the urban and suburban context, without all the schemes looking like BedZED. If this supply chain were adopted by English Partnerships or some of the regional development agencies for even a tiny percentage of their development programme, somewhere between 2,000 and 5,000 homes a year would result in no additional cost for this aspirational step-change specification. ZEDfactory wish to actively encourage other delivery teams to adopt this supply chain, and would prefer to work with the government to make these standards accessible to the entire industry. It is important that this initiative is formulated to be in the national interest rather than to benefit any individual companies.

BEDZED: THE NEW ENGLISH GARDEN-CITY PROTOTYPE

BedZED tries to show how we can reconcile density with amenity – achieving a step-change reduction in environmental impact at the same time as increasing most residents' quality of life. With a typical UK family's annual carbon emissions being spent thus: a third for heating and powering the home; a third for transport, commuting and private car use; and a third for food miles – with the average UK meal having travelled over 2,000 miles from farm to dinner plate – there's just no point in addressing any one of these issues without addressing the others, so at BedZED we have tried to make it so easy and convenient to lead a near carbon-neutral lifestyle that most people simply default into this way of living without conscious effort. Built to densities that mean we could meet almost all the new homes required by 2016 on existing stocks of brownfield sites, without losing valuable agricultural land and green belt to low-density traditional development. At the same time as providing most new homes with a garden, a south-facing conservatory, and the opportunity to avoid commuting by working on site, BedZED re-introduces the Victorian back-to-back, with housing facing south, and commercial space facing north. This very deep plan format provides two active frontages, minimising external wall surface area, and minimising the overall site area required by the super-insulated wall thickness. This creates single-aspect dwellings looking south over their own gardens, with high daylight levels maintained in a deep plan by triple-glazed roof lights over stair voids. Wherever possible, the housing ground-floor level is raised 1,200 mm above the pavement and workspace, allowing residents to look down at workers and public passing in the mews streets. Terraces are never longer than six units, allowing the development to be porous to pedestrians and cyclists, while parking is flung to the perimeter of the site using Homezone principles.

Environmentally benign innovation will cost more, so we have enabled the developer to buy a site with outline planning permission for a housing estate with a maximum permitted density, and then add an office park without having to pay for the land. We have placed gardens on the workspace roofs, which allow virtually every home to have a garden, showing how density can be increased at the same time as increasing amenity. The adjacent mid-1980s' Laing homes development over the fence has the same residential density as BedZED, but without any private gardens on three-storey walk-up flats. The money the developer would normally have spent buying land for the office park is then re-invested in the ZED super-green specification. We have set a national precedent for this legally, by expanding a normal Section 106 planning gain agreement with the local authority to officially include reduced environmental impact targets. This is a real breakthrough, as it allows carbon-neutral new mixed-use development to be built without always requiring government grants. Resale values at BedZED are a minimum of 15 per cent higher than exactly the same size unit immediately over the fence, and often around 30 per cent higher on larger flats and townhouses. Over 1,000 members of the public have registered an interest in moving to a ZED community.

SKY ZED, WANDSWORTH

How do you replicate as many of the social and environmental features of BedZED on a compact inner-city site? We found an unloved Wandsworth traffic island in public transport tariff Zone 2, with excellent public transport nodes, right beside an underused overground railway station on the Waterloo line. The site had never been considered for housing, and is currently a pedestrian no-go zone, housing a large advertising hoarding. Wandsworth Council is currently occupying many short-lease dysfunctional office buildings up the road, so we designed a four-storey car-free office plinth for the local authority, capped with a communal roof garden complete with crèche and residents bar/café. Above, two 35-storey aerodynamic blades house around 300 affordable key worker one and two-bedroom shared-ownership flats. The blades are connected every six floors with communal enlarged lift lobbies incorporating communal herb gardens and shared play space for residents. The homes are placed high enough above the traffic to dilute air pollution to normal London standards, and the super-insulated, thermally massive construction with triple glazing and heat recovery ventilation not only reduces thermal requirements to about one-fifth of a normal home, but also provides excellent acoustic isolation. Double-glazed balconies with opening windows are provided for every home. The building has been designed to focus the prevailing wind on to building-integrated wind turbines – providing all the homes' annual electrical requirements from renewable energy generated within the site's boundaries. The same wind turbines can already be found in urban areas outside petrol stations and supermarkets in this part of London and make the same noise in high winds as a car passing in the street. The careful shape of the building means that a SkyZED turbine in Wandsworth has the electrical output of the same unit sited on a hillside in Wales. The existing underpass system has been renovated and a series of glazed courtyards has been created, making it safe and easy to cross from the station to the new Wandsworth riverside quarter, effectively healing the damage to the urban fabric done by traffic engineering in the 1970s. SkyZED provides over 300 homes with no loss of open space in the borough at the same time as creating a landmark green gateway as the urban focus to one of the most important approaches to London.

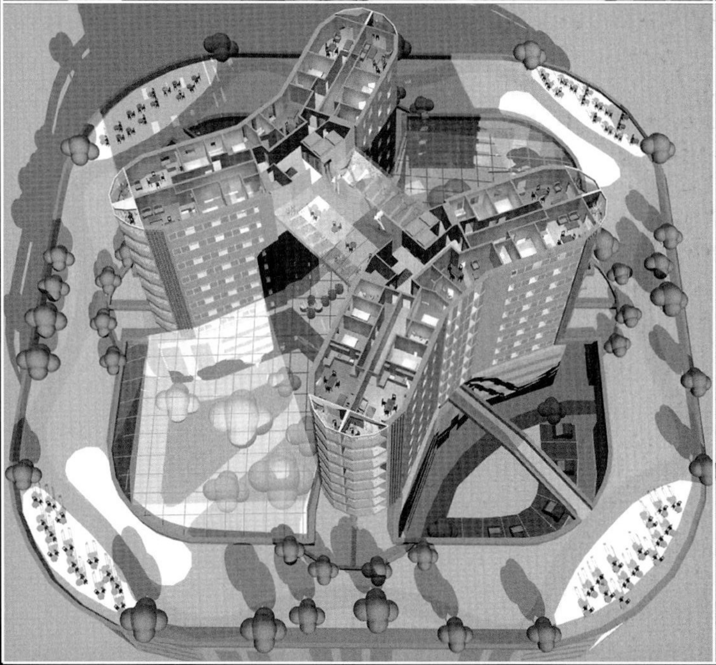

15.12 SkyZED Wandsworth, aerial view. Two 35-storey aerodynamic blades house around 300 shared-ownership flats.

15.13 Cut-away perspective. Blades connected every sixth floor with communal enlarged lift lobbies including gardens and play space.

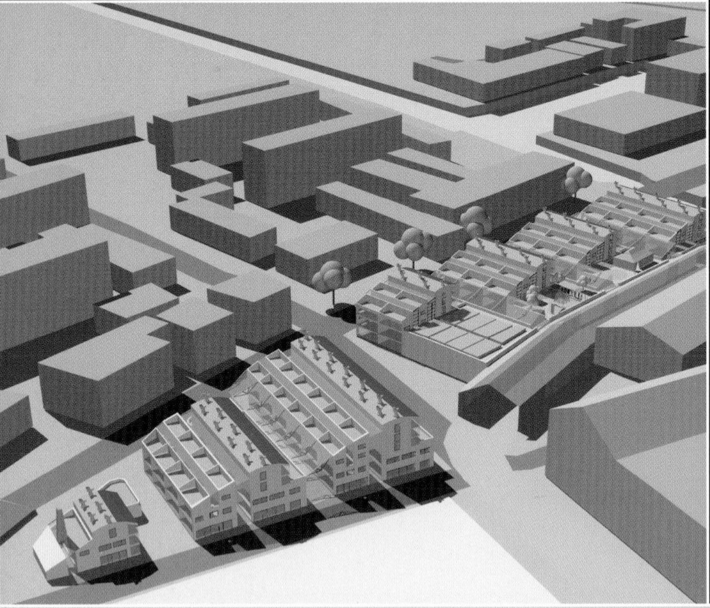

ZEDQUARTER AT KING'S CROSS

Developer Argent St George have commissioned Bill Dunster architects to produce a feasibility study for a carbon-neutral ZEDquarter on disused railway land behind King's Cross station. We had to work within the constraints of the existing tunnels, incorporate a listed Victorian potato market arcade – and work within the rules set by the masterplanners. A two-storey commercial base containing office and retail space is top lit by east-west axis central arcades feeding into the listed glazed street. Above, roof gardens are placed wherever storey heights are restricted by underground tunnels, with south-facing three-storey family and live/work residential accommodation above more solid load-bearing zones. Reclaimed London stock brick will tie the new mixed use development into the tough street scene and existing historic railway buildings, providing the urban context in this part of town. We believe this project shows how higher density solar urbanism can work in inner city areas with high land values.

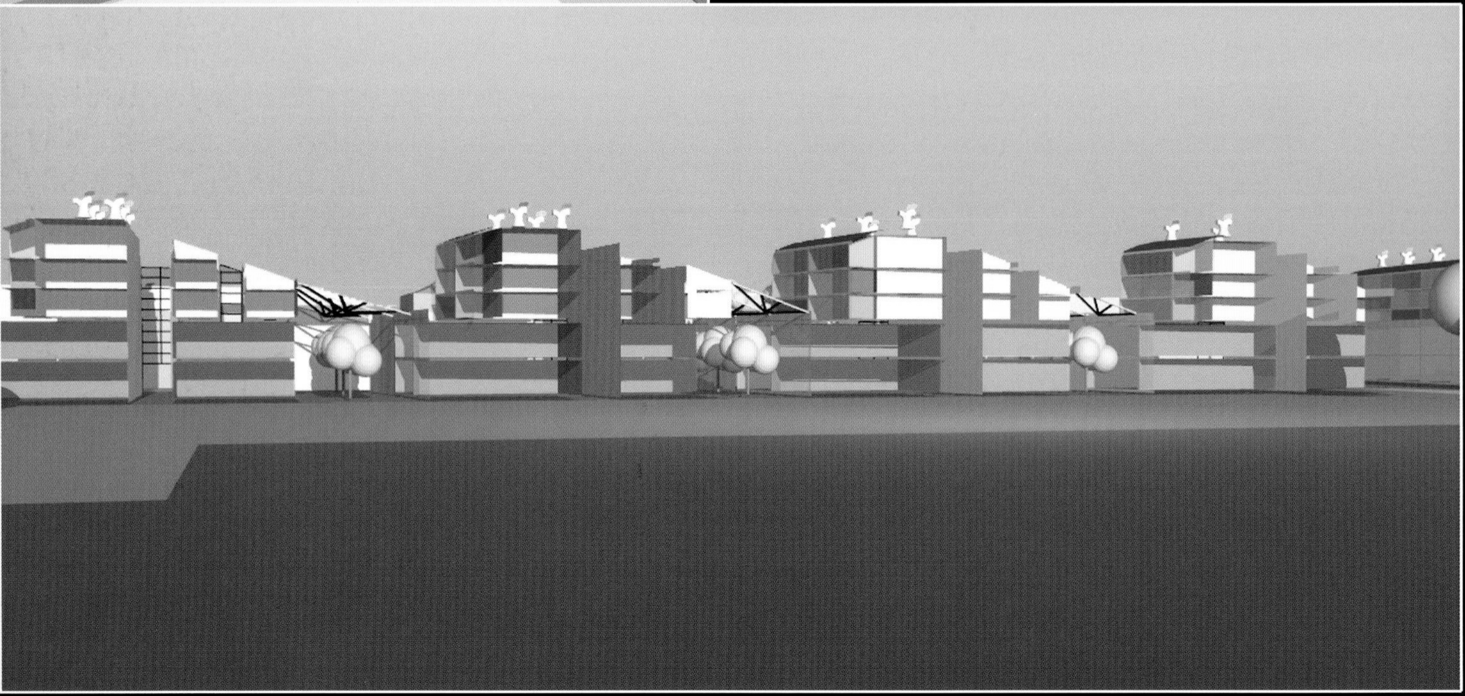

15.14 ZEDquarter, King's Cross, aerial view of low-rise option from north. Feasibility study for disused railway lands behind King's Cross station.

15.15 ZEDquarter, King's Cross, cross-section

BROUGHTON PARCEL D

As climate change accelerates, it is increasingly important to plan urban quarters around the physical properties of the construction proposed. This is particularly important if lightweight timber-framed or steel-framed systems are proposed. Conventional lightweight construction places thermally massive brickwork or rendered blockwork on the outside face of any habitable space, effectively removing any potential for passive cooling or solar thermal storage in winter. With this construction it becomes important to use small windows to limit summer solar gain, and if possible keep to east-west orientation.

Working within English Partnership's design codes requiring perimeter block layouts, ZEDfactory have proposed placing thermally massive ZED standard housetypes on all terraces within 20 to 30 degrees of due south, and conventional timber-framed housetypes from a volume housebuilder's standard range on all other orientations.

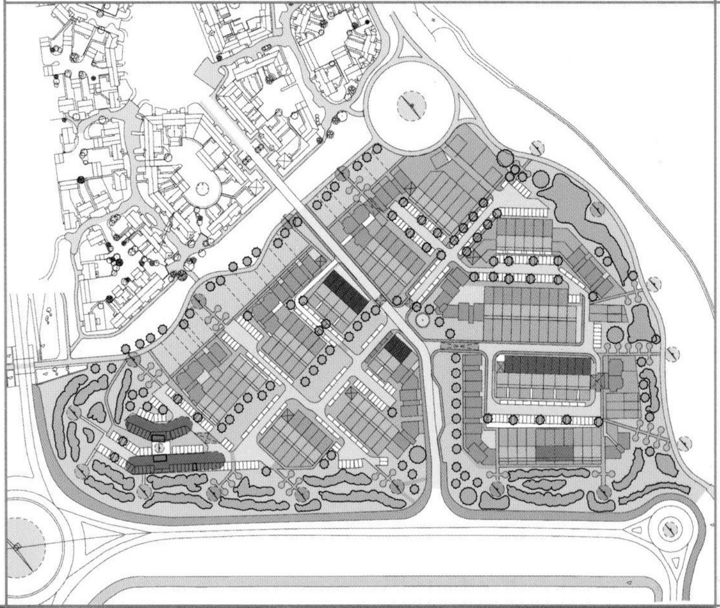

The east-west facing homes all have individual gables maximising the surface area of south-facing roof surface. This allows future installation of large areas of solar electric panels and the opportunity for every household to install solar thermal panels for domestic hot water at some stage in the future. By using the large areas of 'green space left over after planning' for installing small 15 kw output wind turbines (making more or less the same noise at 20 metres per second wind speed as a car passing in the street), we found it was possible to meet the government target of a 60 per cent

15.16 Broughton, coloured site plan. Seventy homes/ha with the majority of homes having their own garden.

15.17 Perspective view from south. The target of 50 per cent of affordable homes was met.

15.18 Street view showing ZED homes juxtaposed with traditional. Addressing the new bioclimatic challenge will inevitably lead to a new urban language.

carbon reduction by 2050 at the targeted completion date for the project – autumn 2005.

Thermal modelling by Arup of both timber-framed and ZED housetypes shows ZED units to require 25 per cent less winter space heating than exactly the same spec east–west facing unit. By combining the benefits of passive solar gain and the mounting opportunities for active solar collection, it is clearly beneficial to maximise south-facing domestic frontage. By placing live/work and workspace units in the shade zone of the purely residential accommodation on the ZED units, it was also possible to achieve two active frontages, with parking courtyard home zones working well as a more commercial zone. The big difference between these ZED units and the original BedZED design is that all live/work units have their own roof gardens, allowing the allowing flexibility to move towards purely residential use if market conditions suggest this may be more appropriate. The flexibility to use the north-facing units as community spaces, bars, cafés, shops, offices, live/work units – as well as residential – will ensure that this community will adapt easily to a future suggesting far lower levels of private transport. Significantly, the Broughton masterplan proposed a density of 45 homes/ha. The ZEDfactory scheme achieved around 70 homes/ha, with the majority of homes having their own garden, and, although requiring a higher overall construction cost to meet the low carbon specification, the residual land value still substantially exceeded that achieved by a more conventional ecohomes excellent rating built to the original planning brief density. The target of 50 per cent affordable was still met. Using this worked example, we believe it is possible to demonstrate how the government's sustainable communities programme can be fitted on less land, with higher numbers of affordable homes, and with significantly lower overall carbon emissions.

NOTES

1 According to DEFRA climate change conference, London, March 2004.

2 According to Pierre Williams, House Builders Federation spokesman.

3 The PPS22 is where new buildings have a minimum quota of their annual energy load met from building integrated renewables.

What urban design needs to make its theoretical basis complete is a vertical theory of urban design. Urban design must extend from just horizontal considerations to those which rise vertically upwards and into the public and semi-public realms of buildings themselves. Systemically, urban design needs to be integral to interior architecture and to the internal spatial configurations within buildings.

This is particularly crucial in the case of many of today's new intensive urban buildings, many of which are literally cities within buildings. We see these dense building types emerging in the increasingly intensifying urban areas in our cities. Whether these structures are simply tall buildings or actual skyscrapers – or are other large mixed-use complexes, such as super-large shopping malls (also found in suburban areas) and public/institutional buildings where people gather in large numbers – we find an increasing provision of enclosed, or partially-enclosed, public spaces within their densley packed and intensively built forms.

CHAPTER 16

A VERTICAL THEORY OF URBAN DESIGN

KEN YEANG

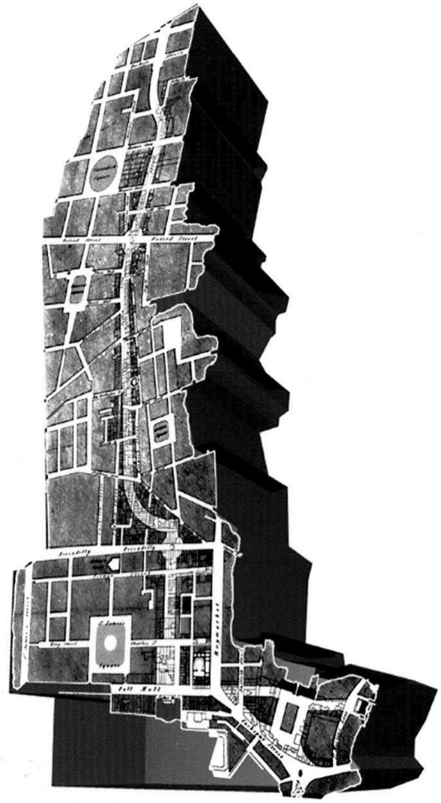

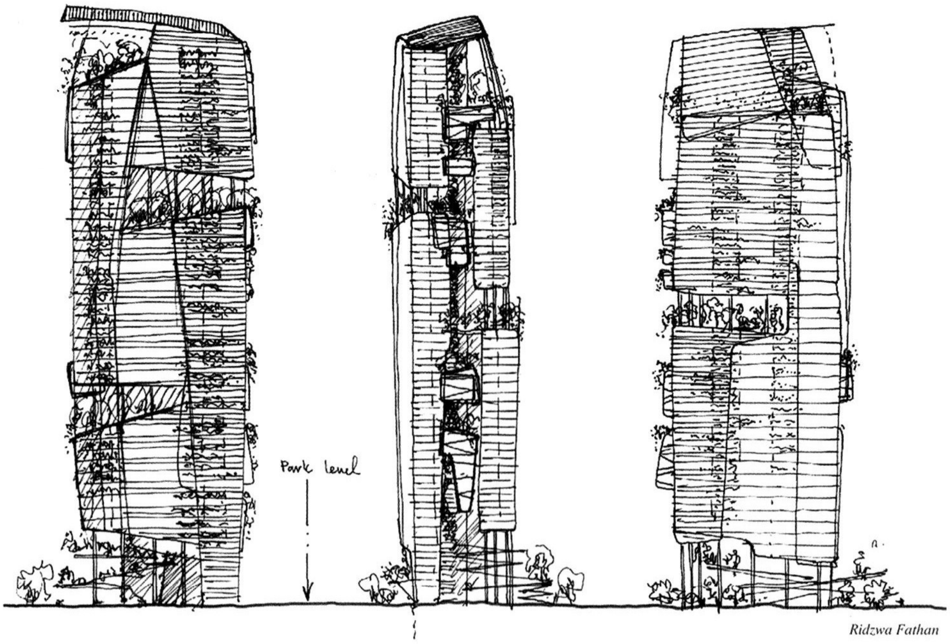

16.1 A vertical theory of urban design, Georgian London. Successful existing urban design concepts as models for designing the skyscraper built form.
16.2 Sketches of Eco Tower, Elephant and Castle, London, by Ridzwa Fathan. Greening opportunities within the high rise.
16.3 Masterplan. The skyscraper as a vertical extension of the city.

A recurrent central issue in urban design is of course how to organize groups of buildings to contain space and public activities, as distinct from the modernist view of buildings as objects in space. For instance, the skyscraper has inevitably been regarded as an object in space and more often considered as a pristine and prestigious symbol or landmark denoting an important place or node, than judged on its contribution to the public realm at the ground plane.

Simply stated, many of the new urban buildings today are now so densely populated and such intensively concentrated built structures, that it would be totally useless to plan and to design these as if they were just endeavors in architectural or engineering design. We need to add the urban designer's spatial, social and public-realm dimensions to their design.

By making the intensive building type's design and planning become much more of an urban design endeavor, it is clear that their design must take into account (of course, in addition to the normal engineering and architectural considerations) those usual urban design concerns, such as the creation of communities, of place-making and public realms, of providing multiple accessible linkages, of creating vistas and a sense of enclosure in the semi-public spaces.

The design challenge now becomes one of how these urban design factors can be achieved and interpreted satisfactorily at the upper reaches of the new urban type's built form, and not merely at the ground level.

It is, of course, at the ground plane that the design issue of resolving this junction, where the vertical parts of the intensive urban building type meet the ground, needs to be resolved in a satisfactory manner. The question might be, how do we bend and stretch the public realm at the ground up into the built form's circulation and the spatial programmes at the upper parts of the structure?

What is proposed here is the need for a vertical theory of urban design to provide the basis for the design of these new intensive building types. In developing a vertical form of urban design, or as urban design that is now 'vertically considered', we can start to have an unprecedented and new way of looking at the city's intensity and at the city's intensively built-up areas, as a lateral version of existing urban design as we know it at present.

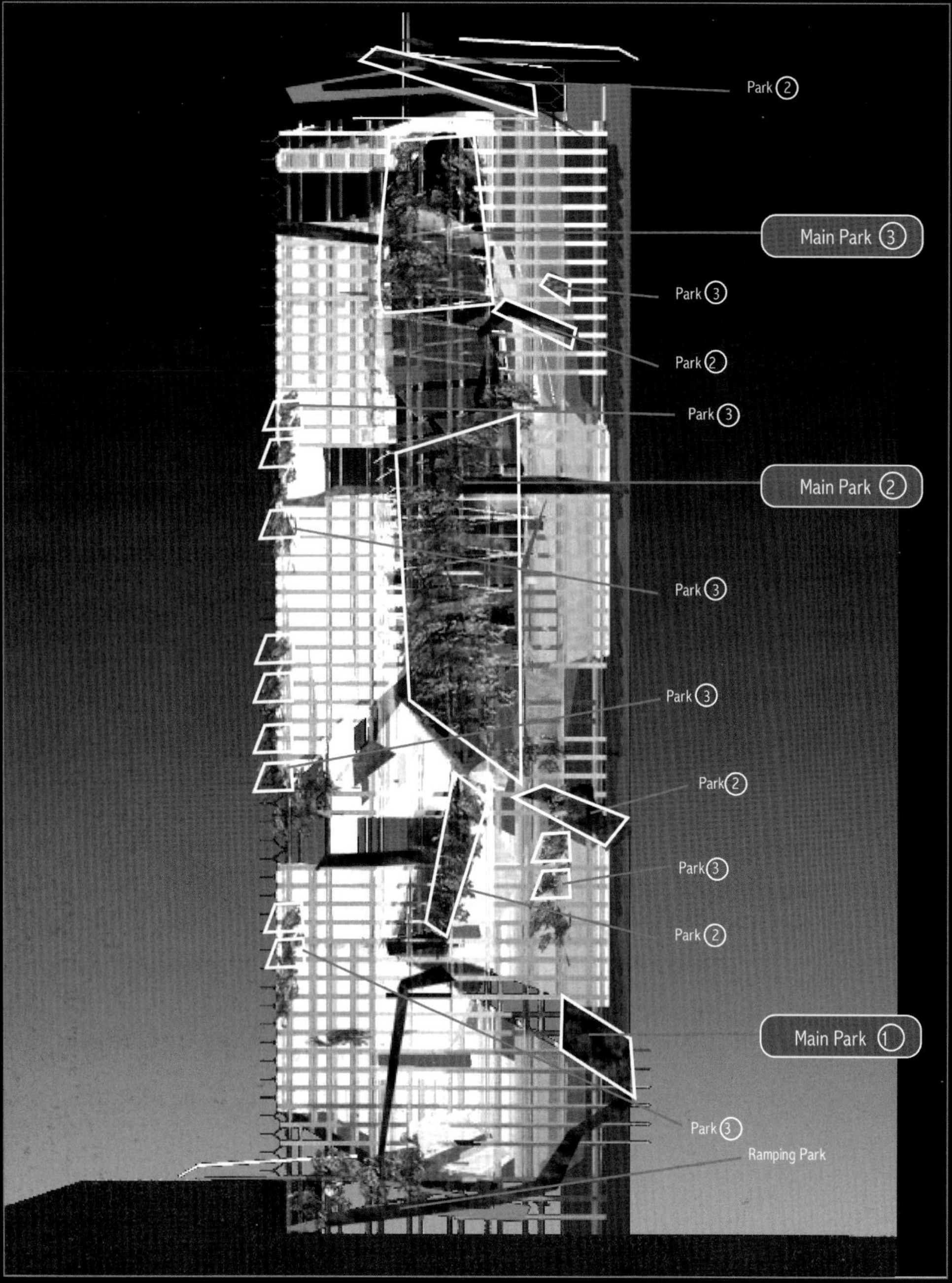

16.4 Parks in the sky. We need a vertical landscape plan that consists of large parks, pocket parks and smaller green areas for communities and their activities.

For planners, this vertical theory will reposition existing horizontal urban patterns and propositions into the vertical realm, with the city seen as truly three-dimensional, as a vertical matrix of land uses and spaces.

What are the beneficial outcomes of this theory? These are as follows: it will influence (and benefit), first of all, the practice of urban design today by expanding its role into the vertical built-form of the increasing numbers of intensive mixed-use buildings that are being built where large numbers of people congregate. It will improve the future quality of life of the inhabitants of these densely populated buildings by making them more habitable and humane, by seeking to resemble the ideal conditions that we currently find at the ground plane but are now attempting to build up in the sky. Finally, it will cause us to rethink the existing development and techniques for the design and the planning of our city's densely built-up urban zones.

When implemented, we will likely find that future tall and intensive urban buildings in our cities will no longer consist of similar homogeneous floor plates, with one stacked on top of the other, as most are today. Now as vertical built resolutions of urban design, they will be more humane and pleasurable working and living environments with a greater diversity and differentiation of internally enclosed and semi-enclosed spaces, considerably more internally accessible and, of course, leading to better and more comfortable public realms in the sky. The greater provision of internal linkages and mobility opportunities will take place making as an essential precept for their design at the outset, and they will be pleasurable communities in the sky, healthier living and working environments, with greater interaction with and awareness of the external natural environment and landscaping, and, of course, they will be environmentally-friendly and green.

Simply stated, developing this vertical theory of urban design is the opposite of existing urban design ideas, taking concepts adopted and concepts adopted at the horizontal plane, but now flipped vertically into the intensive built form. What would urban design (in the sky) mean if the prevalent concepts and ideas of urban design are now flipped vertically?

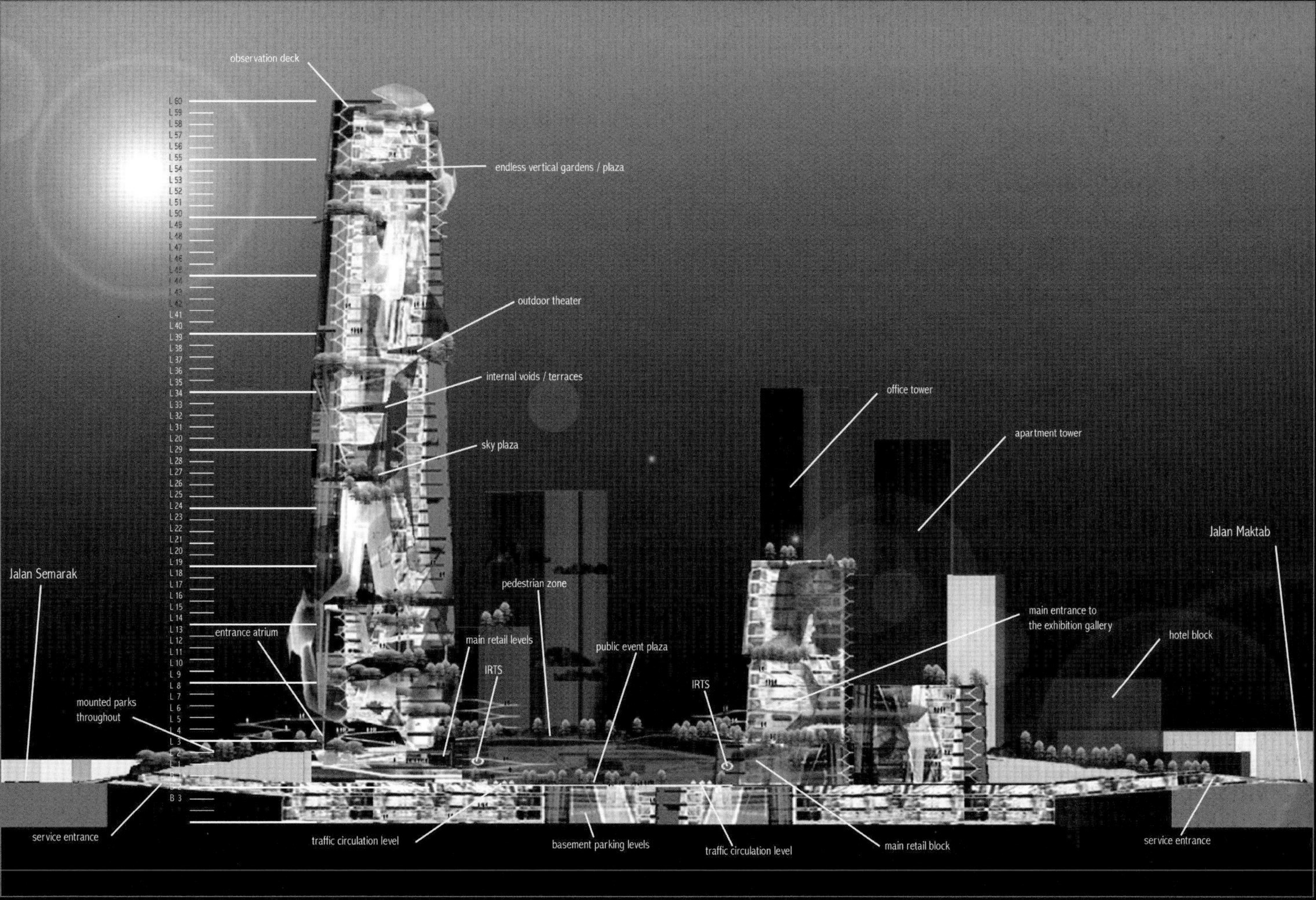

For instance, we might ask, what is place making and the creation of a destination and public realm in the sky? How can we create useable and safe public realms and places in the upper parts of the skyscraper? Would merely the provision of atriums suffice? How should these be shaped to create a sense of place?

What are linkages in the sky? How can we increase the mobility and connectivity of people within the upper parts of buildings beyond the elevator cores and escape stairs? Can we introduce secondary and tertiary circulation systems such as escalators, ramps, short-travel elevators, additional stairs, etc.?

What is the figure-ground relationship in the sky? Can there be articulated spatial relationships at the upper parts of the intensive building type beyond the relationship between the elevator cores and the net useable spaces and the vertical stacking of floors?

What is community making in the sky? How can we create habitable communities in the sky and avoid having to place all the communal amenities only at the ground plane?

How can we have parks and green spaces in the sky? How can we have a green vertical landscaping plan for the skyscraper that can consist of large parks, smaller parks, pocket parks, and smaller green areas for the communities and their activities?

All at once, we now find a whole new realm of possibilities opening before us, both for the architect and for the urban designer. This applies

16.5 **High rise should have a multiplicity of uses. Like the city at the ground plane, all the essential amenities should be accessible and provided at the upper levels of the high rise.**

even to the real estate developer who may be building the next generation of high rises, and is trying to make the high rise more habitable and marketable in a competitive market, and will need to take account of these new considerations. The design impact will also be the reconfiguring of the skyscraper's built form and spatial dispositions beyond the current range of bland towers.

Urban designers will suddenly find that their existing field of expertise and relevance has significantly expanded. They will be needed now more than ever in the design of tall structures and other intensive buildings in the city.

In application, the idea will advance the development of practical knowledge of the urban design of skyscrapers and other intensive buildings, and at the same time provoke a theoretical debate on the idea of a vertical theory of urban design. Urban design has much to teach architects and developers in the design of such intensive buildings.

With the current trend by many of our countries' leaders to intensify developments within existing cities and with the continued proliferation of the high rise and other intensive building types, the application of urban design principles and techniques to a vertical theory of urban design vertically is even more pressing.

16.6 The application of urban design techniques has much to teach architects and developers in the design of such intensive buildings.

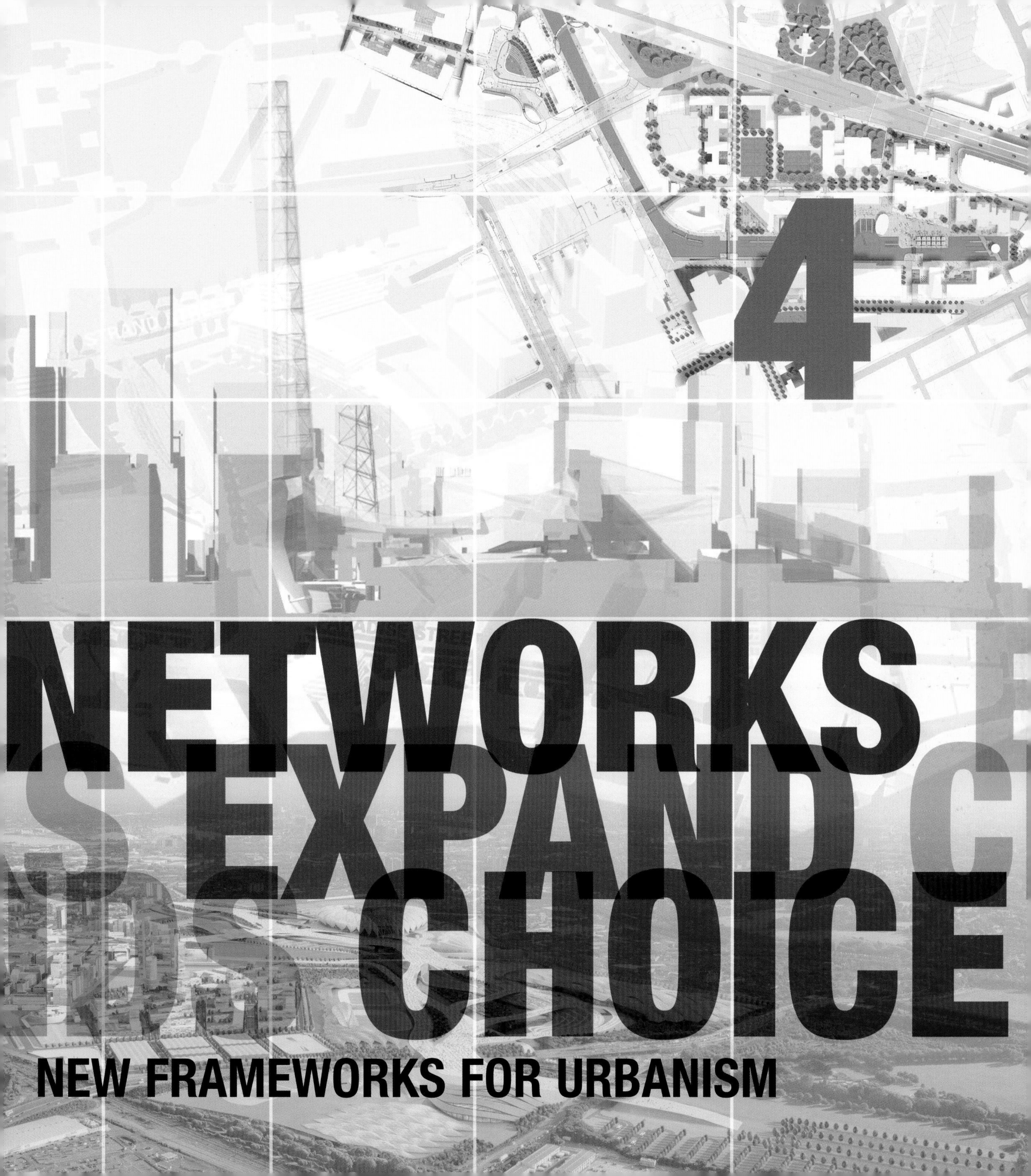

4

NETWORKS EXPAND CHOICE

NEW FRAMEWORKS FOR URBANISM

The BRAND NEW AUTHENTIC RETAIL EXPERIENCE is all around us and is being developed in new forms of architecture at an alarming rate. The snobbishness that has accompanied High Architecture's approach to retail design now has to disappear in the face of the sheer proportion of new space being created that has a retail component as its core use. All architects and urban designers have to confront the issues raised by the rise of retail. Theoretical discussions, most notably, *The Harvard Design School Guide to Shopping*, have made the subject fashionable and indeed essential reading for anyone interested in the future of urban design.[1] But all this does not mean that the professions generally understand the implications of embracing the commercial, indeed, many haven't the least idea as to what the key ingredients of retail design are and how they affect urban space.

I have chosen the 'Brand New Authentic Retail Experience' as a title as each word in this phrase encapsulates a key aspect of the nature and future of the rise of retail and its impact on urban design. I will highlight in turn the focus of ideas related to each word.

CHAPTER 17

THE BRAND NEW AUTHENTIC RETAIL EXPERIENCE

THE COMMERCIALISM OF URBAN DESIGN

RICHARD REES

BRAND[2]

The rise of the Global Brand is one of the most significant cultural phenomena related to retail success. A brand is a form of super-image that transcends the limitations of the product it identifies. This is best exemplified by a brand such as Nike. The Nike swoosh is a universal trademark that does not rely on language to convey its meaning but encapsulates a whole series of meanings in relation to lifestyle, fitness, health and other similar aspirational goals for a wide section of the population. It has been argued that there is a process of deification now taking place in relation to brands with consumers acting like acolytes. Therefore, there is a need for 'temples' for the service of brand deities. One such, designed by BDP in 2000, is Niketown in London. This is the conversion of an existing large store premises into a 'town' where consumers simultaneously experience a museum (sporting artefacts from famous athletes), a miniature city (houses for each sport) and entertainment in the form of constant video displays and music. The shopping seems almost secondary yet the formula obviously works with the brand-conscious shopper as this is one of the most successful stores in London in terms of turnover.

The message here is that more and more stores are going to be driven by brand considerations and more consumers are going to shop to experience the brand environment. This implies a completely different perceptual emphasis in relation to brand shopping from older forms of retail grazing. The further implication is that the shopper does not read a street as a series of shops or buildings so much as head for a brand destination and experience other brands on the way. The power and reach of brands are such that the street has difficulty in distracting the shopper from this shopping pattern.

The most visible recent brand building in the UK is Selfridges in Birmingham. This is a deliberately provocative form created by Future Systems to give immediate identity to the store. The façade is the building and its scale-less lustre created from a surface of shimmering ceramic panels suggests all sorts of readings. However you choose to look at it (it particularly reminds me of a giant handbag), it transmits all the right messages inspirationally to the potential Selfridges customer. It is a one-off and Selfridges will have difficulty replicating its impact elsewhere but the iconography of the façade has still managed to find its way into the typeface used for the building signage.

NEW

The one constant in retail is that it is always changing. The word 'new' is at the core of the mantra of its continual re-invention and therefore customer satisfaction and continually expanded spending. Retail change is arguably a key barometer of change in general in twenty-first-century society and exhibits the characteristics of a natural virus. Viruses adapt and change to suit their environment, mutating so that they can spread successfully. Other commentators are very aware of the issues this raises in the more static realm of urban design:

> **Shopping, rather than being a stable urban building block, is best described in terms of cycles, births, declines, and measured in terms of life spans.**
>
> **The rift between planning and shopping ignores the extent to which shopping pervades the conceptualisation of the urban. Because the influence of commercial retail has so permeated the idea of the city that it is impossible to separate the notion of urbanity from shopping, the issue of resisting shopping's spectacular lure has become irrelevant. Architecture's antagonism towards shopping is due in part to its historical preoccupation with form and composition. By imagining space in terms of bounded, stable, and unchanging entities, architecture has been largely unable to accept the excessive and formless nature of shopping.[3]**

17.1 Niketown, Oxford Street, London. Niketown epitomises the new wave of brand-exploiting stores and each one is unique to its location. Source: BDP

17.2 Selfridges, Birmingham's revitalised Bull Ring. The skin and form of this building are deliberately ambiguous and memorable to reinforce the uniqueness of the Selfridges brand. Source: Future Systems

17.3 Selfridges seen across Birmingham. Seen from the perspective of the Birmingham cityscape, the impact of the Selfridges building is even more pronounced.

The difficulty for urban design in embracing retail is in this nature of change. Urban theory recently has predicated concepts of relatively permanent environments whose key values, once established, are based on a permanence of character. There are no examples of urban theory that I am aware of where flexibility and commercial values are celebrated. Even ten years from now you can guarantee that a retail environment will be very different from what has been designed now. It is guaranteed that there will be a number of waves of change even in the near future as retailers look for what the *Harvard Design School Guide* calls 'The Next Big Thing'. The danger of embracing change in this way is that obsolescence is inevitable and makes creating the right urban environment and architecture with a coherent typology that contributes to the retail environment supremely difficult.

It is in its very nature that new urban retail development is expensive and requires a lot of land acquisition and compulsory purchase. The risk imposed on the developer is high so they will not usually undertake these projects unless they give a high premium return. This means in the UK that they look first to create value by encouraging the big stores such as John Lewis to come into the picture and demand large-scale developments. Incremental development is therefore difficult to create. However, once a threshold of value has been created, the possibilities of creative urban design start to become much greater.

AUTHENTIC

Public space, as it was once classically defined by generations of architects and city planners, no longer truly exists. This is because historic public space had not just a physical identity, but also had a social identity bound to the activities that took place in it. Social interaction and identity have been taken up and removed by media with much wider reaches and through which information can now be presented, debated, and transformed: public space has been succeeded by newspapers, journals, magazines, television, radio and the Internet. For decades the media has been the primary means of public expression, where many initial impressions of reality have been created, where prominent events have been experienced.

The idea of public space as functioning in the current historic pattern is generally now outdated. Very few public spaces can function as outlets for spontaneous public demonstrations because of the diffuse nature of modern constituencies. Trafalgar Square is still an occasional national focus for demonstrations but the authorities have prevented it for a number of years from being the focus of New Year celebrations in London. The whole public domain is now up for grabs in terms of being part of the backdrop to new sorts of public expression. The way that the squares in Sydney were taken over for the Olympics by installing cinemas to watch events, the colonisation of streets by protest groups that deliberately set out to undermine the street's normal operation and the conversion of the Seine motorways in Paris into beaches in August are all examples of the way we have deconstructed space and expected it to respond in a more flexible way to our changing needs. This is a great opportunity for cities if it is understood properly and seen to be positive rather than (as is sometimes the case where politicians are concerned) being seen as an unnatural development of the way we interact with our cities.

This idea of the fake and the authentic is becoming meaningless if the authentic is not recognised

17.4 Tesco and Tesco Express. The ubiquitous chain food retailer has mutated the Tesco retail building to adapt to the smaller sites now available in town and city centres.

17.5 Bournemouth Library. The library as social centre and shopping experience in Bournemouth – a highly successful combination. Source: BDP as such by the spectator and can be challenged on a large number of theoretical levels. The development and sophistication of virtual reality space will lead to an even greater acceptance of the non-reality or non-physical space experience and, in the face of this, the competition from any sort of 'real' experience will become an issue. I doubt very much if the concept of authenticity will even feature in the debate in a few years time when electronic parallel realities are common.

At the moment the new urban retail street can now only be read as an open mall in the city. A mall is a shopping street where the primary experience is retail and the street is structured to maximise this. The city in a post-'out-of-town'-mall world has to accept this and come to term with the 'inauthentic' implications. The danger that is inherent in accepting the supremacy of the retail imperative that other important design generators are absorbed as second-hand and in a romanticised and meaningless form. As the *Harvard Design School Guide to Shopping* succinctly puts it: 'As the processes of gentrification, commercialisation, and 'theme-ing'– all forces implied by the logic of shopping – become increasingly accepted as strategies to revive the city, the artificial effectively becomes the real.'[4]

Even great urban theorists such as Jane Jacobs have failed to see the inherent contradictions in the ideas of gentrification and have helped the creation of what many see as theatrical backdrops to commercial environments. Given what we have just discussed about the nature of change in retail environments, then the implication is that retail environments become theatrical backdrops that change every so often to match the latest retail trends.

This scenario has not yet happened outside the confines of the theme park, and in the UK the latest designs for the new retail street embrace the concept of mixed use and a number of the other main tenets of good urban design as set out by the Urban Design Renaissance. In the BDP study for the BCSC (2002) on retail development and urban design, we looked at the compatibility of good urban design as laid out by English Partnerships and others in relation to retail design, and questioned developers, practitioners

17.6 Cribbs Causeway, Bristol. One of the last of the conventional out-of-town shopping malls, Cribbs Causeway is now changing into a focus for other development – the town is coming out to the Mall.
Source: BDP

17.7 Smaralind Shopping Centre, Reykjavik. An example of where shopping has created a social focus and allowed leisure to develop in the adjacent multi-purpose space.
Source: BDP

and the public on their views.[5] The outcome of that report demonstrated the wide gulf between retail developers, on the one hand, and the planners, regional agencies and other arbiters of good urban taste, on the other. Given that the current urban renaissance in relation to city centres desperately relies on the value inherent in retail developments, some form of reconciliation is necessary.

RETAIL

In an era of a blurring between activities, retailing has become the leisure and aspirational activity *par excellence*. It is the number one activity of the planet's most influential consumers and exists at the very top of their consciousness. Wal-Mart's sales are larger than the gross domestic products of three-quarters of the world's economies. Sainsbury's beats countries like Uruguay, Ecuador, Luxemburg and Sri Lanka.

Major institutions now rely on their retail arm to generate sufficient income to keep them in existence. Airports, art galleries, churches, hospitals, schools, railway stations and a wide range of other institutions are all now impelled by retail values as a key element in their nature and very existence. Is this an implication that institutions need to change more in the future in order to be competitive, with all the implications that has for architecture and urban design?

There are signs that the big brands and supermarket chains are becoming more flexible in their sizes and styles of shop unit. This has been evidenced by the emergence of such stores as Tesco Metro. This is good in providing more choice for customers but could drive out even more of the independent small shops by providing even more competition. In France, legislation prevents the invasion of the town centre by large stores and small independent retailers are encouraged. Nevertheless, if the big brands become more flexible in selecting shop sizes, the same competition could emerge there. This flexibility is good news in one way; the more varied the size of shop unit, the more possibility there is to create a richer urban environment. Also, with customers now targeted by computerised loyalty cards, it is possible that the diversity of goods already provided in some branches of stores such as Sainsbury's will become even more pronounced. However, this will not make up wholly for the proliferation of the major brands.

That the retail virus has spread so far and so efficiently is no surprise, given the science behind consumer spending that has developed in the past few decades. For example, psychogramming, the use of psychoanalysis, motivational analysis, focus groups or ethnographic research in order to sell commodities helps in the aim of controlling the consumer and following his or her whims with perfect flexibility.

The idea of intense competition in all areas and the wooing of the individual has led to the greater commercialisation of public space. Even classic streets such as Regent Street have their own organisations dedicated to maintaining competitive edge. Town centre manager roles are being created all over the UK and are very much in demand. Competition is now between cities rather than between suburb and city. The ultimate development of these trends is that shopping is homogenising the environment and all environments are being impelled to behave like shops.

EXPERIENCE

In a relatively grim climate like that of the UK it was inevitable that the experience of shopping in comfort provided by the covered shopping mall was going to be popular.

> **In providing a year-round climate of 'eternal spring' through the skill of architects and engineers, the shopping centre consciously pampers the shopper, who reacts gratefully by arriving from longer distances, visiting the centre more frequently, staying longer, and in consequence contributing to higher sales figures.[6]**

The out-of-town shopping mall has been discredited in the UK and accused of destroying city and town centres, as it has done in the USA. The problem for the new urban city-centre retail environment is how to lure the shopper back when some of the experience will have to contend with the weather and other inconveniences such as long walking distances to parking or poor public transport. The cities that will succeed will provide the best balance of comfort and variety of experience. There will be covered streets in new developments, but they will look like a street with a roof over it rather than an internal roofed environment in the manner of the traditional mall. There are advantages to providing covered space if it can be utilised for other purposes. In BDP's Smaralind shopping centre in Reykjavik, the covered space at the end of the shopping mall is now booked for events for three years in advance.

The public is now on the look-out for layers of pleasure in their city environment and will not be short-changed any more by low environmental aspirations. They demand a feel-good factor and a degree of environmental comfort but without complete isolation from the weather as in the traditional covered mall. This comfort factor has now to be combined with a lot of built-in stimulus – it's the theme park principle moderated for the city: a combination of stimulus and safety. The exemplars of this sort of environment do not yet exist and they will require strong and diverse imaginations if they are not immediately to descend into public access film sets.

There are parallels with the way that the retail environment is manipulated and the way classic urban design principles work. As long ago as the 1970s, Barry Maitland, in his book on retail design, talked about the need to have major points of incidence at a maximum of 200-metre centres within new retail developments. Large department stores are known as 'anchors' in retail design and are used as landmark destinations within shopping developments. Incidence is created along shopping streets by including 'MSUs' or medium-sized units such as Next, to vary the size and impact of shops. Retail architects have been manipulating these elements to create varied interior-scapes for years and are now transferring their skills to exterior-based schemes and absorbing the urban design agenda.

This shift to the outside is partly driven by the need to create more variety in the retail experience and therefore different moods. It has led to the development of terms such as 'sunshine retailing' and 'café culture' to define new ways of attracting people and custom. This celebration of the outside has given rise to more emphasis on restaurants as a major feature of the street scene, coinciding with the cultural changes caused by people cooking less for themselves. This escape to the outside does not mean that the covered street or even the mall has been abandoned but that the palette for designers combining all the elements has been expanded. Psychological reactions to places are as important for the retail designer as they are for the urban designer. They are the key to enjoyment, reputation and repeat visits and therefore to customer service and loyalty. This needs the designer to consciously assess the types of imprint and memory that are being aimed for and why. This is often not done successfully.

In the work of John Jerde, the intensity and variety of forms and juxtapositions are carried to expressive extremes. The intent is to keep shoppers in a state of heightened excitement and anticipation that keeps them in the mood to spend. The move towards mixed-use development and the inclusion of civic elements such as libraries actually gives the retail urban designers even more elements with which to structure their new designs. Changes in level, fountains, and cafés that interrupt the pure retail programme are also part of this kit of parts to play with.

With the increase in mobility provided by both the private car and air travel, cities will not only compete locally, but globally as well. Why shop in a drab local city centre if you can nearly as cheaply find the same shops in Paris or Prague with their inherent historic urban quality? What happens also when there is a true conflation of global experience created by virtual reality and the Internet? Being able to experience Paris in your sitting room is actually going to challenge the experience you will get from your local shopping area. You will be able to literally wander around Sears in New York, so why bother to go down to the local Boots? Uniqueness is therefore going to become a fundamental selling point in the success of a place.

THE NEW URBAN RETAIL-LEAD DEVELOPMENTS

Having gone through the key issues in the retail/urban design debate I have chosen to illustrate three schemes (two of them by BDP) and analyse how they react to this debate. They are in different parts of the world and have widely different briefs but still have to deal with the same issues.

Nijmeigan, Holland

One of the few completed two-level outdoor street developments with residential above, Nijmeigan has been highly influential in Europe and elsewhere in demonstrating the potential of this form. The developer, ING, employed two different architects to design the two sides of the street and the resultant richness and variety of character add immensely to the urban and retail experience. Lifts and escalators are treated as objects of street sculpture and are integrated into the design.

Paradise Street, Liverpool

This development by Grosvenor, designed by BDP, will transform a city that has lagged behind its English competitors in commercial terms for several decades. The aim is to create a subtle balance between its historic context, the city's existing retail core and a new entertainment focus adjacent to the Albert Dock. Its design programme is complex but is based on a major retail extension of 100,000 m^2 to the existing Church Street. This requires the creation of two new department stores, one being a relocation of John Lewis. There are long-term plans to have a new tram link through the site and a bus station will be incorporated into the scheme. A simple triangular retail diagram of anchor stores and retail streets is superimposed onto the city fabric and it is the synthesis of these elements that gives the scheme its strength, along with the creation of a variety of different street types and the complex use of levels.

Retail change will be absorbed by providing blocks with varied column grids and good depths to allow a variety of shop sizes. The character of each block is being enhanced by employing different architects to design each one. This avoids any possibility of descending into pastiche or creating an uneventful townscape. The mix of uses is also important in creating a unique destination. The scheme is aimed at completion for Liverpool's European City of Culture year 2006.

17.8 Paradise Street, Liverpool. By 2008 Paradise Street will realise many of the ambitions of the Urban Agenda and deliver a really sustainable retail-based mixed-use scheme. Source: BDP masterplan

Waterfront City, Melbourne

The pattern of retail in Australia is similar to the European one in the major cities. Melbourne has similarities in terms of architecture to a number of English cities but is laid out in a classic US grid system and in that way bears more resemblance to the US models. Waterfront City is a docklands development combining retail, residential and entertainment in a concentrated development surrounded by new high-rise residential. The concept is of a major waterfront plaza linked by two dense shopping and residential streets to an entertainment area dominated by a 110-metre diameter observation wheel surrounded by other entertainment facilities and restaurants.

The scheme is a combination of intense entertainment and waterfront activity book-ending the retail and residential development in between. Again, the retail diagram is simple, consisting of

17.9 Waterfront City, Melbourne. Waterfront City in Melbourne is a striking mixture of retail, leisure and residential that promises to deliver a rich new environment. Source: BDP and Hassell

17.10 **Sheffield, new retail. The proposed Pinstone Street development in Sheffield is almost impossible to differentiate from the surrounding existing city fabric – which was the intention.** Source: BDP

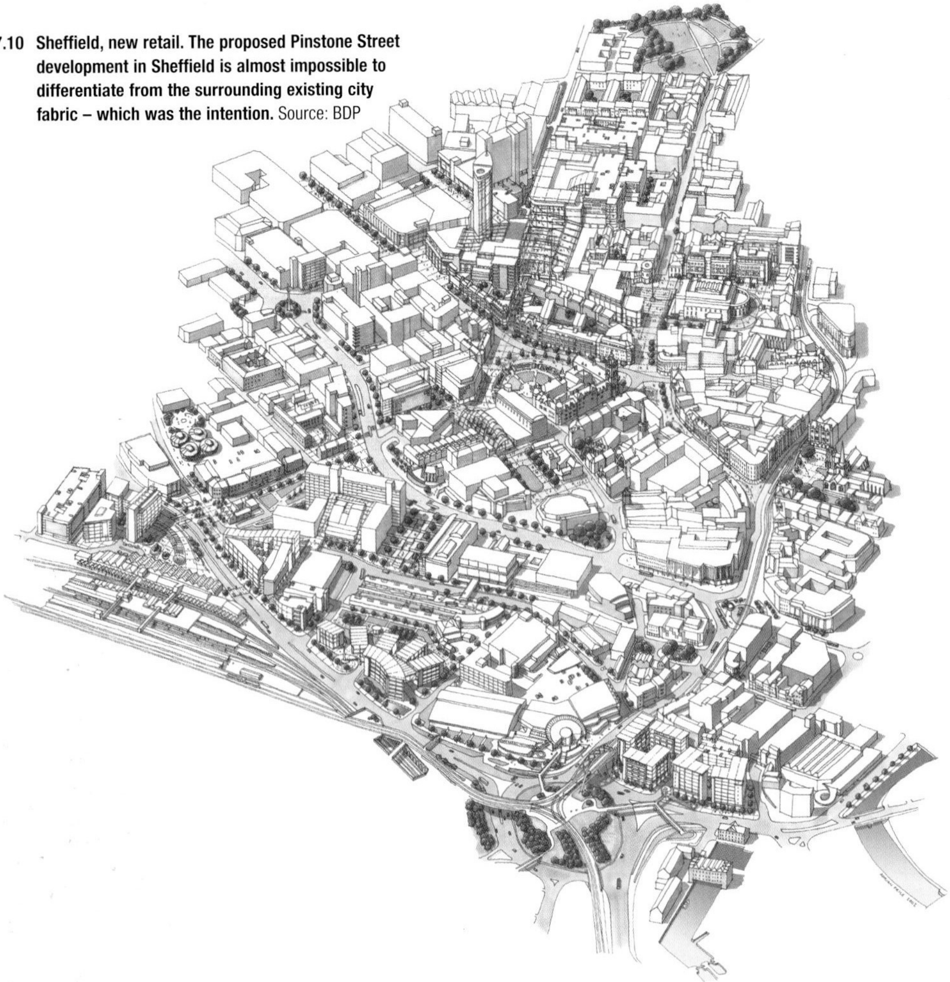

two parallel streets with a cross-link connecting the waterfront to the entertainment area.

In Liverpool, a portion of the two-level street is justified by major drops in the topography of the ground. In Waterfront City, there is no such justification in terms of topography but the two levels throughout the retail streets represent a more deliberately intense street experience. The canopies over walkways provide shelter from the harsh extremes of the local climate whilst maintaining the nature of the street and providing a reference to the main downtown retail area. Block depths allow for the same degree of flexibility as at Liverpool. There are fewer architects involved than in Liverpool as there are fewer streets, but uniqueness is still provided by them working separately on the different streets (BDP and Hassell, Melbourne). The potential for different uses and events on this site is huge and the main public spaces are already earmarked for major events.

The first phase will be completed for the Commonwealth Games in 2006 and will consist of the core street pattern and most of the retail and residential buildings plus the observation wheel.

CONCLUSION

We are at a point of great change in the way people experience and view the urban environment and it is likely that the pace of this change will continue. Retail development has become an essential element of this change and is one of its generators. Our perceptions of good urban environment will have to evolve and take into account the way that people's perceptions of their environment are being influenced by technology and the media. The role of retail in changing these perceptions has finally to be acknowledged.

A lack of flexibility in thinking at this stage could be disastrous and lead to another wave of problems with the urban environment within a generation. Changes in shopping patterns are already under way with the emergence of Internet shopping or 'e-tailing'. However, it appears that there is a synergy between the bricks and mortar retailers and e-tailing. The balance in the future may be a mixture of both in order to keep brand awareness in both the high street and on the net.

Will e-tailing finally kill the High Street? I think not, as the shopping experience of each is still very different. The High Street can compete as it gives a social experience in addition to the shopping experience. Combinations of different activity in relation to retail, as at Waterfront City, will become the norm to attract people away from their computers. To stay successful, the High Street has to build on its unique strengths, stay flexible and finally emphasise and keep vibrant the additional social and physical experiences it can draw in.

NOTES

1 *The Harvard Design School Guide to Shopping*, Cologne: Taschen, 2001.

2 I have cheated here by using the word as an adverb in the headline phrase but discussing the noun. This sort of shift is typical of the world of retail.

4 *Harvard Design School Guide*, Cologne: Taschen, 2001

5 BSCS, *Urban Design for Retail Environments*, London: 2002

6 Victor Gruen, *Shopping Towns in USA*, New York: Van Nostrand Reinhold Company 1960

In an essay entitled ‘Roads belong in the landscape’, the American commentator on landscape J.B. Jackson asked the question ‘Which came first, the house or the road leading to the house?’[1] Not an easy question to answer, however, if one were to rephrase this question in terms of which do we value more, then the answer is likely to be easier to find: the house, of course. More significant to Jackson’s original question though – and also not easy to answer – is the wider more fundamental question concerning the nature of place and our relationship to it. Is place exclusively a site of permanency or can it be something more temporary or a site without clear demarcation? Can place be an experience defined more easily by movement?

The networks that link economic and industrial activity are becoming increasingly complex. There are more people and more amounts of stuff moving around today than at any previous time and the trends indicate that the amounts and distances will increase. The number of points which movement is to and from is also increasing. At the same time, economic activity no longer conforms to traditional notions of geography and architecture and, as a consequence, is becoming more difficult to read in terms of its location. It is no longer located in the places that it used to be such as city centres and ports, nor in buildings that look like ‘proper’ factories or shops. Economic activity is now located in places similar to Swindon, Ontario Mills and Crick. If this is anywhere at all, it is beyond what is commonly recognised as the urban fringe. This activity can be seen locating itself near motorway junctions and airports and is evident by the amount of commercial traffic that flows between these points.

CHAPTER 18

PLACE, EXPERIENCE, MOVEMENT

ANDREW CROSS

This greater movement of goods and people is closely tied to contemporary consumer lifestyles, which are generally identified with a life oriented towards the urban centre. Contemporary life – at least affluent contemporary life – is very much defined by the principle of being able to travel to an almost limitless number of destinations and obtain goods and services from around the world almost as quickly as one can type a credit card number. The distribution centres, out-of-town shopping centres and business parks, along with airports and motorways, are very much the channels along which this flow of people and goods moves. And it is constantly moving. Goods move in and out of distribution centres as quickly as people do at airports.

These channels of movement are also growing at an alarming rate. So much so that that they can seem to be on the verge of overwhelming the communities they may actually serve. Not only this, but it would appear that the relationships between our contemporary lifestyles and the infrastructures that underpin them is now very difficult to conceptualise – especially if contact is only via a computer screen. With so much movement, with so much dispersal of goods and services, it becomes difficult to really know where something – the manufacture of a product or origination of a service – is happening. We might believe it has happening in one place when in fact it is probably happening somewhere else altogether. In terms of a perception of an economic landscape, it is possible there is now a kind of disembodiment occurring between activity and place. At least, with what is usually thought to mean place.

In more traditional understandings of place, settlement and activity have a direct relationship with physical geography. Work is linked to the location of raw materials and markets and people generally settle where the work is. This traditional image no longer applies. Today the situation appears much more fluid as activity and labour migrate around the world without really changing form. Yet, seemingly contrary to this fluidity, interest in and emotional attachment to place appear to be local and very particular, even if the places under consideration are themselves dispersed and in some cases notional. For example one might like to think of a local High Street with an attendant localised economy and that food sold in this High Street is grown in a specifically 'rural' situation. Or, that a house in southern Europe or a tropical beach that are visited for holidays are considered authentic and 'unspoilt'. Equally, it might be the 'cultural energy' so closely identified with the concentration of a thriving city.

What tends to characterise such places is a sense of permanency and the recognition in them of some kind of cultural value, a value that other sorts of place apparently lack. While such places become very important to people, and indeed for very good reason, there are many other kinds of 'place' which are possibly just as important but the experience of which is very different. Certainly, there seems to be little interest in or love for motorways, airports or, indeed, distribution centres, out-of-town shopping centres and call centres, and their lack of value is compounded by what is identified as a homogeneity of design and experience. Except, of course, the importance or real value of these 'non-places' is in the services they provide, which can often be the means of connection, or channels of movement, between the more valued places.

Interestingly, it is within the channels of movement, or places that are more temporary, that most people spend their time; either working, travelling or consuming. Whether we ourselves are moving or other things are moving, these places matter to us. But why do such places tend to be overlooked and how much is understood about their relationship to the places that indicate a desirable contemporary lifestyle? Do we think that they are ultimately dispensable? Is it simply the case that the only sense of place possible is with the qualities only associated with the places of recognised value? Another thing that characterises places of cultural worth is that they are easily visualised and comprehended. They are easily identified as a more authentic experience over something that is less certain. So is this a question of image over substance? Is the image of a particular kind of place more important than the reality of how places actually function or of what our true relationship to them is?

What, if any, is the exact relationship between the seductive images of portable telecommunications, 'authentic' world cuisine and designer outdoor clothing with the telecommunication masts, distribution centres, and airports that increasingly dominate an anxiety about landscape? Is it better not to know? Despite an overall growth in information, it would appear that less and less is known about how specific things happen, where they come from and how they reach us. In a sense, it is as if more and more things from unknown origins pass through our landscapes – and we ourselves travel further distances to ever-increasing destinations – without ever really 'touching the sides'.

Is it possible a kind of slippage is occurring between an understanding of place and the channels of movement? With the increasing movement becoming more evident, there is a growing perception that the objects of movement – roads, vehicles, airports, mobile-phone masts – represent a threat to the authentic experience of place. What this perception overlooks is that the channels of movement – not only the objects but the time-space continuum that people occupy – may be just as real if not more so. As J.B. Jackson concluded: 'Roads no longer merely lead to places; they are places.'[2] In future, what will be required is to either enhance the image of the authentic place – the house – to the greater exclusion of everything else – the road, or give much more credence to a less fixed and more variable kind of place. Either way, in terms of actual experience it is much more likely to be spent along the road.

THE RENAULT PARTS DISTRIBUTION CENTRE IN SWINDON

Built by Foster and Partners in 1982 to much critical acclaim and reputed to be the building that has spawned numerous airports worldwide – none of the building's walls are supporting. Around the time Figure 18.1 was taken in 2000, it was announced that Renault was to reorganise its distribution in the UK and was moving out of Swindon. On hearing this news, local people in Swindon – whom one assumes are rather proud of this award-winning structure – were eager to learn what would happen to the building. Quickly a rumour started to circulate. Renault were to take it with them! You can laugh, however, although the building remains in Swindon, it is not known how close to truth this rumour actually was because there was nothing to stop Renault from doing so. Foster's design could be dismantled and erected elsewhere with relative ease and was preferable to constructing a new building.

For over a hundred years Swindon was a single-industry, single-company town: home of the Great Western Railway. Now companies move to and from Swindon with relative ease. And if people and organisations can move so easily, why not buildings?

18.1 Renault Parts Distribution Centre, Swindon, UK.

ONTARIO MILLS SHOPPING MALL IN FONTANA NEAR SAN BERNARDINO, CALIFORNIA

Or, to be precise, at Exits 58 and 109 on I-10 and I-15. The Ontario Mills mall is situated on a site that used to be agricultural land before being selected in 1942 as the location a vast new steel plant. Largely due to cheap imports from the Asia-Pacific region, the plant closed in 1984. Located at the intersection of two transcontinental highways, Ontario Mills is not only an 'out-of-town' shopping centre serving the Los Angeles area but, like many malls in the USA, it also provides an attraction to long- distance travellers. An opportunity for them to break their journeys and exercise a bit of retail therapy.

As a building and a place, the Ontario Mills mall makes little pretence as to what it is: one of the largest retail malls in the USA – a massive shed situated in the middle of a giant car park. Little attempt has been made to embellish the exterior of the shed with any additional character, except to advertise its presence. While by no means at all like the Renault Building in Swindon, this shed is, however, also of a design that is easily erected and dismantled. Internally, the building shows clearly how it functions. Quite literally as a shed, housing many shop stores belonging to numerous popular retail chains – in a sense free-standing temporary structures housed within the outer structure.

Compare Ontario Mills with another building in Swindon, the Great Western Shopping Centre. This 'designer outlet mall' is housed in part of what was the famous Great Western Railway works. This particular building retains much of its original character of an early Victorian factory yet it provides a comfortable home for the outlets of a number of popular retail chains. Due to the listed status of the building, the numerous retail units had to be

18.2 Ontario Mills shopping centre, San Bernardino, California.

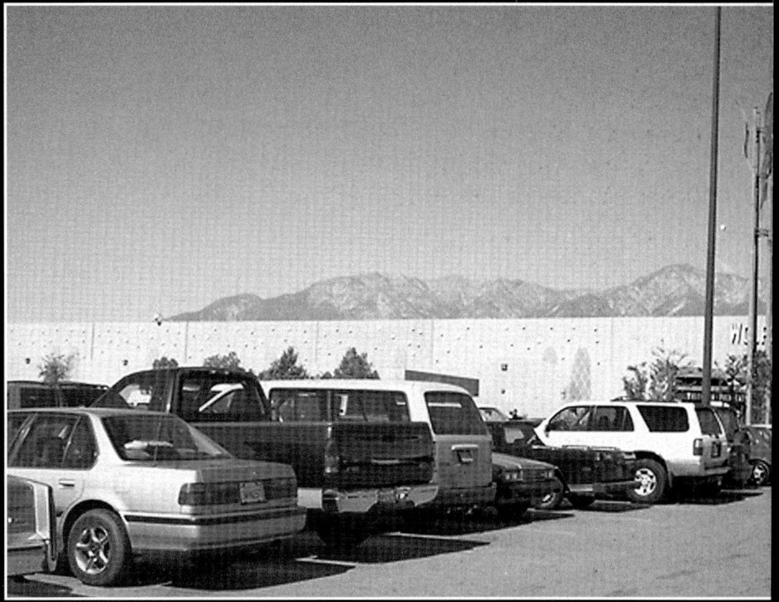

constructed without altering in any way the fabric of the original building. In a sense, what you have is free-standing temporary structures housed within the outer structure. In many respects both Ontario Mills and the Great Western Shopping Centre are simply sheds housing a particular economic activity that could be replaced reasonably easily by another without really changing the building. The main difference is that one is 150 years old and pretty permanent and the other ten years old and probably fairly temporary.

Ontario Mills and the Great Western Shopping Centre were both created as a means of regenerating an area following the demise of a principal industry. Don't forget Swindon didn't exist before Brunel decided to service his trains there in the 1830s. Interestingly, though, unlike Ontario Mills, the Great Western Shopping Centre is at the heart of the original town. However, being situated not too far from the M4 motorway, the shopping centre attracts visitors from as far as as Bristol, Oxford and even London. Swindon's new economic activity, like the Renault building, is concentrated on the outskirts.

CRICK

You might say this is Middle England – literally. It is the area around Rugby and the junction of the M1 and M6 motorways and home to some of the largest distribution centres in the land. At Junction 18 near a place called Crick are giant sheds used by Tesco, the Royal Mail and 'logistics' companies like Tebbit & Britten, W.H. Malcolm and Eddie Stobart. Eddie Stobart also has a large servicing facility for the firm's lorries. There is no reason for these sheds to be in this particular location except for its relationship to other places. (Incidentally, in the foreground is the old roman route of Watling Street.)

18.3 Watling Street, Middle England, but could be anywhere

A bit like the railway junctions of old; in terms of road freight transportation Crick is probably the contemporary equivalent of Crewe junction. And even rail has a role to play. As well as serving as regional distribution for central and southern England, Crick is also a point for transhipment and sorting of loads travelling to and from as far as continental Europe and Scotland. Among the big sheds of Crick is located DIRFT (Daventry International Railfreight Terminal), and trains regularly arrive from Italy and France as well as the container port at Felixstowe. Containers and trailer 'swap-bodies' are quickly transferred from train to road. (W.H. Malcolm runs its own connecting train from Coatbridge in Scotland.) Also it is no coincidence that Rugby has been discussed as a site for a possible new airport for Central England.

These days everyone has a distribution centre, or so it seems. Of course Amazon.co.uk has one. It is the enormous new building to the east of the M1 near Milton Keynes. But so do Pearson educational books. Theirs is near Lutterworth further up the M1 along with BT, Argos and a number of others. Gap has recently relocated their entire UK distribution and administration to Junction 1 on the M6 near Rugby – the centrepiece of a new business park curiously entitled Central Park. Some of these buildings are so vast that GPS is sometimes used to navigate their interiors.

Don't be fooled into thinking this kind of infrastructure is tied to a low-quality level of goods. Whatever the quality, or origin of the goods being distributed and sold, the economies of scale demand an infrastructure of this kind to ensure the goods are constantly available at retail outlets. Even Waitrose have distribution centres and giant fleets of lorries.

18.4 Droxford Busines Park, Sunderland, UK

DROXFORD BUSINESS PARK

This building is part of a special high-tech business park near Sunderland called Droxford. Established to specialise in modern telecommunications, the business park is home to a number of call centres and administrative centres belonging to some established national companies such as Barclays Bank and T-mobile as well as local companies like London Electricity. The park is conveniently situated on the A19 (along with 'new' industries including the Sunderland Nissan plant), providing swift access to a large predominantly young workforce travelling from as far away as Tyneside and Teesside. One of the reasons for the location of this business park is partly a large catchment of potential labour, economic assistance from regional development agencies, and relatively cheap land. Droxford is built on the original site of a coal-washing plant.

Droxford is situated in what used to be the County of East Durham. In 1934 at the height of the Depression the playwright J.B. Priestley visited the area and recalled in his book, *English Journey*:

> **But who knows East Durham? The answer is nobody but the people who live and work there, and a few others who go there on business. It is, you see, a coal mining district. Unless we happen to be connected in some way with a colliery, we do not know these districts. They are usually unpleasant and rather remote and so we leave them alone. Of millions in London, how many have ever spent half an hour in a mining village?**[3]

Well, the area around Sunderland is now by no means the unpleasant place that J.B. Priestley spoke of, far from it. But of how much concern is this to the people of somewhere like London and the South-East? Indeed, are we any more knowledgeable about Sunderland or Swindon or elsewhere than in J.B. Priestley's time?

NOTES

1 J.B. Jackson, 'Roads belong in the landscape', *Landscapes: Selected Writings of J.B. Jackson*, MIT Press, 1970

2 Ibid.

3 J.B. Priestley, *English Journey*, London: Penguin Books Ltd, 1977

In August 2003 a consortium led by EDAW was appointed by the London Development Agency to prepare visionary regeneration masterplans for the Lower Lea Valley, located in the boroughs of Hackney, Newham, Tower Hamlets and Waltham Forest. The plans were to map out the area to facilitate the 2012 Olympic Games and Paralympic Games, and crucially, the legacy – what the area would look like after the Games.

The masterplans are a vital component of London's 2012 bid as they provide the 'design blueprint' needed to transform one of the poorest parts of the UK into a stunning development, capable of staging the greatest sporting show on earth.

CHAPTER 19

LOWER LEA VALLEY OLYMPIC AND LEGACY MASTERPLANS

JASON PRIOR

The proposals will help to meet the aspirations for London to become a sustainable city. The proposals will help to drive regeneration throughout the Lower Lea Valley and set a benchmark for the whole of the Thames Gateway. This vision deals with a range of masterplanning principles throughout the Valley.

The proposals also set a new standard of urban design in the UK. They establish a series of layers, each of which can act as an individual programme but which can also be brought together to create a total design. This allows a range of projects to be implemented.

This menu of interventions include:

- **A focus on communities**. Preparation for the plans are built on existing aspirations within the boroughs and involve one of the largest public consultation events ever undertaken in the capital. The aspirations of existing communities and the anticipation of those of new incoming communities are an issue that resonates in London. The history of the development of London Docklands has meant that great emphasis has been put on easing the relationships between the two groups and creating inclusive public spaces. These include both green space in the parks and 'blue' space through remediation of rivers and canals; and integration, creating new connections within and across the valley.
- **A celebration of the area's unique character**. London lost many of its rivers into culverts and drains during the Victorian era. The opportunity to achieve an active relationship with the rivers and canals in the area will not only enhance the 'green' credentials of the area, but raise its status with London's different character areas. The waterways will provide new experiences in recreation and pleasure. Rivers will run through the park and canals through built areas, creating an integrated urban water environment.
- **Greening the city**. Its five key aims are: (1) to link the Lea Valley Regional Park to the Thames; (2) to integrate the park to the wider green space network; (3) to make use of waterways and

19.1 Olympic Park aerial perspective. Views show the location of the Olympic site, north of the Isle of Dogs on the bend of the River Thames.

topography; (4) to integrate water management and ecological systems with landscape; and (5) to encourage active and intense use of green areas. It does this by setting up a networked park structure, which will be designed to integrate with local systems and incorporate great diversity of spaces, vegetation and habitats. Unlike many conventional parks there will be no 'green deserts'.

- **Reconnecting the city**. A key driver for this project is to provide the connections to the rest of the city that have eluded the area for so long. The valley is well served by strategic transport infrastructure, yet its internal transport system is almost non-existent. Bridges, major land bridges, pedestrian and cycle routes, and a new road network will re-integrate different areas through a series of new routes and connections.

It is not only external connectivity that is critical. Linking the area together so that it functions more effectively is a key principle. This has to work for the Olympics, by providing major access routes and using them to channel movement to the right venues and to link up the main areas of the Olympic Park, as well as for the post-event movement through the area where the nature, form, enclosure and vitality of the routes will be addressed by post-games development of mixed-use communities.

- **Densification, consolidation and change**. Many existing low-intensity uses will be relocated to consolidated sites within the valley or to other areas. New development will bring in housing, offices and retail areas, as well as more and better-quality open space. In addition, as part of the government's urban agenda, there is a recognition of the need for a more sustainable approach to the delivery of housing and its associated services such as transport. This has led to a raising of housing densities and an extolling of urbanism as a way forward.

- **Delivering regeneration**. With development on the scale proposed, sophisticated infrastructure systems are needed to handle the inputs (power,

19.2 Olympic Park, aerial view. The landscape setting of facilities emphasises the Park setting in the wider green network.

Clockwise from left

19.3 Legacy Masterplan. Visionary regeneration masterplan for the site after the Games.

19.4 Olympic Masterplan. The design blueprint of Britain's 2012 bid to host the Games in the Lower Lea Valley, East London.

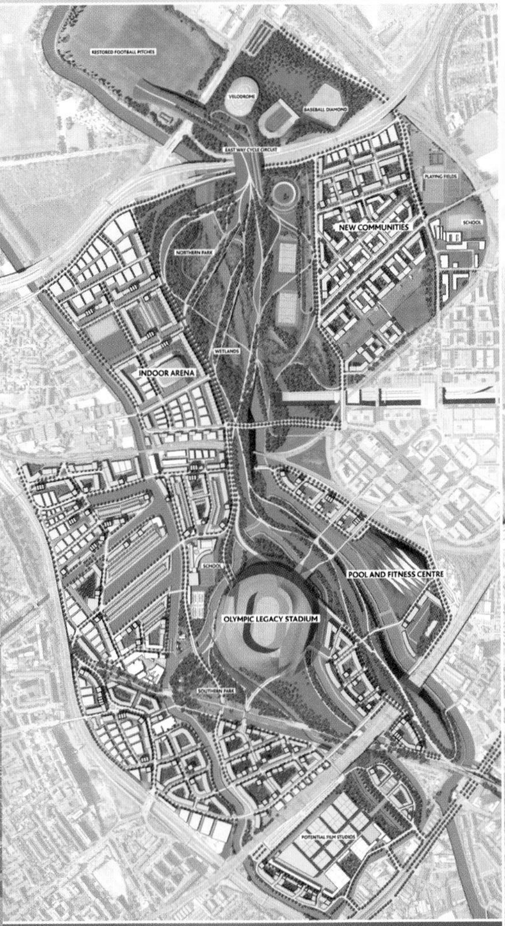

19.5 Village Plaza view. The heart of the village.

19.6 Stadium external view. An iconic architectural design statement.

19.7 The built environment legacy.

19.8 Village water view. The Lea River is a key feature.

19.9 Sketch, Olympic Park. Networked park structure.

19.10 Sketch, legacy. Footpaths and cycle network for local population.

water, energy, etc.) and outputs (waste and drainage). The scale of this development offers the opportunity to introduce innovative systems that demonstrate a new way forward for sustainable urban living.

- **A city for people**. With regeneration of the Lower Lea Valley many new jobs, homes and social facilities for local people, will be provided, including new health and community centres and two new schools. These communities will be formed in a radically enhanced physical environment, one that is easily accessible to all people.

London will define the Games through its architecture, its iconic venues, its cultural programme and its people. The Olympic venues within the Olympic Precinct will be set in an evocative river landscape, through which visitors will pass between venues, gather around video screens, or find quiet places to picnic near the water's edge.

The Olympic and Legacy Masterplans would bring forward one of the largest and most significant urban regeneration projects ever undertaken in the UK. The Games would transform the Lower Lea Valley, turning it into a vibrant new urban quarter and a place of local and national pride.

The Legacy Masterplan provides 9,100 new homes and thousands of permanent jobs and a major parkland along the River Lea linking Hackney Marshes with the Thames. The new park system will create 127 hectares of publicly accessible open space, an increase of 66 per cent. A number of Olympic venues, including the velodrome and the aquatics centre will be retained as major assets.

The plans would accelerate London's expansion eastwards to accommodate the expected population growth in the capital over the coming decades. It would also redefine aspirations for London's urban landscape, as new buildings and open spaces are planned across the capital for the future.

ACKNOWLEDGEMENTS

Prepared by the EDAW-led Consortium (EDAW, HOK Sport, Allies & Morrison, Foreign Office Architects, Mott MacDonald, Buro Happold, Faithful & Gould, Mace and Fluid working also with Capita Symonds, Eversheds, GVA Grimley and Economic Research Associates).

Today, cities have a very different structure from those of fifty years ago. Information and communication technology, over the last half of the century, has had a massive impact on the form of our urban settlements. It has reduced distance, increased mobility and allowed freedom of choice. Cities with traditionally centralised urban forms, through improved communications, have linked up to surrounding centres to create sprawling, networked metropolitan regions. However, much of the current urban design debate is focused on returning to the values, urban structures and visual language of pre-twentieth-century cities. Laudable as these values are, they only provide half the picture of the issues that are likely to confront us in the emerging twenty-first-century city.[1]

European cities, such as Copenhagen, Amsterdam and Düsseldorf are, today, all part of sprawling metropolitan regions. Copenhagen, a city of half a million population, with the completion of the Oresund Bridge, is now part of the Oresund, a city region of 3.5 million spread across two nations. Amsterdam, with Utrecht, Rotterdam and The Hague, created the Randstad – a world-class city of 6 million people. Australia's fifth-largest city is the Gold Coast, a low-density corridor of over 100 miles, running south from Brisbane with a population of over 425,000 with Surfer's Paradise as its focus.

CHAPTER 20

GIVING MEANING TO THE EXPERIENCE ECONOMY

USING URBAN DESIGN TO RE-ESTABLISH A PLACE IN THE NETWORKED CITY

JOHN WORTHINGTON

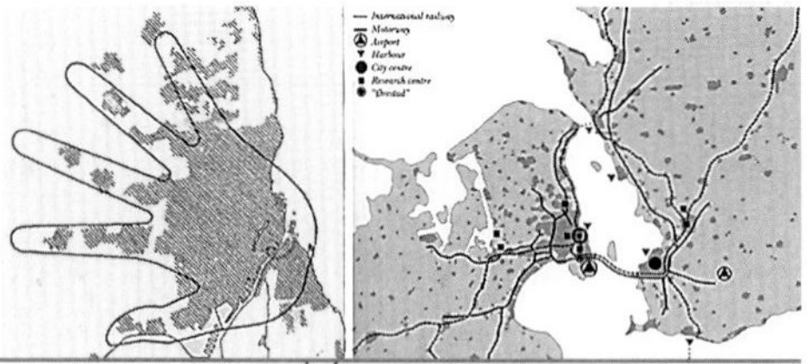

20.1 Oresund Region. The hand image depicts the network of settlements.
20.2 Twenty-first century city. A low-density city in a high-density landscape.
20.3 Retail park. Convenient and accessible shopping.

The twenty-first-century city is a city of paradox. It has points of intense concentration, while also being dispersed, forming a low-density city in a high-density landscape. It has an increasing ethnic diversity, while at the same time celebrating enclaves, such as 'China Town', with a single dominant culture. It aims, at the macro-scale, to improve accessibility by speeding up traffic flow, while at the micro-level it aims to reduce through-movement and by so doing enhance the pedestrian experience. Urban planners are faced with the dilemma of accommodating both our desire for reliable, convenient and accessible shopping, as reflected in the out-of-town 'retail park', with our search for the unusual, individual, and authentic. The networked city crosses traditional political boundaries, blurs accepted planning use classes and questions accepted models of urbanity. Faced with these paradoxes, planning has tended to focus on reinforcing traditional centres. The discourse is framed as a choice between centre or periphery, rather than recognising it can be *both central and dispersed*, each finding their appropriate strengths, linked within a networked conurbation.

In 1938, Lewis Mumford published the *Culture of Cities*, and sixty years later the sociologist, Sharon Zukin, published *Cultures of Cities* (1998).[2] One letter separates the titles of the two books, while the landscape they portray is vastly different. Mumford's image of the city is founded on civility, creativity, continuity, inclusion, a concern for the past and the vibrancy of heterogeneity. Zukin's city, as reported through the eyes of an urban sociologist, is one of ethnicity, consumption, discontinuity and exclusion. From the inclusive city we have moved to exclusive enclaves with a paranoia for security. Joel Garreau in *Edge City*[3] describes these emerging (sub)urban centres, growing around transport intersections, where land is available to support new combinations of functions, such as retail, offices, education and leisure. These clusters are market-driven, invariably happening despite the planners. Major transport interchanges, such as at airports, rail stations and highway intersections, have become destinations in their own right. At Schiphol Airport, in the Netherlands, over 20 per cent of the total 25 million passengers a year are transit passengers, who dwell in or pass through the airport. The immediate airport generates 35,000 jobs and at least treble that in the vicinity. Schiphol is marketed as an 'airport city',[4] with a casino, museum, chapel, retail, leisure, offices and hotel. All it lacks is a resident population and an elected council. Tyson's Corner, Virginia, with over 18 million square metres of corporate office space, and two large regional shopping malls, is Joel Garreau's model of edge city. Access is predominantly by private car, with large expanses of car parking, and inward-focused retail malls and office atria as the emerging meeting places. These new centres, unlike traditional urban cores, which have grown organically with a diverse mix of activities, are uniform in their offering and conceived as precisely functional 'machines' to maximise the customer experience and financial return to the operator. The new centres are a reflection of the experience economy,[5] where the cost of the physical product is a small percentage of the total cost to the consumer, who is choosing a product for the values it represents and service it affords. The 15 cents that the coffee distributor pays for coffee beans is translated into the $5.00 we are prepared to pay to achieve a total experience.[6] The dilemma is that these instant environments at the periphery, with their focus on efficiency, functionality and convenience, have lost the chance encounters and unplanned authenticity of the experience they are aiming to create.[7] The retail mall, conceived as the local community centre, has become exclusive, homogenous in its quality and pricing, and planned to maximise throughput. These super-functional, themed locations have lost the qualities they set out to achieve. It is not surprising that in some out-of-town centres developers are beginning to consider the ways they can intensify use, attract a wider mix of retailers by price, quality and function and re-establish community uses such as libraries, schools and public offices.[8] The challenge for today's urban designers, perhaps, is to understand the attributes of these peripheral nodes, giving meaning to both centre and periphery, and coherence to the journey between the points.

Kevin Lynch, over forty years ago, recognised the need for urban design to address a variety of scales.[9] He identifies three levels from *project design* where 'there is a definite client, a concrete programme, a foreseeable time of completion and effective control over the significant aspects of the form' to *system design* 'which considers the form of a functionally connected set of objects'. These may be distributed over extensive areas, e.g. a highway network or a signage system. Finally, at the level of the city or region, *city design* can provide legibility and meaning to the wider context we inhabit. I would argue that the role urban design can play, in a continually changing context, is to provide meaning through programme, identity through form, and character and quality through materiality and detailing, within a development framework that will absorb changes over time. The opportunity for urban design is to address the paradox of centre and periphery, and understand why the new typologies at the periphery have been so successful and where they may be found wanting. New typologies are continuing to emerge, while existing nodes will need intensification and retrofitting. Both, if they are to become embedded in the community, will require intelligent programming (briefing) and imaginative design.

It is in the Netherlands that one can, perhaps, most clearly experience the vision of the twenty-first-century city. Centre and periphery have become blurred into a network of distinctive places, to form the Randstad. The Randstad, or Delta Metropolis,[10] is a conurbation of 6.5 million inhabitants, comparable in population to Paris or London but taking up over five times the land area. It is composed of 12 communities of over 100,000 people, dominated by four major cities and one 'inner city' airport, Schiphol. Within this conurbation, as with Paris or London, it has distinctive quarters: Amsterdam, for finance and culture; Utrecht, for learning and media; The Hague, for government; and Rotterdam/Delft for work and learning. Though separated by distance, they are close in convenience and time. The highway becomes 'main street', inter-city rail the 'metro' and it is effectively 45 minutes between any two nodes within the city.

In the Netherlands with its strong tradition of public housing, the boundaries between the disciplines of architecture, urbanism and landscape have always been vague. In the early 1920s, housing layouts were synonymous with city planning. The tradition continues, strengthened by the majority of land being in municipal ownership. The change, with the impact of the new information and communication technology, is that we no longer need to work, play and support ourselves where we live. The CIAM

- 39.6 million Passengers per annum
- 54,000 jobs
- Rail and road connections
- Destination in its own right

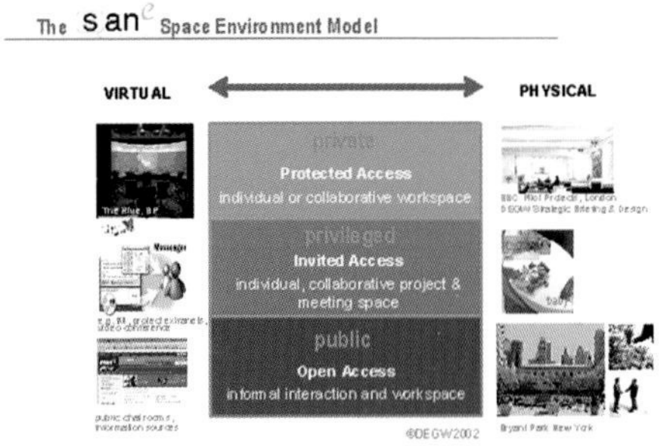

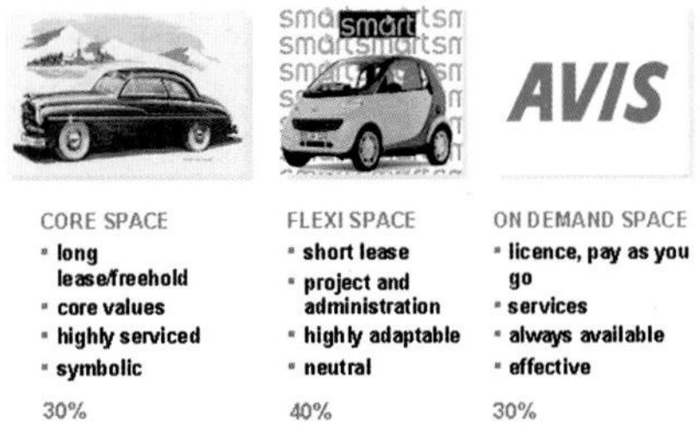

20.4 SANE study explored the implications of the distributed workplace.
20.5 On-demand flexibility of pay-as-you-go.
20.6 Aesthetic of mobility. Mecanoo assessed the highway experience.

(Team 10) model[11] of the neatly zoned self-sufficient community, is splintering into the desire for both local community, and the freedom of choice of being linked to a wider network of opportunities. The Netherlands is finely tuned to this debate, supported by government funding for design competitions, publications and exhibitions. Publications such as *Post Ex Subdis: Urban Fragmentation and Constructions*, a collection of essays edited by GUST, address the phenomena of sprawl and the challenges of 'designing contemporary cityscapes'.[12] Similarly the work of practices such as MVRDV, Mecanoo, and West 8, both in print and built outcomes, explores a new sort of place-making which draws on a close understanding of the relationship between 'programme', form, and function.[13]

The Dutch Ministry for Planning and Housing (VROM) has recognised the phenomena of the new knowledge economy, and the opportunities for a networked city within a wider networked region.[14] Its fifth report (*Making Space, Sharing Space 2000-2020*) sets the context by recognising:

> Less processes are becoming dispersed spatially within the Netherlands The growing competition and costs of knowledge development rendered increased co-operation between business and institutes necessary. More and more people are working with other people and information; fewer and fewer people are required for physical production. As a result, all the elements of communication are becoming more important, and the economy is increasingly taking on the character of a network economy, at both the international and regional scales.[15]

The VROM fifth report is based on the understanding that to meet these needs and overcome the lack of space and decreasing car accessibility in cities 'more and more businesses are moving to the urban periphery or locating along infrastructure routes'. The report concludes:

> The development into a network society is evidenced spatially by the emergence of urban networks; no longer is everything centred around one city or one conurbation. Instead, various centres are developing and citizens are zigzagging across greater distances based on their individual choices and desires.[16]

In today's 'shattered' world, I would argue, each of us perceives the city on three levels: the virtual 'city of the mind' which can range across geographic boundaries, and is made of the places special to us – Venice for pleasure, Boston for learning, or Camden for living and working; the metropolitan networked region for *convenience*; and high-density localities for our sense of physical *place*. Ironically, none of these definitions of the city synchronises with the political boundaries which formally define the city space.

The new generation of wireless and mobile technologies is resulting in new paradigms of work. Increasingly, work is becoming liberated from the confines of the traditional office building, and taking place in a continuum of different times and different places. DEGW have recently completed SANE (Sustainable Accommodation in the New Economy),[17] a two-year research project funded by the European Commissioner's Information Society Technologies Programme. SANE explored the implications of the *distributed workplace* and the physical and virtual worlds of the different types of space now inhabited by many organisations. Companies are increasingly managing a portfolio of space types from *private* (e.g. personal office/home working) to *privileged* (e.g. company conference centres/airport lounges) and *semi-public* (corporate atria/hotel lobbies). A number of global organisations have already adopted real estate strategies, which run counter to the traditional view of 'head office' space primarily in 'downtown' locations. Firms are looking to reduce their long-term commitment to space in high-value locations, by readjusting their portfolio to a three-way model of Fixed Space, Flexi Space and On-Demand Space.[18] Nokia, for example, with their 'M-Office' programme, have outsourced 25 per cent of their office portfolio to Regus as a 'pay-as-you-go' solution to provide a mix of workspace in a variety of locations.

In the sprawling networked city a new typology of places is beginning to emerge.[19] Their common characteristics are that they have a variety of modes of public and private accessibility; an overlap of functions, with synergetic and complementary uses both within the node and as part of the wider urban network; and a recognisable image. Such places are forming around events venues (stadia); transport nodes (rail and air); institutions of learning or health; production clusters (e.g. film studios); and retail, leisure complexes. These new focal points have grown rapidly, as a response to market forces, on either 'greenfield' sites or from the kernel of an existing use. Their rapid growth has invariably been supported by the availability of large land holdings under single ownership. The outcome has been massive 'schemes', 'instantly developed' and conceived and executed comprehensively. They are market-driven, rather than user-led; designed to maximise efficiency; and 'over-functionalised', with a 'semi-public' cocoon. Maarten Hajer and the urban sociologist Arnold Reijndorp, in their work, *In Search of New Public Domain*,[20] perceptively describe the new semi-public spaces that are emerging and the need for a new language. They present 'place' as a consumer commodity and the urban field as an archipelago of enclaves. The authors highlight the differences between public spaces: the 'Urban Realm', owned and controlled by the city; and the 'Urban Domain', or semi-public space, that is privately owned and managed, though perceived and used as public space (e.g. the retail mall, stadium or airport). This public domain is not so much a place as an experience, which fails through over-functionalisation, a lack of authenticity and insufficient diversity. The experience is a themed fantasy, rather than being owned by a dominant culture. The challenge for urbanists, they argue, is to provide 'more friction please', a looser fit of functions, and opportunity for connectivity between sub-cultures within a dominant set of values. It is heartening that the Dutch are embracing the phenomenon of the periphery as a key element of our future cities.

The Randstad has become a laboratory for these emerging nodes. Some are becoming distinctive places in their own right, others are points along the highway. The 2005 Rotterdam International Architecture Biennale, curated by Francine Houben, was dedicated to mobility.[21] The introduction to the exhibition,

20.8 Gateway to the city core. Primary coloured forms straddle the highway.

entitled *A Room with a View*, sets the challenge to give the aesthetics of mobility some form. Mobility, Houben states, 'is not just about traffic jams, asphalt, delays and tollgates, but also about people deriving a sensory experience from their everyday mobility. Every day . . . millions of people experience the changes of the city and countryside, for them, the train and the car are also "A Room with a View". Mecanoo's study of the Randstad circuit (Holland Avenue)[22] assessed the quality and character of the highway experience, so as to develop an aesthetic of mobility from the viewpoint of the user. Pointers already exist. The multi-storied glass clad 'go-kart' circuit, between Delft and the Hague, ablaze with lights at night; the car showrooms and Smart-Car sales towers; and the unexpected views of the high-rise clusters of Rotterdam. The highway can have a unique character, with strategic interventions; designers could give the landscape of the 'edgeless city' meaning and legibility. Melbourne, the second city of Australia, prides itself on its quality of design. One of the leading architectural practices, Denton Corker Marshall[23] has, through a series of independent, though strategically located, projects, provided a visual coherence to the city core. Entering from the airport the gateway to the city core is a collection of primary-coloured forms that parallel and straddle the highway, followed by two huge concrete verticals that mark the crossing of the river and the entrance to docklands. As one moves around the grid, key points at the edge, such as the convention centre and museums area, are highlighted by the continuing use of primary colours and powerful forms.

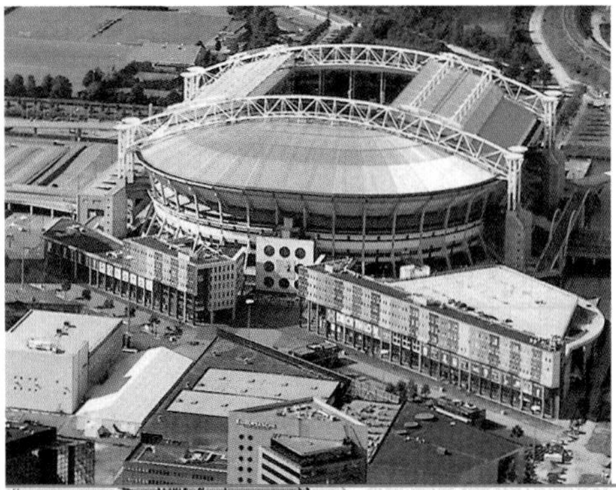

20.8 Ajax Stadium, Amsterdam sits in a fast-developing office and logistics area.

20.9 Papendorp, a greenfield site.

Schiphol Airport, and its surrounding sites, is arguably the fifth urban node within the Randstad. It covers an area the size of Amsterdam and, with the completion of the high-speed train, will encompass Amsterdam 'Zuidas', a 2.5 million square metre mixed-use development proposal, no more than eight minutes from the airport by public transport.[24] As the airport reaches 30 million passengers a year, it's clearly more than a box to facilitate passenger through-put. It's a place for leisure, retailing, exchange and work, with the main business service centre having in excess of 20,000 users a month. The area is in continuous change. Today, the primary design focus is on providing a meaningful building infrastructure within which functions and activities can adapt. Reinforcing the identity of the airport and its hinterland, linked as it is by every mode of transport, is an exciting challenge, given the overlap of political boundaries and the originally limited functional perception of its use.

The Ajax Stadium in South Amsterdam, connected by rail and road to both the historical centre of Amsterdam and the wider region, is a developing node. The stadium, while acting as a landmark, sits in a fast-developing office and logistics area, with a specialist furnishings diagonal boulevard linking it to the railway station and working living area beyond. The parking, to maximise usage, is conceived as a transfer stage, providing cheap parking, convenient access and public transport to the centre. Unlike the traditional mall, the Boulevard access to the arena provides the public domain, with connections to the surrounding area. Over time it will be interesting to see whether the plan will allow for intensification, increased diversity and linkages back to the surrounding stand-alone elements of office parks and the Amsterdam Medical Centre complex.

At the periphery of the Randstad, on the mainline to Enskede, is the Hilversum Media Park. Originally the campus of the public broadcasting service, with the liberalisation of broadcasting services it has developed into a media park for a wide range of media firms and their supporting service. With good connections by public and private transport and close access to the Hilversum centre, the area with the media park as its core has attracted the leading media and marketing firms, with small support firms settling in the surrounding lower-rent building stock. Like so many of the new nodes, it has grown up in response to market demand, adapting the existing residential housing stock or piecing together larger landholdings for new development as appropriate. Today, this area of Hilversum, at the periphery of the town, has emerged as a key 'cluster' for the media, with its links outward to the Randstad.

Utrecht, one of the four major cities in the Randstad, is also the largest Vinex housing growth point identified in the VROM fourth report (1990).[25] The Leidsche Rijn development, a site of 2,500 hectares for 30,000 dwellings and a population of 100,000, is at the edge of Utrecht and easily accessible from the Randstad highway systems and the Utrecht, Rotterdam, Den Hague railway. Papendorp, an area of 25 hectares, was zoned as a main employment neighbourhood to eventually provide for jobs and houses. Papendorp Business Park, with Donald Van Danzig (OMA) as masterplanner and DEGW responsible for the development brief, is planned to provide for a mixture of uses ranging from corporate headquarters in a parkland setting, to commerce and technology parks associated with a high density central zone. Initially, Papendorp was seen to be in competition with the city's other major redevelopment project, the Central Station Site (UCP).[26] In reality, each site had its unique characteristics, and attraction to specific activity mixes often associated with the same sector or company. Papendorp, being a greenfield site, could be developed rapidly, provide ease of access to the highway and a variety of building typologies to reflect changing ways of working. However, unlike the central station area with its mixture of old and new building stock, connection to fast train links and proximity to the historical centre, it could not provide the same variety of accommodation and economic diversity. The central site is attractive to 'front office', showroom, creative and marketing functions, while Papendorp is more suitable for support 'back office' functions or regional offices of professional organisations. Both sites have a role to play in the wider Randstad market, and will be able to work in synergy with the proposed light-rail link.

The Netherlands, with its ambitious urban programme and desire to innovate, is providing a pointer to a wider view of the role urban designers can play. The way forward is far from clear. However, some pointers can be recognised. First, in a paradoxical world, cities will be both concentrated and dispersed: concentrated into high density, easily accessible enclaves within a decentralised urban network. The designers' challenge will be to give meaning and legibility to the wider region and the links between. Second, the market-focused, highly functionalised, car-dominated nodes at the periphery, as they mature, are recognising the need to look outward and recognise the potential symbiotic relationships with other centres in the networked region.

The Don Valley stretching from Sheffield to Doncaster, and intersected by the M1 motorway, highlights these paradoxes and opportunities.[27] Meadowhall retail mall, adjacent to the M1 at the edge of Sheffield, with good road and rail connections, was perceived as a competitor to the city centre. However, with 33 million visitors per annum, it can also be seen as a major draw for the wider city, the opportunity being to extend the time visitors stay and attracting them to go to the centre for the diversity of experience difficult to create at Meadowhall. As the area changes from industry, so the retail can link outwards, taking advantage of the river, recreating public spaces, inserting a wider mix of functions and integrating with the surrounding area. With changing expectations, the twenty-year-old shopping mall will be as much in need of renewal and intensification as our traditional industrial cities. This pressure for rethinking 'out-of-town' developments will be fuelled by a search for authenticity, rather than the themed Disneyesque environment of the retail mall. Forward-looking property investors and developers are recognising that precision in function with no space for the unprogrammed, reduces spontaneity and the opportunity for diversity.

In a world of continuous flux, masterplans as blueprints are being superseded by frameworks that set infrastructure, typologies and value systems within which a programme of built projects and events can unfold. In the past three years, DEGW have worked with a team within the City of Utrecht, re-establishing the brief and formulating a development framework for the Utrecht Central Station area.[28] The lessons have a wider significance for managing the process of change in the emerging networked city nodes. The time initially spent establishing the different stakeholder expectations, what can be changed, and the relevant themes and values of importance to the constituents has been invaluable. Website questionnaires, town meetings, focus groups with specific stakeholders and, finally, a referendum, were all part of a process to establish transparency and commitment to change. The framework to manage a twenty-year strategy, tackled in parts and completed in stages, has four key drawings and a programme of proposed small and large projects, as an unfolding sequence of events (exhibits 11, 12). The drawings cover the following:

1 The long-term 'fixes', e.g. listed buildings and urban character of the area.

2 Proposed infrastructure and structure landscaping, funded by the public sector, which compose the 'capital web'.

3 Urban framework, describing the grain of proposed development, mix of functions and quality of place.

4 Vision for the area, expressed through diagrams and aerial perspectives.

Such a framework allows for the inevitable changes that will occur through time. It is robust enough to integrate social, economic and physical expectations and allow for changing political viewpoints.

The new information and communication technologies have both dispersed and intensified our cities, while at the same time speeding up the process of change. Urban design in response is searching for ways to engage at both the neighbourhood (project) and the metropolitan scale, and at the same time create responsive frameworks to manage and moderate change. Design has a unique role in providing meaning and authenticity in a 'shapeless' world. At the broad level, the designer's role is focused on establishing programme and form; and at the specific level, quality through detail and materiality. Some pointers can be recognised. First, that the framing of urban problems will be less about defining alternatives (it is *either* this *or* that) but more about accommodating alternatives (*both* this *and* that) by celebrating paradox.[29] Second, that to ensure authenticity, rather than a themed Disneyesque environment, we should search for a dominant culture, around which subcultures can flourish. Precision in function, with no space for the unprogrammed, reduces spontaneity and the opportunity to create a 'lived-world' of place, 'giving pace, variety and orientation to man'.[30] Finally, masterplans as blueprints are being superseded by frameworks that set infrastructure, typologies and value systems, within which a programme of built projects and events can unfold.[31] The networked city offers a challenging canvas for urban designers.

NOTES

1 See the paper given to the Association of Dutch urban Designers and Planners (BnSP) at the 5th Van Eesteren/Van Iohuigen memorial lecture 2000, Juan Busquets and John Worthington, Technical University Delft. BnSP, April 2000.

2 Lewis Mumford, *Culture of Cities*, 1938, and Sharon Zukin, *Cultures of Cities*, 1998.

3 The phenomena of the urban centre located at a freeway interchange was first identified by Joel Garreau, *Edge City: Life on the New Frontier*, New York: Doubleday, 1991. Robert Lang, *Edgeless Cities: Exploring the Elusive Metropolis*, Washington, DC: The Brookings Institution, 2003, takes the proposition a stage further in describing the many faces of sprawl.

4 I describe the emergence of the airport as a destination in J. Worthington and Briggs. Guller Guller, *From Airport to Airport City*, Barcelona: GG, 2004, provides an overview of the growth and change of ten European airports.

5 Pine and Gilmour, *The Experience Economy: Work is Theatre and Every Business is a Stage*, Boston: Harvard Business School Press, 1999.

6 Ibid.

7 Leading property companies in the UK, such as Bovis Lend Lease and British Land, are reviewing how to diversify the limited functionality of the retail mall to take on the role of the town centre. A recent publication, sponsored by the National Endowment for the Arts, by Smiley and Robbins, *Sprawl and Public Space: Redressing the Mall*, Princeton, NJ: Princeton Architectural Press, 2002, addresses these issues, with case studies.

8 Ibid.

9 See Kevin Lynch, *City Sense and City Design*, edited by Banerjee and Southworth, Cambridge, MA: MIT Press, 1991. On the writings and projects of Kevin Lynch, see 'City design and city appearance', in *Principles and Practice of Urban Planning*, 1968.

10 See Dirk Frielings' chapter on the Delta Metropolis in Echenaque and Saint, *Cities for the New Millennium*, London: Spon, 2001. See also the Delta Metropolis website: www.deltametrapool.com.

11 The Dutch section of CIAM (Van den Broek and Bakema with Van Eyck) prepared a plan for Nagele in the NE Polder, which reflects these principles. See Aldo van Eyck, *Three Schools in Nagele*, Architects Year Book 9, London: Elek Books, 1960.

12 GUST, *Post Ex Subdis: Urban Fragmentation and Constructions.*

13 OMA (Rem Koolhaas) have always been fascinated by the programme as the stimulant for architectural form, which was developed by the next generation practices which grew out of OMA. See R. Koolhaas and MAV, *S, M, L, LX*, Rotterdam: 010 Publishers, 1999. Also Hatye Carty, *The Region Makers: Rhein Ruhr City*, Düsseldorf: NRW-Forum Kultur and Wirtschaft, 2003.

14 DEGW studies for the Dutch Ministry of Planning and Housing (VROM) on high-speed rail interchanges and their impact on urban strategies, sets out the characters of these emerging centres.

15 VROM (Dutch Spatial Planning and Environmental Communication Directorate) See also Graham and Martin, *Splintering Urbanism*, London: Spon Press, 2004.

16 Ibid.

17 Summaries of both the fourth and the fifth reports are published in English. See also Harrison, Wheeler, and Whitehead, *The Distributed Workspace*, London: Spon Press, 2004.

18 John Worthington, 'Accommodating change: emerging real estate strategies', *Journal of Corporate Real Estate*, January 2001, 3(1): 81–95.

19 See John Worthington, 'Learning to live with the networked city', in proceedings of conference organised by Dublin Institute of Technology (DIT) and Harvard University Graduate School of Design, *Metropolitan Corridors: Planning for the Future*, Dublin, 2001.

20 M. Hajer and A.Reijndorp, *In Search of New Public Domain: Analysis and Strategy*, Rotterdam: NAI Publishers.

21 F. Houben and Calabrese (eds.), *Mobility: A Room with a View*, Rotterdam: NAI Publishers, 2003. Catalogue for International Architecture Biennale, Rotterdam, 2003.

22 Mecanoo, *Holland Avenue*, The Hague: Ministry of Transport, Public Works and Water Management, 2003, considers the motorway, not only as a means to go from A to B, but as an environment that in itself is a place to be. A design road atlas.

23 See Jackson and Johnson, *Australian Architecture Now*, London: Thames and Hudson, 2000, and Philip Goad, *Melbourne Architecture*, Sydney: The Watermark Press, 1999.

24 The masterplan has been prepared by Pi de Bruijn (Architekten Cie) for the City of Amsterdam, Zuidas Project Group, to include 985,000 square metres of office space, 1,056,000 square metres of housing and 322,000 square metres of retail and cultural facilities, associated with the high speed rail station. See *Profession Architect*, Rotterdam: 010 Publications, 2002.

25 *Landscape Architecture and Town Planning in the Netherlands*, 95-97, article on Leidsche Rijn. Uitgeverij THOTH, Bonsum, 1998, pp. 98–109.

26 DEGW, *Two Sites One City: Strategic Brief for UCP and Papendorp Sites*, Utrecht, London: DEGW, 1997.

27 DEGW undertook a strategic review of opportunities either side of the raised section of the M1 motorway for a consortium of landowners.

28 DEGW were members of the development team, preparing the development brief for the Utrecht Central Station Area, setting up the communication process and preparing information for a public referendum (www.stationiedutrecht.nl). See DEGW First Annual Founders Lectures, in John Worthington, *Making Change Work: Design as a Catalyst for Organisational Innovation*, 2003. Response by Stuart Lipton.

29 See John Worthington, 'Learning to live with the networked city', in proceedings of conference organised by Dublin Institute of Technology (DIT) and Harvard Graduate School of Design, *Metropolitan Corridors: Planning for the Future*, Dublin 2001.

30 E. Relph, *Place and Placelessness*, London: Pion, 1976.

31 CABE, *Creating Successful Masterplans: A Guide for Clients*, London: CABE, 2004.

In August 2002, *New York Magazine* invited Morphosis to propose a design for the World Trade Center site. We thought through several programmatic and design issues in our initial proposal. The results of the short time we spent brainstorming and designing were published in the September 16, 2002 edition, which appeared on the newsstand the week of September 11.

We attempted to express to the city and the world, through architectural gesture, both memory of the terrible losses and destruction as well as hope and optimism through the decisive intention to rebuild. Each focal point we envisioned would function to these concurrent ends.

CHAPTER 21

GROUND ZERO

THOM MAYNE

Starting with rethinking the concept of the tower, we asked ourselves what type of new vertical structure would most suitably mark the New York skyline of the twenty-first century. As a critique of the concept of the tower, our primary structural component exists as a tower-like form, but is not habitable above the 10th floor. Rising above the level of the 10th story is a scaffold covered by skin onto which commemorative, educational, commercial or entertainment imagery can be projected. This empty tower houses communications equipment on the inside while providing a forum on the outside to be used by owners and residents as they see fit. We chose to resist placing an isolated object building onto the site. Rather, our building bends, folds and penetrates the earth to actively engage the ground below as it spirals into the site, where the lower floors can be illuminated by light streaming into the cavernous forms exposed on the west side. In order to address the magazine's requirement of reclaiming a significant amount of the interior space formerly provided by the destroyed towers, we envisioned our towers laid horizontally, long and low structures which would frame the site and lead to the river.

At Ground Zero, a large park swells up and covers the footprint of the north tower, which is expressed as a large underground room. Submerged and opening up to the park through a square oculus, this room would house an official memorial to the victims of the attack. On the footprint of the second tower we proposed an open plaza, where people will circulate and gather. In an effort to expose the depth of the original site, a large canyon remains open to the sky. From above one can gaze down onto both the infrastructural elements such as escalators and subway tunnels, as well as onto commercial and recreational frontages.

We hope each architectural gesture resonates with imagery that will subtly honour the past while forging a new paradigm of architecture and urban design, providing the requisite square footage in a configuration that physically engages the site and its users.

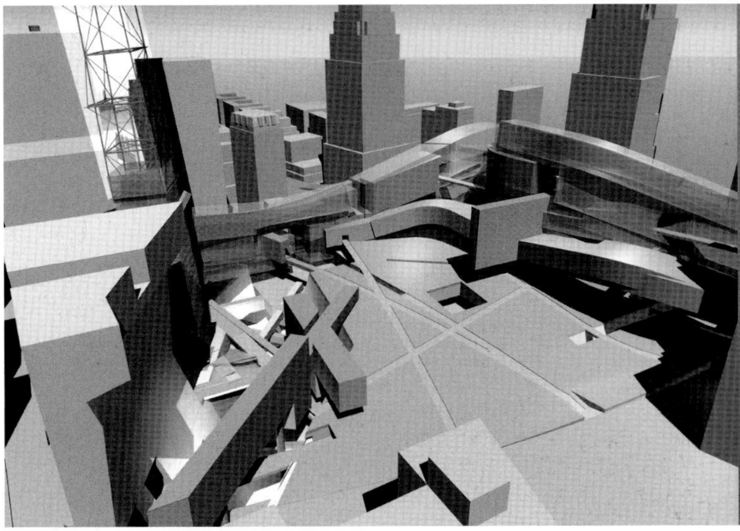

21.1 North perspective

21.2 Canyon perspective

21.3 Cross-section

21.4 West perspective

21.5 Dynamic spaces

We are disinclined to trust anyone who says they can predict the future, and with good reason. The desire to know what happens next is nothing new and the kind of people who until recently have set about fulfilling this need – necromancers, gazers into crystal balls, science fiction fantasists, not to mention town planners – don't inspire much confidence.[1]

Such a warning is certainly a disincentive to a comfortable and agreed prognosis for the future of urban design. The litany of utopias and dystopias that have been and gone, from the Garden of Eden to *Bladerunner*, remind us not only of the fragility of any sensible dialogue but also of the numerous voices and critics out there who have their own individual ideals. Sometimes they complement each other and the beginnings of a movement or manifesto comes to the surface. Most often they are the hum that goes on in the background of the busy practitioner's world that, like a radio news channel, every now and then demands attention and changes of practice.

This chapter is in three parts: the first sets the scene, the second reviews the contributions in this book and the final section presents some thoughts on the ways forward.

CONCLUSION

URBAN DESIGN FUTURES

JON ROWLAND

SETTING THE SCENE

Urban design has emerged as an important tool in redefining how we address our urban environment. The focus of activity in the past few years has been on gaining acceptance for urban design principles as part of the mainstream approach to such issues as urban regeneration and the design of new settlements. It moved us out of our 'silo thinking' and has helped us realise how complex designing our cities can be. Having achieved that, urban design is now at a crossroads. Many urban designers are pondering where we go from here. This state of flux, in what was until recently essentially a cohesive intellectual approach, is illustrated in the different contributions in this book. This collection of polemical essays is a sounding board for some current notions in urban design that set out a number of scenarios for its future direction.

It is important to recognise at the outset that much of the urban design discussed in this book reflects a Western cultural view. As Tony Lloyd-Jones in his contribution reminds us, we are working increasingly within a global urban design context that reflects not only a form of cultural imperialism but also local aspiration. There are large swathes of Third World cities that are the product of informal settlement. These follow a pattern of simple streets/routes and a flexibility that enables a building to act as both residence and workplace. The urban design is simple, robust and functional. There is no masterplan, but a framework of movement corridors and networks. However, many of these cities also seek to emulate a more Western ideal of Central Business Districts, high-rise housing, and large-scale movement corridors for the private car. It is these latter aspects that are addressed here.

Urban design is not new. It just is forgotten every now and then, after which we have a period of rediscovery, re-invention and re-definition. All civilisations attempt to describe their ideal cities. In physical terms, for example, gridded cities go back thousands of years. We still have much to learn from places like Pompeii. This is not confined to Western cultures. Islamic cities with their geometric urban grain of walled compounds and religious spaces represent a hierarchy of private to public thresholds that replicate a relationship with Paradise.

Urban design has always tried to tie in the physical form together with philosophical, social and economic considerations. These contexts change from generation to generation. Cities which represented the eighteenth-century Age of Reason differ from those reflecting nineteenth-century industrialisation or the Garden City as the antidote to the 'satanic mills'. Twentieth-century modernism and individualism reduced the concept of the city to simple ideas of structure, commodification and monetary value. Utopia here has shifted to global profits, where the fit of emerging cities, like Shanghai, no longer relates to their local surroundings, but to their position in the world. The language in which that is expressed pays homage to Western culture as a means of expressing its new context.

In philosophical terms, because of urban regeneration or renaissance, urban design is now coming to terms with impermanence. To a certain extent this is inevitable. The moral and philosophical climate has engineered an eclectic, pick-and-mix response to our built environment where disposable commodities now include houses, office blocks and neighbourhoods. For areas in the process of de-industrialisation, this poses particular problems as developers are often unwilling to invest in anything that does not give quick returns. The effect of this is a 'sheds-r-us' approach to the environment and recognition that housing need only have a thirty-year life span before it is replaced. Globalisation of trade and culture, media and now urban design has left us with a sense of cultural ambiguity. The question of how to deal with the gap between what we might call the 'tradition of fixity' (are we here to replicate an image of a static past?) and the 'prognosis of transience' (where change is an integral part of the environment), is now becoming apparent.

In the political sphere, urban design has come a long way in recent years, from the periphery of consideration, to a central plank of UK government policy. This achievement has been due not only to the positive influence of organisations such as the Urban Design Group, but also to the negative influences of those architects, planners and other professionals who lost the plot when it came to designing our towns and cities.

In the UK one of the key turning points in the transition of urban design's profile was Prince Charles' comment about the 'monstrous carbuncle' proposals for the National Gallery extension. His subsequent involvement in developments, most influentially at Poundbury, an extension of the town of Dorchester that was designed by Leon Krier on Duchy of Cornwall land, helped change the agenda. In fact, Krier was a key player setting the intellectual tone for much of the debate on urban design in the 1980s and 1990s, not only for his work at Poundbury, but also at IBA in Berlin and at Seaside in Florida.

In 1990 Geoffrey Broadbent in his book, *Emerging Concepts in Urban Space*, described two broad schools of urban design thought.[2] The key protagonists in one group were Rob Krier and Aldo Rossi, who were seen as 'neo-rationalists'. The other school of thought comprised the old bulls of urban design, Kevin Lynch, Gordon Cullen and Christopher Alexander, who were deemed to be 'neo-empiricists'. Leon Krier somehow straddled both these paradigms. Geoffrey Broadbent points to Krier's view that today we think of earlier street patterns and so-called organic structures as having grown 'as unconsciously as flowers in the field'.

> **People like to forget the plasticity, perspective and symbolic precision of these apparently free-formed stone masses are not the fortuitous product of a spontaneous zeal for building, but represent, on the contrary, the highest sense of ordering the realisation and consolidation of the highest ethical artistic consciousness.**[3]

But as Malcolm Moor says in the Introduction, there is no such thing as unconscious planning, and towns have rarely been designed for such arbitrary reasons.

Broadbent went on to promote the idea that three broad components would shape the city of the future:

- **Monuments**: those symbolic aspects of a city in which Aldo Rossi believed the memory of the city resided, and without which a city lacks particularity or identity. He was talking soul! While that might be appropriate for towns or cities with a historic core, it poses problems when their original functions move to faceless office blocks at urban edges that offer a better real estate value, leaving churches to become residences, banks to become pizza parlours or just holes in the wall, and civic halls to become the haven for tea dances.
- **Urban texture**: the 'touchy-feely' quality issues of townscape, a sort of artists' view of street scenery.
- **Out-of-town housing**: suburban development that drew from the powerful images of garden cities to present inhabitants with a place to sleep but not much else. Here Broadbent saw that the skilful planting of trees, hedges and the use of fencing could overcome the lack of sense of urban enclosure between buildings.

By these three components customer choice would be maximised and the city of the future would be judged. What the Broadbent critique reflected was a continuation of the idea of urban design as essentially a physical and spatial set of tools to help regain elements of traditional urban forms that had got lost in the post-war drive for reconstruction and growth.

Responsive Environments[4] represented a more rational approach to understanding the components that make up our cities and the rules to assemble them. It began the cataloguing of typologies, processes and practices of urban design, and acknowledged the complexities of the endeavour. This document remains an important tool for urban designers.

When the UK government defined urban design as 'the complex relationship between built and unbuilt space', it was drawing on Krier's ideas on urbanism, on the bedrock of *Responsive Environments* and a political agenda for a better urban environment as exemplified by *Quality in Town and Country*[5] that would eventually lead to the Urban Task Force and Urban Renaissance reports and the *Urban Design Compendium*.[6] This conflation of ideas represented a seismic shift in both the perception of urban design and in the recognition that we could do something about the dire state of our built environment and the quality of output of our developers and volume builders. Like all such changes, the surface ripples were substantial. Concepts in urban design were discussed, the vocabulary of urban design, once a secret and almost Masonic language, was exposed, and the *lingua franca* of 'permeability', 'legibility', 'activity nodes', and so on, was unleashed on the unaware public.

What the embrace of urban design has done is to bring together those elements that had previously been seen as separate items, such as transport, land use, economics, planning and design, with an understanding of the complexities of the interdependencies between these elements. The analysis of the 'layers' of the city would be reflected in a better understanding of the urban environment. Like a chronometer, the transport cogs would be linked to the economic spindles and the community springs all working in different timeframes but all linked and well accommodated, to produce an effective product that would both guide and control the way we experience the world, its quality, and our movement through it. In looking at the layering of our urban environment we are in fact also looking at how we deal with time.

22.1 Kentlands. The intention to create a series of places through urban design codes.

22.2 BedZED, UK. Creating new design orthodoxies which rely on expensive technologies that mass production could make affordable.

REVIEW

In reviewing the contributions to this book, five broad interdependent and overlapping urban design themes emerge. Much of the dialogue is still about the physical design of space but the emphasis within each theme differs. I will review these as follows:

- the new fundamentalism: urban design and regulatory mechanisms;
- the new battleground: urban design, sustainability and townscape;
- the culture of inclusion: urban design, social space and movement;
- choice and the lack of it: urban design, lifestyle and experience;
- 'blurring the edges': urban design and change.

Each of these has elements that cross boundaries to inform other themes. Let me start with urban design as a tool for regulating our environment.

The new fundamentalism: urban design and regulatory mechanisms

The desire to improve our social and environmental surroundings is inherent in the human condition. In the West we see it represented in Thomas More's *Utopia* where the codification of that condition is set out:

> The city is compassed about with a high and thick stone wall full of turrets and bulwarks . . . the streets shall be appointed and set forth very commodious and handsome, both for carriage and also against the winds. The houses be of fair and gorgeous building, and on the street side they stand joined together in a long row through the whole street without any partition or separation. The streets be twenty foot broad. On the back side of the houses, through the whole length of the street, lie large gardens enclosed round about with the back part of the streets. Every house hath two doors . . . who so will may go in, for there is nothing within the houses that is private or of any man's own.[7]

And now some 500 years later we see the same concern raised by the proposition that codes are an essential tool in the control of the 'sense of place'. In America, the New Urbanists' codes reflect a set of fundamental principles of town-making. However, More's *Utopia* included social and economic rules, while the New Urbanists rely on the carefully controlled creation of a physical realm that tends to be peopled by like-minded consumers who buy into a common brand (clapperboard, Georgian, etc.). Paul Murrain from the Prince's Foundation is an advocate of such an approach but sees the public realm as more than just the physical place. It is part of a collective statement encapsulated by the word 'Civitas' – a concept for establishing order and hierarchy out of chaos.

John Punter is less starry-eyed. His view of an urban design future is firmly locked into the practicalities of legal procedures that urban design ultimately has to address. This includes the role urban design will play in spatial, regional and neighbourhood policies. It also involves the battle for hearts and minds that needs to take place to embed urban design mechanisms, such as planning obligations and design codes as well as new skills, into our culture.

These two aspects of control and legislation will form a major strand of work, within the urban design umbrella. The issue, of whose code, whose vocabulary, the implicitness of the aesthetics, and the cultural context could be a major battleground, so too would be the process of achieving that code. Whether legislation takes urban designers down a legal cul-de-sac will be another issue. The links between urban design and regulatory mechanisms are clear. The questions are what form regulation takes, how it is managed, and by whom.

The new battleground: urban design, sustainability and townscape

Harriet Tregoning is a leading advocate of 'Smart Growth' in the USA, and her analysis praises the sustainability programmes and projects there. New forms of development are being created that question current practices and policies. But she also recognises the importance of legislation:

> There's a lesson in it: policy-makers and smart growth advocates need to become a little more subversive in how change is sold. You can only get so far by telling people to live differently for the good of the planet. They need to be shown how they benefit right now, in their waistlines, their wallets, and their own backyard.

22.3 Ecolonia, the Netherlands. Sustainability is the driving principle of this new neighbourhood with its woonerfs and green roofs.

22.4 Ecolonia, the Netherlands. Sustainability also has a social dimension.

Urban design has some way to go in making sustainable development relevant to the wider population. Nevertheless, anecdotal evidence suggests that New Urbanist developments increase sales values. Developers get more money, consumers achieve their aspirations and their own self images, and (relatively speaking) a more sustainable form of development is built.

Pioneers in this country have taken a less subversive role. Bill Dunster's BedZED development at Sutton is an in-your-face, take-it-or-leave-it developments that flies its sustainability flag for all to see. This is not a traditional townscape. It represents a challenge to many urban design orthodoxies. Its success or failure will be judged not only on its energy efficiency but by the 'sense of place' it creates and its resale value. BedZED is the first of a series of developments that could, over time, develop into a brand that will encapsulate a set of aspirations and meanings that is missing from the housing provided by the volume builders.

Lucien Kroll *has* been subversive. His development at Ecolonia not only has the emblematic green roofs and solar panels, but is carefully planned with community involvement to achieve the 'civitas' that Paul Murrain strives for, but without the coating of nostalgic architecture. Shared-surface streets, sustainable drainage, 'walkability'/'cyclability', public transport, multi-use space, all evoke the openness and self-responsibility of Dutch society. The UK obsession with privacy gives way to the Dutch view of neighbourliness, individualism to communalism, 'health and safety' to well-being, single use to multi-purpose. This understanding of the complexities and different 'layers' involved in the creation of a neighbourhood sets a lot of European urban design apart from the Anglo-American approach.

David Rudlin provides a link between sustainability, urban design and the need for greater control. His practice, URBED, promotes similar ideals to Smart Growth through its programme for Sustainable Urban Neighbourhoods. He draws on historic townscape, advocates urban repair, and promotes a contemporary townscape. The plan for the Telford Millennium Community, one of the UK government's demonstration projects, carried out by JRUD, Lifschutz Davidson and URBED to test new forms of urban development, exemplifies how responding to a range of sustainable criteria can challenge more mainstream urban design.

The concept of townscape in every age has led to a range of powerful images. The Garden City, Ville Radieuse, Archigram, Seaside, all have been instrumental in changing visions and with them the concept of urban design. At each crossroads, some of us take comfort in tried and tested approaches to the design of our urban environments, and some 'boldly go' to explore new urban design programmes. Here is an MVRDV vision:

> What is more important is the idea that we are all involved in designing real three-dimensional spaces, in generating a city with three dimensions . . . We think there is great potential for future sustained development if we consider urban agglomerations as integrated and interdependent units. We are currently working with the idea of mixing functions, integrating differences and designing objects that are capable of modifying their qualities and characteristics in the future. We are also concerned with the social aspects, and we propose a way of working with a mixture of functions, making it something interesting and desirable under circumstances of spatial density and compactness.[8]

These concepts of use of space, movement and what we might term 'blurring the edges' are worth exploring further.

The culture of inclusion: urban design, social space and movement

One of the directions of urban design is towards a culture of inclusion. We are multicultural societies. We bring a range of experiences to our neighbourhoods. We also collect experiences through travel and replicate them in a sanitised form either internally in our large shopping malls or as part of our street scene.

Jan Gehl's contribution to this idea of the quality of experience arose from his analysis of Copenhagen city centre. He points to the differences between the 'welcoming environment' and the price we pay for moving fast and thus creating an unwelcoming environment. The unwelcoming environment is exemplified by development that presents us with blank walls and turns its back on its surroundings. The 'welcoming environment' is the modern meeting place, the space enclosed by buildings with activities that spill out into that space and create the vitality that makes that space memorable.

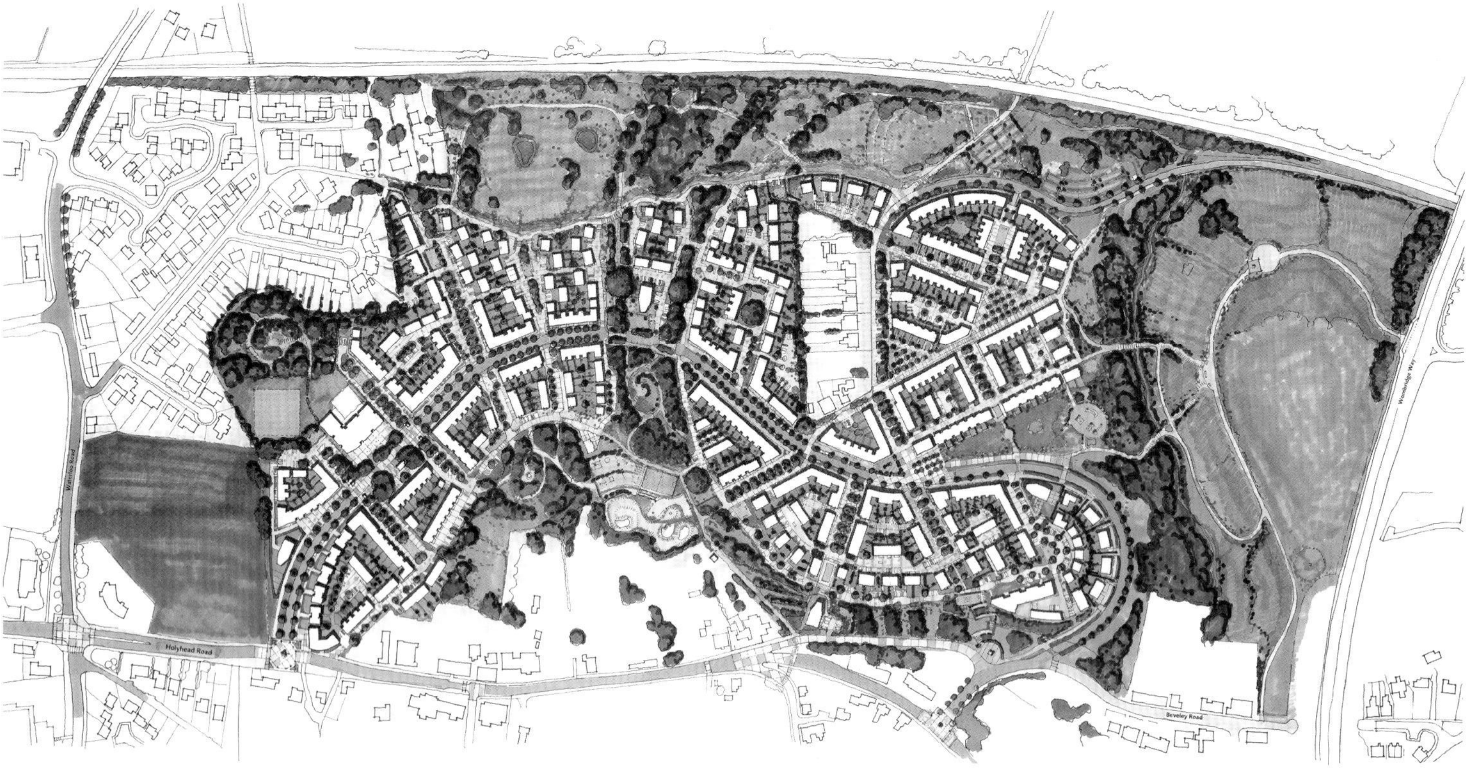

22.5 Telford Millennium Community masterplan, UK. Built on a redundant coal mine at Ketley, the plan explores new urban forms to deal with issues of remediation, ecology, sustainable drainage, solar orientation and new forms of housing. This results in a plan form that combines traditional and contemporary elements.

Enclosure rather than object buildings can help create that sense of city comfort, which enables us to engage in what we are best suited – being sociable. Jan Gehl and Tim Stonor of Space Syntax both promote the primal experience of walking and stopping and meeting people, that makes up much of the context in which our public life is played out. For urban designers this means a grasp of social movement, animation, risk, gender, institutional, retail and economic issues, as well as the physical elements of function, density, orientation, height and so on. Not only do these experiences have to reflect the cultural context in which they exist, but they also need to be connected or they become boring. 'Permeability' and 'connectivity' are words we use for this aspect of linking experiences – and that link, that bond, should be enjoyable.

Comfort and pleasure become important in the design of our cities. Both Jan Gehl and Tim Stonor are concerned with places that encourage enjoyment, happiness, interchange and time. These also mirror the principles of the 'città slow' movement – where the aim is to create an environment that resists the pressure to do everything faster, and therefore to improve the quality of our urban life. The movement is not fuelled by some vicarious nostalgia but by a view of conduct and self-regulation that preserves cultural traditions. Carl Honore in his book, In *Praise of Slow,*[9] suggests that until we rewrite the rules that govern every sphere of life – the economy, the workplace, urban design, education and medicine – decelerating will be a struggle.

Ken Worpole builds on this idea in his contribution. His view is that the use of space can only be understood through the medium of time. There are 'surges' or 'intensities' of use that vary depending on time and protagonists. A space that is comfortable for older people during the day, can also be the environment for people to meet, flirt and embrace at night. But this pulsing of space is only one aspect of the complex layering that makes up successful space between buildings. Ken Worpole promotes the idea of a further three aspects:

- the 'physical realm';
- the 'symbolic realm' that encapsulates the meaning and values of that place and brings to mind both Krier's and Rossi's views of the importance of memory;
- the 'relational realm'.

This last category is interesting because it can encapsulate both political control of the space and/or its democratisation, and the notion of the surges and

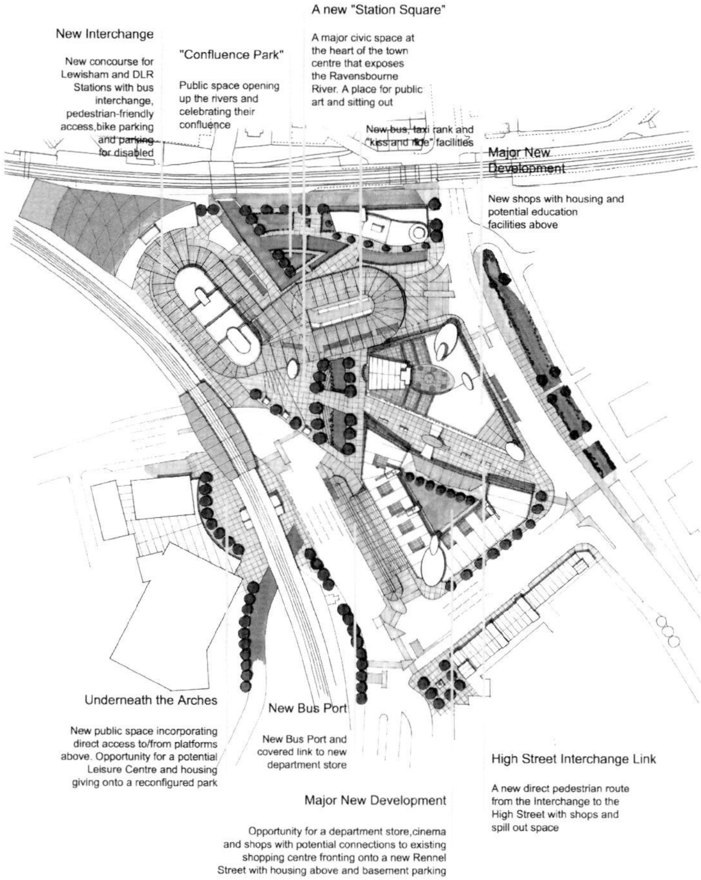
A new "Station Square"
New Interchange
New concourse for Lewisham and DLR Stations with bus interchange, pedestrian-friendly access,bike parking and parking for disabled
"Confluence Park"
Public space opening up the rivers and celebrating their confluence
A major civic space at the heart of the town centre that exposes the Ravensbourne River. A place for public art and sitting out
New bus, taxi rank and "kiss and ride" facilities
Major New Development
New shops with housing and potential education facilities above
Underneath the Arches
New public space incorporating direct access to/from platforms above. Opportunity for a potential Leisure Centre and housing giving onto a reconfigured park
New Bus Port
New Bus Port and covered link to new department store
High Street Interchange Link
A new direct pedestrian route from the Interchange to the High Street with shops and spill out space
Major New Development
Opportunity for a department store,cinema and shops with potential connections to existing shopping centre fronting onto a new Rennel Street with housing above and basement parking

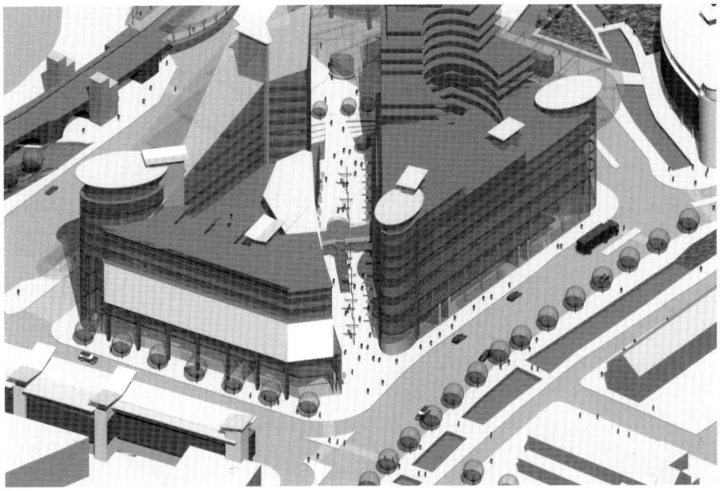

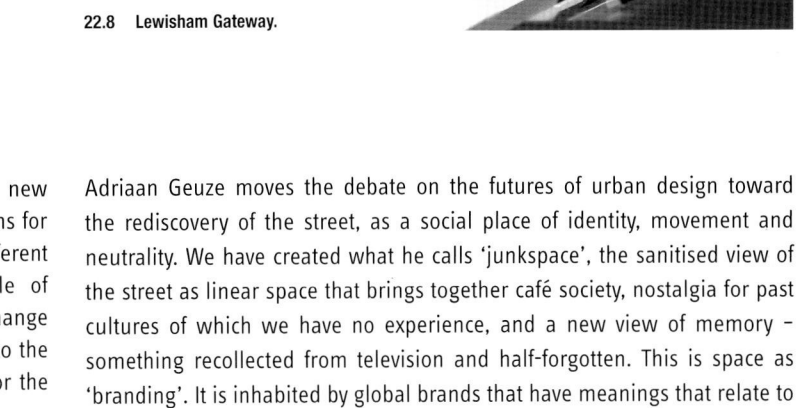

22.6 Lewisham Gateway, UK, Urban Design Framework. Part of a development brief for a key transport interchange in South London which creates a new street block with riverfront public spaces and a mix of uses linking the railway station to the town centre to replace a large roundabout.

22.7 Lewisham Gateway.

22.8 Lewisham Gateway.

pulses that might generate new movement strategies and promote new forms of linear spaces. Thom Mayne explores this concept in his designs for urban environments. Implicit in the 'relational realm' is the view of different time that different individuals or activities inhabit. The principle of 'Eigenzeit', what we might call 'own time' or 'own pace', reflects a change in the way we use space. The continuing incursion of private space into the public arena through, among other technologies, the mobile phone or the lap top, complicates our view of the design of urban space.

Time scarcity has led to the inclusion of personal private space into public space. The mobile phone leaves its user no place to be alone, it has externalised our intimate space. We need public space to be private and talk to business colleagues, family and friends. This is not just about the decorous world of Gordon Cullen and the physical design of urban space, but a more inclusive and flexible approach to the design and management of our public realm. Alex Lui's case study of Lan Kwai Fong shows how the change in the way the public realm was used has assisted its regeneration. Designing for such spontaneity and change is difficult. Success is often an issue of timing, not only from a property market perspective, but also in terms of consumer perception. Just as Alex Lui reminds us about 'location, location, location', Gehl's riposte might be 'something happens, because something happens, because something happens'.

Adriaan Geuze moves the debate on the futures of urban design toward the rediscovery of the street, as a social place of identity, movement and neutrality. We have created what he calls 'junkspace', the sanitised view of the street as linear space that brings together café society, nostalgia for past cultures of which we have no experience, and a new view of memory – something recollected from television and half-forgotten. This is space as 'branding'. It is inhabited by global brands that have meanings that relate to choice within a very limited palette. The street has become a corporate entity.

'Please, please, please give us back our streets' is his cry. Yet it was not that long ago that Le Corbusier roundly condemned the landscaped streets of the Garden City ideal. His view was that the idea of the street must be abolished. Streets were an obsolete notion and we needed to create something that would replace them.

The influence of this exhortation changed the role of the street from a carrier of social communication to one of physical communication. If we add to this new orthodoxy the advent of the professions of highway engineer and planner, with their separate desires to achieve fast-flowing traffic and match the zoning of uses and their own codes and performance specifications, we see the intellectual gap that practices like West 8 are fighting to close.

22.9 Bull Ring, Birmingham, UK. Future Systems' design for the new Selfridges department store creates a new brand for the city. There are only limited opportunities for such iconic events and urban design needs to understand how to use them effectively.

22.10 Bicester shopping village, Oxfordshire, UK. The artificial has been used to create a comfortable backdrop to retail therapy.

Yet movement is a dynamic component of place-making and urban structuring that the urban designer can harness to create exciting places. It has inspired architects to create great examples of dramatic interchanges. The symbiotic relationship between such transport infrastructure and urban design is starting to be exploited. In the UK the government is proposing Transport Development Areas, (a direct take on Peter Calthorpe's proposals for Transit Oriented Developments), as a means of concentrating development as part of an overall strategy for the expansion of London as a polycentric city. We still have some way to go. The recent projects for Stratford and Lewisham Gateway in London are new success stories.

In Lewisham, urban design, public consultation, and a realisation that new transport connections had put the area on the property map guided the process. The programme is to replace a traffic roundabout with a new mixed-use street block, a new public square, and transport interchange, and to bring the existing shopping centre to the station. This urban design approach of proposing a street-based solution has helped change the design agenda from the standard retail proposal for a large monolithic development to a framework of development blocks. This is becoming a model for development around stations.

The design of social space goes to the heart of urban design. We can continue to create places and encourage activities that determine what type of people will be using them, where law-abiding users can establish a safe environment for themselves – whether through the design of gated communities or privately owned malls. Yet such control can be boring – and perhaps that is what Adriaan Geuze is railing about. J.G. Ballard, in his book *Cocaine Nights*, promotes the idea that the utopian ideal relies on the insertion of a virus or friction to threaten the quality of life in a gated community (in that case it was murder and arson) and thus create the essential ingredient of 'community' or 'togetherness' that architecture or urban design cannot create.

On the other hand, we can move towards a more inclusive design approach that not only views the public realm as an outside room with equitable access, but also as a welcoming place where different activities can attract different people at different times, and reduce the likelihood of a viral attack. This approach is being pursued by cities like Leeds, Manchester and Rotterdam where culture, inclusivity and neutral space are concepts being used to 'rediscover' the streets and social spaces.

People now know what is achievable. They have enjoyed the piazzas in Italy, walked the boulevards in Paris, sat at the Ramblas pavement cafés of Barcelona, appreciated Starbucks' coffee shop lifestyle, *Friends* and New York loft living, and wandered around pedestrian-friendly town centres virtually everywhere. They are fed up with their own lifeless town centres, and this is the difference between the current cycle of change and renewal, and previous cycles. We now live in a consumer society, and the exercise of choice is right.

Choice and the lack of it: urban design, lifestyle and experience

We live in a pluralistic world where we increasingly adopt a consumerist approach to virtually all aspects of our lives. People have never had so much freedom of choice nor been better informed of what is on offer and where the best places are to access it. Choice extends to the dozens of types and colours of cars, 30,000 items on supermarket shelves to 100-channel TV and the vast range of entertainment on offer in clubs and restaurants. There is a selfish, liberated, mobile, informed, opinionated and infuriatingly capricious population, and urban designers are creating the setting for their lives. An increasing number of families adopt a peripatetic lifestyle where they shop in town B with the best retail offer or use the Internet and stay at home, live in town C to get children into the school with the best league table results, go out for a evening in town D with the smartest clubs and bars and commute to work in city A to access the best highest-paying jobs.

The irony of so much choice is that there is so little regarding the biggest item of expenditure, the house. House builders appear to compete with each other to offer the blandest housing designs with the most grandiose names. The most affluent segment of society could exercise their power to choose but are limited to a scaled-up version of the usual housing offer. Middle earners have little choice between the similarly boring products of a building industry still living in the 1950s with 'Austin Allegro' architecture, while the lower-paid house buyers have no choice as their only criterion is affordability.

22.11 Paddington Basin development, London. A masterplan as vehicle for architectural branding. Source: Gillespies

22.12 Masterplan, Paddington Basin development. The role of public space is to hold the plan together and make sense of the architecture. Source: Gillespies

22.13 Paddington Basin development, London. Source: Gillespies

The range of choice and the lack of it are epitomised by Kate Muir, recently describing her life as a 'burb' wife in the USA, visiting her local mall:

> **Mall-ennui set in: that purposeless, rootless wandering, that feeling of isolation. All the shops – and there must have been hundreds – were cloned by The Gap . . . In this useless profusion there's an aftertaste of deception. There are a thousand possibilities but they're all the same.**[10]

This reflects Richard Rees' view of the power of retail and volume builders to homogenise the environment and our experience of it. Choice and diversity are controlled. According to Rees, urban design can help change this dominance by learning from its promoters about experiential design, lifestyle, and branding. He sees urban design moving in three directions:

1 As part of the homogenised environments of global trademarks, where instead of signal buildings with symbolic meanings, we will have 'universal trademarks that do not rely on language to convey their meaning, but encapsulate a whole sense of meanings'. Our spaces and buildings will be organised around our response to these emblematic signs. Instead of the church or temple, we have the trademark building as a brand. Rees' example is of Future System's Selfridges department store in Birmingham: a one-off piece of iconography (accompanied in that city by the spatial trademarks of the 'Victoria Square' brand, and the 'Brindley Place' brand) that helps sell cities.

   This appeals to architects and their ideas on vista closures, landmarks and signature buildings. While not all cities can achieve the Guggenheim effect of Bilbao, the idea that urban designers can learn about massing, placement, landmark destinations and the assembly of component parts from retailers in order to create city environments, is not yet part of mainstream practice. Up to now these concepts have been kept within the closed environment of the Mall. But new ideas on how we want to use our streets have led to a re-think. Some architects like BDP are starting to explore this. For others the masterplan with the trademark building is the vehicle for two bites of the lucrative redevelopment cherry: (1) to make a statement about a city; and (2) to establish the opportunity to build the iconic structures around which it is organised.

2 The second direction he suggests is the creation of a total experience through combining the changing ways that public spaces are used with

the 'retail imperative' as the progenitor of the design. So we experience a design of an artificial memory, like Bicester Village retail outlet in the UK, that has no meaning other than as a theatrical backdrop to shopping that changes every so often to match the latest retail trend. This, in his view, is the new authenticity – and it is not designed to last a long time.

3 The third route is to bring together the concept of designing in 'experience' with the perceptual approach to branding and nostalgia, and the establishment of coherent typologies.

In this context, we need to reflect on the work of Bo Grunland at the Danish Academy of Fine Arts in Copenhagen.[11] He builds on the ideas of street socialising pioneered by William Whyte's research in the USA and the retailers' rules of perception. The suggestion is that to enervate a space with social experience, we need to see some 1,000 faces an hour walking past. But that experience is not going to take place unless there is something interesting happening. And this is where the retailing approach to designing the urban environment plays a part.

To keep shoppers interested and to ensure 'through-put' or 'footfall', Grunland suggests the need for 25 'unique works' every 100 metres. These unique works can be shop signs, decorations, interesting façades or displays – what we urban designers call variety and diversity. At walking speed this produces a new work, and a new emotion every four seconds. This idea can be similarly evoked on residential or other development. But it's no good if the 'unique works' are repetitious and a sense of *déjà-vu* is experienced.

So perhaps we will see the emergence of different forms of 'branding' based on design consumerism – the way people actually use and experience buildings and spaces – which will promote choice and diversity. Closed systems and inward-looking monolithic structures will cede to the open structure of streets, squares, and more flexible types of buildings, perhaps even managed in order to ensure greater experiential uniqueness.

But this also presents challenges. Alain Cousseran suggests we have a surfeit of pretend-space and 'sanitised urbanism' that has had the idea of public symbolism removed. These are spaces with no particular function. Nothing much happens in them. The icons become playthings, but the users are disregarded in the quest for a design vocabulary. Cousseran is clear that 'urban space is not a language but its foundation and it is first and foremost a production not a representation'. He sees three-dimensional space as an idea that cannot be characterised in words like street or square but is defined by the notion of limits, edges and emotion: 'The idea of anticipation is essential . . . It must contain the necessary expressive qualities in order to elicit an emotional response in the user.'

Again, his view is not new. The need for variety and messages has been embedded in our urban environment since the beginning of cities. How to sign your goods, how to bring people to prayer, and use buildings and spaces as story-telling elements are all part of experiential design. What has changed has been the nature of the media and the attitude to time. Venturi understood this in the American context of Las Vegas where to get the right emotional hits required bigness, branding, built-in obsolescence and continual change.

Mardie Townsend is right to point out the inequity in the way we produce our urban design experiences. Male perceptions have created our cities and public spaces. One only has to look at Trafalgar Square as a memorial to the army officers who conquered other peoples in far-off countries to see the gulf between the aspirations of women and the reality of public space of the past. One hundred years ago only women of dubious repute walked the streets alone. It is only recently that women have come to design our urban environments and through this the disjunction between women's aspirations and reality are only now being exposed. Mardie Townsend points to a recent research project into the design of new neighbourhoods where the nostalgic myths of the home, based on outdated stereotypes, are played out again and again – through the medium of bathroom colours and kitchen accessories. Her view is that we inevitably end up with an inappropriate and unsustainable approach to addressing the needs of neighbourhoods in the future.

The view of public space as a male place of society, culture and reason, while female space reflects intimacy, nature and passion, has changed little over time. We still see the dominance of male grand gestures in the design of our public realm. A core urban design principle will be to address the issues of plurality and gender so that more democratic spaces are achieved, but are accessible and safe for all.

22.14 Fairford Leys new community, Aylesbury, UK, designed by John Simpson and Partners, uses coding as a development control tool.

22.15 Borneo, Sporenburg, Amsterdam. Its code has an implicit set of values that are not based on traditional aesthetics but explore new design ideas within a traditional street form. Urban Designer West 8

Whether well-designed and visually stimulating surroundings promote happiness as well as physical health is an altogether more difficult matter. Designers would love to believe that their creations brought happiness to their inhabitants. It will take the combined effort of the design professions and behavioural psychologists among others to explore these issues. But if we can entertain the ideas of 'città slow', it is not too far-fetched to consider 'città happy'.

Urban design will continue to address these social and economic agendas, and not just physical issues, in the future. Urban designers will need to collaborate to achieve these new goals. If we do not take this on board, we could be undermining the concept of community and social capital and in turn promoting the anomie of individual choice. Finding the balance is critical.

'Blurring the edges': urban design and change

These dichotomies continue: male and female, big and small, cocaine nights and utopia, exclusivity and inclusivity. The city is a set of contradictions and urban design is there to mediate between them and help blur the edges. John Worthington embraces this 'bothness' in urbanism. The city has high and low densities, it is both centralised and dispersed. The mediation he suggests is in the form of new typologies that will allow the flexibility of use that we increasingly desire. So we look for multi-use spaces, both as a building type and as an element of the public realm. 'Shell' buildings, where the product is space whether for offices, residential or commercial use, are an example. They will be used at different intensities at different times by different people. Another typology reflects events and experiences that bring people together to create spontaneous communities, such as Glastonbury Festival, where place is a consumer commodity.

This approach is similar to that put forward by Andrew Cross. He points to a new form of flexibility demanded in the name of corporate nomadism, where big-box retail and call centres exemplify the disposability of the building and its associated environment. His view is that we could be in the process of a return to a wandering culture. Globalisation, increased movement between cities, and the promotion of greater choice have resulted in lightweight work-shelters that are demountable or discardable. We have moved from the closed communities of herding nomads, through the more open agricultural and industrial settlements to post-industrial 'call-centrism' where we carry our work with us from 'no place' to 'no place'. All we have is a public realm structure that allows for this to happen, but no emotional attachment to place. The place is the movement.

If we take Thom Mayne's interest in change as the constant, then the role of urban design can start to be redefined, away from the Lynchian model of creating a fixed stage within which activity takes place, to one where there is continual reappraisal of 'city transactions, interactions and exchanges. The result of these reassessments would be the evolution from ideal geometry to multi-dimensional systems.'[12] He goes on to reflect on new organisational frameworks 'that supersede plan oriented strategies which privilege order over contingency. Programmatic and spatial adjacencies and the hybrids they engender call for a more three-dimensional organisational matrix that promotes interconnectivity and allows the manifold logics of the city to advance, recede and cohere'.[13]

Perpetual change thus becomes a core urban design principle. And so we arrive at the flexible urban structure or framework around which a range of decisions can be made, which reflects the current desire for choice but ultimately promotes areas of privacy, public interchange, movement and social responsibility.

This is very different from the ideas put forward by Geoffrey Broadbent some fifteen years ago. Urban design then was seen as a set of physical concepts. What Worthington and others are suggesting is that urban design is much more about connectivity, not only along and about physical routes but also along and about flexible structures that respond to the issues of time. The recognition that urban design should address the layers of the city in the way that planning or engineering cannot, presents us with a level of complexity we are just starting to get to grips with. MVRDV in Holland are exponents of this, espousing the idea of 'stacking'. Their housing silo in Amsterdam is an architectural example of this view. Here a mixed-use development of offices, workspaces, shops and public space, all of different typologies and tenures, are stacked together. Their pavilion for Expo 2000 plays with this idea and reflects the conflation of public space and private space, of nature and open space that is both artificial in the environment it creates yet can be seen as contribution to the new urban form. Ken Yeang also uses the idea of stacking by pushing the more conventional form of high-rise buildings to respond to new programmes of sustainability and energy efficiency.

The 'layering' of an urban environment is similarly being explored by a number of other designers. Foreign Office Architects' projects in Yokohama for the Port Authority, or EDAW's for the London Olympic bid exemplify such an approach. Here simultaneity of uses – parkland on the roof, shipping terminal on the lower floors – creates a series of fresh experiences within a new urban form, and challenges many of the current urban design orthodoxies.

CONCLUSION

Urban design futures

So where does this review leave us? I think five things are happening.

1. The democratisation of decision-making.
2. A consolidation of urban design around a set of traditional values.
3. Continuing debate between the demands of sustainable development and traditional townscape.
4. What we might call the urban design of uncertainty.
5. Increasing interest in the urban design of layers and movement.

Democratic urban design

The public realm, our streets and parks, belong to local people. In many countries the process of making decisions on our built environment has been widened. Communities and 'stakeholders' have become more involved. A range of procedures has been established to include more people in the process. Urban Design Assistance Teams pioneered the approach of engaging citizens in the USA in the 1960s. 'Planning for Real', 'Enquiry by Design', community planning weekends, design 'charettes', are all techniques geared to increasing the involvement of the public in having an influence on their local built environment. The UK government's agenda has been to empower communities in regeneration areas. This has exposed differences between those communities who have the capacity to participate knowledgeably, and those where the level of engagement is limited because of gaps in social, educational, and economic skills and resources.

On top of this, we have an increasing series of other interventions geared to improvement in other spheres, such as 'well-being'. Health audits are now as much part of the masterplanning process as urban design audits. The 'mapping and gapping' of skills and resources have also widened the perception for the need for an all-encompassing arena in which to deal with these overlapping issues. This inclusiveness has both positive and negative aspects. On the plus side, involving other conceptualisers such as gender specialists, social anthropologists, artists, community development experts, risk managers, sustainability appraisers, or health enablers can only enrich the process of defining urban design parameters for a particular programme or project. However, this also slows down the process, and can create professional logjams.

Another plus is the gradual improvement in the knowledge base of a public caught up in major projects. However this inclusiveness has also led to an increase in 'NIMBY'ism (not-in-my-back-yard) where empowerment of some communities has been at the expense of others. In many cases it is the most vocal self-selected individuals who claim to speak on behalf of their communities who may not be providing a balanced view. Means of empowering large and more representative elements of the public still eludes many consultation and participation programmes. Mardie Townsend has pointed out some of the gender issues, but ethnic and other minorities, and the youth in particular are often not heard.

A third plus has been the increased awareness of design through television and other media. Architecture and urban design are 'sexy'. Aspirations for places, spaces, and new built environments have been raised.

This, then, is the arena in which the first urban design future will continue to be played out. Urban designers will act as interlocutors, interpreters, arbitrators, and negotiators, trying to balance increasingly complicated technical and design issues with a more pluralistic and diverse set of socio-economic demands. If we do not get this right, urban designers could

22.16 Morphosis competition entry for rebuilding of the Twin Towers, NYC. This explores the challenge of how we bring contemporary 'place', structure and movement together.

22.17 Olympic Park Masterplan, East London. This exemplifies many of the hybrid forms where place and transience can co-exist. Source: EDAW

become emasculated once again, not because of their role as designers, but because of the Sargasso Sea of professional disciplines involved. The Bermuda Triangle beckons. Leave that to the project managers!

The urban design of traditional values

In the UK a more traditionalist approach to urban design that concentrates on the physical aspects of the discipline will become more apparent, especially within new housing developments. This future for urban design is bound up with its increased use as a development-control tool. Coding – and particularly coding that has an implicit set of aesthetic values – will become more common. Current testing of codes by the Commission for Architecture and the Built Environment (CABE) for a series of demonstration projects leans heavily on the New Urbanist experience.

Coding in the UK is also influenced by experience of design guidance as epitomised by such publications as the *Essex Design Guide*, which has set the scene for much developer housing of the past twenty years. Something originally viewed as answering a local concern became a generic model. The current demonstration projects are searching for clues to provide some context. Many schemes borrow from historic centres that may be quite removed from the immediate locality of the development. There is little re-interpretation or attempt to address or express new agendas such as sustainability and energy resource efficiency. So we end up dealing with fragments, an eclectic mix of images, and artefacts. It is as if urban designers are DNA scientists trying to replicate a historical ambience in a different contextual laboratory without the benefit of an overall thesis.

A key element in this fragmentation is the number of agencies and professions involved in such projects. Many are working to different ends, responsible to different agencies or organisations. It is no wonder that few schemes venture far from the accepted image of some English village life. We have lost the benefit of an overarching vision for the future – hence the plethora of neo-traditional developments that are currently being built.

Coding will also follow the retailers' philosophy that a brand with character and authentic style will win the loyalty of more customers than if it targets everyone because this dilutes the brand. Brands that are taking control of their own surroundings can create an experience and emotion for consumers in three-dimensional environments. This is just what Seaside, Celebration and Poundbury have succeeded in doing. In these places, the brand (and its code) perform for the customer.

If coding is to succeed and not get locked into a battle of aesthetics, it will need to be underpinned by a set of philosophical principles that are geared to some of the issues set out in this book. It cannot meaningfully be grafted onto existing procedures that were originally established to deal with different forms of urbanism. Even Leon Krier considers the need for an integral vision of society, but that has to be part of a political struggle or else 'it will merely be reduced to a style'. Coding *will* have a role to play, but if it is to respond to the demands of the new century, such as sustainability, energy efficiency and new typologies, then urban designers should start exploring the contemporary city in a more creative way, focusing on the framework issues of movement networks, accommodating change, and encouraging social interaction, rather than the aesthetics of one form of fenestration or another. Perhaps we might then see the emergence of appropriate frameworks/forms with appropriate levels of codes that reflect the complex systems that make up the built environment. In the UK we can start to see this process emerging. Manchester's *Rebuilding the City: A Guide to Development for Hulme*,[14] part-authored by David Rudlin, is proving successful. Birmingham's Urban Design Strategy is long-standing and has played an important part in the renaissance of that city.

Eco-urbanism and traditional townscape

The third urban design future will seek to resolve the issues between the increasing demands for environmentally responsible development and traditional townscape. This is best seen by looking at BedZED, at one end of the spectrum, and developments such as Fairford Leys, at the other. Some local governments in the UK are starting to demand major changes in energy efficiency from developers proposing new settlements, while at the same time also requiring adherence to local vernacular. The implications are obvious – sustainable materials such as timber replacing brick with its high embodied energy, and solar orientation challenging the twists and turns of traditional towns. Zero-footprint development and high eco-scores demand new morphologies and typologies. Establishing the balance to create a new townscape will be a new urban design future.

The ground rules are changing. While it is easy to follow a traditional agenda and set of design rules, the new agenda for sustainable development is uncertain. That uncertainty is an interesting issue. Whereas the concept of branding is about creating certainty and uniformity, the dissection of the layers of the city and their interdependencies, promote uncertainty, and the need for flexibility. So we can see a divergence appearing between a more dynamic approach to urban design, which explores issues of change, and one which creates the stasis and sameness we see in many of the masterplans currently being produced.

The urban design of uncertainty

Part of the challenge for urban design, then, is to find ways of accommodating such dynamism, where roles and functions can vary within short spaces of times. This is the fourth urban design future. Public spaces and buildings become multi-functional, used differently at different times. Streets become 'theatres of activity' – a vision that is pure Fellini. His view that all life is theatre and can be found on the street echoes the interests of Jan Gehl, Thom Mayne, Tim Stonor and others. The emphasis will be on the importance of connectivity, choice, and a framework that encourages movement, activity and pulse. This builds on the ideas that David Gosling and Barry Maitland put forward in *Concepts of Urban Design*.[15] Their view was that the basis of urban design was all about acknowledging the levels of complexity, promoting some form of framework based on the way the city was used that would be able to accommodate change, and reconciling the single-use zones of the modern city. The flexible framework will therefore be key to this urban design future. It will enable development to respond to uncertainty. We need to reflect on the implications for the design of 'place', form, security, comfort, convenience and meaning. How do we create 'place' or character in a flexible structure? Such adaptability will also see the emergence of new typologies and spatial components to inhabit the framework. Multi-purpose space, shell buildings, 'caravanserais', cinemas that show live football, venues, residences that are workplaces and so on. West 8's Adriaan Geuze's take on this is not to consider standard urban forms, but to advocate an integrated urban design approach of connectivity and convenience, individuality, pleasure and intimacy, and the provision of adaptable space.

A critical part of the framework is the movement network along which different experiences can be achieved, what Cousseran calls the existential process. At key interstices, centres for particular activities can cluster, creating a democratic and polycentric set of communicating lines. Some of those lines are virtual, but some reflect the changing importance of particular connections and the transient nature of different developments. How we 'dress' those routes, the scale, sight lines the '4-second hits', the havens and contact with the surrounding neighbourhoods within the concept of change, are areas that this urban design future will address. Establishing such a flexible structure which can allow for a disposable building, or Paris Plage, or Notting Hill Carnival, or street markets, or temporary park will also be key to making the city pleasurable. This is not the static townscape of Gordon Cullen, but the design of a set of sequences, 'events', incidences and experiences into what Bernard Tschumi calls an urban 'assemblage'.

This brings us back to John Worthington's 'bothness' or what the cultural guru Homi Bhabha calls the 'hybridity' where 'place' and transience can co-exist. This is certainly a view endorsed by Jon Jerde who designed Fremont Street in Las Vegas as a sequence of experiences:

> **The Fremont Street experience is four blocks long . . . It provides hyper entertainment; the audience is totally immersed in an environment that is without predictability. What we have created with Fremont Street is a new kind of instrument for which there is no street music. We used the best solution available to us at the time converting what had originally been three-dimensional into anamorphic illusion, but the possibilities for this instrument are unknown and limitless. We now have a new language of architecture that encompasses light, illusion and change. We are at the beginning of a paradigm shift.**[16]

The urban design of layers

This brings us neatly to another urban design future. Multi-usage of space, enclosures and movement corridors, have to work both in three dimensions

22.18 Freemont Street, Las Vegas.

22.19 Freemont Street, Las Vegas.

but also in time. That infers continuous vertical and horizontal integration and an understanding of the layers of the urban context. This spatial integration is the playground of the Landscape Urbanists: Morphosis, Rem Koolhaas, Foreign Office Architects and others. Morphosis' competition work for IFCCA and the replacement of the Twin Towers, both in New York, exemplify this aspect. Thom Mayne's plan for downtown Los Angeles has the idea of permanent change and urban transience built into the urban design concept.

This is a different approach from that of many European practitioners, although Rem Koolhaas has been the conduit for much of this stream of urban design. His role as interlocutor has helped synthesise ideas on movement through public space and through buildings. His masterplan for the Illinois Institute of Technology or his recent Dutch Embassy in Berlin project the idea of 'trajectory' with its attendant variety of experience. This starts to bring together Richard Rees' and Ken Worpole's views of experience, the variety of 'events' proposed by Bo Grunland, and the concept of layering.

In a recent *Saab Magazine* (accompanied by the strap lines: 'Creative thinkers are the driving force behind modern life, bright-eyed people whose vision extends to include possibilities and opportunities the rest of us miss, and who want to shake everyone else by the shoulders to get them to see the light. They know there's "a better way".'[17] How's that for a branding statement?), Koolhaas provokingly both embraces the idea of branding (part of his Harvard shopping tome) yet rejects the idea of identity, character and con-centricity as concentration of power. Much more democratic or 'generic' is the move to the poly-centricity, and 'blurring of edges' that John Worthington has celebrated. The fixity of the centre versus the transience at the edges or the ephemerality of typologies within the centres could well be the arena in which this facet of urban design will be played out in the future.

> The Generic City is the city liberated from the captivity of the centre, from the straitjacket of identity. The Generic City breaks with the destructive cycle of dependency . . . It is a city without history . . . It is easy . . . If it gets too small, it just expands. If it gets old, it just self-destructs and renews. It is equally exciting – or unexciting – everywhere. It is superficial – like a Hollywood studio lot it can produce a new identity every Monday morning.[18]

The transience and genericism promoted by Koolhaas reflect our obsession with individualism and personal choice. However, identity, dismissed by Koolhaas as a straitjacket, is a cultural touchstone that we urban designers often use to help define 'place'. It is a recognition that 'place', however inauthentic, can provide a remedy in helping to heal many cities as part of their urban renaissance. The creation of memories and 'place-making' is part of the vocabulary of urban designers. The celebration of the vicarious and received fragments of historical memory is there for comfort and resonance. The big challenge is how we bring these layers of framework and 'place', structure and movement together.

All the contributors to this book pose prickly issues. Do we move down the road of maximum choice? Is our route a celebration of a framework that is geared to transience and change? Should urban design encourage the concepts of communalism and self-responsibility that Lucien Kroll and Ken Worpole promote? Is the inexorable logic of New Traditionalism and coding the consolidation of a brand of communities and the celebration of the private sphere? Can we learn from Harriet Tregoning and Bill Dunster how to confront the straitjacket of 'townscape' with the urban design of sustainable development? The futures for urban design will depend on how we address these questions. However, this will not happen until better skills and greater understanding of urban design are established for all involved in the built environment, whether professionals through their formal university experience such as foundation courses, or the community through both informal routes to knowledge and through changes in our school curricula. If we are going to participate in the creation of our own environment then we need the tools.

Ultimately, it seems to me that urban design is a mediating mechanism that attempts to reconcile the different layers and intensities of the built environment. That mediation is not just functional, but should be imbued with meaning and principle that recognise the complexities, pluralities and democracies of our societies today – and they will vary and change. Perhaps we need to redefine our ideas on space and enclosure.

This is an exciting time for urban design. In the next few years these themes will be explored more fully and the boundaries of urban design extended. Some urban designers will move away from the broad consensus that has informed practice in the past few years, hopefully challenging today's orthodoxies. Others will investigate the overlaps and seek to understand the interdependencies between them. Thus a continuing programme of enriching urban design will proceed as a means of analysing, changing and regenerating our cities. As long as we continue to see this as an integrated process, then we may begin to reach a new utopian ideal.

Perhaps Alex Krieger is correct and urban design is no longer a technical discipline but is really a state of mind.

NOTES

1 James Collard, 'Tomorrow's People', *The Times*, 27 December 2003.

2 G. Broadbent, *Emerging Concepts in Urban Space*, Van Nostrum Reinhold International, 1990, p 338, discussing Leon Krier's 1987 Atlantic plan.

3 Ibid.

4 I. Bently, *et al.*, *Responsive Environments*, Oxford: Butterworth, 1985.

5 Department of Environment, *Quality in Town and Country*, London: Department of the Environment, 1994.

6 Llewelyn Davies and English Partnerships, *An Urban Design Compendium*, London: The Housing Consortium and English Heritage, 2000.

7 Thomas More, *Utopia*, London: Phoenix, 1994, pp. 8–9.

8 MVRDV, *Stacking and Layering: MVRDV 1998–2002*, El Croquis, 2002, p. 14.

9 Carl Honore, *In Praise of Slow*, Orion, 2004.

10 Kate Muir, *The Times*

11 'Streets Ahead', an unpublished report to BT on the future of the street by Landscape Design Associates and Jon Rowland Urban Design, 2000.

12 LA Now, V2, 'Shaping a new vision for downtown Los Angeles: Introduction', by Thom Mayne, University of California Press 2002.

13 Ibid.

14 See *Rebuilding the City: A Guide to Development for Hulme*. Hulme Regeneration Limited, June 1994.

15 David Gosling and Barry Maitland, *Concepts of Urban Design*, London: Academy Editions, St Martin's Press, 1984.

16 Jon Jerde, 'Revitalised city', *TATE*, Issue 24, Spring, 2001.

17 Rem Koolhaas, 'The generic city', *SAAB Magazine*, 02/2003, p. 36.

18 Ibid., p. 37.

INDEX

accessibility 30–1, 33, 37–9, 51, 55, 67, 98, 102, 112, 138, 156, 158, 160, 162–3, 165–6, 182
accountability 4, 129
adaptability 30, 34
administration 19, 51, 55, 153
Advocacy Planning 115
aesthetic advisory committees 51, 55
affluence 7, 91, 150, 180
affordable housing 33, 53, 91, 122–3, 127, 131, 134, 180
Africa 34, 36
Age of Reason 174
agriculture 36, 124, 127, 129–30, 151, 183
air conditioning 14, 123, 128
airports 149–52, 160–1, 163, 165
Ajax Stadium 165
Aker Brygge 72–5
Albert Dock 147
ALEA, Alençon 120
Alexander, Christopher 30, 67, 175
Alexandria, Virginia 47
alienation 3, 100
Alpha-aan-den-Rijn 117
Alsop, Will 64
alternative energy 105
Amazon 152
amenities 52–3, 55–6, 90, 125, 130, 139
America *see* United States
America City Beautiful 21–2
American Automobile Association (AAA) 39
American Comprehensive Plans 56
American Dream 40
American Planning Association 43
Amsterdam 11, 44, 53, 87, 159, 161, 165, 183
anchors 146–7
animal urbanism 114–20
Annapolis 44
anthropology 30, 97, 111, 184
anticipation 111
appeal mechanisms 51, 55
Appleyard, Donald 30, 37
Archigram 177
architect-urbanists 22
Architectural Advisory Panels 55
Architectural Review 5
architectural style 31, 49, 57, 63, 68, 74
Arendt, Hannah 47, 49
Argent St George 132
Argos 152
Arup 134
Asia 9, 34, 36, 88–93
Atlanta 39
attitudes 43, 102, 107, 115–16
Augé, Marc 97
Australia 54, 102, 147, 159, 165
Austria 129
authenticity 142, 144–5, 150, 160–1, 163, 167–8, 182, 185
automobile industry see cars
avant-garde 12, 87
Aylesbury 183

back office 166
backlashes 63
Bacon, Edmund 18
Baker, Charles 68
Ballard, J.G. 180
Bangkok 10
Barcelona 52, 67, 86–7, 180
Barclays Bank 153
Barnet, London 19
Barnett, Jonathan 20
Barton, Huw 56
Bastille 96
Bath & North Somerset Council 98
battleground 176–7
Bauer, Eddie 40
Bauhaus 106, 116
BCSC 145
BDP 143, 145–8, 181
Beacon Councils 56
Beaux Arts 21–2
Beddington Zero Energy Development (BedZED), Sutton 9–10, 105, 124, 127–8, 130–1, 134, 176–7, 185
Beijing 9
Belem, Brazil 35
Bentley, Ian 30
Berkeley 30
Berlin 23, 56, 66, 174, 188
Best Value 55
Bethoncourt-Montbeliard 119
Bicester 180, 182
big architecture 12
Bilbao 181
Billingham, John 95
biodiversity 10, 55, 115–16
Birmingham 52, 56, 61, 97–8, 143, 180–1, 185
Birmingham City Council 97–8
black arts 80
Bloomsbury 61, 66
Bois de Vincennes 96
Boots 146
Bordeaux 11
Borneo, Amsterdam 183
Boston 39, 162
Bournemouth Library 144
Bouwfonds 117
Bradford 60

brain drain 43
branding 142–3, 145, 148, 176–7, 179, 181–2, 185, 187–8
Brazil 352
BRE ecohomes 128
Brennan's Law 51–2
Brighton 60
Brindley Place, Birmingham 56, 61, 181
Brisbane 14, 159
Bristol 59, 144, 152
Britain 3, 5–7, 10–11, 50–3, 55–6, 88, 93, 95, 99, 102
British Broadcasting Corporation (BBC) 66
British Telecom (BT) 152
Brixton 80
broadband 60
Broadbent, Geoffrey 175, 183
Broadcasting House 66
Broughton 133–4
Browne, Kenneth 6
brownfield sites 11, 33, 43, 56, 126, 130
Brunel, Isambard K. 12, 152
Buchanan Street, Glasgow 22
Buckingham Palace 15
budget 95, 119
Buffalo, NY 6
building industry see construction
Building for Life 55
building regulations 123, 127
Bull Ring, Birmingham 180
Burchell, Robert 42
bureaucracy 27
Burnham, Daniel 19, 27
By Design 30

café culture 146, 179
California 42, 48, 60, 151
Calthorpe, Peter 11, 41, 62, 180
camaraderie 14
Cambourne 62
Cambridge City Council 55
Camden, London 162
Campo, Venice 14
Canada 53
Canary Wharf, London 4
capital web 167
carbon economy 122–3, 125–30, 132, 134
carers 100, 102–3
cars 2–4, 24, 31, 33, 37, 39, 43–4, 71–3, 83–4, 91, 98, 103–4, 129–31, 146, 160, 162, 165–6, 180
Carson, Rachel 8
Castleford 96
Catalonia 86–7
Cato Institute 89
CCTV 14
Ceausescu, N. 116
Celebration 62, 185
Central Business Districts (CBDs) 90–1, 93, 174
Central Park 152
Central Station Site 166
centre-periphery links 160–1, 166–7
Cerda, A. 67
Champs Elysées 19, 73, 112
Channel 4 96
Channel Tunnel Rail Link (CTRL) 24
channels of movement 150
character 30
charettes 52, 184
Charles, Prince 61, 174
Chesterton, G.K. 48
children 95–6, 98–9, 101–2, 104
Chillingworth Road, London 53
China 9, 27, 88–9, 91, 93
China Town, Singapore 9
choice 180–3
Christmas 14, 91
Christo 15
CIAM 3, 18, 161–2
Cirencester 26
citizenship 47, 97–9
cittä slow movement 178, 183
City: Rediscovering the Center 96
city design 161
City of London 4, 97
City Plan 52
cityscapes 89, 162
civic realm 48–9
civil engineering 1, 19, 43–4
civitas 47, 176–7
Clarksdale 72
climate change 105, 123–5, 129, 133
clutter 111
co-operative planning 52
Coatbridge 152
Colchester 81
Cole, Richard 95
Colindale, London 26
collaboration 41, 56, 68, 78, 92, 183
collage approach 7
collector roads 48
colleges 42
colonialism 36, 93
commercialism 88–93, 143–7, 149–53, 166
Commission for the Built Environment (CABE) 7–8, 11, 16, 26, 50–1, 55, 68, 95, 99, 185
Commonwealth Games 148
communications 31, 86, 102, 117, 159, 161–2, 167, 179
Communities Plan 58–9
Community Strategies 52
commuting 44, 130
compact cities 33, 36
compartmentalisation 107
competitiveness 42–3
complacency 40, 49, 57, 115, 122, 125
Concepts of Urban Design 187
configurational studies 79
conflict resolution 55–6
congestion 23, 71, 87
Congress of the New Urbanism 42
consensus 31, 40–1, 102, 189
conservation 4, 7–9, 23, 51, 55
Conservative Government 4, 59
construction 10, 31, 66, 71, 101, 104, 107–8, 111, 122–3, 126–9, 131, 133–4, 152, 180
consultants 11, 76–8, 81, 104, 122
consultation 13, 15, 55–6, 96, 101, 155, 180, 184
consumers 8, 11, 55, 59, 145–6, 150, 160, 163, 177, 179–80, 182–3, 185
context 9–10, 31, 34, 36, 55, 72, 78, 118, 130, 161, 174, 178, 185
Continent 6
contractors 66, 98, 115
control process 51, 55–6
Copenhagen 52, 71–3, 94, 159, 177, 182
Le Corbusier 2, 7, 9, 20, 26–7, 40, 106, 115–16, 179
Cornell University 6
Cornell Urban Design Team 6
Cornwall, Duchy of 174
Corporation of London 98
corporatism 4, 31, 52, 67, 90, 160, 163, 166, 179, 183
Council for the Protection of Rural England (CPRE) 97
Council Tax 56, 127
Counter-Attack 6
Countryside Lobby 58
Cousseran, Alain 3, 106–13, 182, 187
Covent Garden, London 8–9
covered space 146
Crane, David 30
Crewe 152
Cribbs Causeway, Bristol 144
Crick 149–53
crime 14, 34, 36, 43, 58, 79
critical mass 92
Cross, Andrew 149–53, 183
Crown Street, Glasgow 61
Cullen, Gordon 6, 30, 175, 179, 187
cultural institutions 42
Culture of Cities 160
Cultures of Cities 160
cycles 10, 73, 130, 156, 177

D'Aguilar Street 90–1
Dali, Salvador 87
Danish Academy of Fine Arts 182
Darwin, Charles 2–3
Daventry International Railfreight Terminal (DIRFT) 152
Davis, Mike 11
Davos 115
Day, K. 102
dead zones 81
decentralised concentration 36
DEGW 162, 166–7
deification 143
Delft 161, 165
Delta Metropolis 161
democracy 98, 111, 115–16, 125, 182, 184–5, 187–9

demography 10, 59, 92, 101–2
demonstration projects 127
Denmark 73, 87, 94
Denton Corker Marshall 165
Depression 3, 153
deregulation 50–1
desertification 124
design codes 47, 54–5, 124, 126–7, 129, 133, 176, 185
design levels 161
design origins 5–6
design panels 55
despair 95
developers 4, 16, 21, 31, 43–4, 51, 53, 56, 66–7, 86, 122, 126–7, 130, 132, 140, 144–5, 147, 161, 167, 174–5, 177
developing world 7, 9, 30–1, 33–4
discotheques 91
distributed workplace 163
distributor roads 48
divorce 10, 102
Docklands, London 155
Don Valley 166
Doncaster 166
Dorchester 174
dormitories 33
dot.com revolution 60
downtowns 38–9, 43, 63, 90, 93, 148, 163, 188
drainage 34
Droxford Business Park 153
Duany, Andres 27, 42, 62
Dublin 94
due process 51, 55
Dunster, Bill 10, 122–34, 177, 189
Düsseldorf 159
Dutch Embassy, Berlin 188
Dutch Ministry for Planning and Housing (VROM) 162

e-tailing 148
Ealing, London 62
earthquakes 73
ease of movement 30, 34
East Durham 153
Eckbo, Derek 18
Eco Tower 136
eco-urbanism 185–7
ecology 1, 10, 23, 26, 56, 102, 115–18, 127, 129, 156
Ecolonia, Alpha-aan-den-Rijn 117–18, 177
Economic Freedom Network 89
economics 33, 42–4, 52, 57, 59–60, 76, 89, 91, 93, 97, 101–2, 104, 123, 125, 145, 149–50, 152–3, 159–69, 175–6, 178, 184
economies of scale 31, 123, 127–9, 153
Ecuador 145
EDAW 23, 154, 184
Eddie Stobart 152
edge cities 31
Edge City 160
edgeless cities 165
Edinburgh 61, 66
education 18, 42–4, 48, 51, 53, 55–6, 99–100, 102, 118, 160, 178, 184
Eigenzeit 179
Einstein, Albert 3
elections 43
Elephant and Castle, London 136
Embarcadero Freeway 73
Emerging Concepts in Urban Space 175
enclosure 30
energy efficiency 55, 105, 177, 184–5
enforcement 51
engineering 1, 7, 11, 19, 24, 26, 43, 53, 58, 86–7, 98, 108, 115–16, 131, 136, 146, 179
England 3, 58, 63, 97, 147, 152
English Heritage 50
English Partnerships 129–30, 133, 145
Enquiry by Design 184
Enskede 165
entrepreneurs 43, 92
environment 2, 6, 40, 42, 51–2, 54–5, 57, 59, 76, 98–9, 101, 117–18, 122, 126–7, 129–31, 138, 146, 148, 185
Environmental Protection Agency 41
Erskine, Ralph 94
Essex Design Guide 185
ethnicity 89, 160, 184
ethnography 146
Europe 11, 18, 21–3, 29–31, 36, 49, 51, 53, 55–6, 83, 86–7, 94–6, 98, 102, 108, 116, 123–4, 129, 147, 150, 152, 159, 177, 188
European City of Culture 147
European City Structure Plans 56
European Commissioner's Information Society Technologies Programme 162
European Football Championships 86
European students 6–7
European Union (EU) 33, 86, 124
Euston Road, London 66
exchange schemes 103–5
Exchange Square, Manchester 23
exclusion 31, 51–3, 100, 160–1, 183
exercise 71
experience 142, 146, 159–69, 180–3
experts 102–4, 123, 125
Expo 2000 183

failures 31
Fairford Leys, Aylesbury 183, 185
Falk, Nicholas 68
False Creek 53
farmers' markets 14
Farrell, – 80
fascism 116
fast food 4, 86, 98
Felixstowe 152
Fellini, F. 187
feminism 102
Fielden Clegg Bradley 21
financial consultants 11
fiscal policy 41, 44
fitness centres 71
fixed space 163
fjords 75
Flachenutzungsplan 56
flexi space 163
flood zones 127
Florida 174
fly-posting 98
fly-tipping 95
focus groups 102–3, 105, 146, 167
food 124, 130
footfall 80, 182
footprint analysis 127, 129, 185
Ford, Henry 72
Ford Motor Company 72
forecasting 79, 81
Foreign Office Architects 184, 188
Forest Hills Gardens 41
form-function link 78
fossil fuels 125, 127
Foster, Norman 66, 80
Foster and Partners 77, 151
France 14, 98, 106, 112, 116–17, 119–20, 145, 152
Frankfurt 4
Fraser Institute 89
Fredericksburg 94
freeways 11
freight 152
Fremont Street, Las Vegas 187
Freud, Sigmund 3
functionality 31, 114, 160–3, 165–8
fundamentalism 176
Furnass, B. 103
Future Systems 143, 181
Futurism 26

Gap 152, 181
gap funding 53
garden artistry 108
Garden Cities 41, 174, 177, 179
gardens 112
Gare du Nord, Paris 24
Garreau, Joel 160
gas 125
gated communities 31, 36, 63, 180
Gathorne-Hardy, Flora 97
Gaudí, A. 87
Geddes, Patrick 26
Gehl, Jan 8, 70–5, 94, 177–9, 187
Gehry, Frank 12
gender differences 102, 178, 182, 184
general problem solving (GPS) 115–16
Geneva 87
gentrification 9, 16, 41, 53, 145
geography 149–50, 162
Georgian design 7, 13, 58, 62, 94, 176

Germany 106, 126
Geuze, Adriaan 7, 179, 187
ghettoes 34
gibbets 14
Gideon, Sigfried 27, 40
Gillespies 21–2
Gladwell, Malcolm 44
Glasgow 60–1, 94, 96
Glastonbury Festival 183
Glazer, Nathan 48
Glemme, Erik 96
Glendening, Parris N. 41–2
global warming 125–6
globalisation 29, 33–4, 92, 174, 183
Gloucester Docks 21
Gold Coast 159
Golden Jubilee 15
good life 44
The Good Place Guide: Urban Design in Britain and Ireland 95
good practice 30, 33, 36, 104
Gosling, David 187
Gospel Oak, London 3
government duty 125
GPS navigation 152
graduates 15
graffiti 8, 86, 95
Grahame Park 19–20
Grainger Town 61, 66
Grand Prix 14
Grand Projets 87
grant mechanisms 53
Great Notley 62
Great War 3
Great Western Railway 151
Great Western Shopping Centre 151–2
Greater London Authority 7
Greece/Greeks 47, 111
green movement 8–10, 15
Green Spaces, Better Places 95
green stickers 116
greenfield sites 10, 33, 56, 107, 126, 163, 166
Greensboro 39
grids 3, 6, 31, 36, 47, 78, 147, 165, 174
Grimshaw, – 80
gross domestic product 145
Ground Zero 170–2
growth 42, 92–3
Gruen, Victor 18
Grunland, Bo 182, 188
Gueze, Adriaan 83–7, 180
Guggenheim Art Gallery, Bilbao 12, 181
Gulf Stream 123
GUST 162

Hackney 154, 158
Hackney Building Exploratory 99
Hadid, Zaha 64, 68, 80
Haeckel, Ernst 115
The Hague 159, 161, 165–6
Hajer, Maarten 163
Hakim, C. 102
Hall, Peter 10
Les Halles 84
Hammersmith Flyover, London 4
Harlow 52
Harvard 5, 18, 20, 28, 30, 188
The Harvard Design School Guide to Shopping 142, 144–5
Harvey, David 27
Hassell 148
Haussmann, Baron 7, 19, 27, 68
Hayek, Friedrich 114
head offices 163
Heritage Foundation 89
Heritage Lottery Fund 95
high streets 4, 48, 97, 148, 150
high-rise housing 2–4, 13, 30–1, 36, 41, 140, 147, 165, 184
Highbury Initiative 52
highways 84, 160–1, 163, 165–6, 179
Hillier, Bill 30, 47, 78
Hilversum Media Park 165–6
historicism 62, 68
Holland *see* Netherlands
Holland Avenue 165
Hollywood 84, 188
homeopathic architecture 114–20
homeowners 39–40
Homezone 130
Homi Bhabha 187
homogenisation 15, 97, 146, 150, 161, 181
Hong Kong 9, 88–92
Honore, Carl 178
Hopkins, – 80
hospitals 42, 102, 145
Houben, Francine 163, 165
House Builders Federation 127
Houses of Parliament 52
housing associations 4, 117
Howard, Ebenezer 2–3, 19, 27
Hulme, Manchester 58, 60–1, 185
human capital 43, 103
hutongs 9
hygienic space 107
hyper architecture 12

IBA 174
Icknield Loop Master Plan, Birmingham 13
iconography 12, 143, 181
identity 15, 30–1, 33, 84, 86, 144, 161, 165, 179, 188
ideologies 23, 63, 115–16
IFCCA 188
Illinois Institute of Technology 188
impact fees 53, 56
In Search of New Public Domain 163
inclusion 52–3, 102–3, 160, 177–80, 183
Indies, Laws of 19
industry 3, 10, 33, 59–60, 103, 107, 122, 126–7, 149, 151–3, 167, 174, 180, 183
information technology 31, 102, 159, 161, 167
infrastructure 24, 26, 31, 33–4, 36, 42, 52–3, 56, 60, 66, 89, 100–2, 104, 150, 152–3, 156, 162, 165, 167–8, 171, 180
ING 147
inorganic kingdom 115–16
inscribed space 3, 106, 108–12
integrated planning 11
intensive building 135–6, 138, 140, 160
interior-scapes 146
Internet 86, 144, 146, 148, 180
interventions 1, 34, 50, 55
investment 11–12, 39–40, 42, 55, 58, 75, 122, 127, 129, 167
invitations 72–3, 75
Ira Keller Foundation Park 53
Ireland 14
Islam 36, 174
Isle of Dogs Enterprise Zone 4
Islington 53
Italy 14, 26, 67, 71, 107, 152, 180

Jackson, J.B. 149–50
Jacobs, Jane 18, 27, 30–1, 145
Jakarta 33
jargon 80
Java Island 53
Jenks, Charles 68
Jerde, John 146, 187
jobs 43, 56
John Lewis 144, 147
Joint Centre for Urban Design 7
Jon Simpson and Partners 183
JRUD 21, 26, 177
Jubilee Line, London 11
Junkspace 86–7, 179

Kalvebod Brygge 71
Karl Johann Gaten 72
Katz, Bruce 63
Katz, Peter 42
Kentlands 176
Kettel, B. 102
key workers 123, 131
Kings Cross, London 132
kitsch 116
knowledge industry 59–60, 102, 162
Koetter, Fred 7
Koolhaas, Rem 9, 22, 27, 118, 188
Krieger, Alex 5, 8, 18–28, 189
Krier brothers 3, 22, 30, 108, 174–5, 178, 185
Kroll, Lucien 13, 114–20, 177, 188
Kwartler, Michael 20

Labour Government 3, 55, 59
Laguna West 62
Laing 130
laissez-faire 89
Lan Kwai Fong Association 91–2
Lan Kwai Fong, Hong Kong 9, 89–93, 179
land use 5, 40–4, 54, 67, 76, 78, 81, 89, 138, 175
land value 42, 127, 134, 144, 153, 163
landscape architecture 1, 11, 18–20, 26, 43–4
Landscape Practice Group 97–8
The Landscape Urbanists 188
Langham Place 66
language 67–8
Las Vegas 108, 182, 187
laser lights 15
Latin America 34, 36
Lawrence, David 18
layers 184, 187–9
leakages 77
Leeds 60, 64, 180
Lefebvre, Henri 27, 102
Legacy Masterplans 154–8
legibility 30, 37, 175
legislators 126–7
Leidsche Rijn 166
Lenné 68
levies 53, 56
Lewisham Gateway, London 180
Libeskind, Daniel 64, 68
Lie of the Land 97
lifestyle 12, 14, 102–4, 129, 143, 150, 180–3
Lighthouse 94
lightweight construction 123, 127–8, 133
Lilla, Mark 48
Lima 34
limited pallet 65–8
Lisbon 11
Liu, Alex 179
Liverpool 60, 94, 147–8
Living Places: Cleaner, Safer, Greener 95
Livingstone, Ken 60
Lloyd-Jones, Tony 7–8, 29–37, 174
local authorities 30, 34, 52–3, 55–6, 98, 130
logistics 152, 165
Logo Cities 86
London 4, 7–9, 11, 13–14, 44, 53, 60–4, 77–9, 81, 87, 92, 95, 97–8, 123, 131–2, 136, 144, 152–8, 161, 181, 184, 186
London Development Agency 154
London Electricity 153
London Marathon 14
Los Angeles 11, 151, 188
Louvre 19
low carbon agenda 127
Lower Lea Valley 154–8
loyalty cards 145
Lui, Alex 9, 88–93
Lutterworth 152
Luxemburg 145
Lynch, Kevin 6, 30, 37, 108, 161, 175, 183
Lyons 117

M-Office programme 163
Macanoo 165
Macao 14
Machado, Rodolfo 28
McHarg, Ian 26
main streets 48
mainstream urban design 12–13, 29–30, 33–4, 36, 177
Maitland, Barry 146, 187
makeover programmes 96
Malcolm Moor 1–16
malls 4, 18, 31, 61, 78, 86, 102, 135, 145–6, 151, 160–1, 163, 165–7, 177, 180–1
Manchester 58, 60–1, 180, 185
Manthorpe, Walter 6
manuals 30, 50
Margate 79
Marina Quay, Singapore 9
market forces 4, 8, 91–3, 114, 160, 163
marketing 22–3, 123, 129, 140, 166
Marseilles 123
Marsh Farm Estate, Luton 2
Marshall Mills 64
Marx, Karl 3
Maryland 41–2, 44
mass production 107
Mass Transit Railway 90
Massachusetts 42
massing 67–8, 181
masterplanning 12, 19, 21–3, 31, 52–4, 56–7, 60–8, 126, 129, 132, 134, 154–8, 166–8, 181, 184, 188
Mathieux, Phillippe 96
Mayne, Thom 170–2, 179, 183, 187–8
Mayor of London 7, 60, 66
mayors 7, 31, 60, 66
Meadowhall retail mall 166–7
Mecanoo 161–2
media 43, 71, 86, 98, 144, 148, 161, 166, 174, 184
medical centres 42
Mediterranean 14, 123
medium-sized units (MSUs) 146
meeting places 72–3, 87, 91, 111, 177
Melbourne 52, 147–8, 165
merchandising 115
metropolitanisation 31
Michigan 42
Middle Ages 112
middle class 36, 43
Middle East 125
migration 33–4
Milan 87
military intervention 125, 127
Millau 115
Millenium Footbridge 79
Millenium projects 12, 79, 177
Milton Keynes 3, 129, 152
Miró, Joan 87
Mirralles, – 68
mises en scène 96
MIT 6, 30, 37
Mitchell, Bill 14
Mitchell, Joni 8
Mitterand, François 87
mobs 13
Modern Movement 3, 7–10, 29, 31, 40–1, 61, 63, 106, 114–17, 136, 174
modular construction 104
Monaco 14
monitoring 51
monocultures 122
monopolies 89
monuments 175
Moor, Malcolm 175
More London Bridge Masterplan 66
More, Thomas 176
morphology 30–1, 34, 36, 127, 187
Morphosis 188
Moses, Robert 19, 40
motivation 93, 116, 146
motorisation 31, 36, 39
motorways 31, 37, 126, 144, 149–53, 166
Moule, Elizabeth 42
movement 149–53
Muir, Kate 181
multi-family 44
multi-functionality 102–3, 187
multiplier effect 11
Mumford, Lewis 18, 20, 160
Murrain, Paul 7, 46–9, 176–7
MVRDV 162, 177, 183
Myer, George Val 66
Myer, J.R. 37

Nairn, Ian 5
Napoleon III 19
Nash, John 66, 68
National Audit Office 11
National Curriculum 99
National Gallery 174
National Urban Summit 48
neighbourhood committees 54
neighbourhood managers 92
neo-colonialism 115
neo-Georgian design 62
Netherlands 51, 55, 63, 98, 117, 147, 160–3, 166, 177, 183
networks 141, 159–63, 167–8
new 142–4
New England 42, 48
New Jersey 48
New Ordinary 122–34
new town blues 3
New Towns 106
New Urbanism 10, 22–3, 30, 33, 36, 41–2, 47–9, 58, 62–3, 116, 176–7, 185

New Vision for Planning 55
New Year 91–2, 144
New York 4, 20, 40, 63, 92, 115, 146, 171, 180, 186, 188
New York Magazine 170
Newcastle 61
Newham 154
Next 146
Nijmeigan, Netherlands 147
Nike 143
Niketown 143
Nissan 153
Nokia 163
Nolli Map 22, 26–7
nomadism 183
Non-places: Introduction to an Anthropology of Super-Modernity 97
Norr Mälarstrand 96
North America see United States
North Carolina 39
North Sea 125
Norway 74
not in my back yard (NIMBY) 43, 56, 184
Le Nôtre, – 112
Notting Hill carnival 187

obesity 39, 44
obligations 53, 56, 176
observation programme 96
obsolescence 144, 182
O'Donoghue, Bernard 15
Office of the Deputy Prime Minister (ODPM) 55, 95
Office of Metropolitan Architecture 96–7
Ohio 48
oil 125
Oldham 65
Olmsted, Frederick Law 19, 26, 41
Olympic Games 24, 86, 144, 154–8, 184, 186
OMA 166
on-demand space 163
Ontario Mills, San Bernadino 149–53
open space 3–4, 6, 10, 21, 23–4, 26–7, 41, 43, 53, 93, 103, 107, 131, 156, 184
open-air dissent 13
Orange County 53
Oregon 39, 52
Oresund 159–60
organic kingdom 115–16
orthodoxy 55, 177, 179, 184, 189
Oslo 72–5
out-of-town shopping centres 4
outline applications 50–1, 67, 130
outsourcing 163
Oxford 152
Oxford Brookes University 30
Oxford Polytechnic 7
Oxford Street, London 15

Paddington Basin, London 181
Pallio 14
Papendorp Business Park 165–6
para-military uniforms 98
Paradise Street, Liverpool 147
Paralympic Games 154
Paris 14, 19, 68, 73, 84, 87, 96, 98–9, 112, 123, 144, 146, 161, 180, 187
Paris Plage 14, 187
participation 13–15, 27, 184
paternalism 13
pavilion architecture 31
Peace Gardens, Sheffield 98
Pearl River Delta 93
Pearson 152
pedestrians 2–3, 6, 10–12, 30–1, 33–4, 36–7, 41–2, 71, 73–4, 77, 79, 90, 95–8, 116, 130–1, 156, 160, 180
peer review 55
Pennsylvania 48
People, Parks and Cities 95
performance 30, 55, 127
permeability 77, 175
permitting process 51–2, 55
Perseigne 120
Peru 34
Petrarch 111
Pew Center for Civil Journalism 43
Philip II 19
photography 95–6
physical realm 178
physics 15
Piano, Renzo 15
pillories 14
piloti 12
Pinstone Street, Sheffield 148
Pirai, Brazil 33
Piranesi, G. 22
Pittsburgh 18
Place de l'Homme de Fer, Strasbourg 10
Plan Voisin 7, 9, 116
Planning Act 7
planning authorities 51
Planning and Land Compensation Bill 52
Planning Policy Guidance Notes 50
Planning for Real 184
planning system 2, 50–6, 67
Plater-Zyberk, Elizabeth 42, 62
pluralism 51, 180, 182, 184, 189
polis 47
politics 2, 4–5, 10, 43, 55–6, 59, 68, 71, 74, 92, 98–9, 101, 108, 111, 125, 127, 144, 160, 162, 165, 167, 174, 178, 185
pollution 3, 39, 107, 131
Polyzoides, Stefanos 42
Pompidou Centre 15
Popper, Karl 5
population growth 39
Porritt, Jonathan 101
Portland 39, 52–3
Portland Place 66
Post Ex Subdis: Urban Fragmentation and Constructions 162
post-modernism 4, 57, 63, 106–13
post-permission amendments 51
Poundbury 6, 22, 62, 174, 185
poverty 34, 43, 58, 118
power supply 34
Prague 115, 146
pre-fabricated concrete 4
Prescott, John 59
preservation 23, 28, 43, 93, 127
pressure groups 8
prettification 96
Priestly, J.B. 153
Princes Circus 81
Prince's Foundation 10, 129, 176
principles 30, 36–7, 48, 51–5, 57–8, 62–3, 98, 130, 146, 150, 182, 185
Prior, Jason 154–8
Priority Funding Areas 42
private finance initiatives (PFIs) 67
privatisation 4, 31, 103
privileged space 163
procurement 51
professionals 2, 4, 13, 18–19, 23, 27–8, 51, 55–6, 76–81, 99–100, 102, 123, 127–8, 142, 166, 174, 179, 184–5, 189
profit 10, 56, 92, 122, 127, 174
Promenade PlantE 96
property crash 4
prototypes 127
Pruitt-Igoe, St Louis 4
pseudo-science 80
psychoanalysis 146
psychogramming 146
psychology 146, 183
The Public Face of Architecture 48
public goods 40
public life 46–7
Public Parks Initiative 95
public realm 46–7, 49, 52–3, 66, 68–9, 77, 84, 95–8, 100–5, 135–6, 138–9, 176, 180, 182–4
Public Realm Strategy 98
public space 108, 111, 144, 148
public space designers (PSDs) 86–7
Public Spaces 95
publicity 12
Punter, John 7, 30, 50–6, 176

quality 8, 30, 40, 42, 50–6, 58, 63–5, 95–6, 98–9, 105, 130, 138, 153, 161, 165, 167, 175, 180
Quality in Town and Country 175
quantitative methodology 80
Quarter Studies 52, 56

Radburn Estate, London 19

Radburn, New Jersey 2
Raleigh 39
Raleigh Park 104
Randstad 159, 161, 163, 165–6
real estate 9, 20–1, 39, 41, 92, 140, 163, 175
Rebuilding the City: A Guide to Development for Hulme 185
recessed space 106
recycling 40, 105
red-light districts 90
Rees, Richard 12, 181, 188
referenda 43, 167
Regent Street, London 61, 66, 146
Regents Park 66
Regional Development Agencies 55, 130, 153
regulatory mechanisms 176
Regus 163
Reijndorp, Arnold 163
relational realm 97–8, 178–9
Renaissance 7, 12, 20, 43, 67
Renault Parts Distribution Centre, Swindon 151
renewable energy 126–7, 131
rents 9, 75, 166
repair 67
Responsive Environments 30, 55, 175
retailing 4, 12, 31, 33, 142–8, 151–2, 156, 160–1, 163, 165–7, 178, 180–3
retirement 33
retrofitting 161
reviews 51–2, 54–5
Reykjavik 144, 146
RICS 11
Ridzwa Fathan 136
Rifkind, C. 48
ring roads 2–4, 13
Rio de Janeiro 34
roads 149–50, 152, 156, 165, 167
Rochdale Road, Manchester 2
Rockwell, Norman 62
Rogers, Richard 7, 15, 64, 80
romanticism 48
Rome 19, 22, 67
Ronan Point 4
Rossi, Aldo 30, 107, 175, 178
Rotterdam 96–7, 159, 161, 163, 166, 180
Rotterdam International Architecture Biennale 163
Rotterdam Museum Park 96–7
roundabouts 6, 180
Rowe, Colin 3, 6–7, 22
Rowland, Jon 173–89
Royal Fine Art Commission 7
Royal Mail 152
Royal Town Planning Institute (RTPI) 50, 55–6
Rudlin, David 57–68, 177, 185
Rugby 152
rules 115–16, 187
rural development 10
Rutgers University 42
Sainsbury's 145–6
St Botolph's Quarter 81
St Paul's Cathedral 4
sales figures 146
San Bernadino 151
San Francisco 39, 73
Santayana, George 2
Sant'Elia, A. 26
Sao Paulo, Brazil 35
Saratoga Springs 44
Sasaki, Hideo 18
Saunderson, W. 101
Scandinavia 37, 123
Schiphol Airport 160–1, 165
schools 102, 145, 158, 161
Schumacher, E.F. 8
Schwartz, Martha 23
scientific method 5
Scotland 152
Scraton, S 102
Scruton, Roger 47
Scully, Vincent 42
sculpted space 108
Sears 146
Seaside, Florida 62, 174, 177, 185
Seattle 54, 56, 115
security 14, 31, 36, 89, 98, 102–3, 187
sedentary lifestyle 39
Seine, River 14, 19, 98–9, 144
self-cleansing 55
Selfridges, Birmingham 12, 143, 181
Selfridges, London 14
semi-public space 163
Sennett, Richard 27
Sert, José Louis 19, 28
service space 108, 111–12
Shane, Grahame 7
Sharing Space 162
shattered world 162
shed developments 4, 12, 31, 33, 151–2
Sheffield 60, 98, 148, 166–7
Sheffield City Council 98
Sherwood Energy Village 105
Shoemaker, Robert 13
Shonfield, Katherine 98
shop-houses 9
shopping malls 4, 18, 31, 61, 78, 86, 102, 135, 145–6, 151, 160–1, 163, 165–7, 177, 180–1
Sienna 14, 71
signage 111, 143, 161
Silicon Valley 60
Silvertown 61
Simpson, Jon 183
Singapore 9
single parents 104
single-person households 10, 33, 36, 59
siting 67–8
Sitte, Camillo 19, 22
Sixtus, Pope 19, 67
skills shortages 127
Sky Zero Energy Development (Sky ZED) 131
skyscrapers 4, 135–6, 139–40
slums 3, 30–1, 34, 67
Smaralind Shopping Centre, Reykjavik 144, 146
smart growth 23–4, 40–4, 58, 176–7
Smart Growth and Neighbourhood Conservation Initiative 41
Smart Growth Network (SGN) 41
Smith, Adam 114
smoking ban 14
sociability 94
social change 2, 10, 30, 102, 126, 143–4, 180, 183–4
social malaise 78
socialism 7
socio-economics 78–9, 184
sociology 160, 163
Soja, Edward 27
solar power 10, 124, 126–7, 129, 132–4, 177
Solomon, Daniel 42
Sorkin, Michael 64
Southall Gasworks 62
Space Left Over After Planning (SLOAP) 6
Space project 95
Space Syntax 30, 78–81, 178
Space, Time and Architecture 40
Space Unit 95
space/form 76, 78, 80
spaces between 71, 75, 94
Spain 19, 86–7
Sparks, Les 8, 68
spatial models 78–9
Speakers Corner, London 14
specialisation 15, 19, 31
speculation 56
Spokane 72
Sporenburg 183
sport 14
sprawl 38–45, 73, 107, 124, 159, 162–3
squatters 119
Sri Lanka 145
stacking 183–4
stalls 90
standards 122–3, 127, 130
status 84
Stein, Clarence 2
Stevenage 52, 56
Stewart, Potter 38
Stockholm 72, 96
Stockley Park 64
Stonor, Tim 76–82, 178, 187
Strasbourg 10–11
Stratford City, London 24, 180
street furniture 14, 83, 86–7, 97
street life 14, 47, 71, 75, 83, 86, 90, 92, 146, 177, 179–80, 182, 187
street lighting 14
streetscapes 11, 27, 111
Der Strype, The Hague 25

students 15, 27
Stutz, Chris 82
Sub-Saharan Africa 36
suburbs 5, 22, 31, 33, 36, 38–9, 41–3, 49, 55, 59–61, 63–4, 101–2, 135, 146, 175
subways 3
Summer Schools 7–8
Sunderland 153
sunshine retailing 146
supermarkets 71, 145, 180
supply chains 122, 126–30
Supreme Court 38, 52
Surfer's Paradise 159
surveillance 80
surveyors 1
sustainability 1, 8–11, 15, 26, 30–1, 33–4, 37, 41–2, 44, 51–3, 55–7, 96, 102, 105, 121, 155–6, 158, 176–7, 184–5, 187, 189
Sustainable Accommodation in the New Economy (SANE) 162–3
Sustainable Communities: An Action Programme 95
Sustainable Communities Initiative 50
Sustainable Communities Programme 128–9, 134
Sustainable Urban Neighbourhoods 177
Sutton 177
SUVs 40
Swindon 103, 149–53
Sydney 54, 56, 144
symbolic realm 97–8, 178
system design 161

T-mobile 153
Takoma Park Metro 44
Tan, Sacha 82
tariffs 53
taxation 42, 82
Team 10 18
Tebbit & Britten 152
technology 31, 102, 104, 123, 126, 159, 161–2, 166–7, 179
Teeside 153
telecommunications 31, 150, 153
Telford Millenium Community 177
Temple Quay 59
Ten Commandments 30
tendering 66
terrorism 14
Tesco 144–5, 152
Thames Gateway 127, 155
Thames, River 7, 155, 158
Thatcher Government 4, 50
theme-ing 145, 163, 168
Third World 9, 34, 174
Tiergarten 68
Tiger Economies 9
time-lapse photography 96
Tokyo 63, 92
Tollitt, Penelope 98
totalitarianism 115
Tour de France 14
tourism 33, 89–90
Towards an Urban Renaissance 50, 95
Tower Hamlets 154
town centres 3, 11, 38, 42, 107, 145–6, 180
Town and Country Parks 95
Town and Country Planning Association 99
town planning 1, 4–6, 15, 31, 71, 86, 100–2, 107, 173
Town-Country Magnet 2
townscapes 6, 30, 94–5, 97, 99, 147, 175, 177, 184–7, 189
Townsend, Mardie 13, 100–5, 182, 184
trademarks 143
tradition 7, 10, 12, 22, 31, 46–9, 51, 60–1, 63, 101–2, 105–6, 127, 130, 150, 159–60, 163, 167, 174, 177, 184–8
Trafalgar Square 77, 79, 144, 182
traffic 1, 3, 14, 26–7, 30–1, 36, 38–41, 43–4, 53, 71–2, 74, 86–7, 90–1, 98, 107, 111, 131, 149–53, 160, 165, 179
training 16, 23
trams 11, 147
Transit Oriented Development 11, 180
transport 1, 11, 24, 26, 30, 36–9, 41–3, 59, 71, 73–4, 76–7, 79–81, 84, 86, 96, 102, 108, 130–1, 134, 146, 152, 156, 160, 163, 165–6, 175, 177, 180
Transport Development Areas 180
trees 112, 118, 175
Tregoning, Harriet 11, 38–45, 176, 189
Tricorn Centre, Portsmouth 10
trolleybuses 11
trophy architects 66
Tschumi, Bernard 187
Tuileries Gardens 112
Tunick, Spencer 14
Turner, John 34
turnover 143
Tuscany 67
Tyneside 153
Tyson's Corner, Virginia 160

UCP 166
uncertainty 187
unconscious design 30
unemployment 34
unit-mix regulation 53
Unité, Marseilles 2
United Kingdom (UK) 3–5, 7–8, 10–11, 16, 30, 36, 49, 53, 57–8, 62–3, 95, 98, 101, 103–4, 122, 124–5, 127–8, 130, 143–6, 151–2, 154, 174–5, 177, 180, 182, 184–5
United Nations Declaration on Human Rights 101
United States (US) 3–7, 11, 18, 20–3, 29–31, 33, 36, 38–44, 48–9, 51–8, 62–3, 71, 104, 123, 146–7, 151, 176, 181–2, 184
universities 42, 79
University College London 30, 78
Unwin, Raymond 19, 27
Upton 10
urban decay 42
Urban Design Assistance Teams 184
Urban Design Associates 62
Urban Design Compendium 175
urban design definitions 19, 28, 175
Urban Design Group 16, 50, 55, 174
Urban Design Panel 55–6
Urban Design Strategy 185
Urban Development Plans 52
Urban Green Spaces Task Force Report 95
Urban Parks Programme 95
Urban Renaissance 58, 63–4, 174
Urban Renewal 27, 31
Urban Space 3
Urban Splash 59
Urban Task Force 10, 175
Urban Villages Forum 127
urban villages movement 30
Urban White Paper 58, 95
urbanism 48, 108, 112, 156
URBED 57, 62, 67–8, 177
Uruguay 145
Utah 42
Utrecht 159, 161, 166–7
Utrecht Central Station 167

Van Danzig, Donald 166
Vancouver 52–5
vandalism 2, 8, 95–6
Vaulx-en-Velin, Lyons 117
velodrome 158
Venice 12, 14, 162
Ventoux, Mont 111
Venturi, Robert 37, 108, 182
Vergeley, Jacques 96
vernacular architecture 62, 87, 185
Versailles 40
vertical design theory 135–40
vested interests 56
Victoria Square, Birmingham 97–8, 181
Victorian design 7, 127, 130, 132, 151, 155
Ville Radieuse 26, 177
Vinex 166
Virginia 47, 160
virtual communities 102–3
volume housing 123, 126–9, 133, 175, 181

W.H. Malcolm 152
Waitrose 153
Wal-Mart 145
Wales 131
Waltham Forest 154
Wandsworth Council 131
Ward, Colin 99
Washington DC 33, 35, 44, 47
Washington Monument 14

Wasted Space campaign 95
water 23–4, 34, 105, 155–6, 158
Waterfront City, Melbourne 147–8
Waterloo 95, 131
Watling Street 152
Watson, B. 102
way-finding 111
West 8 162, 179, 187
Westfall, William 48
WFSchutz Davidson 177
Whitaker, Craig 44
Whyte, William H. 22, 74, 95–6, 182
wilderness recreation 43
wind power 10, 131, 133
Wirth, Louis 27
Women and Housing Towards 2020 102–3, 105
women's liberation 100
work paradigms 162
World Trade Center 170, 186, 188
World Trade Organisation 93
World War II 41, 89
Worpole, Ken 8, 94–9, 178, 188
Worthington, John 159–69, 183, 187–8
wow! factor 12
Wright, Frank Lloyd 40
Wyoming 48

Yale 42
Yeang, Ken 135–40, 184
yes in my back yard (YIMBY) 44
Yokohama Port Authority 184
young turks 63

Zero Energy Development (ZED) 127–30, 132–4
zero-heating homes 127–8
zoning 5, 20, 51–5, 89, 107, 116, 162, 166, 179, 187
Zukin, Sharon 160